Western Images

Images

—— of ——

China

COLIN MACKERRAS

HONG KONG
OXFORD UNIVERSITY PRESS
OXFORD   NEW YORK

Oxford University Press

Oxford   New York   Toronto
Petaling Jaya   Singapore   Hong Kong   Tokyo
Delhi   Bombay   Calcutta   Madras   Karachi
Nairobi   Dar es Salaam   Cape Town
Melbourne   Auckland

and associated companies in
Berlin   Ibadan

First published 1989
Second impression 1991
Reissued in Oxford Paperbacks 1991
Published in the United States
by Oxford University Press, Inc., New York

ISBN 0 19 584915 9 (cloth)
ISBN 0 19 585342 3 (limp)

British Library Cataloguing in Publication Data available

Library of Congress Cataloging-in-Publication Data available

Printed in Hong Kong
Published by Oxford University Press, Warwick House, Hong Kong

Preface

As one long fascinated by China, both past and present, I have often been struck by the contrasting attitudes which different and equally competent specialists have adopted towards matters relating to China. The controversial nature of Western images of China was borne in on me with particular strength when from 1964 to 1966 I got what was at that time for a Westerner the most unusual opportunity of teaching English in the People's Republic of China, at the Beijing Institute of Foreign Languages. I was able to compare and contrast what Westerners were saying about China in their home media and elsewhere with my own interpretation of what I saw and heard going on around me. Images are a worthwhile area of study because they bear on how people of one culture perceive and relate to those of another.

In the first half of 1986 I was invited to give a series of lectures on Western images of China at the same Beijing Institute of Foreign Languages where I had taught 20 years before. Although I had long been very interested in this subject, I had never before set down ideas and information about it in a coherent form. The present book derives in large measure from the lectures I gave. However, I have read, seen, and learned an enormous amount on this subject since that time, and expanded, reorganized, and changed greatly the material given in the lectures. Part III of this book has been published in a somewhat different form by the Centre for the Study of Australian-Asian Relations at Griffith University, Brisbane, as its Australia-Asia Papers No. 41.

I should like to thank those various people with whom I have discussed the ideas and material in this book. These include colleagues and students both at the Beijing Institute of Foreign Languages and Griffith University in Brisbane, Australia. I have learned an enormous amount from them. In particular, I should like to thank Professor Nancy Viviani who, as Director of the Centre for the Study of Australian-Asian Relations, gave me permission to rethink, rework, and republish the section on images of the People's Republic of China for a wider readership. Thanks are due also to the copyright-holders of the photographs for permission to use them; credit is given individually on the plates themselves. I should also like to thank my wife Alyce for her encouragement to research and complete this book.

Colin Mackerras
December 1987

Contents

Plates

1

Introduction

MARCO POLO has become legendary both in the West and much of the rest of the world as an early representative of one major civilization who lived and worked in another and took the trouble to understand and appreciate what he saw and heard. Actually, Marco Polo (c. 1254–1324) was not the first European to visit or even live in China, but he was the first not only to return afterwards to his own country but also to leave an account describing his experiences and impressions. This explains his quite justified fame in world history.

It also makes him the first major formulator of Western images of China. The aim of this book is to present and analyse such images; to trace how they have changed from time to time, and to relate both the images and the changes they underwent to the politics or intellectual environment — or both — in the West. The subject of this study is the West, China the object. Though the theme of cross-cultural relationships is never far from the surface, this is primarily a study of one aspect of Western intellectual history.

An image is a view or perception held by a person or group. In the present context, however, it is more specifically a perception which holds sufficient priority with the viewer to impinge upon the consciousness. Under this definition, a completely trivial perception is not an image at all. Thus, for Marco Polo to have remembered a detail clearly enough to include it in his account of his travels suggests that it was important enough to be regarded as an image under the definition offered above. But what is noteworthy for one viewer may not be so at all for another. In this book the concern is only with part of the range of views of China, those which are not trivial and relate to Western preoccupations with China.

One aim *not* within the scope of this book is the presentation of the reality of China. Though I have tried to handle the images critically, I have not normally commented on who is 'right' or 'wrong' when observers present rival or conflicting views. Images are not and have never been necessarily the same as reality. At all times there is an infinity of realities. What all observers of China appear to have done is to filter what they see through the spectacles of their own backgrounds, ideologies, biases, and experiences. It is a nearly universal, and perfectly understandable and natural, pattern for observers of another people to remain firmly planted in their own culture. Some make more attempt at understanding, even appreciation, than others. Some are quicker to draw comparisons with their own civilization than others. Some are by temperament more eager to expose weaknesses in or criticize, or alternatively to admire and exult in, what is foreign. But while there can be common ground between images and realities, they rarely or never overlap completely.

None of this means that the present author has no point of view. On the contrary, like the Western observers who are the subject of the book, he is bound by his own culture, upbringing, training, and temperament. Here, as elsewhere, phraseology and the selection of material inevitably reveal a point of view or sympathy. My aim is to be fair to all, including in the presentation of images which may be extremely contentious, while acknowledging that what appears fair to one person may not seem so to another.

Two related theories have been suggested which bear on knowledge and interpretation and are of great relevance to a study of images. Both are by well-known scholars and have exerted considerable influence, including on the formulation of my own position as enunciated in the preceding paragraphs. It may be possible to determine their applicability in the light of the Western images discussed in the following chapters.

The author of the first of these theories is the distinguished French historian and philosopher Michel Foucault (1926–84), one of the most influential thinkers of our age. He has described his theory simply as 'power/knowledge' (pouvoir-savoir). In a book published first in 1980, one scholar of Foucault's ideas stated that this concept 'constitutes the strategic fulcrum of his recent work'.[1] It argues in essence that knowledge or 'truth' is in effect a function of power. Those who hold power can and do use it to further their own interests, to exercise power or to keep themselves in power. Foucault says:

Truth isn't the reward of free spirits, the child of protracted solitude, nor the privilege of those who have succeeded in liberating themselves. Truth is a thing of this world: it is produced only by virtue of multiple forms of constraint. And it induces regular effects of power. Each society has its régime of truth, its 'general politics' of truth: that is, the types of discourse which it accepts and makes function as true; the mechanisms and instances which enable one to distinguish true and false statements . . . the status of those who are charged with saying what counts as true.[2]

Foucault defines this 'regime of truth' in the following famous sentence: '"Truth" is linked in a circular relation with systems of power which produce and sustain it, and to effects of power which it induces and which extend it.'[3] According to this theory, images of China would tend to become a bulwark for a particular set of policies towards that country, or even for a more general policy. Information would be carefully selected and propagated to justify that policy or set of policies. The relationship between knowledge and reality dwindles in significance beside that between knowledge and power.

The other theory is that of Edward Said, who in quite a few places acknowledges his debt to Foucault.[4] Said designates his theory simply as 'Orientalism'. Although designed specifically as a critique of the Western study of West Asian civilizations, its main points are equally applicable to the study of China. Said argues that Western scholars have misinterpreted or produced distorted accounts of Eastern civilizations because of their ethnocentric attitudes.

If it is true that no production of knowledge in the human sciences can ever ignore or disclaim its author's involvement as a human subject in his own circumstances, then it must also be true that for a European or American studying the Orient there can be no disclaiming the main circumstances of *his* actuality: that he comes up against the Orient as a European or American first, as an individual second.[5]

Said's study is a passionate attack on Western scholarship for its lack of sensitivity to the value systems of the people studied, for its failure 'to be animated by the specific societies and problems' of study,[6] for its general inability to examine Asian countries in their own terms. He believes 'too close a relationship between the scholar and the state' to be inadvisable and a feature of 'Orientalism'. This is one of the respects in which Said is clearly heavily influenced by Foucault's 'power/knowledge' concept. Said calls for an emphasis on *discipline* as opposed to areas studies: 'Interesting work is most likely to be produced by scholars whose allegiance is to a discipline defined intellectually and not to a "field" like Orientalism defined either canonically, imperially, or geographically'.[7] In other words, despite his passionate attacks on Western scholarship, he is quite specific in recognizing the possibility of 'decolonizing' knowledge, in acknowledging 'that there is scholarship that is not as corrupt, or at least as blind to human reality'[8] as the 'Orientalist' type he castigates in such strong terms.

Clearly the two theories just outlined are related to each other, because Said's notion that the West 'colonized' knowledge about Asia means that the West devised the construct of 'the Orient' as part of the process of enhancing the power of the West over Asian peoples.

The term 'China' can be understood in a number of ways. It denotes a geographical entity, a nation, a history, a society, a people. While it is true that the geographical entity which is China and the people who inhabit it are separate, they are related closely to each other. The focus of the present book is on images of Chinese people and what they have created, rather than of the physical country. The particular images of this people I have chosen tend to be social, political, and historical, but there is some attention given also to economic matters. In view of the enormity of the subject, certain important topics have been specifically omitted or treated only very sparsely. These include China's literature and arts and its minority nationalities.

The time-frame of this book is deliberately comprehensive. It covers Western images from the very beginnings of contact between China and the West until our own age. The early centuries from the time of Ancient Rome until the thirteenth century are covered extremely briefly, for the very simple reason that images then were vague and not extensive. It is with Marco Polo's account that detailed Western images of

China begin. Unlike a drama or novel, history does not end, and so images which one culture has of another reach no final conclusion. Nevertheless, it is necessary to place a limit on this study not only at the early but also at the recent end. The one I have chosen is the end of 1987. Again the reason is simple: it is the year that the typescript for this book was completed.

Images exist on various time levels. How people view the China of their own day is a completely separate matter from how they view the China of the past. This dichotomy exists in all ages, even though the 'power/knowledge' relationship may apply both for images of the present and those of the past. To readers of this book, the eighteenth century is the past, but the West Europeans of that time held images of a China which was current to them; they also had perceptions about what was to them China's past. Another problem is that there is no clear boundary between past and present. In the strictest sense, yesterday is the past, but common sense dictates that the very recent past be normally considered jointly with the present. Of the three parts in this book, the first selects specific periods down to 1949, and examines how the China of the day looked to the Western people living at that time, to them the present, even though the past to us. The second part considers only images of China's past, and traces changes over the centuries in Western images of Chinese history. The third part looks at images of the People's Republic. In a sense this implies a belief that the years since 1949 can be regarded as a historical period, which can be labelled 'the present'. Indeed, most chapters in that part consider how China looked in the years which were contemporary with the observers. But there is also a past within these few decades, for example post-1976 images of the Cultural Revolution of the late 1960s and early 1970s constitute a noteworthy and interesting topic. In considering levels of time, it is necessary to choose boundaries in order to present material in manageable and understandable form. The two years 1949, when the Chinese Communist Party came to power, and 1976, when its Chairman Mao Zedong died and his main followers, the 'gang of four', fell from power, are convenient and appropriate time boundaries.

Given the number of 'Western' countries and range of areas

within each, the place-frame also needs definition. In this book 'the West' as a broad generalization is the countries of Western Europe, North America, and Australia. Such a definition will require refinement depending on the period under discussion. So North America and Australia are irrelevant to this book until the nineteenth century.

Over the centuries there has been a strong tendency for one country to dominate Western images of China. In the eighteenth century it was France, in the nineteenth Britain, and for most of the twentieth unquestionably the United States. Foucault's 'power/knowledge' relationship is relevant here, because dominant powers tend strongly to be able to dominate in the field of ideas as·well.

It follows that for any given period, examples from one country are likely to predominate. There are some parts of 'the West' which figure but rarely in this study. This does not mean they are without 'images of China'. However, total comprehensiveness is impossible and certainly not my aim here. What I have tried to do is to allude to 'images' which are most important in the West at any one time. Probably also there has been some degree of internationalization in Western images of China since the earliest contacts. This process has strengthened in the nineteenth and especially the twentieth centuries. Divergences or conflicts in images of China have normally been stronger within the 'dominant' country of the day than they have been among different countries.

The concept of 'the West' takes on meaning mainly if juxtaposed to 'the East', and the boundary between the two fluctuates according to the political, economic, and cultural circumstances of the day. One area which is in this book excluded from 'the West' is eastern and most of central Europe. There are occasional references to the Austro-Hungarian Empire and, for the period since World War I, to Austria. But countries such as Czechoslovakia, Romania, and Greece are not covered here at all. For the period since World War II, Germany means the Federal Republic, not the Democratic Republic. The major omission is Russia and its successor the Soviet Union. Although these countries, or in the case of the Soviet Union a major portion of it, are unquestionably part of Europe, it is a moot point whether they should be considered part of 'the West'. The main reason for excluding them is scale. To this author it appears that 'Central and Eastern European images of China' is an entirely different topic from the one focal here. It would be a significant field of research and include such major matters as Soviet Marxist attitudes towards China, but not one I have aimed to cover in this book.

Images do not exist in a vacuum. Within those countries and areas considered as 'the West', it is worth considering just who or what groups hold the images which are the topics of the following chapters. The answer will vary with the period. Probably few people at any time in any Western country have held clear images about China. But both images and information have filtered more extensively to the millions without specialist knowledge or experience of China since the middle of the eighteenth century. Not only more and more people in absolute terms have held images of China with the passage of time, but a higher proportion. In the early centuries few Westerners other than the educated held images of China, but the groups have expanded as the numbers have done so. Increasingly since the nineteenth century, and especially since World War II, the holders of 'Western images of China' have come to include the proverbial 'ordinary people': students, journalists, business people, members of religious or political groups, workers, farmers, and so on. But the identity of these 'ordinary people' is extremely unclear, let alone their depth of knowledge and how they perceive China. Of course this writer can, and to some extent will, appeal to opinion surveys for the recent period when they exist, but these probably do little more than refer to a particular place and time and consequently are not central to this study.

Putting the question round the other way, one can ask who are the formulators or creators of images. Some are specifically *not* China specialists. A few of these, such as Georg Friedrich Hegel or Karl Marx, contributed enormously to Western intellectual history and their view on China was influential, even though they were in fact not interested in it and it never occupied centre stage for them. At the other extreme are a few who simply used China as a background for an adventure story. An example is Captain W. H. Johns, the author of the Biggles books. Novels or films set in China create images of that country, even if it is totally incidental to the story at hand. While Johns would not rate a mention in a treatment

of serious literature, let alone of sinology, he does figure in
the chapter on contemporary images of China in the 1950s.

Most image-formulators about China are specialists on that
country, or have a deep interest in it. They are travellers,
missionaries, priests, diplomats, merchants, business people,
government personnel, novelists, journalists, and academics,
among others. The priority one suggests in this list depends
upon the age. In the days of Marco Polo the traveller clearly
took precedence, while the diplomats and academics mattered
not at all and the journalists did not exist. In the nineteenth
century, diplomats and missionaries made significant contributions, probably greater for contemporary studies than academics but less in the field of history and literature. Since
1949, the influence of missionaries as a source of images of
China has declined drastically. For immediately current images
it is journalists who matter most, but they obtain a great deal
of their information and perceptions from diplomats. For images
of the past, either recent or distant, academics take priority.
A scholarly work refers to the past by the time it is published,
even if it intended to concern the present, and the same is
so of a television documentary. Journalists tend to be specialists
less on China than on reporting. Thus it is that advisers to
the creators of television documentaries are more often academics
than journalists or diplomats.

In some ages there is overlap among the professions which
contribute most to formulating images of China. In the nineteenth
century some diplomats and missionaries went on to become
distinguished academics. Since World War II, academics have
often moved to government service or journalism, and vice
versa. There is overlap also within the list suggested. Priests
can be academics and anybody can be a traveller. The
overwhelming majority of image-creators have been intellectuals in the sense of being literate people capable of con-
structing images in written form.

The function of travel to China among image-formulators
is problematic. In the thirteenth century almost all reliable
information, though not all images, came from those who
went there. In the eighteenth century not many Westerners
either resided or travelled in China. J. B. Du Halde, the greatest
author of the age on China, never visited the country. In the
1950s and 1960s much was written by journalists and academics,

and said by government spokespersons, who did not visit China. Yet travel is at all times one part of image formulation; its priority, *how* important it is by comparison with other sources, depends on circumstances.

Another variable among image-formulators is language. Some of the greatest works on China of the past were written by people who did not know Chinese at all. Most journalists both of the past and present know little or no Chinese. Especially in the 1950s and 1960s, quite a few academics were in the same position. Yet many of those with greatest mastery over the classical or contemporary language have either been or become academics. Looking at the China-specialists over the centuries, one can see that knowledge of the Chinese language has been useful, but by no means necessary, to becoming an image-formulator.

Images may be conceptual, visual, aural, or olfactory, or a mixture. Due to the constraints of the print medium, virtually all the images discussed in this book belong to the first two categories. Until the present century, those Westerners who did not actually visit China derived the overwhelming majority of their images of China from reading books or magazines, either of them with or without pictures. Nowadays, people derive their ideas about China from seeing television programmes, films, or pictures, listening to radio items, stories from friends, or lectures from people who claim to know something about the country. They may read books, newspaper or magazine articles, or travel or live in China itself. Print remains vital for imparting images, but to nothing like the extent of the age before the invention of radio, and especially television.

The images discussed in this book are those presented in books and magazines which were or are widely read, or contained important or path-breaking ideas. For the recent period it is necessary to add popular films and television programmes, which can be used either in the original form or as recorded in print. Books, articles, films, and television programmes may aim to document fact, or they may portray fiction. Either way they are sources for images. The assumption is made that such works, whether by China specialists or not, exert an impact on the way people perceive China. In other words, it is valid to cite what is written or screened about China as an 'image' of China, even if I can offer no evidence on how many people actually read or saw the relevant work, or remembered or believed it if they did.

This leads to the problem of reading or viewing. This writer shares the theory put forward by Louis Althusser that reading is not an 'innocent' or neutral activity, but rather a process of interpretation, governed, at least in part, by the questions the reader brings to the text.[9] It appears that different people may read precisely the same book or excerpt and get something different out of it. They may remember different points, or derive a completely different priority of images from the same extract. This is because they approach it in different ways, and with different questions, interests, experiences, and biases. This problem assumes particular force in reading novels or sources which show China merely as background. The fact that a novel's author is much more concerned about a good story than accurate detail about the background does not mean that such a work conveys no images. But precisely *what* those images are may vary from one reader to another. The same problems exist for viewing films or television programmes, with the added complication that a feature film is always the director's interpretation of the novel on which it is based.

Even though I have discussed with other people reactions to many works about China, it is impossible to carry out detailed surveys showing popular reaction to the various sources I have used. Consequently, the images discussed in this book are essentially my own interpretation of what I have read or seen. I have tried to use passages which the context suggests the author regarded as important on any particular topic. But it is quite impossible for me to be sure that someone else with different questions, interests, experiences, and biases might not have read into the sources something different from what I have seen.

Finally, why write such a book as this? There are both negative and positive reasons. There are already treatments of Western attitudes towards China covering particular periods or the people of one country.[10] But there is room for a new evaluation of old ideas and a need for an account of the recent period, in particular that since the fall of the 'gang of four' in 1976. So far there is no consolidated general treatment of

Western images of China from the earliest to the most recent times, even given the fact that the term 'recent' is entirely relative and for somebody writing in 1900, the year 1890 was 'recent'.

A positive reason for researching Western images of China is that the country and its people have been for centuries, and remain, controverial in the West. This is partly because China is so large and populous and consequently so important, and because its tradition is so long and grand. In addition, Western images gain significance because they bear upon the West's relations with China, upon how one major civilization relates to another. Though the images have tended to fluctuate, the West has been concerned about China for a very long time. The signs are that this situation will continue into the indefinite future.

At certain times, particular dominant groups — whether consciously or not is not the issue here — have designated China in a range of ways, as worthy of admiration, sympathy, curiosity, fear, ridicule, hostility, conversion to Christianity, or as a means of profit. Western images of China are not only interesting but also an active part of a series of power relationships. They are consequently a prominent area of study well worth exploration.

PART I

WESTERN IMAGES OF CHINA'S PRESENT
DOWN TO 1949

2

Early Western Images of China

THE ancient Romans knew of the existence of China; they called it Serica and its people the Seres or Sinae. The term Seres derives from the clearest image in their extremely hazy knowledge of China: that it traded silk. The famous *Historiae Naturalis* (*Natural History*) of Pliny the Elder (AD 23–79) mentions the labour involved in making silk fabrics: 'so has toil to be multiplied; so have the ends of the earth to be transversed: and all that a Roman dame may exhibit her charms in transparent gauze'.[1] However, he was unaware that silk was produced by silkworms. Like Virgil (70–19 BC) and many other Roman poets down to Claudian (*c.* 370–*c.* 404),[2] he believed silk was combed from the leaves of the forest.

It is possible that Chinese traders entered Roman territory from the first century BC, but no official Chinese missions visited the city of Rome itself. Pliny believed the Seres to be 'inoffensive in their manners indeed'. They keep to themselves, he adds, and do not seek trade with other people, but are prepared to engage in it if others seek it.[3]

The first Western writer to discuss China coherently in detail extending beyond a paragraph or so is the Egyptian Greek Theophylact Simocatta, whose work dates from the early seventh century. He calls the Chinese Taugas and names their ruler as *Taissan*, identified as the great Tang emperor Taizong (reigned 626–49). We are now in the era when Christianity had become dominant in the Byzantine Empire, so it is not surprising to find Theophylact Simocatta raising the criticism that 'the nation practises idolatry'. Still, his comments are broadly positive. The Chinese 'have just laws, and their life is full of temperate wisdom'. This is a large, powerful, and rich country with a thriving commerce. The emperor is said to have 700 concubines.

'The king's women go forth in chariots made of gold, with one ox to draw them', while the women of the chief nobles use silver chariots. Already China comes over as a rich and exotic marvel, an idea which was to dominate Western images for many centuries. And, of course, Theophylact praises the Chinese for their 'skill and emulation' in raising silkworms and producing silk filaments of various colours.[4]

Theophylact's work was not particularly influential in his own time. Despite his remarks on Chinese silk production, the silk trade between Byzantium and China had fallen on bad times simply because Nestorian monks had smuggled silkworm eggs from China to the West, and Byzantium had begun its own silk industry. Theophylact Simocatta was roughly contemporary with Muhammad (c. 570–632) and not long afterwards Muslim power placed a curtain between China and the West. Europe forgot about China. It was not until the medieval crusaders began returning from the east 'with their tales' that 'the store of factual knowledge' was again increased.[5]

The First Great Age of Sino-European Contact

Although the legend of the Eastern Christian ruler Prester John began to circulate in the middle of the twelfth century, the medieval era of European consciousness of Eastern Asia reached its height through a sense of threat from the Mongol empire. The feeling of threat was not without foundation. In the early 1240s, Mongol troops scored substantial victories in Poland, Silesia, and Hungary. In the spring of 1242 they reached within a few miles of Vienna and were about to attack it when news reached them of the death of the Great Khan Ögödei on 11 December 1241. 'The presence of all the princes and military leaders was immediately required for the convocation' which elected the new khan.[6] Central and Western Europe's escape was indeed a narrow one.

Yet for Western Europe there could be advantages in the Mongol conquest. Up to this point it had done incomparably more damage to Russia, not to mention the arch-enemy Islam, than to Western Europe. Why not attempt to convert the Mongols to Christianity and use them as allies against Islam? The Pope, Innocent IV (reigned 1243–54), despatched two embassies to

Mongolia. One of them was never heard of again; the other, led by the Franciscan friar John of Plano Carpini, returned to Europe in 1247 after a voyage to Mongolia of about two-and-a-half years. According to one writer, 'although the Mongols had carried many European slaves into Asia, John is the first European on record to proceed east of Baghdad and return to tell his tale'.[7] He is thus historically important, but he did not succeed in converting the Mongol khan or persuade him to co-operate with the Christians against Islam.

Although John of Plano Carpini wrote extensively of his travels and heard about China, he did not actually visit it. The image he conveyed of the Chinese was of an affable, kind, and hard-working people, fine craftsmen, with a language of their own. He believed they worshipped one God, and honoured Jesus Christ, but needed to be baptized. China itself he believed 'very rich in corn, in wine, gold, silver, silk, and in every kind of produce that tends to the support of mankind'.[8] His was an idealized view which included a measure of wishful thinking. Yet he appears to be the first Western writer to mention China who had actually seen a Chinese. He is also the first to call them Cathayans.

John of Plano Carpini was followed by others. William of Rubruquis, a Flemish Franciscan, stayed eight months at the Mongol capital of Karakorum from December 1253 to August 1254. Like John, he did not visit China. However, he did meet many Chinese in Karakorum and was generally impressed with them. 'They are first-rate artists in every kind of craft, and their physicians have a thorough knowledge of the virtues of herbs, and an admirable skill in diagnosis by the pulse', he writes. And later he continues, 'they do their writing with a brush such as painters paint with, and a single character of theirs comprehends several letters so as to form a whole word.'[9] William's account also contains its share of myths, but although he was struck by several of the same features mentioned by his predecessor John, he does not make the mistake of seeing the Chinese as quasi-Christians.

In 1264 the Mongols extended their control south of the Great Wall and made Khan-balik (Beijing) their capital. In 1279 they completed the reunification of China by conquering the south. Meanwhile the first visitors from Europe were arriving in China itself, including the Polo brothers Niccolò and Maffeo from Venice. Khublai Khan (1215–94) received these two in audience and asked them about Europe. When they proved unable to satisfy his curiosity, he dispatched them to request the Pope to send to his capital 100 learned men who could teach his court about Europe and debate there with people from other countries.

The Polos were appointed apostolic delegates to the Khan's court and left Europe again for Khan-balik in 1271. This time they took with them Niccolò's seventeen-year-old son Marco. They went overland through Persia and what is today Xinjiang; they crossed the Gobi desert, passed Chang'an (now Xi'an), and arrived in the capital in 1275.

The Polos stayed in China for seventeen years. At Khublai's request Marco travelled widely, including to Yunnan, and took notes for the Khan on his experiences. However, the claim made in most, though not all, the manuscripts of his travels that he was Governor of Yangzhou for three years is not confirmed in Chinese sources and is very unlikely.

The Polos left China in 1292, accompanying a Mongolian princess who was travelling by sea to marry a Mongol ruler in Persia. The intended husband had actually died in 1291, even before they left China, so instead she married his son. The Polos pressed on to Italy, arriving back in Venice in 1295. Marco was later a naval officer and was a prisoner-of-war for nearly a year in 1298 and 1299. It was during his imprisonment that he dictated to a fellow captive, Rustichello of Pisa, an account of his experiences in China. The fact is of profound significance and makes Marco Polo's extraordinary fame quite natural.

Other Europeans lived and worked in China during the thirteenth century, but Marco Polo was the only one, so far as is known, to travel and work there and to write an account of his experiences. For the first time in history Europe possessed a detailed narrative about China and its neighbours based upon more than hearsay and speculation.[10]

The book he dictated is usually called in English *The Description of the World* or *The Travels of Marco Polo*. Probably Rustichello's original manuscript was destroyed, but well over 100 copies and adaptations survive, in various languages. The book was immediately popular and consequently influential as a source

of images of the China of its time, though it is only fair to
add that Marco Polo had a reputation as a story-teller and
did not always command belief. Even today, his account has
to be treated cautiously, and there are signs that Rustichello
was not above embellishing what Marco Polo had told him
if he thought the romance of the story demanded it. There
are also some curious omissions, such as any mention of the
Great Wall, tea cultivation, or foot-binding. For the present
purposes, however, what matters is not so much its accuracy as the view of China it imparted to Europe.

Khublai Khan comes out of Marco Polo's account very well;
there are no criticisms of his policies. The overall thrust of
The Description is immensely laudatory of China and its
civilization, but not so positive about relations between the
Mongol rulers and the Chinese people.

A few salient points should be recounted. Marco Polo was
very impressed by China's richness and prosperity. Indeed,
because of his account, Cathay, as he called North China,
'became for over two centuries synonymous with Eldorado
— a fabulous land of wealth on the far side of the world'.[11]

Marco Polo was also much struck with the flourishing
commerce and inter-regional trade he found in China. In
particular, he admired the emperor's personal concern for his
people's well-being. The Great Khan 'sends emissaries and
inspectors throughout all his dominions' to find out if there
has been a crop failure anywhere. 'And if he finds that any
have lost their harvest, he exempts them for that year from
their tribute and gives them some of his own grain to sow
and to eat.' Marco Polo calls this 'a magnificent act of royal
bounty'.[12] It is but one of a whole list of imperial kindnesses
to the people, which gave Marco Polo the impression of a
happy country indeed.

Polo was completely bowled over by Chinese cities. Kinsai
(Hangzhou) he states flatly is 'without doubt the finest and
most splendid city in the world'.[13] He describes the West Lake
in the city: 'And all round it are stately palaces and mansions,
of such workmanship that nothing better or more splendid
could be devised or executed. These are the abodes of the
nobles and magnates.'[14] It is also a very prosperous city with
numerous and well stocked market-places.

Khan-balik is nearly as magnificent and prosperous. Palaces

and fine houses abound. 'The streets are so broad and straight' that 'you can see along the whole length of the road to the gate opposite'. There is much traffic but all is well controlled. 'The whole interior of the city is laid out in squares like a chess-board with such masterly precision that no description can do justice to it.'[15] Strong words indeed! Marco Polo does not dwell on the poverty he must have seen around him, perhaps because it was not as bad as what he was used to at home.

Marco Polo records the use of coal, which was apparently new to him and not in use in his native Italy, although it was certainly used in Britain in his time. All over the country of Cathay 'there is a sort of black stone, which is dug out of veins in the hillsides and burns like logs'. Wood exists in plenty also but the stones burn better and cheaper.

But the population is so enormous and there are so many bath-houses and baths continually being heated, that the wood could not possibly suffice, since there is no one who does not go to a bath-house at least three times a week and take a bath, and in winter every day, if he can manage it. And every man of rank or means has his own bathroom in his house, where he takes a bath. So it is clear there could never be enough wood to maintain such a con-flagration.[16]

In the manner of his day, Marco Polo categorized people according to religion, not culture or race. Given the circum-stances of Europe in his time, it is not surprising to find him extremely hostile to Islam. Yet towards the Buddhists he was very tolerant, even admiring. Although he called them 'idolators', the term was clearly not intended as insulting. He gave to the 'sages of the idolators' credit for the fact that the Great Khan provided alms to the poor.[17] He marvelled at the 'huge monasteries and abbeys, of such a size that I assure you that some resemble small cities inhabited by more than 2,000 monks'. The feasts they made for their 'idols' were splendid and accompanied by 'the most magnificent hymns and illumina-tions that were ever seen'.[18]

On the other hand, Marco Polo was not oblivious to certain political problems. He was well aware that the Mongols were overlords in someone else's country. 'The Great Khan had no legal title to rule the province of Cathay, having acquired it by force.' For that reason he put authority not in the hands of Chinese, but in those of 'Tartars, Saracens, and Christians'. Polo recognized that, because of the domination of foreigners, 'all the Cathayans hated the government of the Great Khan'.[19] He is also quite open about the savage punishments meted out to rebels, such as being flayed alive, and about the dreadful beatings suffered by criminals.[20] His wording, however, everywhere suggests support for Mongol rule and the assumption that the Great Khan's opponents are in the wrong.

The Polos were travellers, merchants, and servants of the Mongol government, and there were others like them. Italian merchants, especially from Genoa, remained active in China up to the middle of the fourteenth century. Trade existed and Chinese silk was still sold in Europe, even though by this time there were also thriving silk industries in Sicily, Spain, and other places nearer home than China.

Franciscan friars travelled in China for missionary and other religious work. Among them the one to leave the most detailed record was Odoric of Pordenone (c. 1286–1331), who lived in China for some three years in the 1320s. Like Marco Polo he was much impressed with the splendour of Chinese cities; he described Hangzhou as 'the greatest city in the whole world'[21] and shared Polo's awe at Khan-balik and the Great Khan's court.[22] Unlike Polo, he noticed the custom of foot-binding and is the first Westerner to write of it: 'And with the women the great beauty is to have little feet; and for this reason mothers are accustomed, as soon as girls are born to them, to swathe their feet tightly so that they can never grow in the least.'[23]

The lack of any criticism of China's government or customs, even of so unfamiliar and cruel a custom as foot-binding, is symptomatic of Odoric's extremely positive attitude towards China. If anything, he is even more enthusiastic than Marco Polo. Constantly he uses superlatives, the biggest or finest, to describe something he has seen.

It is true that some people in the fourteenth and later centuries refused to believe Odoric's story. Yet it became extremely famous in his own day. Indeed, among the various medieval travelogues of the monks, which, of course, do not include Marco Polo's narrative, Odoric's was 'the only one that enjoyed great popularity throughout the ages',[24] and that is ample testimony to its role as a creator of images.

In the middle of the fourteenth century China and Europe again became cut off from one another. The collapse of the Mongol dynasty in China made the overland route to the west much more difficult to pass. Trade and interest in Europe or its religion dried up. The Black Death, which killed about a third of Europe's population between 1348 and 1351, created conditions which stopped European merchants or missionaries from travelling to far-off places. The first great era of Sino-European contact was over.

The Century of Discovery

In 1508 the Portuguese King Manuel I sent Diogo Lopez de Sequeira to reconnoitre Malacca and gave him the specific instruction to 'ask after the Chijns, and from what part they come, and from how far'.[25] For the next century or so, a revived interest in China centred on Portuguese and Spanish authors.

Three men produced eyewitness accounts of parts of southern China which formed the basis of sixteenth-century European knowledge and images of China. Galeote Pereira was a Portuguese soldier, sailor, and merchant adventurer who was captured off the coast of Fujian for smuggling in 1549 and unfortunate enough to be held under arrest for several years. Gaspar da Cruz was a Portuguese Dominican, while Martin de Rada was a Spanish Augustinian priest whose writing reports his visit to Fujian in 1575. All three wrote accounts of their stays in China, but only the first two were printed in their own day, Pereira's in Italian translation in 1565 and da Cruz's in its original Portuguese in 1569–70. Pereira's work covered not only China but also other places as well and circulated fairly widely in its time. Da Cruz's book, by contrast, remained rather rare, possibly because it was published in Portugal during a plague epidemic. Being in Portuguese it could not hope to achieve as wide a readership as Pereira's account.

Pereira emphasizes the large size and population of China. He has quite a bit to say about the officials who 'are served and feared'. He describes them as 'an idle generation, without all manner of exercises and pastimes, except it be eating and drinking'.[26] Having been closely involved with it himself, Pereira also describes the legal system in great detail. He notes the beatings with bamboo whips, which make 'the standers-by tremble at their cruelty',[27] and the effects they produce on the sufferer, as well as the severe prisons from which escape is impossible. At the same time, Pereira's experience made him believe the Chinese law system fair. The public trials rendered false testimony out of the question. His summation is that the Chinese are better than Christians 'in doing justice' and 'more bounden than they to deal justly and in truth'.[28] Clearly Pereira's favourable verdict resulted from the outcome of his own case. Viceroy Zhu Wan, who was initially responsible for his arrest, committed suicide after losing a power struggle over his strong enforcement of anti-smuggling and foreign-trade laws. Though he may not have known it, Pereira's own trial probably functioned to gain incriminating evidence against Zhu Wan.

Gaspar da Cruz's *Treatise in which the Things of China are Related at Great Length* 'may fairly be claimed as the first book devoted to China which was printed in Europe'.[29] Unlike Marco Polo's book, much of which is about other countries, da Cruz's is about 90 per cent directly concerned with China. It thus occupies a major place in the history of Western literature on China, even if its relatively narrow circulation puts it lower in the scale of sixteenth-century Western image-formulators of China than Pereira's account.

Gaspar da Cruz spent only a few months in China altogether, and much of his work is based on Pereira, a debt which he frankly acknowledges. Yet da Cruz was a most observant and honest traveller and his book contains many interesting and perceptive comments. Like many others he was impressed with China's prosperity, and while he saw poverty he could state that 'these poor people notwithstanding do not live so poorly and beggarly in their apparel as do those who live poorly in Portugal'.[30] He also commented favourably on Chinese agriculture, and on the industriousness of the people. 'China is almost all a well husbanded country', he observed, where the people 'are great eaters' and 'every one laboureth to get a living, and every one seeketh ways to earn their food'. But they are not so kind to the underdog or the lazy, as da Cruze goes on to point out: 'A great help . . . is that idle people be much abhorred in this country, and are very odious unto the rest, and he that laboureth not shall not eat, for commonly there is none that do give alms to the poor.'[31]

The only chapter to be designated 'notable' in its title is that which deals with those 'who are sentenced to death, and . . . other matters that pertain to justice'. Although this chapter is at least partly based on Pereira's experience, the overall impression it gives the reader is in fact very much more critical. While da Cruz follows Pereira in suggesting that open trials made false testimony very rare, he has more to say in more gruesome language about the savagery of the penal and prison system which obtained in the China of the sixteenth century.[32]

As is to be expected, Gaspar da Cruz suffered from the religious intolerance of his age. Yet in some respects he was remarkably, even extraordinarily, broadminded. For instance, he was the first, and for quite a long time the only, European writer to remark upon Chinese music. Moreover, he took the trouble to understand some of the various musical instruments and singing styles, and did so not to condemn but to appreciate. He describes the Chinese as 'commonly very ingenious and cunning with their hands' and comments on their achievements in the arts, with 'many inventions in every kind of work', especially masonry and painting.[33] In fact, Gaspar da Cruz's *Treatise* was a remarkable achievement, which deserved a wider readership in its own day than it got.

About 1583, in response to considerable and growing interest in China among educated Europeans, Pope Gregory XIII (reigned 1572–85) ordered the composition of a comprehensive history of China. The chosen author was the Augustinian priest Juan Gonzalez de Mendoza. Basing himself on Pereira's, da Cruz's, as well as de Rada's and other accounts, he produced the best-selling and pathbreaking *History of the Great and Mighty Kingdom of China*, published in Rome in Spanish in 1585.[34] He never realized his dream to visit China and was the earliest of a number of great European scholars whom circumstances prevented from setting foot in the country which fascinated them so much.

Mendoza tried, and largely succeeded, in collecting together in one volume everything which was known in the West about China, the first man ever to attempt such a task. This alone makes his *History* very significant. It was also very successful, and consequently influential. No other book created images of China in late sixteenth-century Europe as this one did. By the end of the sixteenth century it had been reprinted

46 times in seven European languages: Spanish, German, Dutch, Italian, French, English, and Latin. As the scholar C. R. Boxer aptly writes: 'It is probably no exaggeration to say that Mendoza's book had been read by the majority of well-educated Europeans at the beginning of the seventeenth century'.[35] Its authority was so great that 'it became the point of departure and the basis of comparison' for all later works on China written in Europe before the eighteenth century.[36]

Like Marco Polo and other early writers, Mendoza is much impressed by the size of China. It is 'the most biggest and populous that is mentioned in all the world'.[37] The title of the book itself, with its reference to 'the great and mighty kingdom', already shows the thrust of Mendoza's view of China. The cities he writes of in exuberant terms, emphasizing the magnificence of their walls, and the splendour of their streets, which are 'very well paved, and so broad that 15 horsemen may ride together in them'.[38] The highways everywhere in China are, according to Mendoza, 'the best and gallantest paved that ever hath been discovered'. Both in their streets and their houses, the Chinese are 'marvellous clean'.[39]

Mendoza writes of the central and local bureaucracy in much detail and with admiration. The highest officials he says 'generally have a marvellous moral virtue, and that is, they be all very patient in hearing any complaint'.[40] He is aware of the examination system by which men entered the public service and describes it in enthusiastic terms.[41]

On the other hand, Mendoza is harshly critical of the legal system. He notes the savage punishments given out by the courts and describes in great detail the 'cruel torments' used to extract confessions. Admittedly, he is defensive even here: 'yet do they execute none of them [the tortures] except first they have good information',[42] as if innocent people hardly ever confessed under torture, but the picture is pretty grim all the same. The prisons are 'as terrible and as cruel' as the punishments, and since the population is so large, 'so have they many prisons and very great'. In this way the officials can 'keep in peace and justice this mighty kingdom'.[43]

Like most other relevant writers of his time, Mendoza was very favourably impressed by the Chinese family system. The women are not only attractive but also virtuous, 'secret and

honest',[44] meaning that one does not often see them in public.
And foot-binding he discusses in some detail without criticism.
'She who hath the least feet is accounted the gallantest dame',
he says, quite correctly. The reason for the custom he believes
to be to immobilize women, both in the home and outside
it,[45] almost certainly a very incomplete analysis.

Finally, Mendoza treats the subject of religion in China
with spectacles rosily tinted by his own Christian beliefs. He
does not appear to have understood Confucian rationalism
at all and his accounts of monastic life read like descriptions
of Christian monasticism. He states directly that the Chinese
believe in the immortality of the soul: the soul of a virtuous
person 'shall live eternally with great joy, and shall be made
an angel' whereas that of an evil one 'shall go with the devils
into dark dungeons and prisons'.[46]

Mendoza's book was strongly attacked by the Constable
of Castile, D. Juan Fernández de Velasco, soon after it was
published. The basic ground was that Mendoza's account extolled
China's greatness too much.[47] What is crucial is that Mendoza
appears to have carried the public with him and European
images of China followed his version rather closely. In other
words, they remained dominantly positive and more detailed
than at any earlier time.

It is necessary to remember that what most concerned Mendoza
and many others was the conversion of the Chinese to
Christianity. There were even some who wished to impose
Christianity on China by military force. In 1576 the governor
of the Philippine Islands, Dr Francisco de Sande, formally
proposed a military attack on China, but King Philip II of
Spain fortunately rejected the suggestion the next year and
instead suggested 'good friendship' with the Chinese. Mendoza
was clearly in the 'peace camp', but the eyes with which he
viewed China were just as dedicated to Christianity none
the less.

The sixteenth century was, for Europe, the age of discovery.
Although India, the East Indies, and the Philippines had loomed
larger in Europe's consciousness in the first half of the century,
China and Japan replaced it in the dominant place from about
1550 on. Most of the authors and readers on China were not
only genuinely interested in it, but also very favourably disposed
towards it. Their aim to convert it to Christianity was senseless

and futile but not yet imperialistic. At the end of the sixteenth century, Europe may have believed it could teach the Chinese, but was still prepared to admire them.

3

Jesuit Missionaries and the Philosophers

WHILE Mendoza was working on his great book about China, other developments were occurring in Catholic Europe which were to lead on to the first great age of European sinology. In 1540 the Society of Jesus was founded by Ignatius of Loyola (1491–1556). Part of the Catholic Reformation of the sixteenth century, the Society saw the conversion of non-Christians to Catholicism as part of its brief. Among Loyola's earliest followers was Francis Xavier (1506–52) who in 1534, even before the Jesuits' formal establishment, had pleged himself to missionary work in Loyola's service.

Xavier went to Goa in India in 1541 and to Japan in 1549. He was enthusiastic about the Japanese and their culture. Although he had heard about China as early as 1546, it was in Japan that he came to realize China's importance if he was to succeed in his aim of Christianizing Eastern Asia. He wrote of China as 'an immense empire, enjoying profound peace'. Portuguese merchants had informed him that it was 'superior to all Christian states in the practice of justice and equity'. The Chinese themselves he believed very wise. Those he had met in Japan were 'acute, and eager to learn' and 'in intellect, they are superior even to the Japanese'.[1] These latter held 'a very high opinion of the wisdom of the Chinese', he wrote on several occasions. 'They used to make that a principal point against us, that if things were as we preached, how was it tha. the Chinese knew nothing about us?'[2]

Xavier died in Macao while waiting for a Chinese merchant he had bribed to take him to China. He never realized his dream to go to the Chinese empire.

Xavier's policy had been that 'to win converts a missionary had to become an "integral part" of a particular civilization'.[3]

Such a broadminded concept was extraordinarily contentious in his day. Yet it was followed also by Alessandro Valignano, who succeeded Xavier as the head of the Jesuit missions in East Asia. Valignano was extremely impressed by the Chinese. He encouraged his followers to learn to speak Chinese. It was at his command that Matteo Ricci learned as much as possible of the language, society, politics, and culture of China from 1582 on. In 1601 Ricci reached the Chinese capital Beijing, the first European on record to do so for 80 years, and lived there until his death in 1610.

Later Jesuits built on the foundations which Ricci had laid. At the end of the Ming dynasty, the Jesuit Johann Adam Schall von Bell (1591–1666) gained the favour of the court itself through his knowledge of astronomy and the manufacture of cannon. The new Qing dynasty retained his services, appointing him head of the Department of Astronomy (*Qin tian jian*). It is true that he was disgraced at the death of the Shunzhi Emperor (reigned 1644–61), but Kangxi (reigned 1662–1722) later rehabilitated him posthumously and appointed another Jesuit, the Belgian Ferdinand Verbiest, to head the Department of Astronomy.

The Manchu emperors forbade the Jesuits to involve themselves in politics and appear to have trusted them because they came from a remote civilization and were not part of the system. One scholar has called them 'unbiased sources of information' and 'impartial witnesses from outer space'.[4] However, it is worth remembering that only a small number operated at court and the vast majority of missionaries never went near so exalted a place.

In the seventeenth century, missionaries of other Catholic orders, especially the Dominicans and Franciscans, began working in China. All orders became embroiled in a sharp controversy of the 'rites'. The Jesuits believed that ceremonies in honour of Confucius and one's ancestors were compatible with Christianity under certain circumstances, while the Dominicans and Franciscans adopted the alternative attitude. The matter was taken to Rome and involved several popes.

In 1715 Pope Clement XI condemned the tolerant missionary practices of the Jesuits, insisting on European forms of Christian practice in China and forbidding the use of Chinese rites. In 1742, Pope Benedict XIV not only reaffirmed the ban, but even prohibited further debate on the matter. After Kangxi's death the decline of Jesuit influence gathered momentum. Most were expelled from China; the final blow came when, in 1774, news of the decree dissolving the Society of Jesus reached Beijing. Writing in an inscription for the Jesuit cemetery at the time, the most famous of the last generation of Jesuits in China, Joseph-Marie Amiot (1718–93), recognized that this event marked the effective end of the Society's influence at both the Chinese court and in the country as a whole. By the end of the eighteenth century there were only about thirty European missionaries left in the whole of China.

The policy of 'integration' which Xavier had originated was thus a permanent one for the Jesuits in China. It meant that, in order to convert the Chinese to Catholicism, the Jesuits must learn as much as they could about the land and its people. Certainly they must speak the language. Ricci had aimed at the top, in other words he began by trying to convert the mandarinate and made a practice of adopting their dress. This approach was in sharp contrast with the Dominicans, whose policy was to try and convert the ordinary people first, the ruling groups later. Adam Schall, Verbiest, and other Jesuits worked at the court itself. Otto van der Sprenkel sums up the results of Jesuit policy thus:

The fact that so many of the missionaries, from Ricci at the beginning to Amiot at the end, were as indefatigable in scholarship as they were devoted in religion, ensured that while they failed in their mission to interpret Christianity to the Chinese, they were brilliantly successful in interpreting China to the West. In letters, pamphlets, and folios, in travel notes, translations, and learned monographs, they sent back a flood of information to Europe on every aspect of China's past history and present condition.[5]

These voluminous writings include two particularly famous series. The first and more important is the Lettres édifiantes et curieuses,[6] which began publication in 1703 and continued until 1776, about one-third dealing with China. The other is the Mémoires concernant . . . des chinois,[7] which ran for seventeen volumes from 1776 to 1814.

The Dominicans took a very different, and much more negative, view of China and its society than did the Jesuits. The net political result of the Rites Controversy was defeat for the Jesuits. But in terms of images of China conveyed to Europe, the Jesuits were incomparably more influential during the seventeenth and eighteenth centuries than any of the rival religious orders.

Matteo Ricci

The first of the major Jesuit works on China was, of course, that of Ricci. His diaries were taken to Rome by Father Nicholas Trigault, a fellow Jesuit, who translated them from Italian into Latin and had them published in Augsburg in 1615.[8] In the next decade or so the work was reprinted four times in Latin and translated into German, Spanish, French, and Italian, and excerpts were translated into English. Like Mendoza's work, Ricci's was widely read and popular. One contemporary scholar considers the diary 'is not reliable as evidence for Ricci's own view' of the Jesuit interpretation of Confucianism,[9] but there is no reason to doubt that it was an extremely influential source of images of China in its day.

Ricci appears to have been the first European to become fully aware of the Chinese intellectual tradition and transmit that knowledge to the West. His book describes Chinese achievements in mathematics, astronomy, and medicine, as well as the crucial role of the Confucian classics in Chinese society. He also discusses the official examinations in great detail, including their various levels, the conditions under which they were taken, and their Confucian contents. Ricci was probably the source for the knowledge, still new in Europe, that the Chinese examinations were written.[10]

Ricci recognized the place of rationalistic and this-worldly moral philosophy in Chinese society. He also tried to come to grips with Neo-Confucianism and he shows some understanding, albeit rudimentary, of the complicated philosophy which it entailed. The reason was not so much broadmindedness as his attempt to convert the *literati* to Christianity. He could see that it was necessary for him to gain some idea of how they thought if his efforts were to bring any success, and it was his conscious policy to interpret any ambiguities in Confucius' writings to suit Catholic Christianity.[11] Ricci was not impressed with China's various other religions such as the 'sect of idols'; astrologers, fortune-tellers, and such people he regarded as 'the blind leading the blind'.[12] As one scholar has aptly commented: 'For tactical purposes Ricci wished an alliance with the Confucians against the Buddhists.'[13]

The earliest reference to Confucianism in Trigault's version of Ricci's diaries is the following passage:

The only one of the higher philosophical sciences with which the Chinese have become acquainted is that of moral philosophy, and in this they seem to have obscured matters by the introduction of error rather than enlightened them. They have no conception of the rules of logic, and consequently treat the precepts of the sciences of ethics without any regard to the intrinsic co-ordination of the various divisions of this subject. The science of ethics with them is a series of confused maxims and deductions at which they have arrived under guidance of the light of reason. The most renowned of all Chinese philosophers was named Confucius. This great and learned man was born five hundred and fifty-one years before the beginning of the Christian era, lived more than seventy years, and spurred on his people to the pursuit of virtue not less by his own example than by his writings and conferences. His self-mastery and abstemious ways of life have led his countrymen to assert that he surpassed in holiness all those who in times past, in the various parts of the world, were considered to have excelled in virtue. Indeed, if we critically examine his actions and sayings as they are recorded in history, we shall be forced to admit that he was the equal of the pagan philosophers and superior to most of them. He is held in such high esteem by the learned Chinese that they do not dare to call into question any pronouncement of his and are ready to give full recognition to an oath sworn in his name, as in that of a common master.[14]

The condemnatory first sentences of this passage are not from Ricci's hand at all. They are Trigault's embellishment of Ricci's observations that dialogue, not logic, is the form Chinese philosophers use to present their views.[15] Just as Ricci's views on Confucianism had taken on a political twist in China to favour his missionary work, they immediately began to become enmeshed in theological debate in Europe itself after his death.

Like many of his European predecessors, Ricci took a very favourable view of China's size and variety of produce. He was also struck by its prosperity: 'everything which the people need for their well-being and sustenance, whether it be for food or clothing or even delicacies and superfluities, is abundantly produced within the border of the kingdom'.[16] The reasons for this prosperous life he believed to have been the fertile soil, the mild climate, and the industry of the people. As far as the first two are concerned it is necessary to note that he was referring to south China, not the north; this is clear from his reference to two or even three harvests a year.

Another point that struck Ricci very favourably was how peace-loving China appeared. He regarded it as remarkable that, though China possessed a well equipped army and navy, 'neither the King nor his people ever think of waging a war of aggression'. They are content with what they have and lack any ambition for conquest. 'In this respect they are much different from the people of Europe', Ricci observes.[17]

However, Ricci also dwelled on several of the most abhorrent aspects of Ming China. These include slavery, female infanticide, and the castration of 'a great number of male children' in northern China so that they can serve the emperor. Above all, he was horrified by the power of the magistrates. Although he found the penal laws of the country 'not too severe', he describes in some detail the frightful beatings which certain people suffered. He notes specifically that 'as many are illegally put to death by the magistrates as are legally executed'. Because of the magistrates' 'lust for domination', Ricci believed that 'everyone lives in continual fear of being deprived of what he has, by a false accusation'.[18]

Ricci's picture is thus only partly a favourable one and he pulls no punches in criticizing. It is to be noted that he lived in China when the Ming dynasty was in decline. Hardly more than a decade after Ricci's death China was in the grip of the notoriously tyrannical eunuch Wei Zhongxian (1568–1627). Not long afterwards the dynasty itself collapsed. Perhaps what is striking under these circumstances is how positive Ricci's impression was. It is by no means to cast doubt on his honesty or withhold credit for his achievement to suggest that his aim to Christianize China influenced his view of that country.

The Jesuits after Ricci

The Jesuits were tremendously impressed by the early Manchu emperors. In the second half of the seventeenth and all the eighteenth centuries they presented Europe with an extremely, indeed unduly, flattering picture of China.

It is worth remembering that Loyola had specifically ordered full reporting of their activities by Jesuit missionaries in the field, but had distinguished those that might be published from those which should be 'reserved for the eyes of the superiors of the Society'.[19] The editors omitted sections which might undercut the value of Jesuit missionary work, or show differences of opinion about China which rival orders could exploit. Since the Jesuits had chosen to work from the top down it was in their interests to show the ruling classes as effective and to get on well with them. Hence there was a tendency to downplay criticism of China in public statements.

In 1687 there appeared in Paris a book entitled *Confucius Sinarum Philosophus* (*Confucius Philosopher of the Chinese*). This was the first complete translation into a European language of any of the Confucian classics to be published in Europe, and included the *Lunyu* (*Analects*), the *Zhong yong* (*Doctrine of the Mean*), and the *Da xue* (*Great Learning*). The Jesuit translator claimed his work to be a literal rendering of the original, but in fact there is also a considerable infusion of European moral philosophy. In places 'Confucius speaks not only in the language, but also with the thoughts of the medieval scholastic philosophers and theologians'.[20] The reason was partly due to the conviction of the Jesuits of Christian veracity. But much more noteworthy is that the translator was actually imputing to the Chinese a knowledge of truth irrespective of Christian revelations. Indeed the introduction to the translations asserts specifically that the ancient Chinese must have had knowledge of the true God and must have worshipped him.

Among the earliest Jesuit missionaries in China to publish an account of the country in his own lifetime was Louis Daniel Le Comte (1656–1729), whose *Nouveaux mémoires sur la Chine* appeared in Paris in 1696. It was immediately translated into several languages and widely read, in the context of its time certainly an image-formulating work. In fact it was somewhat too influential for the Catholic authorities of the day. Le Comte formed a very positive view of Chinese government and law. 'As if God himself had been the legislator, the form of government is hardly less perfect in its origin than it is at present after the more than 4,000 years that it has lasted.'[21] More dangerous still from the point of view of certain Catholic superiors was his view of Chinese religion and morality. The Chinese may be heathens, but 'I have everywhere noticed a chosen people who adore in spirit and in truth the Lord of heaven and of earth',[22] by implication a direct challenge to the exclusiveness of the Judaeo-Christian divine relevation. He even thought that the Chinese worship of the true God could serve as an example for Christians. Issues of this sort had been under debate in Catholic circles for some time. In 1700, the theological faculty of the Sorbonne investigated several books including that of Le Comte and ordered them to be burned.

By far the most important of works on China in the seventeenth and eighteenth centuries is Jean-Baptiste Du Halde's *The General History of China,* which, according to part of its immensely long subtitle, contains 'a geographical, historical, chronological, political, and physical description' of China, Chinese Central Asia, Korea, and Tibet. Du Halde edited Volumes IX to XXVI of the Lettres édifiantes et curieuses (1709–43) and they are his main source; his work is in a sense a digest of what they say. Du Halde himself was among the great sinologists never to have visited China. Du Halde's work, in four volumes, is the largest and most comprehensive single product of Jesuit scholarship on China. It is a truly spectacular accomplishment and in all senses a major landmark in the history of sinology. Among the many in Europe who referred to China and relied on Du Halde as a principal source of information were Montesquieu, Joseph de Guignes, the Encyclopedistes, Rousseau, Voltaire, Hume, and Goldsmith. It is clearly crucial as a source of Western images of China in its day.

Du Halde was immensely positive about China. He praises virtually every aspect of its people and society, and where he offers criticism it is in a defensive tone as if he regarded himself as an advocate for China. He frequently makes comparisons with Europe, mostly to show better conditions in China. Du Halde and other editors of the Lettres apparently made a conscious policy of selecting and publishing material favourable to China in order to refute their opponents' image of an atheistic culture.

The work is so comprehensive that it is not easy to select points needing mention. The following are illustrative only.

Du Halde believed China very well governed. He could

see the power of the mandarins, but believed it generally benign. 'They would not be able to maintain themselves in their offices', he wrote, 'if they did not gain the reputation of being the fathers of the people, and seem to have no other desire than to procure their happiness.'[23]

China is extremely prosperous, says Du Halde. It is 'one of the most fruitful countries in the world, as well as the largest and most beautiful'. He ascribes this 'plenty' to the industry of the people and to the large number of lakes, rivers, and canals.[24]

Du Halde's view of the Chinese people was favourable. They 'are mild and peaceable in the commerce of life', although they can be 'violent and vindictive to excess when they are offended'.[25] He found their modesty 'surprising' in that 'the learned are very sedate, and do not make use of the least gesture but what is conformable to the rules of decency'. As for the women, decency 'seems to be born' with them, as shown by the fact that 'they live in a constant retirement' and 'are decently covered even to their very hands'.[26] Du Halde seems to have been impressed by the demeanour and social position of women. He is not shocked even by foot-binding. 'Among the charms of the sex the smallness of their feet is not the least', he writes.

When a female infant comes into the world, the nurses are very careful to bind their feet very close for fear they should grow too large. The Chinese ladies are subject all their lives to this constraint, which they were accustomed to in their infancy, and their gait is slow, unsteady and disagreeable to foreigners. Yet such is the force of custom, that they not only undergo this inconvenience readily, but they increase it, and endeavour to make their feet as little as possible, thinking it an extraordinary charm, and always affecting to show them as they walk.[27]

Clearly Du Halde was aware of some shortcomings in Chinese society. Despite the 'plenty' to which he draws attention, he knew there was also great poverty. He was perceptive enough to attribute this partly to overpopulation. 'Yet it must be owned that, however temperate and industrious these people are, the great number of inhabitants occasions a great deal of misery', he writes. Some people expose their children to die because they cannot afford an upbringing.[28]

Finally we may note Du Halde's rather positive view even

of the Chinese law system of his day. The 'prisons are neither so dreadful nor so loathesome as the prisons of Europe, but are much more convenient and spacious, and are built in the same manner almost throughout the empire'.[29] The generally favourable judgement, even in comparison with Europe, is quite characteristic of Du Halde's work. Although he was aware of the use of torture he goes some way towards excusing it by stating that 'the Chinese have remedies to diminish, and even to destroy the sense of pain, and after the torture they have others to make use of to heal the criminal'.[30] He appears to have believed that punishments meted out were usually well deserved.

The Jesuit writings on China, at the pinnacle of which Du Halde's work stands, were much read and produced a big impact on Europe. The Society's scholars were, in a real sense, the fathers of Western sinology, and the earliest secular writers on Chinese history, to be discussed in a separate chapter, owe their learning to the Jesuit efforts. The net result was that eighteenth-century Europe knew quite a lot about China.

The Philosophers

Many philosophers of the day admired the Confucian rationalism which contrasted very strongly, they believed, with the religious conflict so prevalent in Europe. In Germany, the Lutheran logician and mathematician Gottfried Wilhelm Leibniz (1646–1716) was appalled at the immorality of his own time and country and argued that China ought 'to send missionaries to us to teach us the purpose and use of natural theology, in the same way as we send missionaries to them to instruct them in revealed theology'. He believed China and Europe, at the opposite ends of the vast Eurasian continent, to be the greatest of the world's civilizations.[31] Leibniz worked much of his life for cultural interchange between China and Europe, and his efforts bore some fruit.

Among the thinkers of the French Enlightenment, the most influential of those positive about China was Voltaire (1694–1778). Highly laudatory about Chinese government, he departed from a view widely held in his time that China was an 'enlightened despotism' and denied that it was a despotism at all. Such a view he believed to be false and based on the purely external factor that people often had to prostrate themselves before superiors. Voltaire's contrary opinion was that China's governance was based on morals and law, and the respect of children for their fathers. The educated mandarins were the fathers of the cities and provinces, and the king that of the empire.[32]

One of the points which struck Voltaire most positively about China was the secular nature of Confucianism. The religion of the emperors and the tribunals he claims 'has never been troubled by priestly quarrels'. He praised Confucius for claiming to be not a prophet but simply a wise magistrate who taught old laws. This was a doctrine of virtue, which preached no mysteries and taught that mankind was naturally good. At the same time, Voltaire rejected utterly the charge that the Chinese were atheists, although he did see their religion as primarily concerned with the present world, not that which follows death, and appears to have regarded their approach as a point in their favour.[33]

Voltaire was much impressed by China's large population, which he estimated at some 150 million and much more than all of Europe, where he believed there were some 100 million people. He comments on the large cities and the considerable prosperity of the country as well as the range of foods and fruits available there. He was aware that the Chinese had known about printing long before Europe.[34]

Almost exactly contemporary with Voltaire was François Quesnay (1694–1774), the leader of the first systematic school of political economy, known as the Physiocrats. Quesnay's *Le despotisme de la Chine* (*Despotism in China*) was published in Paris in 1767. It is enthusiastic about China, even though, as its title shows, its author sees that country's government as despotic. Quesnay regarded China's despotism as benign, in contrast to that of his own country.

The Emperor of China is a despot, but in what sense is that term applied? It seems to me that, generally, we in Europe have an unfavourable opinion of the government of that empire; but I have concluded from the reports about China that the Chinese constitution is founded upon wise and irrevocable laws which the emperor enforces and which he carefully observes himself.[35]

Quesnay considered agriculture as by far the most economically productive activity and China was his model. Here was a rich and prosperous nation with fertile soil and a multiplicity of rivers, lakes, and well maintained canals, where peasants were free and ran no risk of 'being despoiled by arbitrary impositions, nor by exactions of tax collectors'.[36] Yet Quesnay did recognize much poverty in China. Like Du Halde he attributed this largely to overpopulation: 'in spite of . . . the abundance that reigns, there are few countries that have so much poverty among the humble classes. However great that empire may be, it is too crowded for the multitude that inhabit it.'[37]

Though China was much less focal for the great Scottish political economist and philosopher Adam Smith (1723–90) than for Voltaire or Quesnay, he does merit mention here because of the enormous influence of his work *The Wealth of Nations* in the history of political economy.

For Smith, China had for a long time been 'one of the richest, that is, one of the most fertile, best cultivated, most industrious, and most populous countries in the world'.[38] Smith to some extent shared Quesnay's enthusiasm for Chinese agriculture but in contrast saw the large population as a positive factor. He praises China for not going backwards and its 'lowest class of labourers' for making shift 'to continue their race so far as to keep up their usual numbers'. Still, Smith was keenly aware of the 'poverty of the lower ranks of people in China' which, he claims, 'far surpasses that of the most beggarly nations in Europe'. So bad is this poverty that in the great towns several children 'are every night exposed in the street, or drowned like puppies in the water'.[39]

The other point to strike Adam Smith most strongly is the extent of domestic, but lack of foreign, trade. Because of its agricultural wealth, its enormous extent, its large population, the variety of its climate, 'and consequently of productions in its different provinces, and the easy communications by means of water-carriage between the greater part of them', the domestic market is perhaps 'not much inferior to the market of all the different countries of Europe put together'. But Smith regarded the resultant lack of foreign trade as a serious drawback for the Chinese political economy. Foreign trade would open the possibility of learning about the machines and industry of other parts of the world, and 'could scarce fail to increase very much the manufactures of China, and to improve very much the productive powers of its manufacturing industry'.[40]

Despite trenchant and perceptive criticisms, Smith's view of China was basically positive. A very different and very negative image of China came from Charles Louis de Secondat Montesquieu (1689–1755). He agreed with Quesnay that China was a despotism, but saw little benign about it.

Montesquieu was noted for his division of governments into three types: republic, based on virtue; monarchy, based on honour; and despotism, on fear. He argued, further, in a theory which was to assume great importance in later periods, that the natural environment was the main social determinant. Climate takes pride of place, but terrain also ranks high. Montesquieu believed that in hot climates people were weak, lazy, and cowardly, so despotism was the norm, but in cold places people were courageous and free. Montesquieu posed a dichotomy between free Europe, where the temperate zone was large, and Asia, where it hardly existed at all. In China the cold north had conquered the hot south and inflicted despotism everywhere. China seems unable to win; even though some of it is in fact cold, none of it is free.

Despite the fear by which as despots they rule, the Chinese emperors are not without saving graces: they have and are themselves subject to very good laws. Moreover, they are forced to govern well because they know that otherwise revolutionaries will rise up to attempt their overthrow. This is no doubt a reference to the doctrine of the Mandate of Heaven (*tianming*).

Montesquieu knew of the strong family system in China and apparently admired it. The relationship between rulers and people was that of father and children. The legislators required the people to be submissive, peaceful, and industrious. 'When everyone obeys, and everyone is employed, the state is in a happy situation.'

Unfortunately, however, 'by the nature of the soil and climate, their subsistence is very precarious'. As a result the Chinese, Montesquieu believed, were 'the greatest cheats on earth', despite their good laws. 'Let us not then compare the morals of China with those of Europe', he wrote.[41] So whatever good points he may have found in China's society, he was hostile to its people, whom their environment had driven to deceit. His view verges on environmental racism.

Conclusion

Montesquieu leads on to a very much bleaker picture of China in the imperialist nineteenth century. Yet despite the existence of men such as he, it is almost certainly fair to see European images of China from about the middle of the seventeenth to the middle of the eighteenth century as more positive than at any other time before or since.

This was the period of the passion for *chinoiserie* in artistic tastes, which extended from products of craftsmanship and architecture to literature and the theatre. The most famous example of the last was Voltaire's *Orphélin de la Chine*. First produced in 1755, it was based on a translation by the Jesuit J. Prémare of the Chinese drama *Zhaoshi guer* (*Orphan of the Zhao Family*), which was included in Volume III of Du Halde's great work. There were some strange political consequences of the sinomania. In 1764 Mirabeau's *Philosophie rurale* bore as its frontispiece a picture of the Chinese emperor ploughing a small plot of ground to set a good example to his subjects. In 1768 the French dauphin and in 1769 the Emperor Joseph of Austria copied him.

It is of course true that the first half of the Qing was a relatively stable and prosperous period of China's history. Yet the images which the West came to accept were somewhat more flattering to China than the realities could warrant. The transmission of these images to Europe was primarily the work of the Jesuits. It is ironical that they should have been so successful in such a task, when what they were really trying to do was convert the Chinese educated classes to Christianity.

The politcal and ideological dimensions of these images remain significant, despite the sincerity and pioneering work of these thinkers and sinologists. Du Halde and others had political and theological points to score through presenting Chinese society in a favourable light. For Voltaire, a splendid China was at the heart of a new and original view of civilization and its history. For several major philosophers China was a model constructed to criticize their own society. Both the Jesuits and the philosophers were like the great majority of people in all ages. What mattered most to them was not so much the foreign culture — in this case China — as home.

Meanwhile the main European centres of interest in China

had moved north. Marco Polo was Venetian, Rada and Mendoza Spaniards. Ricci, the founder of the Jesuit mission, was Italian, but it was France that led the way in informing Europe about China from the middle of the seventeenth to the late years of the eighteenth centuries. The reign of the great French 'sun-king' Louis XIV (reigned 1643–1715) was contemporaneous with Shunzhi and Kangxi, and made France politically dominant in Europe. In any case, the countries of southern Europe, which had led the way up to the time of Ricci, have never again become the West's main centre of the study of China.

4

Nineteenth-Century Imperialism
and China

JUST like earlier centuries, the nineteenth produced a variety
of views in the West about China. However, the balance between
positive and negative images shifted decisively away from
the former and towards the latter.

There were various reasons for this. The cults of *chinoiserie*
and sinophilism which characterized the Enlightenment 'had
run their natural course and completely lost their impetus'.[1]
The Chinese empire itself was declining quite rapidly from
the late years of Qianlong's reign onwards, and the downhill
move gathered momentum throughout the nineteenth century.
But by far the main reason was the rise of European, and
especially British, imperialism from the time of the Industrial
Revolution. For the first time Britain became a leader as a
formulator of Western images of China.

Chronologically, the beginning of the change from the dominantly positive images of the eighteenth towards the negative
of the nineteenth century occurs in the middle of the eighteenth
century. Baron George Anson returned from a long voyage
around the world in 1744 and his account was published by
his chaplain Richard Walter in 1748. It is the first full-scale
attack on the rosy images of China which the French Jesuits
were pushing. For a variety of domestic reasons, which had
but little to do with China, opinion both in France and Britain
moved strongly against China in the second half of the eighteenth
century. After the rupture of relations occasioned by the
withdrawal of the Jesuits from China in the 1770s the event
which brought about the beginning of a new wave of interest
in China was the embassy of Lord Macartney in 1793. On
the whole the newly industrializing and supremely confident

West now saw a declining China with eyes totally different from those with which their predecessors of not long before had viewed an empire which appeared to be at the height of its glory.

In his diary recording his embassy to China, Lord Macartney remarked of its political system that its aim was apparently 'to persuade the people that they are themselves already perfect and can therefore learn nothing from others'. Macartney thought this an unwise approach: 'A nation that does not advance must retrograde, and finally fall back to barbarism and misery.'[2] Even this brief observation illustrates beautifully three points which were to move centre stage in the formulation of Western images of China in the nineteenth century. One is the assumption that China would be learning from the West in future; China would no longer be the model which Voltaire and others had seen in it. The second is the belief in change. Macartney expressed a view typical of nineteenth-century Europe when he stated that if China refused to change it would sink back into misery.[3] He was right in his perception that Chinese ideology at the time was intensely conservative and thus eschewed change. Finally, Macartney's implication that change meant progress brimmed over with the optimism that was characteristic of nineteenth-century Europe.

Macartney put forward another view which was in contrast to these assumptions. One of the last remarks he makes in his diary under its final day, 15 January 1794, is that 'nothing could be more fallacious than to judge of China by any European standard'. But his next sentence says: 'My sole view has been to represent things precisely as they impressed me'[4] and that seems perfectly fair. Yet it raises and bypasses the issue of by what standards he himself judged China if not the European ones with which he had been brought up. Macartney was aware of the problem and his diary on the whole suggests that he coped with it honestly according to his own lights. Yet the whole tone of nineteenth-century writings on China shows that realistic attempts to take account of non-European, for example Chinese, standards grew fainter and fainter, rarer and rarer, as the century wore on and the military, economic, political and social impact of Western imperialism strengthened. This was the period when the 'Orientalist' approach to China reached its height, when Europe colonized not only parts of China, but also knowledge about it.

Macartney's journal was not published in full until 1962. However, John Barrow, who was a member of Macartney's suite, published selections from his writings in 1807, and several members of the party wrote and published their own accounts of the embassy. The 'official' version was that of Sir George Leonard Staunton,[5] who was Macartney's deputy and Minister Plenipotentiary in his absence. One twentieth-century writer has written of Staunton that he 'interlards his description of the embassy with occasional unqualified eulogies of Chinese society which are reminiscent of the reactions of earlier ages'.[6] He maintains the generally uncritical attitude which had characterized Du Halde, the Physiocrats, or Voltaire.

More interesting as representative of a new and very different point of view on China is John Barrow's *Travels in China*, published first in 1804. This book focuses less on the embassy itself that on Barrow's comments on Chinese life and society, based on his travels there. Before Chapter 1 is an 'advertise-ment' in which Barrow declares his strong disagreement with 'the almost universally received opinion' and pleads his own comments as 'the unbiassed conclusions of his own mind, founded altogether on his own observations'.[7] He seems to be excusing himself for differing so basically with Staunton. It was, after all, through Staunton's patronage that he had gone to China in the first place; moreover, after returning to England he lived in London with Sir George and helped him write the official version of the embassy. He feels called on to warn his readers that, in contrast to the bland 'authentic version', his own book will represent a blistering attack on China, its government, institutions, society, and people.

Barrow saw a country with a bad government, describable only in 'terms of tyranny, oppression, and injustice', exciting feelings of 'fear, deceit, and disobedience' from the governed.[8] The laws are so cruel as to 'exclude and obliterate every no-tion of the dignity of human nature'.[9] The murder and expo-sure of infants are common, induced by the 'extreme poverty and hopeless indigence, the frequent experience of direful famines, and the scenes of misery and calamity occasioned by them'.[10] As for the people themselves, they are dirty and 'their bodies are as seldom washed as their articles of dress';[11] they are cunning cheats and thieves and their 'general character . . . is a strange compound of pride and meanness, of affected gravity and real frivolousness, of refined civility and gross indelicacy'.[12] The reference to refined civility shows Barrow's willingness to allow relieving features in the Chinese and it is necessary to point out, in fairness to him, that he blames for the evils of China not 'the nature and disposition of the people' but rather the 'system of government', including the Manchus' failure to change either the 'forms' or 'abuses' of the previous ancient and stagnant political structures.[13] But the overall picture and images which emerge from Barrow's account, both of China and the Chinese, are very grim indeed.

Protestant Missionaries

The embassy of Lord Macartney in 1793 foreshadowed the rise of British and other encroachments on China, but these did not begin for several decades. On the other hand, the British Protestant missionaries of the early nineteenth century followed Macartney rather quickly. As it happened, they created very little impact in China at first and there were less than 100 converts in 1840. They encountered great difficulty in gaining admission to China and their contact with the people was very sparse indeed. It was British gunboats that gave them the impetus they needed to make greater headway in China. The irony is that whereas their initial progress in converting the Chinese to their religion was negligible, their impact on Britain and the West was substantial in that it was they who played the major role in changing Europe's attitude towards China and its people.

The contrast between the slight impact on China and the considerable one on the mind of the West recalls the experience of the Jesuits. However, the British Protestant missionaries of the early nineteenth century were 'narrow-minded, conservative and unimaginative', qualities quite unlike the humanism of the Jesuits.[14] Britain was in the throes of a general conservatism which resulted, at least in part, from a reaction against the doctrines of the French Revolution of 1789. At the same time its mood was, ironically, expansive as regards the missions. The last years of the eighteenth and first of the nineteenth centuries saw the establishment of quite a few new missionary societies by several Protestant denominations.

One of them was the London Missionary Society, set up in 1795, which was to provide the first of the British Protestant missionaries in China, Robert Morrison (1782–1834), who arrived in Guangzhou in 1807. Morrison made few Chinese friends and hardly any converts, but spent his time on a dictionary and Chinese translations of the Bible, the latter published in 1818. In addition, he wrote on the Chinese language itself and among his works are a Chinese grammar, printed in 1815. Morrison believed that the clue to converting the Chinese was to know their language. His overwhelming, more or less exclusive, interest in the people was their conversion to Christianity.

Other early Protestant missionaries included the Englishman W. H. Medhurst (1796–1857), and the Americans David Abeel (1804–46) and Samuel Wells Williams (1812–84). All three wrote substantially on China. The Protestant missionaries regarded China mainly as a country of heathens 'who lacked the light of God and must be rescued from eternal damnation',[15] and the images they conveyed to the West were correspondingly condescending and negative.

S. Wells Williams was the author of the famous general work *The Middle Kingdom*. It was first published in 1848, and later went through quite a few imprints and editions. It was in its day and remains the best known of the many nineteenth-century compendiums about China and Chinese life in general. It can certainly claim to be image-formulating, and in view of its eminence as a general account of China it may be worth looking at more closely.

There is no doubt that *The Middle Kingdom* is extraordinarily broad in its coverage, in scope very similar to Du Halde's monumental work. There are chapters on geography, population, natural history, law, government, education, language, classical and 'polite' literature, architecture, diet, social life, science, history, religion, commerce, foreign relations, and other matters.

Williams took the trouble to learn Chinese. Indeed, he believed that 'the contempt which the people feel for their visitors, and the restricted intercourse' which had characterized the last century were due to the deplorable ignorance of foreigners of the Chinese language. And, of course, 'far above all in importance', knowledge of the language can help missionaries convert the people and 'accept the proferred grace of their Redeemer'.[16]

Williams believed himself sympathetic to China and the Chinese people. In his preface he states it as one of his objects in writing his work 'to divest the Chinese people and civilization of that peculiar and almost undefinable impression of ridicule which is so generally given them; as if they were the apes of Europeans; and their social state, arts, and government, the burlesques of the same things in Christendom'. Williams knew well of the *du haut en bas* attitude which Westerners of his own time held towards China. He himself was trying to be fair. For him China was 'the most civilized pagan nation in her institutions and literature now existing'.[17]

Yet Williams describes these same institutions as 'despotic and defective, and founded on wrong principles'. 'They may have the element of stability', he goes on, 'but not of improvement'. They do not make people 'honourable, truthful, or kind'. In short, 'this civilization is Asiatic and not European, pagan and not Christian'. What is surprising for Williams is 'that this huge mass of mankind is no worse'.[18]

As far as Chinese literature is concerned, S. Wells Williams regards it as worth looking at for its curiosity value and because it is 'the literature of so vast a portion of the human species'. Yet he also denies that it contains 'much to repay investigation . . . to one already acquainted with the treasures of Western science'.[19]

Despite the narrow ethnocentrism obvious in such views, there are even sharper barbs reserved for the people themselves. His summation of 'the moral traits of Chinese character' is devastating. It is true that he does find some points to praise, such as that 'industry receives its just reward of food, raiment, and shelter, with a uniformity which encourages its constant exertion', a comment which is actually far too kind about the social system. But the people themselves he found 'vile and polluted in a shocking degree'. 'Brothels and their inmates occur everywhere on land and on water' and 'young girls going abroad alone' risk 'incarceration in these gates of hell'. But all is not lost; Williams has a solution, though only one: 'As long as they love to wallow in this filth, they cannot advance, and all experience proves that nothing but the gospel can cleanse and purify its fountain.'

The Chinese, according to Williams, are ungrateful and mendacious. This is no small matter: 'their disregard of truth has perhaps done more to lower their character in the eyes of Christendom than any other fault'. They are avaricious and deceitful. He quotes Abeel, whose portrait, incidentally, appears at the front of Volume II, as trusting a servant, whom he 'had taken to be peculiarly honest for a heathen', only to find him guilty of fraud. Williams found that 'thieving is exceedingly common', and 'public and private charity is almost extinct'.

Williams concludes that the Chinese 'present a singular mixture' of virtue and vice. But 'if there is something to commend, there is more to blame'. The list of virtues is short, of vices long. The result is 'a full unchecked torrent of human depravity . . . proving the existence of a kind and degree of moral degradation, of which an excessive statement can scarcely be made, or an adequate conception hardly be formed'.[20] This is actually a much more damning indictment even than Barrow's overall conclusion.

Another and somewhat later American missionary was Arthur H. Smith, who lived in China for 22 years and in 1890 published what one authority as late as 1979 described as still 'the most comprehensive survey of Chinese characteristics'.[21] Its function as image-formulator and reflector is obvious from the fact that it went through five editions within a decade of its first publication. By the nature of its subject, it concerns not China as an abstract entity but the Chinese as people. Much narrower in its scope than Williams's great work, it covers some of the same ground and is in general only slightly less damning and patronizing, but in some respects it can be even more so.

Smith devotes a chapter to each of 26 characteristics, beginning with face and continuing with others, including economy, industry, politeness, the disregard for accuracy, intellectual turbidity, contempt for foreigners, the absence of public spirit, conservatism, filial piety, benevolence, mutual suspicion, and the absence of sincerity. These 'characteristics', a mixture of positive and negative, are embellished to include others and garnished with illustrative stories conveying verisimilitude.

Smith proclaims that 'many old residents of China', presumably meaning Westerners, are 'in substantial agreement' with his views about the Chinese,[22] and there is no reason to doubt that most ordinary readers accepted his ideas as well.

One 'characteristic' was 'the absence of nerves' and its concomitant, the ability to endure physical pain. 'Those who have any acquaintance with the operations in hospitals in China, know how common, or rather how almost universal, it is for the patients to bear without flinching a degree of pain from which the stoutest of us would shrink in terror.'[23] The Chinese can sleep anywhere and under any conditions. They do not need or want peace and quiet when sick. Smith does not present these features as condemnation, indeed he even quotes with approval a letter of George Eliot to the effect that the ability to bear pain betokens 'the highest calling and election', but to this reader at least his style is so condescending as to imply criticism.

A chapter exemplifying an attempt at balance but with an exceedingly grim overall thrust is the one entitled 'the absence of sympathy', among the longest chapters in the book. It begins with an explanation of the Chinese absence of sympathy through their poverty. Smith also praises the Chinese as a people of mild disposition and acknowledges he has seen many instances of devotion by Chinese towards the sick, even when total strangers.[24] However, he gives far more space to proving his point that the Chinese lack sympathy and are cruel. Their 'whole family life' illustrates their lack of sympathy. The worst relationship of all is mother to daughter-in-law. 'Cases of cruel treatment which are so aggravated as·to lead to suicide, or to an attempt at suicide' on the part of the son's hapless wife 'are so frequent as to excite little more than passing comment'.[25] Either inside or outside the family, the overall indifference of the Chinese to the suffering of others 'is probably not to be matched in any other civilised country'.[26] Not surprisingly, one of his main examples in support of this contention is the punishments meted out by the legal system. Since the time Gaspar da Cruz had praised Chinese justice, European law had progressed enormously while China's had, if anything, worsened. Smith was quite typical of his time in his utter condemnation of China's punishment system. While this is a perfectly reasonable point of view, Smith is less fair in suggesting that the punishments are cruel because that is the Chinese national character. A footnote spells out what the rest of the chapter implies: 'the Chinese being what they are, their laws and their customs being as they are, it would probably be wholly impracticable to introduce any essential amelioration of their punishments without a thoroughgoing reformation of the Chinese people as individuals'.[27] Barrow had blamed bad Chinese national characteristics on the government, Smith implies the reverse causation.

Although he has some praise for the Chinese people, Smith's overall evaluation of their characteristics is extremely harsh. Their needs are few. 'They are only Character and Conscience. Nay, they are but one, for Conscience *is* Character.'[28] This castigation that the Chinese lack any character leads Smith to a discussion of how this serious defect can be overcome. Experience shows that no solution can be found within the people themselves or their country, so obviously reform must come from without: 'To attempt to reform China without "some force from without", is like trying to build a ship in the sea; all the laws of air and water conspire to make it impossible.'[29] The force from without clearly means the West, or more specifically Christianity. China 'needs a new life in every individual soul, in the family, and in society'. These many needs boil down to 'a single imperative need. It will be met permanently, completely, only by Christian civilization'.[30] In its essentials, Smith's judgement of Chinese national characteristics is the same as that of S. Wells Williams before him.

This peroration concludes the book and thus emphasizes its high priority for its author. Smith is justifying the 22 years he spent in a country he did not particularly like. It would be easy to accuse him of self-righteous bigotry. Of course, it would be an accurate charge but perhaps misses the point. He looked at China with eyes very strongly moulded by his own beliefs, a common and natural phenomenon, but with no attempt at all to consider any Chinese point of view. An eminent historian from the period since World War II considers that Smith 'expressed the tolerant but sometimes acerbic frustration of missionaries who found the Chinese villager impervious to progress and the gospel',[31] a charitable interpretation. Smith happened to publish at the beginning of the decade which probably represents the acme of imperialism in China, as shown by the scramble for the concessions in 1898 and the eight-power invasion in 1900. The effect of the images he portrays is support for cultural, even military, intervention.

Raymond Dawson has argued that the missionaries became more liberal towards Chinese civilization in the second half of the nineteenth century owing to the development of Darwin's theory of natural selection and other scientific ideas which challenged the fundamentalist interpretation of the Christian scriptures.[32] In support of this view one could point to James Legge, who after many years as a missionary in China went on to become the first Professor of Chinese at Oxford University. He prepared a translation of the Chinese classics which even today is regarded as authoritative. He was prepared to see elements of true religion in those of the Chinese and in Confucianism, and his style lacks the haughtiness of Williams. Moreover, his own mind broadened substantially with time as he grew older.

Dawson's is a fair view but should not be overstated. If Williams is a reasonable representative of missionary opinion in the middle of the century and Smith towards the end, then the change in attitude can be seen as no more than marginal. It is instructive also to compare the mid-century editions of Williams's great work with one published in 1883, somewhat over three decades later. By that time Williams had become Professor of Chinese Language and Literature at Yale College. The preface of the later version has been more or less completely rewritten. He opens it by affirming that 'a greater advance has probably been made in the political and intellectual development of China than within any previous century of her history'. He also claims to have tried to show the better traits in their national character. There are, indeed, substantial changes made. The reference to Chinese literature saying that it contains little to repay investigation 'to one already acquainted with the treasures of Western science' is qualified by the rider that 'in fairness, such a comparison is not quite just'.[34] Yet he has not for that reason eliminated the comparison. Moreover, all the caustic comments earlier quoted about the national characteristics of the Chinese remain essentially unchanged: their mendaciousness, dishonesty, their moral vileness, and pollution, even the statement that the vices of the Chinese prove 'the existence of a kind and degree of moral degradation of which an excessive statement can scarcely be made, or an adequate conception hardly be formed'.[35]

Images Conveyed by Non-Missionaries

The imperialist onslaught on China brought with it the opening of consular diplomatic missions not only in Guangzhou and Beijing but in other cities as well. The staffs of these missions included many people with a serious attitude to the study of China. Many learned the language and produced studies on general and particular aspects of China, some of them pioneering works.

One of the earliest official missions to China was the French one of 1884, led by Théodose de Lagrené, the aim of which was to conclude a commercial and navigational treaty. On the staff were several people who later wrote much on China. An example is Natalis Rondot, author of a substantial work on French textile trade with China which included comments on many aspects of Chinese society, such as infanticide.

Among the Dutch Gustaaf Schlegel (1840–1903) and Jan Jacob Maria de Groot (1854–1921) stand out. Both worked in China (and Java) as interpreters in the government service, though Schlegel left in 1872 and later took up a chair at Leiden specially created for him. Both wrote widely on Chinese society. Schlegel's area was law, and he also wrote a pioneering essay on prostitution. De Groot is the author of a major work on religion in China. Published in Leiden in six volumes from 1892 to 1910, it is extremely thorough but very condescending in tone. This is already clear from the work's first sentence, where he refers to the Chinese as a 'barbarous and semiciv-ilized' people.[36] Nevertheless, the diplomatic missions of the nineteenth century do signal the first major Dutch contributions to the Western scholarly study of China.

British missions also produced writers of note. A well-known author is Thomas Taylor Meadows, an interpreter in the British consulate in Guangzhou with over a decade's personal experience in China in the 1840s and 1850s. He wrote a book called *The Chinese and their Rebellions*, published in 1856, which covers very many aspects of China such as philosophy, law, and administration. A substantial portion is given to the Taipings, whose rebellion began and expanded while Meadows was in China. There is also a long essay on 'civilization' with comparisons of China and the West.

The tone of Meadows's book is decidedly self-important. He gives much space to attacking the views of other China specialists, including both British and French. But what is striking is that he usually puts himself in the minority view of defending Chinese characteristics, customs, and ideas against criticism.

An illustrative case in point concerns the relationship between the intellect, morality, and progress in the physical sciences. Meadows denounces the French explorer and sinologue Evariste Régis Huc (1813–60) for his criticisms of the Chinese as 'destitute of religious feelings and beliefs' and 'pursuing only wealth and material enjoyments with ardour'. He describes such accusations, all too common in his own day, as 'baseless calumny of the higher life of a great portion of the human race'.[37] Again, he attacks T. F. Wade, whom he describes as 'one of our official sinologues' and who later became British Minister in China, for his description of the Chinese as 'short-sighted utilitarians, industrious and gain seeking' with an 'infinitely vicious' national mind. Meadows's conclusion on all this is worth quoting:

The chief reason why the Chinese have made so little progress in the physical sciences is not a mental 'incapacity', or 'tenuity of intellect', of which Mr Wade accuses them, but a disregard or even contempt for things material as opposed to things intellectual or moral. In war, which is more especially a fight of physical or material forces, they paid the just penalty of this undue contempt when they became involved in a contest with the possessors of the highest material civilization the world has yet seen: the British people.[38]

Meadows attacks what he appears to perceive as outright racism, but he remains ethnocentric and a supporter of imperialism. The Chinese contempt for the material was 'undue', the penalty for it 'just'. And no defence of China weighs against the ringing nationalism of the last sentence.

As well as missionaries and diplomatic personnel, another category of those with experience in China included explorers or travellers, some of whom had special purposes. The nineteenth century in the West saw a self-confident and prosperous middle class which spawned people with the time, money, and inclination to travel, even under the most uncomfortable of conditions. An example of a scientific traveller is Robert Fortune (1813–80) who went to China in 1843 as Botanical Collector to the Horticultural Society of London. In that capacity he travelled in China and wrote a book on both his scientific and more general experiences. The number of travellers grew as the century progressed. The Frenchman Jules Léon Dutreuil de Rhins (1846–94) was a sailor, who travelled in Africa, Siam, and China and was murdered by Tibetan villagers near Xining. The Australian George Ernest Morrison (1862–1920), whom President Yuan Shikai was to appoint as political adviser in 1912, travelled up the Yangzi River and overland through Sichuan and Yunnan to Burma in 1894. There were also women in this company, the outstanding one being Isabella Lucy Bishop (1831–1904). Despite poor health she journeyed all over the world. In the late 1870s she travelled to Southeast Asia, including Southeast China, and in the 1890s she went up the Yangzi, roamed in Sichuan and to Tibet; she covered about 11,000 kilometres in over a year, much of it alone and on horseback.

The tone of Fortune's book on his 'three years' wanderings in the northern provinces' is very high-handed towards the Chinese. Although he does sometimes make a favourable judgement about them, it is always based on the assumption of the superiority of British and Western civilization over Chinese. He claims to be 'far from having any prejudice against the Chinese people',[39] but he scoffs at the suggestion that the Chinese are 'for a moment to be compared with the civilised nations of the West' in agriculture. His summation is that the Chinese 'are not entitled to the credit of being equal to, much less in advance of the nations of the West in science, in the arts, in government or in laws'[40] However, he does consider them 'considerably in advance of the Hindus, Malays, and other nations who inhabit the central and western portions of Asia'.[41] Sweeping generalizations ranking the peoples of Asia, below those of the West of course, were a typical characteristic of nineteenth-century 'Orientalism'.

The Australian Morrison in his younger days was more tolerant and definitely saw himself not only as a friend of the Chinese but also as one who had undergone something of a conversion. 'I went to China possessed with the strong racial antipathy to the Chinese common to my countrymen, but that feeling has long since given way to one of lively sympathy and gratitude.' He recalls his journey with great pleasure and claims to have met everywhere with 'uniform kindness and hospitality, and the most charming courtesy'.[42] Isabella Lucy Bishop found China 'intoxicating' and 'enchanting'. After being carried all day around and in Guangzhou she wrote that she had for the first time drunk of that water 'of which it may truly be said that who so drinks "shall thirst again" — true Orientalism',[43] by which term she obviously means something desirable and expressing a powerful image of exoticism. Though she understood by 'Orientalism' something quite different from Edward Said, her work no doubt falls under the pejorative sense of the word, as he has defined it in his book.

The travellers quite naturally cover a vast range of topics and though their works probably reached a wider readership than did the scholarly or diplomatic literature, the images portrayed by the writers of the various callings do not necessarily differ essentially. Two perennial themes suffice as illustrations of the travelogues: the law, and the status of women.

Fortune criticizes China not so much for the barbarity of its system of punishments, but rather because 'the government is powerless, and has not the means of punishing those who break the laws'. As a result, 'the only thing which keeps the country together is the quiet and inoffensive character of the people'.[44] Morrison attacks the problem from the opposite end. He is appalled at the shocking cruelty of the punishments and the widespread use of mutilation. While this is a perfectly reasonable view and an image justly very common in the literature, he has drawn a less justifiable conclusion about the Chinese people, one we have already seen in the work of the missionary A. H. Smith: that the Chinese are physically insensitive. 'The sensory nervous system of a Chinaman is either blunted or of arrested development. Can anyone doubt this who witnesses the stoicism with which a Chinaman can endure physical pain.' Another curious comment on the Chinese punishment system is Morrison's suggestion that the Chinese practice of compelling a culprit who has just been beaten to thank the magistrate for correcting his morals 'might with good effect be introduced into England'.[45] Morrison seems to be looking for factors which mitigate his horror at the mutilations he has just been describing in grim detail. Isabella Bishop dwells at length on a prison and lawcourt in Guangzhou. Her summative image is uncompromising and to the point: 'If crime, vice, despair, suffering, filth and cruelty can make a hell on earth, this is one.'[46]

Fortune attacked China for its treatment of women: 'The females here, like those of most half civilised or barbarous nations', which presumably include China, 'are kept in the background, and are not considered on an equality with their husbands'. To prove his point he cites an example that 'they do not sit at the same table'.[47] This is perhaps a reasonable point, but to include it yet ignore foot-binding or concubinage shows a curious set of priorities. It had clearly never occurred to Fortune to doubt that British women were equal to their husbands.

Isabella Bishop was impressed with Chinese women. In contrast to Fortune, foot-binding does loom large as an image of their treatment for her, but she is strikingly defensive about it. Her comments are worth quoting in detail:

I like the faces of the lower orders of Chinese women. They are both strong and kind, and it is pleasant to see women not deformed in any way . . . The small-footed women are rarely seen out of doors; but the serving-woman at Mrs Smith's has crippled feet, and I have got her shoes, which are too small for the English baby of four months old! The butler's little daughter, aged seven, is having her feet 'bandaged' for the first time, and is in torture, but bears it bravely in the hope of 'getting a rich husband'. The sole of the shoe of a properly diminished foot is about two inches and a half long, but the mother of this suffering infant says, with a quiet air of truth and triumph, that Chinese women suffer less in the process of being crippled than foreign women do from wearing corsets! To these Eastern women the notion of deforming the figure for the sake of appearance only is unintelligible and repulsive.[48]

Morrison shows himself aware of several of the more horrific aspects of the treatment of females in China in the late nineteenth century. He has quite a bit to say about wife-beating, the sale of girls into slavery, foot-binding, and female infanticide.

But whereas Fortune's contrasts with the West are aimed at showing its superiority, Morrison, like Bishop, is quite equal to comparisons which defend China. 'The prevalent idea with us Westerners appears to be, that the murder of their children, especially of their female children, is a kind of national pastime with the Chinese', he writes. But this perception of the dominant Western image on female infanticide introduces his own research into quite a few scholarly sources which put forward an alternative view. He cites a former French Consul in China, G. Eugène Simon, to the effect that 'infanticide is a good deal less frequent in China than in Europe generally, and particularly in France'. His own general conclusion on this subject is to doubt 'whether the crime, excepting in seasons of famine, is, in proportion to the population, more common in China than it is in England'.[49] Morrison also reaches a general conclusion about Chinese women, like the one on infanticide comparative, though not with the West: 'speaking as an impartial observer who has been both in Japan and China, I have never been able to come to any other decision than that in every feature the Chinese woman is superior to her Japanese sister'.[50]

The impression which emerges is of Morrison as a nineteenth-century observer more than usually defensive of China. Yet the general picture he paints of the situation in those parts of China where he travelled is exceedingly grim. Moreover, despite his comments on infanticide, he most certainly did see the West as superior to China, as made clear by comments such as 'we, who live amid the advantages of Western civilisation, can hardly realise' the severity of particular hardships in China.[51] And as far as the people themselves are concerned, his enjoyment of his journey did not prevent him from caustic generalizations about their character. He quotes a French missionary as telling him: 'If you ever hear of a Chinaman who is not a thief and a liar do not believe it, Monsieur Morrison, do not believe it; they are thieves and liars every one.'[52] And this is followed by a little story which appears to show the priest right. It was symptomatic of the age that even an observer as perceptive and tolerant as Morrison could allow to go unchallenged so hostile a comment, not about the country, its conditions, or its institutions, but about the character of an entire people with which he claimed to sympathize.

Encyclopedias

The dominantly negative images of the nineteenth century were to some extent spawned but also strongly reinforced by encyclopedias. There was of course nothing new to the nineteenth century about this source of instant knowledge, either in the West or for that matter in China. But entries on countries such as China grew enormously both in length and sophistication during the nineteenth century because of the leap in knowledge which went together with the expansionism, colonialism, and confidence of the Western countries. Correspondingly, the view which comes over from the encyclopedias is heavily coloured by colonialist attitudes. At no time has the weight of encyclopedias as formulators of perceptions about China been greater in relation to the whole range of sources of Western images than in the nineteenth century.

There were numerous types of encyclopedias: general, family, women's, technical, and others, and the tendency was for them to go through several editions. Some were illustrated, others not. Three specific entries on China or the 'Chinese Empire' can illustrate the kinds of images which emerged from this large range of encyclopedias: those of the ninth edition of the *Encyclopædia Britannica*, published in 1876, the 1874 edition of *Chambers's Encyclopædia*, and the tenth edition of the Brockhaus *Conversations-Lexicon*, which came out in 1852. These three encyclopedias could claim as reasonably as any other to be called respectively the two most influential British encyclopedias and the most image-formulating in Germany. All three, especially the first and third, created a strong impact in countries other than the one where they originated.

The *Encyclopædia Britannica* was designed as more scholarly than the other two. Brockhaus calls itself a 'conversations-lexicon' designed for the educated classes, whereas the title of *Chambers's* specifies that the work aims to provide 'universal knowledge for the people'.

Of the three entries on China that of the *Encyclopædia Britannica* is by far the longest, but the most substantial section within it is the one dealing with language and literature, which are given a separate entry in Brockhaus. There is an enormous amount of factual information in these entries, especially in the *Encyclopædia Britannica* and Brockhaus. The tone of all three is extremely condescending, regarding China as an exotic, backward, only semi-civilized, and in some ways rather barbaric country. Of the three, Brockhaus is the most negative, and *Chambers's* the least so.

Chambers's takes its discussion of Chinese government largely from T. T. Meadows and is thus in places quite laudatory. The administrative machinery is described as 'very perfect in its organisation', and the 'normal government' as 'less a despotism than a morally supported autocracy'.[53] The emphasis in the *Encyclopædia Britannica*, by contrast, is on despotism, corruption, and a cruel law system. The system of government is 'a patriarchal despotism'. The emperor 'holds autocratic sway over his household — the empire . . . Whom he will he slays, and whom he will he keeps alive.' Corruption in high places demoralizes the people with the result that 'dishonesty prevails to a frightful extent, and with it, of course untruthfulness'. The fact that the Chinese 'set little or no value upon truth' offers 'some slight excuse . . . for the use of torture in the courts of justice'. There is graphic and detailed description of the torture not only of criminals, but also of witnesses, provoking the by now familiar reaction: 'The Mongolian race is confessedly obtuse-nerved and insensible to suffering, and no doubt Chinese culprits do not suffer nearly as much as members of more sensitive races would under similar treatment.' However, the fact that Chinese do not feel pain to the same degree as Westerners cannot be seen as justification: 'even granting this [the Chinese insensitivity to pain], the refined cruelties perpetrated by Chinamen on Chinamen admit of no apology'.[54]

We have already come from government to national character. All three encyclopedia entries convey generally caustic images of the Chinese and their society. Brockhaus dubs Chinese domestic life as 'in general cold and boring'.[55] For *Chambers's*, social relations are 'regulated by a tedious and elaborate etiquette'. Women are hardly better than slaves. The people are hypocritical and inscrutable. One authority is quoted in *Chambers's*, with approval, as saying that 'a Chinaman . . . has wonderful command of feature; he generally looks most pleased when he has least reason to be so'.[56]

The *Encyclopædia Britannica* concedes 'quiet, happy, domestic life' for those many lucky enough to escape 'the clutches of the mandarins and their satellites' and even 'much that might be imitated by European families' in the ordering of a Chinese household. At the same time, the author is shocked by the prevalence of the smoking of opium, 'a drug which seems to have a greater attraction' for the Chinese 'than for any other people on the face of the earth'.[57] He also addresses the problem of female infanticide and, although like Morrison he is at pains not to exaggerate its prevalence, he does include some devastating material concerning parts of Fujian province. 'The people make no attempt to conceal the practice' of female infanticide, he claims, 'and even go to the length of defending it. What is the good of rearing daughters, they say'.[58]

For the Brockhaus encyclopedia, the first point to make about the Chinese character is their lack of individuality: 'In their national character the Chinese form such a peculiarly marked whole that individuals disappear as members of the nation.' A discussion of the facial and other bodily features of the Chinese leads on to more detail about what they are like as people.

Hard work, politeness, the love of peace and mildness are the hallmarks of the Chinese character. Nothing is more sacred to him than the love of a child or the fidelity of a subject. On the other hand, lust, gluttony, deceitful cunning in trade and traffic, cowardice and false flexibility, an intolerable national pride, rigid adherence to tradition, pitilessness, vindictiveness, and corruptibility form a strong dark side. The innate ability of the Chinese for manufacturing work, his knowledge and opinions are still the same as centuries ago.[59]

The list of virtues is quite short, of vices long, just as with S. Wells Williams. But with the addition of the last sentence, even the virtues tend to dwindle into weaknesses, for it seems that after all this is a people which does not change, even over centuries.

Images of the Taiping Uprising

An impression of Western images of China in the nineteenth century can be gleaned not only from what was written about the country and people generally, but also about a particular period. The first specific and major domestic event in China to be covered in detail by Western observers contemporary with it was the Taiping uprising (1851–66). Indeed, Western reports on the movement are probably nearly as voluminous as Chinese. It will thus be worthwhile to single out the Taipings as an example of Western reporting on the domestic scene in nineteenth-century China. Many Westerners wrote on the uprising; in terms of nationality, most were British, American, or French; of calling, government officials, adventurers, journalists, and above all missionaries.

The initial impressions were mixed. Some people saw the Taipings as just another rebellion, but others, such as Meadows, began to pin hopes on it to change China's politics and religion. One newspaper report in the *North China Herald* (7 May 1853) cited Meadows as having been impressed by how well he was treated in Nanjing, which the Taipings had captured nearly two months earlier and made their capital. On the streets Meadows 'did not hear one of those abusive and derogatory epithets applied to himself or companions, which have always been so liberally bestowed on passing foreigners by the heathen Chinese'.[60]

The phraseology highlights the narrow-minded and condescending attitude, even of those friendly to the Taipings. The missionary W. H. Medhurst is another example of the same point. In a letter to the *North China Herald* (26 November 1853), he expostulates on the marvels of the Taipings who could 'induce 100,000 Chinamen, for months and years together, to give up tobacco, opium, lust and covetousness'. The conclusion he draws is that this 'is confessedly a moral revolution — it is the wonder of the age'.[61]

In 1853 and 1854 the British, French, and Americans sent several fact-finding missions to the Taipings. These were the first official contacts between the Western powers and the movement. Robert McLane, the United States' Minister to China, who led the American mission, concluded that they 'neither profess or apprehend christianity' and gave no grounds at all for the earlier 'hopes of the enlightened and civilized nations of the earth'.[62]

Meadows advocated that the powers befriend the Taipings, but without any intervention. He believed their claims of supremacy for the sovereign were no worse than the Manchus. The Qing, despite the 'British war and in opposition to the spirit of the treaties', was persisting in 'the old national policy of "making a distinction between natives and barbarians", of "avoiding friendly relations" with the latter and of "keeping them off"'. The Taipings, on the other hand, had 'manifested a decidedly friendly feeling'.[63] It was thus in Britain's interests to return the friendship. It appears clear that Meadows supported the major actions of the British in China. His political wish to see the Taipings victorious was due not to any positive image of the Taipings but to his own perceptions of which side would suit British interests best.

For most of the late 1850s contact between Westerners and the Taipings was minimal. When it was re-established, the missionaries were the main group observing the Taipings at close quarters. By the early 1860s few were sympathetic to the movement. The majority had become convinced that a Taiping victory was neither likely nor desirable; they no longer believed in the practicability of effective missionary work in the rebel-held areas.

Government and commercial circles were even more hostile. In August 1860 and again in 1862 the Taipings attacked Shanghai and hence threatened Western interests directly. In December 1861 they actually took one of the treaty ports, Ningbo in Zhejiang. The Westerners saw the experience as confirming their already held view that they could not maintain satisfactory relations with the Taipings. The following is an extract from a report by Frederick Harvey, British Consul at Ningbo. Harvey saw himself as impartial, but still delivered himself of an attack on the Taipings which is unusual in its vitriol and self-righteousness.

The first impression of a sensible and reasoning Englishman, on coming in contact with Tae-pingdom, is one of horror, then of amazement, with contempt and disgust following each other in succession. Tae-pingdom is a huge mass of 'nothingness' (I can find no other word to express my meaning); there is nothing to lay hold of in it. It is a gigantic bubble, that collapses on being touched, but leaves a mark of blood on the finger. In its ten years rampant carousing, what has it ever accomplished? Nothing. . . . Is it a popular movement for the purpose of shaking off a heavy yoke, or is it a sanguinary raid, and an extended brigandage over the country, burning, destroying, and killing everything that has life in it? The answer, alas! is but too obvious.[64]

By the time the Taipings actually fell, there were hardly any Western observers willing to defend them, while in support of the Qing dynasty's cause some foreign troops had actually been prepared to take part. Conventional wisdom in the West on the Taipings was that the movement was a more or less unmitigated disaster, and that the West itself had been decisive in saving China from falling into the abyss of a rebel victory. The summation of a popular encyclopedia on the Taiping rebellion, published about a decade after it collapsed, was that 'after a series of wasteful and revolting barbarities, it was finally suppressed in 1865 by the imperial troops, led by British and American officers'.[65]

Nevertheless, it is only fair to add that there was an alternative view. Its main exponent was Augustus Lindley, a military adventurer with personal experience among the Taipings from 1860 to 1864, who published a book in 1866 on the 'history of the Ti-ping Revolution'. The title itself is significant, because very few people were prepared to credit the Taiping movement as a revolution, using instead the more trivial and pejorative term 'rebellion'.

Lindley defended the Taipings from more or less all charges levelled against them and believed them superior morally and in most other ways to the Qing. They 'never committed wanton devastation',[66] their armies were organized much better than those of the Qing, and observed strict discipline. Speaking as a Protestant Christian himself he believed that the Taipings had genuinely done 'their utmost to enter into the pale and brotherhood of Christendom'.[67]

But his highest praise lay in their treatment of women: 'if one part of their system and organization appeared more admirable than another, it was the improved position of their women'. This factor 'affords strong evidence of the advancement of their moral character'. In particular, the Taipings, says Lindley, 'have abolished the horrible custom of cramping and deforming the feet of their women'. Lindley's view was that women were in general far better off under the Taipings than the Qing dynasty and that their status 'approached that of civilized nations',[68] presumably meaning mainly those of the West.

Conclusion

On the whole, the images discussed above veer towards the centre rather than the extremes of Western opinion in the nineteenth century. There were still the strong enthusiasts. Victor Hugo's painting and poetry shows Chinese influence and in 1848 he drew up a plan which called on the French to educate themselves in Chinese culture. On the other hand, outright racism of the sort found in the London journal *Punch* was quite common.[69]

The rapid technological progress which resulted from the Industrial Revolution made most Westerners extremely sure of themselves and led them to look down on those they regarded as backward or inferior, who included the Chinese. The yardsticks of comparison, the criteria for judgement, were European. Many, even among their 'friends', were not sure whether the Chinese could rate as 'civilized'. Those with experience in China certainly cared about it, and were desperate for profits, converts of just excitement or exoticism. It is surely an exaggeration to argue that in the nineteenth century 'every European, in what he could say about the Orient, was consequently a racist, an imperialist, and almost totally ethnocentric'.[70] Yet on the whole, Western observers conveyed images which conformed with the expansionist aims which had driven them to China in the first place. Their attitudes were entirely consistent with the imperialism of their day.

5

Western Images of Contemporary China in the First Half of the Twentieth Century

I grew up in a double world, the small white clean Presbyterian American world of my parents and the big loving merry not-too-clean Chinese world, and there was no communication between them. When I was in the Chinese world I was Chinese, I spoke Chinese and behaved as a Chinese and ate as the Chinese did, and I shared their thoughts and feelings. When I was in the American world, I shut the door between.[1]

This passage from Pearl Buck's autobiography refers to the period about the time of the Boxer uprising of 1900, when Western images of China were as negative as they have ever been. Pearl Buck (1892–1973) obviously liked the Chinese as a child, and there is absolutely no hint here of the scathing images which most Westerners held at the time. Yet she was already dimly aware of a cardinal rule, that one ought not to encourage too much communication between the Chinese and those Westerners who lived in China.

Pearl Buck played a prominent role in formulating Western images of China in the first half of the twentieth century through her novel *The Good Earth*. In particular, she both influenced and represented a trend resulting in images which were enormously more positive by the time the Guomindang fell in 1949 than they had been when the Boxers besieged the foreign legations half a century earlier.

Buck is representative also both as an American and as a woman. The years 1900 to 1949 for the first time saw the rise of the Americans to a position of dominance among formulators of Western images of China. This was also the first period when women appear among the first rank of those authors whose writings moulded Western views of contemporary China.

The Boxer Uprising

The years leading up to the Boxer uprising saw an expansion of European imperialist penetration in China, including the 'scramble for the concessions' in 1898. Another event relevant to images of the Chinese was the discovery in 1895 of the 500,000-year-old *Homo erectus* known as Java man. On 27 August 1897 an article appeared in the *North China Herald* on 'Darwinism and China'. It argued that the characteristics of the Chinese were as close to those of Java man as to those of modern European 'civilized' man. And when he is angry, he is closer! 'Watch him half bend himself downwards and then spring up with a jerk, his gesticulating arm and twitching fingers hardly under control: he is the very picture of an enraged anthropoid ape.' Unfortunately, the (unnamed) author of this article appears to have been writing seriously, even though it reads more like a joke in poor taste today.

The Boxer uprising merely served to confirm the worst suspicions and fears of the Westerners. A flood of reports flowed back to the West describing what had happened. In terms of images, the main burden of the reports was the courage and generally fine behaviour of the Western missionaries and other residents in the face of attack by the ragged Chinese Boxer peasants.

The main images of the Chinese to emerge from the literature spawned by the Boxer uprising are cruelty, treachery, and xenophobia. 'The awful treachery and base cruelty of the Chinese high officials and the people governed by them are without a parallel',[2] wrote the wife of an American diplomat, who nevertheless exempted the Empress Dowager Cixi, describing her as 'a great woman' with 'a strong character, such as history has seldom recorded'.[3] In particular, their cruelty against foreigners showed how low they had sunk. The well known British traveller in and writer on Tibet and East Asia, Henry Savage-Landor, was shocked to find in the United States a widespread belief that the Boxers and Chinese officials had spared and respected Americans during the uprising. His own view was that 'the massacres of Europeans were by no means trifling nor unimportant, nor due to some personal spite against particular individuals'. He records flagrant cases of high officials determined to 'exterminate all "white devils"' and concludes that the 'attacks were directed against everybody foreign, regardless of age, sex, and condition'.[4]

Chinese cruelty in general and against foreigners in particular was so strong an image that when the *London Daily Mail* reported on 7 July 1900 that the diplomatic community in Beijing had been annihilated, everyone having been 'put to the sword in a most atrocious manner', most people believed it and responded with rage and calls for vengeance. Sarah Pike Conger, whose self-image was of sympathy for China, was among those prepared to argue that the 'Christ-spirit alone' should help the West to 'forgive and forget'.[5] Mrs Conger pointed out, quite correctly, that 'China belongs to the Chinese, and she never wanted the foreigners upon her soil'.[6] But vengeance is precisely what the powers inflicted on China through the Boxer Protocol of September 1901.

The West did not ignore the cruelty which its own people wreaked upon the Chinese. But that was justified, or at least understandable, because the West was merely responding to savage and unprovoked attacks from the Chinese. Witness the following description in one of the many surviving diaries on the Boxer period. It refers to 10 July 1900, during the famous 'siege of the legations' (20 June to 14 August 1900).

Last night twenty Chinese were captured at the French Legation. Three were shot; but the French corporal, saying it would not do to waste so many precious rounds, killed fifteen with his bayonet. Two were kept to be examined.

The flies about the place are something ghastly, being attracted by the unburied corpses of the Chinese . . . Just imagine having to keep watch in the blazing sun from 12 to 2 p.m. as I had to one of these days! My rifle got so hot in the sun that I could hardly hold it, and had to keep it as cool as possible in the shade that /afforded. Add to this steaming heat, a few hundred flies, and you have my picture.[7]

This extract was written by a member of the British consular service in Beijing at the time, Lancelot Giles (1878–1934), the sixth son of the well known sinologist Professor Herbert Allen Giles. Lancelot Giles expresses no disapproval at bayoneting fifteen Chinese because ammunition was short. What interested him, the 'picture' or image he wished to convey, was of flies which made his job of standing in the hot sun for two hours on one occasion that much nastier.

It would, however, be grossly unfair not to emphasize the more liberal currents. At the forefront was a married couple from a Western country which has hitherto been ignored in these pages. During the Boxer period the ambassador to China of the Austro-Hungarian empire, Baron Czikann, was on home leave. In his absence the Austrian mission was headed by Arthur von Rosthorn (1862–1945), the *chargé d'affaires*. According to the authors of a recent large-scale study of Sino-Austrian relations, Rosthorn was 'probably one of the few, if not the only one among the foreigners living in Beijing at the time, who reported on the events with understanding and as a friend of China'. His wife Paula shared his sympathetic views.[8]

Rosthorn denied flatly that there was any inherent hostility to foreigners, or anti-foreignism, among the Chinese. Expanding on a point we have already seen touched on by Mrs Conger, he argued that if the Boxers were angry, and indeed hated the representatives of the great powers, these had only themselves to blame for the acts of plunder they had inflicted on China since 1842. 'We Europeans do not credit to Asians the feelings of patriotism which move us ourselves', he concluded. 'This is a great mistake.'[9] Rosthorn saw the origins of nationalism in the Boxers, not cruelty or hatred of foreigners.

Paula Rosthorn's view, written but not published about the time of the Boxers, is even more forthright, and an adult's view similar to the youthful Pearl Buck's with which the chapter began.

Those Chinese who have not yet been spoiled by Europeans, are an extraordinarily honest people. The country folk are especially touching. We used to go walking a great deal and every time, if we went past a peasant hut, the people would ask us to come in and share their meal. They would always bring fruit and bread (Brot) along and could never be persuaded to accept any recompense for it.[10]

Her image of the Chinese peasant was of a generous and open-hearted person, including towards foreigners, even at the dreadful times at the turn of the century.

More Favourable Images

In his book on American images of China and India in the twentieth century, Harold Isaacs calls one section 'The Attractive People (1905–37)' and thus sees a transition a few years after the Boxers from negative to positive in how Americans perceived China. The eight-power invasion of China in 1900 and its aftermath had 'chastened the Manchu court' and stifled the anti-missionary and anti-Western violence among the rural traditionalists from whom the Boxers had sprung. On the whole, foreigners were physically much safer in China after the Boxers than before. In the United States, meanwhile, 'there was a certain revulsion against the maltreatment of the Chinese', which certainly affected images of China itself.[11]

Academic Opinion

These trends doubtless also affected views in Western countries other than the United States. Arthur von Rosthorn went on to become Austria–Hungary's ambassador in China from 1911 to 1917 and then a sinologist and honorary professor at the University of Vienna. He maintained his opposition to imperialism. When Hitler's Germany invaded Austria he was summoned to join the Gestapo. However, he remained a firm and outspoken opponent of the Nazi regime.[12]

In English-speaking countries a better known representative of the pro-China diplomat turned academic was Professor H. A. Giles, who held the Chair of Chinese at Cambridge University from 1897 until 1932. While in the consular service in China he had compiled his enormous and still famous *Chinese-English Dictionary*, but though he wrote a great deal about China, especially its history, literature, and religion, he never revisited it. According to one writer, himself a diplomat, Professor Giles 'set out to transform current European ideas about China as a country of mystery and barbarism' to an image of a 'country with an unsurpassed record of civilization and culture'. In 1922 the Royal Asiatic Society in Britain awarded him their Gold Medal, saying that he 'beyond all living scholars has humanised Chinese studies'.[13] He even quarrelled with his son Lancelot because the latter wrote him letters criticizing developments in China in the 1920s.[14]

H. A. Giles was enthusiastic about the Chinese people and ever optimistic about their future, on occasion even naively so. In a popular book completed on the eve of the 1911 revolution, he writes with great praise of the innovations brought in by the Manchus. He concludes by predicting that China 'will pass through the melting-pot, to emerge once more, as on all previous occasions, purified and strengthened by the process'.[15] But the assumption is that the changes will take place under Manchu rule, for he failed to show any awareness of the disintegration of the Qing dynasty. To be fair to him, however, he does envisage the certainty of major change in Chinese society, and thus separates himself from the 'unchanging China' syndrome.

In the United States, too, China began to be a notable target of study among academics. The focus was somewhat different from European countries, where historical and philological studies of China predominated. The Americans were not without their historians, but gave greater emphasis to sociology and anthropology. An early example is *Country Life in South China, The Sociology of Familism*, by Daniel Harrison Kulp II, published in 1925. It breaks new ground in being an intensive study of a single Chinese community, that of 'Phenix Village' in Guangdong province. It is based mainly on field work in the village in 1918 and 1919. The author dedicates his book 'to the farmers of forty centuries', but does not betray any obvious prejudices for or against his subjects. Still, the picture of life in Phenix Village that emerges from his investigations is of a rather drab, unfortunate, and tradition-bound, although not unchangeable, existence. Despite its strengths, Kulp concludes that Phenix Village is 'beginning to crack under the stresses and strains of the infusion of modern ideas'. He doubts 'its present independent unity and familist solidarity' will survive, because 'familism does not provide the technic of adjustment to a world dominated by capitalism'. This leads Kulp to hope 'that familism may adopt the technic of capitalism without its exploitative objectives',[16] a statement which shows his political assumptions about the future, especially of China.

A slightly later American sociological study of China, published in 1933, carries the rather pretentious title *The Mind of China*. The author, Edwin Harvey, sees the focus of China's mind as animistic belief. He is optimistic about China's future, in particular the improving status of women,[17] and expects a decline of belief in the world of spirits. His assumption is that this implies 'the acceptance of the obviously effective materialism and industrialism of the West'.[18] Like Kulp's, then, Harvey's view of China is filtered through the spectacles of American liberal capitalism. Yet he was obviously making a sincere and reasonable attempt to apply a social science analytical framework to what he saw around him in Republican China, and to develop the communication between the Chinese and American worlds the absence of which in earlier decades Pearl Buck was later to criticize so severely.

Two Major Chinese Sources for Western Images

Harvey was a great admirer of Hu Shi, whose sentiments he considered expressed 'as enlightened a point of view as that of any civilization'.[19] Hu Shi was one of the leaders of the new culture which emerged in China from the second decade of the twentieth century. He was also among a number of Chinese who tried to influence and improve Western images of China. Of all the works written with this specific aim by Chinese authors in European languages, the most famous and influential was Lin Yutang's *My Country and my People*, which was first published in February 1936 and had reached its seventh reprint by March 1938.

Lin Yutang set out to refute the 'constant, unintelligent elaboration of the Chinaman as a strange fiction, which is as childish as it is untrue and with which the West is so familiar.'[20] One of the two authors he cites as a negative example is Rodney Gilbert, who in 1926 had included the Chinese among the world's 'inferior races'– and China among the 'nations that cannot govern themselves, but must have a master';[21] while Gilbert blamed Western influence for the collapse of China's imperial authority, he believed that the West would be failing in its responsibility if, 'having done the damage', it were to withdraw 'when a firm hold upon the situation might right matters'.[22]

Lin Yutang's appeal is as a patriot who is not ashamed of his country. It is to people of 'that simple common sense for which ancient China was so distinguished' and those 'who have not lost their sense of ultimate human values.'[23] Like A. H. Smith before him, he notes the features of 'the Chinese character'. But his list is very different, and much more positive, than Smith's. The eight characteristics, in the order listed by Lin, are mellowness, patience, indifference, old roguery, pacifism, contentment, humour, and conservatism. The first given is the basic one, being in a sense the source of the others. 'A mellow understanding of life and of human nature is, and always has been, the Chinese ideal of character, and from that understanding other qualities are derived, such as pacifism, contentment, calm, and strength of endurance which distinguish the Chinese character.'[24] Lin continues that 'strength of character is really strength of the mind, according to the Confucianists', and thus makes clear the crucial role he attaches to Confucianism as the linchpin of the Chinese character and culture.

Confucianism looms large also in the image Lin Yutang conveyed to the West of the Chinese family system. Not surprisingly, Lin emphasizes the importance of the family in Chinese culture: 'it very nearly takes the place of religion by giving man a sense of social survival and family continuity, thus satisfying man's craving for immortality'. But he also brings out some points of Chinese society which might go against the grain of a Western reader's values, such as that 'the family system is the negation of individualism itself, and it holds a man back, as the reins of the jockey hold back the dashing Arabian horse'. He is quite clear also that the family system is the root of a great deal of corruption in China, such as 'nepotism and favouritism, robbing the nation to enrich the family' and so on.[25]

The Chinese, and Confucian, system of government Lin calls simply 'parental government' or 'government by gentlemen'. It means that the people should give the government unbounded confidence, and the government, on its side, should look after 'the people's interests as parents look after their children's interests'.[26] There are drawbacks to this system, however, because it means that there are no legal restraints against officials, most of whom turn out to be crooks. Thus corruption is not only rampant but endemic to the system.

Though Lin Yutang does not hesitate to criticize, the overall images which his book conveys are positive. Nowhere is this clearer than in the opening passage of the concluding 'epilogue'.

In the general survey of Chinese art and Chinese life, the conviction must have been forced upon us that the Chinese are past masters in the art of living. There is a certain wholehearted concentration on the material life, a certain zest for living, which is mellower, perhaps deeper, anyway just as intense as in the West. In China the spiritual values have not been separated from the material values, but rather help man in a keener enjoyment of life as it falls to our lot. This accounts for our joviality and our incorrigible humour.[27]

An American writer who claimed to have learned from Lin Yutang an image of Chinese 'finesse and subtlety'[28] probably spoke for many of his generation. Lin identified with the Westernized traditional scholar. His book contains no section on the peasantry, who rate but few mentions throughout, even in the section on social classes. The image of China his book passed on to the West was a highly conservative one, in which the scholar class ruled as it had always done, and that was how things ought to be.

Of all Chinese image-makers, the most influential one in the United States, and especially during the war against Japan and after, was Chiang Kaishek's wife Song Meiling. Not only did she publish in the West, but she made an official visit to the United States in 1943, making many public speeches and addressing both houses of Congress.

The images Song Meiling conveyed both to her own people and to the West were highly optimistic. Her favourite slogan was *resurgam*, a Latin word meaning 'I shall rise again'. This idea of resurgence, of rebirth, summed up for her 'the spirit that is China'.[29] It recurs throughout her articles and was given to the title of her very popular book *China Shall Rise Again*, which was published during the war. An allied image is that of patriotism, the major Chinese quality which will bring about the resurgence.

The images which Song Meiling conveyed to the West were

not all positive. She balanced Lin Yutang's eight Chinese characteristics with 'seven deadly sins', which had held the country
back. They were self-seeking, 'face', cliquism, defeatism,
inaccuracy, lack of self-discipline, and evasion of responsibility. 'Long ago they combined to retard our emergence as
a first-class world power, and they now delay our victory
in this war', she wrote.[30] The invasion by the 'barbaric enemy'
Japan brought one strong advantage, namely that it has 'shocked
the suffering patriotic people into a realization of the nature
of some of our national problems' and would give them the
will to overcome these deadly sins, and lead on to resurgence.[31]
So even a negative image ends up with optimism.

Western Residents in China

Apart from scholars, Western or Chinese, another major group
of image-formulators in the first half of the twentieth century
was Western residents in China. These themselves fell into
several categories, journalists, diplomats and their families,
long-term travellers, and others.

Despite the very low opinion Lin Yutang held of them,
one group of foreign residents worth noting as transmitters
of images to the West was the 'old China hands'. The term
was formerly applied usually to the veteran British business
man, 'the old-time treaty port resident who had never outgrown
the outlooks and attitudes of the previous century'.[32] These
people were attached to their comforts, their clubs, and their
profits. They were mainly imperialist in their views, but were
not without good will towards individual Chinese.

A well-known example is Carl Crow, who wrote several
books about China. At first a newspaper man he later became
an advertising and merchandising agent. His style is flippant
and it is often hard to tell when he is writing seriously. His
book Four Hundred Million Customers, the writing of which
he justifies through his profession,[33] reads mainly like a send-
up, but was certainly serious in attempting to tell Western
business men how to cash in on China's large population.
The book was first published in March 1937 and went through
two more impressions by May 1937. Its fourth was in November
1937, the outbreak of war in China not having diverted the
publishers from yet another impression.

In another book written during the war itself and published

in 1941, Crow exults over the prosperity of his life in the first happy seven months of 1937. 'We foreign devils were making money', he says. 'The reformed National government had been in power for ten years', doing good things such as building public works like railways and hospitals, 'instead of stealing the money more or less openly as had been the immemorial custom in China'.[34] But the good times of profits under Chiang Kaishek were destroyed by the Japanese, and Crow and his cronies had to get out. 'The Shanghai which we left behind as refugees is a city which will live only in memories.' For such people, China was just a playground for the rich foreigners, and basically that was the image they passed on to the West. Crow finishes his book with the sentence: 'The era of the foreign devil is ended.'[35] Flippant as ever, the phraseology ends by being also bitter, yet resigned.

The years 1900 to 1949 saw the climax of Western missionary activity in China, especially from the United States. In 1908 the American Congress voted to use the unused balance of the Boxer indemnity for educational purposes. What this meant was that, under the guise of generosity, the Americans used money, paid to them to help invade China in 1900, for the purpose of imposing their own values on Chinese intellectuals. Foreign missionary schools, and even other sorts of social services like hospitals, mushroomed. The missionaries went as teachers and 'old-fashioned brimstone fundamentalism was still very present'.[36] But many were very impressed by Chinese culture, especially by the politeness and earnestness of their students. As one prominent American missionary educator interpreted the conversion of another missionary: 'He had come to the Far East with a message that he was on fire to give, but in the process of transmission the East had spoken its message to him.'[37] Many who went to change China were themselves changed. Communication between the Western and Chinese worlds was definitely taking place, though not necessarily only in the direction intended by the Westerners. So the image of the Chinese the missionaries presented to the West, in which courtesy and serious-mindedness held a central place, was in general much more positive than that of their nineteenth-century predecessors.

From the 1920s missionaries were forced by circumstances to accept and then become more sympathetic to Chinese nationalism. In 1928 the Jerusalem conference of the International Missionary Council, a body representing Protestants all over the world, accepted a statement from a Chinese Christian that missionaries in China ought to have a 'real love for China' and be 'willing to work with the Chinese'.[38] Moreover, the Guomindang government imposed regulations on missionary schools which forbade religious propaganda and aimed to promote nationalism. There was a strong move in favour of Chinese control of Christian organizations in China. Many American Protestant missionaries came to support revision of the unequal treaties which the Western powers had imposed on China in the nineteenth century, even in the teeth of opposition and resentment from their compatriots in the business and government worlds.[39] The result was that the improved images of China sent home by the missionaries tended to apply not only to the people and culture, but also to the government's political aspirations as well.

Among famous short-term residents was Osbert Sitwell (1892–1969), worth mentioning not only because of his distinction as a writer, but also because he expressed images widely held at the time about China. He lived for several months in Beiping in 1934, calling it Peking, and was much influenced by several Western residents who had lived in the city for a somewhat longer time than he. His motive in going to China was escapism, as he informs the reader in the opening sentence of his preface and in the title of his book. His desire was to exult in the wonders of Peking's past, to 'see the wonderful beauty of the system of life' China incorporated 'before this should perish'. He was aware of growing communist influence among university students, but was not really interested in 'the Social Struggle'.[40] The dominant images he portrays are of a grand and to some extent surviving past, and of a witty and cheerful people, who are 'self-indulgent, fond of food and good things and gossip, kindly and deeply attached to their families' and fond of life.[41] At the same time, he was aware of a darker side of society, and of grinding poverty.

Nowhere in the most backward European states can these crowds of blind people, beggars, cripples, lepers and afflicted of every sort, be seen: and no amount of accidental beauty can excuse their suffering, even though the national temperament of the poor creatures makes them laugh, as they do, between their bouts of professional whining and cringing, at their own misery.[42]

The benign national characteristics may not justify the poverty for Sitwell, but they do go some way towards alleviating its effects.

American Radical Journalism

In contrast to the views of missionaries and other residents in China, the United States produced in the first half of this century a radical tradition of journalism which not only believed that the Chinese Communist Party could win, but also welcomed that possibility. The three famous names are Agnes Smedley (1892–1950), Anna Louise Strong (1885–1970), and Edgar Snow (1905–1972).[43] Much has been written about them and a society was set up in China in September 1984 in their honour. All three wrote widely in newspapers and books to bring the activities of the Communist forces to the world's attention and to promote a favourable image of the changing course of China's history.

Agnes Smedley came from a very poor background. It was her life experiences and those of her family that made her a radical socialist and feminist. Her first major work, published in 1929, was an autobiographical novel called *Daughter of Earth*. That was how she regarded herself. In contrast to Lin Yutang, one of her major concerns was the peasantry, to the extent that she recorded the career of one of them, the Communist military leader Zhu De. 'Eight out of every ten living Chinese are peasants', she told Zhu De to justify why she should write about him. 'If you would tell me your life story, a peasant would be speaking for the first time.'[44] Unfortunately the book which resulted, *The Great Road*, was not published until 1956, several years after her death.

However, Smedley had no time at all for the traditional peasant mentality with its oppression of the poor and especially women. 'Semi-feudal, agrarian China', she wrote in her book on the Jiangxi Soviet and the Red Army, 'is corrupt, degenerate, ignorant, incapable of developing the country, incapable of taking one step that can possibly raise the productive or purchasing power of the Chinese masses.'[45] She believed even in the mid-1930s that only the Communist Party was willing and able to change society; she supported it openly and strongly and predicted its victory. Smedley saw herself as an internationalist. She had been actively involved with German and Indian revolutionaries, as well as in the Soviet Union, before she went to China in 1928. It is not surprising that the authorities of the day kept a close eye on her. Israel Epstein claims that FBI records on her made available under the US Freedom of Information Act 'come to thousands of pages, and some are still kept secret'.[46]

Anna Louise Strong came from a much better educated and more prosperous background than Snow or especially Smedley, she had by far the longest life of the three, and was the only one who got the opportunity actually to live in the People's Republic of China for an extended length of time. She wrote numerous books and articles, not only about China, but also about the Soviet Union, Spain, and Mexico, including 16 books published by prominent commercial American publishers between 1920 and 1946.[47] Her first visits to China were in the late 1920s and resulted in her two-volumed *China's Millions*, which, first published in 1928, later went through several versions and editions. From the middle of 1946 to February 1947, she lived in Yan'an and wrote extensively and glowingly about the society she found there, and about the Communist leaders, especially Mao. She denied absolutely that they were satellites of the Soviet Union. 'There is no indication that they take orders from Moscow and very little that they even seek advice', she wrote.[48] And just before the People's Republic was formally established she wrote that the Chinese, whose past century had been 'determined by every other nation', had now 'conquered their country' so that 'China's future will be determined by the Chinese'.[49] There was no doubt in her mind that the Chinese Communist Party was responding effectively to Chinese patriotism, and would be able to transform the country along socialist lines and to the benefit of the Chinese masses.

For Western images of China, the most influential of these three American journalists is Edgar Snow. He went to work in China in 1928 and in 1936 got what was then a unique opportunity to visit the revolutionary base area of northern Shaanxi and interview Mao Zedong. The Communist Party Chairman told Snow his life history and the reporter simply wrote it all down and combined Mao's narrative with his own vivid impressions and experiences in the base area to form the classic *Red Star over China*. Snow himself modestly attributed its success to its being 'not only a "scoop" of perishable news but likewise of many facts of durable history',[50] but his being the first to record the early life of the eventual victor Mao ensured the continuing influence of his book. The image it transmitted to the West was of 'Chinese dedicated to national integrity and social justice'.[51] The fact that they were Communists made his book controversial but also of strong appeal to the left. In Britain it was due mainly to the active promotion by the Left Book Club that over 100,000 copies of Snow's book were sold within a few weeks.[52]

Novels

Pearl Buck was born in the same year as Smedley. From an American China-based missionary background, she spent almost all the first four decades of her life in China. Although she wrote much about actual events and experiences in China, she is most famous as a novelist, in particular for her best-selling work *The Good Earth,* and she thus brings us to that important image-formulating branch of literature, fiction.

The Good Earth exercized a greater influence in creating Western images of China and the Chinese than any other single work in the period under discussion. The publisher, John Day of New York, and the author were both American, so the novel's main impact was in the United States, but it was read very widely in other countries and was translated into over thirty languages, including at least three in the Soviet Union. According to the John Day Company, that firm alone sold over four million copies in the United States between 1931, its year of first publication, and 1972.[53] No other book on China has ever come anywhere near such sales in the West, either before or since. Moreover, in 1937 *The Good Earth* was made into a film, which its studio estimated in 1955 to have been seen by some 23 million Americans and 42 million others all over the world.[54] One writer claims that 'a safe guess' would put the number of 'Americans exposed to Buck's creation in one form or another' at no less than 40 million.[55]

The Good Earth was unusual in its day in being a Western novel set in China and entirely about Chinese people. The hero of *The Good Earth* is the peasant Wang Lung. The novel opens on his wedding day, when he is poor, but he soon becomes quite rich and then a landlord. He is extremely traditional in outlook and behaviour and very hardworking. His last words to his two sons are 'If you sell the land, it is the end',[56] and this shows the central theme of the novel: the peasant's love for and attachment to land, the good earth.

Pearl Buck saw the peasantry as strong and stable, and the key to China's future. She was the first to give China's peasants, both male and female, a really human face which the West could understand. For this she deserves great credit. She was all her life very critical of the intellectuals, whom she believed had no understanding of or love for the peasants. The overall image she portrays of the peasantry is an extremely positive one.

However, she pulls no punches about their faults. In particular, family matters and customs naturally loom very large in *The Good Earth*. Buck portrays an utterly sexist society in which the rich male gets everything and the women are seriously downtrodden. She does not gloss over the dangers inherent in the excessive emphasis on Confucian family relationships or the sufferings they can cause.

Pearl Buck and her novel have been criticized for lacking complexity in the sense of ignoring politics.[57] To the present writer, this is a valid criticism. It is true that she attacks corruption in the landlord class, and in particular the family from which Wang Lung's wife had come as a slave girl to marry him. Yet the whole thrust of the novel is Wang's ability to move up the social ladder through traditional peasant strengths and virtues. As an old man he asks his grandsons, 'Do you study the Four Books?' And when told that since the revolution nobody studies such Confucian material he answers: 'Ah, I have heard of a revolution, but I have been too busy in my life to attend to it. There was always the land.'[58]

Thus it appears valid to suggest that the image of China Buck got her audience to accept was an inherently conservative one. It is no surprise that though she for a time expressed sympathy for the Communist Party because of its attention to the peasants, she rejected its ideology totally. 'She regarded the innate conservatism of the peasant as the chief bulwark against any effort to force what Buck regarded as the natural and gradual pace of change.'[59]

Though Pearl Buck thus shared with her contemporary and compatriot Agnes Smedley a vital concern with the peasantry as the vanguard of the future, the images the two women conveyed were basically antithetical. The choice of which one portrayed more accurate images depends on one's historical standpoint and from which period one views what they had to say. Seen from the late 1980s, Pearl Buck's vision seems less flawed and Agnes Smedley's less penetrating than they did from the 1950s to the 1970s. But in all periods since the 1930s the Buck view has been very much more acceptable to conventional wisdom than that of Smedley and much more influential in the creation of images.

For images of China during the inter-war years, one other novel besides *The Good Earth* stands supreme. It is *La condition humaine* (*Man's Fate*), by André Malraux (1901–76), a man with a truly remarkable career who, in addition to writing numerous novels and other works, occupied the position of French Minister of Culture under President Charles de Gaulle from 1958 to 1969. Though *Man's Fate* is by far his most famous and influential work, it is not his first book set in China, that being *Les conquérants* (*The Conquerors*), published in 1928, which focuses attention on the abortive Guangzhou uprising of 1925. Malraux spent only a brief time in China itself before the first publication of *Man's Fate* in 1933, yet it is acknowledged by virtually all commentators as a profound study not only of humankind as a whole but of China in particular. Malraux's experience in China could not compare with Pearl Buck's and his target audience is not as vast. Malraux is concerned only with urban people not, like Buck, with the far more numerous peasants. But, to this writer at least, the images he portrays of China in *Man's Fate* are much more powerful than those achieved by Buck.

In one sense this is ironic, because in fact the great majority of the main characters in *Man's Fate* are foreigners. Most of the story is set in Shanghai and Hankou against the background of the 1927 Revolution and it ends as a total disaster with the victory of Chiang Kaishek's troops and the suppression and death of the revolutionaries. Malraux was a Marxist at the time; and his sympathies for the left and for the ultimate dignity of the revolutionaries, even in defeat, are clear. Yet there are absolutely none of the images of optimism and enthusiasm which infuse the writings of Agnes Smedley or Anna Louise Strong. Despite the political import of the novel, Malraux was concerned as much with the destiny of humanity as with the Chinese Revolution itself. He summed up his intentions in the novel in June 1933 as follows:

No one can endure his own solitude. Whether it is through love, fantasy, gambling, power, revolt, heroism, comradeship, opium, contemplation or sex, it is against this fundamental angst that consciously or not, the characters of this novel . . . are defending themselves, engaged as they are to the point of torture and suicide in the Chinese Revolution, upon which for some years the destiny of the Asian world and perhaps the West depended.[60]

The main Chinese character is Ch'en Ta Erh. The novel opens with a graphic description of the anguish he feels as he hesitates to stab a man it is his duty to kill, his baptism in terrorism. Against the wishes of the Moscow-dominated Communist headquarters in Hankou, Ch'en tries to assassinate Chiang Kaishek. As he awaits his proposed victim and his mind ranges, his dominant feeling is solitude: 'the ultimate solitude, for it is difficult for one who lives isolated from the everyday world not to seek others like himself'.[61] Ch'en is fatally injured in the terrorist attack but Chiang is unharmed: Ch'en's final fate is to shoot himself dead accidentally, unaware of Chiang's escape.

The strongest images of China to come from the novel accord with Ch'en's psychology and fate: agony and defeat for the revolutionaries, misery and grim desperation for the poor people, and the total failure of the Chinese to control their own destiny. The concluding section of the novel sums up these images as 'the repression that had beaten down upon exhausted China'.[62]

The gaps between the rich and poor are devastating in this novel, not only in terms of material wealth but in those of life-style. The rich, who are foreign, are able to scoop their profits and indulge in their pleasures through sex or escape through opium. French financial activities in Shanghai are hardly affected by the Revolution. Although there are vivid pictures of poverty among foreigners, the great majority of the poor are of course Chinese, and pictures of teeming impoverished and diseased humanity are many and graphic. Witness the following conclusion to the part of the novel set in Hankou as an example of the novel's haunting power:

The peace of the night once more. Not a siren, nothing but the lapping of the water. Along the banks, near the street-lamps crackling with insects, coolies lay sleeping in postures of people afflicted with the plague. Here and there, little round red posters; on them was figured a single character: HUNGER . . . But . . . how choose the sacrifice, here, in this city to which the West looked for the destiny of four hundred million men and perhaps its own, and which was sleeping on the edge of the river in the uneasy sleep of the famished — in impotence, in wretchedness, in hatred?[63]

The image to emerge from *Man's Fate* is that it is not Chinese people who make the crucial decisions which decide the fate of the Chinese Revolution. The key revolutionary characters in the novel are foreigners. Ch'en merely set himself apart from the Revolution by his individualistic attempt against Chiang's life. It was 'Moscow and the enemy capitals of the West' which were organizing 'their opposing passions over there in the night' and attempting to mould them in ways which suited their own interests. The people were supporting the Communists. 'The Communist propaganda had reached the masses like a flood, because it was what they wanted, because it was their own.'[64] The disastrous collapse of the Revolution in Shanghai was due in part to the failure of Moscow and its clients in Hankou, whose orders Ch'en disobeyed, to provide the necessary support

As a literary figure in the first half of the twentieth century, Pearl Buck stands below a number of other writers with works set in or about China. One who certainly does occupy a position at or near the peak of English literature of the time is W. Somerset Maugham (1874–1965). Though the majority of his 'Asian' works are set in Malaya, Borneo, and Singapore, there are some which concern China, including a travel book about it, and he is, among literary figures, a highly appropriate representative of creators of Western images of China.

About half of Somerset Maugham's novel *The Painted Veil*, first published in 1925, is set in China. It concerns a young married English woman, Kitty, who goes with her husband to a cholera-striken town in Guangdong province on the rebound from a finally unsuccessful love affair with a senior British official in Hong Kong. The story is supposed to take place a few years after the 1911 Revolution. Just as in Somerset Maugham's other works, all the main characters are European, in this novel mostly English, but with some French nuns who run an orphanage in the Chinese town. The great majority of Western novels and short stories of all periods tend strongly to take Westerners as the main characters with the 'natives' confined to subsidiary roles.

Because China is rarely more than background, the images of China are less powerful than those of the Europeans who live there. What is most striking is how kind, even saintly, are the French nuns, who work tirelessly and unselfishly for the locals against the background of a dirty, poverty- and disease-ridden country. Among the strongest images of the Chinese is gratitude for what is done for them. Notwithstanding his acknowledged cynicism, Maugham presents an immensely sympathetic picture of missionary activity in China.

Despite the epidemic, the image of China which Maugham conveys is quite positive. A French nun expresses a strong wish and an English customs official called Waddington the intention never to leave China or return home.[65] Though Kitty begins by finding the Chinese orphans 'repulsive' and 'hardly human',[66] she grows very attached to them when she gets to know them; the lesson seems to be that her racism is based solely on ignorance. In an encounter with Waddington not long after arriving in China, Kitty, who 'had never heard the Chinese spoken of as anything but decadent, dirty, and unspeakable', finds to her surprise that he has adopted the Chinese view of life, namely that 'in China alone was it so led that a sensible man might discern in it a sort of reality'.[67] The image which Maugham seems to be intending is that for all its faults China has a point of view worth hearing and grows upon Western residents to the point where they are quite happy to regard it as their home.

Maugham had travelled in China for some four months in 1919 and 1920. He had met a variety of people but 'concentrated on the British'.[68] In 1922 he had a play premiered set in China, *East of Suez*, and in the same year published his travel notes on China, entitled *On a Chinese Screen*. In the latter work he was himself very proud of his description of the Great Wall, famous as an image of China. Maugham makes a revealing comment on the Chinese coolies, whose faces he thought good-natured and frank. It is similar to the image of cheerfulness within suffering, which Osbert Sitwell was to convey some years later.

It seems natural to feel admiration for their endurance and their spirit. But you will be thought somewhat absurd if you mention your admiration to the old residents of China. You will be told with a tolerant shrug of the shoulders that the coolies are animals and for two thousand years from father to son have carried burdens, so it is no wonder if they do it cheerfully.[69]

The clear message both of this passage and of Kitty's initial reaction to the Chinese orphans as 'half animals' is that Maugham himself felt no racist revulsion against the Chinese, but that he considered other Westerners did so, at least against those of the poorer classes.[70] 'Old residents' surely refers only to Europeans, and especially the British, on whom as we saw he had concentrated his perceptive attentions, hardly to the Chinese. Maugham's comments suggest that racist images of the Chinese may have been more widespread among those who did not write about China and its people than among those who did.

Conclusion

The half-century separating the Boxer uprising from the victory of the Chinese Communist Party thus saw a very wide range of Western images of China and the Chinese, from racist and imperialist on the one hand to radically socialist and feminist on the other, with many in between. But the great weight of published opinion was, in its own terms, positive about, or sympathetic towards, China. Malraux could write with bleak pessimism about one phase of the Chinese revolution, but still supported the revolutionary process. Most of the missionaries, and even business men like Carl Crow, thought they were sympathetic to the Chinese people. And the war against Japan improved China's image still more.

In the United States images became both more active and positive after the country changed its isolationist policy in the late 1930s. The Sino-American relationship from the time Japan attacked Pearl Harbor late in 1941 has been described as 'like marriage after an over-long engagement — a shotgun marriage, if you will, but still a happy union'.[71] An American sampling in 1942, which may well have shown rather similar results in other Western countries, showed the five main 'images' of Chinese people as hardworking, honest, brave, religious, and intelligent, in that order,[72] in other words the Americans held very much more positive perceptions about Chinese as people than did either Lin Yutang or Song Meiling.

The reason for the shift in opinion lay not in China but in the West. Between 1900 and 1949 China did not improve to anything like the extent Western images of it did. The West approved of the Chinese essentially because it believed China was moving in a direction suitable to Western political, economic, and social interests, and wished to encourage the trend. This view is substantiated by the change which took place in the Western image after 1900. Having excoriated the Chinese and imposed a humiliating defeat on them, the West decided it could forge a better and more favourable relationship by appearing to be generous. Western images of China were still part of the 'power/knowledge' relationship of which Michel Foucault has spoken. For all her very genuine sympathy with the Chinese peasantry, Pearl Buck's view was essentially in accord with Western interests, which is why it could be so enthusiastically promoted and received. One scholar has written that 'like most Americans, Buck was inclined to interpret China's history in terms of Western contacts and values'.[73] Her two worlds, with which this chapter began, the 'clean Presbyterian American' and 'merry not-too-clean Chinese' worlds, were still very much in existence in the late 1940s. Communication between them was much better than it had been in 1900, but it was still highly imperfect and selective.

PART II

WESTERN IMAGES OF CHINA'S PAST DOWN TO 1949

6

Sixteenth- to Mid-Twentieth-Century Images of the Past

EARLY European accounts of China are fascinating as historical documents, because they tell us so much of images of China's past, and in some respects can usefully supplement Chinese sources. But in fact works like those of Marco Polo were not conceived as history at all; such authors as he were concerned with the China of their own time and they mentioned the past but little in what they wrote.

Exactly what constitutes history is a moot point. Certainly the early writers on China had no clear philosophy of history in general, let alone of Chinese history in particular, beyond a desire on the part of the more devout Christians among them to glorify God and to assist in converting the Chinese to Christianity.

The Earliest Western Histories of China

Martin de Rada's account of China includes a very brief and chronological section on its 'antiquity' and 'the changes which have occurred therein'. He relates the 'fables' which explain China's beginnings and starts 'authentic history' with the reign of Yu the Great, whom he calls Vitey. He then lists a few emperors, dynastic changes, and rebellions, and concludes by expressing amazement at the long and independent history of the Chinese. 'If this history is true, they began to have kings shortly after the Flood, and they have been without any intermixture with foreigners since then', other than for the short time the 'Tartars' or Mongols ruled them.[1]

The title of Mendoza's pioneering work *The History of the Great and Mighty Kingdom of China* suggests that the reader might expect a focus on history. In fact, however, almost the entire book concerns what was for Mendoza in 1585 the present or very recent past. Yet it does contain a few pages of exposition of China's development from the beginnings.[2] However, the relevant chapter is mainly descriptive and chronological. Its heading tells us the aim: 'how many kings hath been in this kingdom, and their names', and on the whole the content indeed reflects the title. However, there are occasional judgements and comments which show interpretation.

Mendoza's account relies partly on de Rada but also, apparently, on Chinese literary sources. It begins with Yu the Great, whom following de Rada he calls Vitey. It is, however, somewhat more detailed than de Rada's. Other than Vitey, the person to receive the longest treatment is 'a very fair woman' called Bausa who 'did govern the kingdom . . . alone, one and forty years'. Some of the details fit Empress Wu (reigned 684–705), though she is put at the end of what is obviously the Tang dynasty (618–907), not as she should be within its first century. The judgement follows the conventional Confucian one, that she was 'vicious' and indulged in 'ill living'.[3]

De Rada and Mendoza were among the very first Europeans to write about Chinese history. Shallow and inaccurate as their accounts were, they were prepared to begin ploughing into what was for Europe an entirely unknown field. For that they deserve great credit.

In terms of images, one of the most striking results of de Rada's and Mendoza's works was the appearance of a long prose literary work in 1597 set in China. One of the forerunners of the seventeenth-century heroic-gallant romances it was the last literary work of Ludovico Arrivabene (c. 1530–c. 1597) and entitled *Il magno Vitei* (*The Great Vitei*), Vitei being the name Arrivabene, following de Rada and Mendoza, gives to China's first king, Yu the Great. 'China is depicted as the most virtuous nation yet known to mankind.'[4] Moreover, though the author acknowledges that some material in the book stretches credulity, he is specific that his purpose is that 'of bringing to light the fundamental qualities of the glorious Chinese nation',[5] a strikingly strong statement with a ring more reminiscent of twentieth-century China than of sixteenth-century Italy.

The earliest Jesuits to write on China, such as Matteo Ricci, devoted virtually all their efforts to the contemporary situation.

Where history intrudes into their accounts, it is that of the Jesuit missions, with no more than a sentence here and there on China's. Yet the Jesuits most certainly established the first great age of European study of China's past. Antoine Gaubil, who lived in China from the early 1720s until 1759, has been described as 'the greatest sinologist of the whole period of the old Jesuit mission in China'.[6] He not only published widely but exercised enormous influence on European scholars, one of them being his fellow Jesuit J. B. Du Halde.

This great Jesuit's magistral *Description* of China includes well over 200 pages on the country's history.[7] The section is entitled 'Annals of the Chinese Monarchy, or Abridged History In Chronological Order of the Most Remarkable Happenings under Each Emperor', and the content reflects the title faithfully. There is a brief introduction, the main burden of which is to accord Chinese history with the account given in the Bible.[8] There follows a list of dynasties, recording how long each lasted and how many emperors ruled.[9] The overwhelming portion of the historical account simply describes what happened under each emperor.

Du Halde cites it as common opinion in his day that 'the sons of Noah spread into East Asia and their descendants penetrated into China about 200 years after the Flood'.[10] But he is critical in that he claims to accept only what can be substantiated. On the whole he follows Chinese historians closely and praises them because the history they relate 'has nothing of the air of fable such as have the Greeks and Romans in the beginnings of their history'.[11] Of course he supports the Christian view of history, but is prepared to prefer China's to the pagans of Ancient Europe.

Like Mendoza, Du Halde mentions the Empress Wu, and follows the standard Confucian line that she was cruel and a usurper. He even adds to her crimes a fifteen-year persecution against the Christian religion. However, he does not give her unusual prominence and has her correctly placed in the first century of the Tang dynasty.[12]

On the whole, explicit value judgements are rare or follow traditional Confucianism. One emperor, however, about whom Du Halde comes close to waxing lyrical in his praise is Kangxi (reigned 1661–1722). Here was a meritorious emperor with rare qualities, 'one of the greatest whom China has ever had, whose name is respected throughout the East and has yet deserved the attention of all Europe'.[13] The Jesuits had done well under Kangxi, but in 1724 his successor Yongzheng (reigned 1722–35) issued an edict forbidding any Chinese to accept Christianity and ordering the expulsion of all missionaries except those employed at court in Beijing. Since Du Halde completed his great work during the reign of Yongzheng, it is not surprising to find him far better disposed towards Kangxi. It is only fair to add that his favourable view is one most modern historians would share.

Du Halde has included many dates in his history, naturally enough far more for the later than the earlier period. The earlier dates are not correlated to the Western calendar with particular accuracy, but the overall sequence of reigns and events is correct and incomparably the best Europe had produced up to this time. Moreover, Du Halde was the first European to record Chinese history in detail from the beginnings to his own time; the last date is 1732, only a few years before the book's publication. The fact that the historical section occupies only about half a volume of a four-volume work testifies to the truly monumental nature of Du Halde's overall contribution to Europe's understanding of China.

Ironically, many of the earliest major works of French secular sinology deal not so much with the Han people as with those people nowadays regarded in China as minority nationalities. The most prominent of them is the vast *Histoire générale des Huns, des Turcs, des Mogols, et des autres tartares occidentaux, &c. avant et depuis Jesus-Christ jusqu'à present* (*General History of the Huns, Turks, Mongols, and Other Western Tartars Before and During the Time of Jesus Christ to the Present*), by Joseph de Guignes, published in four volumes in Paris from 1756 to 1768. This work owed so much to Gaubil that it has even been suggested that de Guignes simply plagiarized it.[14] Jesuit influence is everywhere obvious in the sinology of the eighteenth century, including in the secular tradition.

De Guignes was also interested in Chinese history as a whole and was one of those to develop a theory on the origins of the Chinese people. Struck by the similarity between the Chinese and Phoenician characters, he concluded that an Egyptian colony had established itself in China in the twelfth century BC and given rise to a new people. This extraordinary theory was quite popular in eighteenth-century France. Of course there were opponents, one of those to pour greatest scorn on it being Voltaire, who argued that there was nothing Egyptian in the appearance, language, writing, customs, or religion of the Chinese.[15]

Voltaire was an admirer not only of China's present, as we saw in Chapter 3, but also her past. He was the first person of any nation to attempt a history of the world which would include not only his own culture but those of distant civilizations as well. His 'universal history' had been in preparation for over twenty years when it came out in 1756, and he continued to work on it for the rest of his life. He included two chapters on China as well as several on other non-European countries. Indeed he was intent to show his countrymen that their own civilization was not the only major one in the world. 'That is why Voltaire began his book by stating quite simply that the Chinese empire was vaster than that of the Frankish emperor' Charlemagne, which Frenchmen of Voltaire's time regarded as 'the climax of human history'.[16]

Voltaire praised China for its historical rationalist sense, free of myth and superstition. 'Other peoples begin their history with the world's origin', he noted. But then he goes on to contrast the Chinese favourably: they 'have never had this folly; their history is only that of historic times'.[17]

One figure to make a particularly favourable impression on Voltaire was Confucius. Here was no prophet, let alone one claiming links with the supernatural, but a wise magistrate who taught old laws. He preached no religion or mysteries but a doctrine of virtue. He taught that mankind was naturally good.[18] Voltaire's two chapters of summation of China's political history also showed it in an extremely positive light.

The first Western general history of China as a whole is *Histoire générale de la Chine* by the Jesuit priest Joseph de Mailla (1669–1748), published from 1777 to 1789. De Mailla had worked at the court of Kangxi and Yongzheng, but after Yongzheng's edict of 1724 against Christianity, de Mailla and the other Jesuits were forced to become sinologists. 'They had both time and opportunity to consult Chinese scholars, to read widely in Chinese literature, and to write.'[19] De Mailla made a special study of Chinese history. Much of the work of these Jesuits was never published, or not until many years later. De Mailla's book was posthumous, being published only some three decades after he died.

De Mailla's history covers the period from the beginnings to the early Qing. It is mainly a translation of the *Zizhi tongjian gangmu*, which is an abridgement by the famous Neo-Confucian philosopher Zhu Xi (1130–1200) of the *Zizhi tongjian* (*Comprehensive Mirror of Aid to Government*), the superb chronological history written by Sima Guang (1019–86) and presented to the throne in 1085. Zhu Xi's principle in rewriting Sima's book was to alter the moral judgements made on particular events to conform more closely to the Confucianism of his day. For the later period de Mailla used other Chinese sources. It follows that what he gave to the West was the Confucian version of Chinese history. His work was, in fact, more or less free of Eurocentrism, despite his being a Catholic priest.

China's Distant Past and Imperialism; The Thirst for the Exotic

De Mailla had, after all, lived many years in China. The period which followed his life was that which witnessed the Industrial Revolution in the West and the rise of imperialism. It also saw a growth in the academic study of China in universities. As early as 1818, the Collège de France, the most prestigious academic institution in France, established a chair of Chinese and Manchu Languages and Literatures. Such sinological activities did not at first focus on history, except in so far as understanding Chinese literature inevitably involved studying the literary development of the past.

The major Western historical work on China in the nineteenth century was undertaken by writers who lived in China as missionaries, such as the German Karl Gutzlaff (1803–51) or the American Samuel Wells Williams. In view of its continuing reputation, and because it contains one chapter on the 'history and chronology of China', Williams's *The Middle Kingdom* is an obvious choice for study as an early representative of nineteenth-century Western writing on Chinese history.

Williams was very concerned with the question of the value of early Chinese sources of history. He saw himself as a moderate standing between two conflicting positions. One was the view that because the oldest books put forward a chronology

comparison with
the Bible — point
example of Said

incompatible with that of the Old Testament, the 'native historians' should be rejected as sources. The result of such an attitude, says Williams, was that 'the whole subject of the settlement and early progress of this ancient race has been considered beyond the reach, and almost unworthy the attempt, of sober investigation'. He similarly rejected the tendency 'to laud the early records of the Chinese to the skies, as the French writers have done'.

Having chosen the middle path, he criticizes the Chinese historians for their attempts to explain the origins of the world without recourse to 'the sublime fact that there is one Creator who upholds his works by the word of his power'.[20] He devotes over half the chapter to trying to sort out the various ancient legends as well as the pre-Zhou history of China, and to finding correspondences in Jewish history as recorded in the Bible. Given his assumptions about the importance of the Bible as a historical source, this is a logical procedure, though to this reader it is a classic example of Edward Said's 'Orientalism' in emphasizing only the values of his own culture and ignoring those of the one he is studying. To be fair to him, however, one should add that the last section of his chapter is a concise chronology of the dynasties and selected main events of imperial China from the Zhou on, which must have been exceedingly useful in its day.

The major nineteenth-century encyclopedias devote a fair amount of space to history, especially that of ancient times. The thrust is descriptive, and chronological, not interpretive. A German encyclopedia spells out what many others, such as the ninth edition of the *Encyclopædia Britannica*, merely imply through their selection and treatment of the material. It characterizes what is recorded about one ancient period as a succession of 'changes of monarch, inner quarrels, usurpations, good and bad regents and a multitude of chance events', specifying that the same comment would apply to 'almost the whole of Chinese history'.[21] The image created is of virtually no meaning at all in Chinese history.

The emphasis on linguistic studies of Chinese, the original impetus of which had come from the missionaries' desires to convert China to Christianity, opened the way to detailed translations of the Chinese classics and history books. Édouard Biot (1803–50) produced numerous works, climaxing in his translation of the classical *Zhouli* (*Rites of Zhou*), published posthumously in two volumes in 1851.[22] A later monumental work is the five-volumed *Les mémoires historiques de Se-ma Ts'ien*, published in Paris from 1895 to 1905. It is a translation by Édouard Chavannes of the first 47 chapters of Sima Qian's *Shiji* (*Records of a Historian*), the first of China's standard histories written in the second and first centuries BC. From Britain came the famous translations by James Legge (1815–97) of many of ancient China's canonical writings, *The Chinese Classics*, published in eight volumes from 1861 to 1885. These three remain landmarks of Western scholarship on China and are but examples of numerous works from the nineteenth and early twentieth centuries which demonstrate the knowledge of classical Chinese language achieved by the sinologists of that era. Such mammoth undertakings could not fail to convey the image that Chinese history and philosophy contained much that was admirable and beautiful, even magnificent.

The European travellers of the same period included some who found remains of ancient civilizations of extreme interest. A particularly significant 'discovery' was made in July 1899 in the Qianfo Caves just south of Dunhuang, Gansu province. It was an enormous deposit of manuscripts and paintings in a sealed chamber, found not by any European but by a Chinese Daoist monk surnamed Wang. Yet because of the imperialist attitudes of the day, it was mainly European (and Japanese) scholars who moved in to take advantage of the finds. The first foreign visitor to the Qianfo Caves was the Hungarian-born Briton Mark Aurel Stein, one of the greatest of the 'historical explorers', whose first major expedition in search of ancient cultural objects and manuscripts had begun in Khotan in October 1900. Among the many to follow him was Professor Paul Pelliot, who in June 1906 left Paris at the head of a French expedition to western China looking for cultural relics and antiquarian manuscripts. The expedition visited Kashgar, Kucha, Turfan, Dunhuang, and other places.

The combination of factors — linguistic ability, explorations in western China, and imperialist attitudes — resulted in an extraordinary outpouring of antiquarian historical work, with the implied image that this ancient period was well worth study. Much of this work concerned the non-Han peoples living in what is today western or northwestern China, such as the Turkish and Mongolian nationalities. Undoubtedly the French were the most prolific. Apart from Pelliot, one could single out Édouard Chavannes who, in 1903, published French translations of many Chinese texts on the Turkish and other peoples from the Sui (581–618) and Tang (618–907) periods. Entitled *Documents sur les Tou-kiue (Turcs) Occidentaux (Documents on the Western Tujue)*, the work was published first in St Petersburg and later in Paris.

Of course the study of the ancient history of China's minority nationalities is a thoroughly desirable activity and men like Stein, Pelliot, and Chavannes deserve credit for such work. However, the explorers, including Stein and Pelliot, assumed it was their right to take precious relics of the past back to Europe to house them there in museums and libraries. The Chinese naturally did not agree. The government of the day was alarmed at seeing so many of the Dunhuang relics being shipped overseas. It ordered the local office to bring all the remaining Chinese manuscripts to Beijing.

The other negative feature of the historical exploration work was the image of China as 'exotic' which it fostered and strengthened in the West. The attitude which many people held was that China and its minority nationalities were worthy of exploration only for their splendid pasts; the present, being miserable, was best ignored as far as possible.

An example is Osbert Sitwell's account of Peking in the 1930s; his concern was much more Peking's past than its current state. The main images to emerge are the exoticism, grandeur, and beauty of China's history. He devotes a whole chapter to 'the wealth of yesteryear' and the magnificent art and culture it produced in its time of prosperity. Like Ancient Rome, it had at one time been 'the greatest city in the world'.[23] He exults in the beauty and splendour of the Forbidden City, and in the elegance of its life. He does mention painful subjects, for example castration and eunuchs,[24] but does not dwell on them, so that the cruelty of the past is not a major image to emerge from Sitwell's account. In general, the exoticism of Sitwell's past Peking is both glorious and desirable.

A very different, and basically negative type of exoticism comes from the grand opera *Turandot* by Giacomo Puccini

(1858–1924), based on a play of the same name by Carlo Gozzi (1720–1806). Premiered in April 1926 at La Scala, Milan, it was Puccini's last work, and he did not live to complete it or see it performed. It concerns the cruel, icy, and beautiful Chinese princess, Turandot, who swears vengeance against men because her ancestress Lou-Ling had been abducted and killed during the conquest of her empire. Any prince who would marry Turandot must answer three questions, if he fails in any one of them he will be beheaded. Many lose their lives but eventually an unknown prince, the son of a defeated Tartar king, answers the questions and teaches Turandot the meaning of love.

Turandot is magnificent as a grand opera, a splendid spectacle with marvellous music. Though designed as fictional, and with the emphasis not on China, but on opera, it nevertheless both created and reflected powerful popular images of China's past. For the country these can be summed up as exoticism and grandeur, and for its people as cruelty and insouciance among those at the top of society, and docility and patience among those at the bottom.

The whole concept of the cold, oriental princess with power to kill and beauty to stun and madden reeks of exoticism. The core Scene Two of Act 2, where the unknown prince answers the three riddles successfully, is set against an enormous marble staircase, on top of which sits the venerable emperor beside whom stands the cruel princess, images of grandeur. References to pain, blood, fire, and death are even more numerous than in Puccini's other operas and the answer to one of the three riddles is 'blood'. Turandot's first words in the opera, in her demanding but thrilling aria 'In questa reggia', tell the masses that the event she is avenging happened 'in this palace thousands and thousands of years ago', giving the impression of timeless and unchanging power, of oriental despotism. The masses play quite a large role in the opera. They offer sympathy to the oppressed, but their function is to do as they are told by the rulers; the impression is of a suitably cowed mob, living in a society where torture is everpresent and life is cheap. Like most of Puccini's music, that in *Turandot* is passionate and melodious. More than the music of any of his other operas, even *Tosca*, it evokes to perfection the combination of exoticism, grandeur, and cruelty.

Major Histories of the Inter-War Period

The years between the two world wars saw further attempts in the West to produce general histories of China, including those on a scale never before attempted. Three deserve special mention: Henri Cordier's *Histoire générale de la Chine*, Otto Franke's *Geschichte des chinesischen Reiches* (*History of the Chinese Empire*), and C. P. Fitzgerald's *China, A Short Cultural History*.

Cordier (1849–1925) had already written and edited an enormous amount, including an excellent bibliography of Western-language works on China, called *Bibliotheca Sinica*, of which one scholar wrote in the 1970s that it had 'not so far been matched, and remains indispensable'.[25] His great general history was published in four volumes in Paris in 1920. Its full title translates into English as 'general history of China and its relations with foreign countries from the earliest times to the fall of the Manchu dynasty' and shows its enormous scope. Volume IV was republished in 1921, including even an epilogue on the decade since the fall of the Manchus to bring the work up to date. Cordier's is the first exclusively historical work on China in any European language to cover all periods from the beginnings to within a decade of publication. The author uses many sources, both Chinese and Western, with a heavy emphasis on French. The sections on domestic history down to the early Qing, are 'generally regarded as little more than paraphrases' of de Mailla's landmark eighteenth-century work.[26]

Cordier's work is mainly descriptive and contains an enormous amount of information, including precise dates of events. It clearly tries and largely succeeds in being simply an objective chronicle, with a minimum of theorizing. Cordier saw historians as of three kinds: the chronicler, the historian who presents marshalled facts to the public, and the philosopher who from facts deduces laws which govern the world. He was quite happy to see himself in the first category.[27]

The 'foreign countries' of the *Histoire générale*'s title are mainly Western and there is a clear bias in their favour. Thus, in Volume III, there are 19 chapters on the Ming period. Of these only seven concern China's domestic history. Chapter VIII is about 'the world in the fifteenth century', Chapters IX to XI the colonial doings of the Portuguese leading them towards China, and the next eight the activities of the Portuguese, Spaniards, English, and Dutch in China itself. Cordier's lifelong ambition was to write a comprehensive study of Sino-Western relations, and it is likely that he saw his *Histoire générale* as fulfilling his original intention in a more modest form.

The *History of the Chinese Empire* by Otto Franke (1863–1946) was published in five volumes between 1930 and 1952. Unlike Cordier's it goes down only to AD 1280, that is to the reunification of China by the Mongols, but its subtitle, which translates as 'an exposition of its foundation, its essence, and its development to the most recent times', shows its author's original intention to deal with later centuries. It relies more on the *Zizhi tongjian* than Zhu Xi's Confucianized abbreviation of the same work. It is documented with extreme care and thoroughness. The third and fifth volumes are given over entirely to annotation based not only on Chinese but also Western sources, and indexes.

In contrast to Cordier's, Franke's work not only contains an enormous amount of descriptive information, it also attempts to be genuinely analytical. The core of his interpretation is to see Chinese history in terms of the rise, development, and conquest of the Confucian state. 'When in China he guessed at the state in which the subject had not yet come to his right, Hegel. . . grasped how conditions were in the Confucian state more sharply than he himself could know.'[28] But Franke rejected Hegel's and Ranke's doctrine of China as a 'nation of eternal standstill' and thus without a history worthy of study; and wrote that 'today no serious historian shares it any more'.[29] The thrust of his work is to demonstrate just how worthwhile and valuable the study of China's history is, as part of world history.

By far the most influential and image-formulating general history of China from the inter-war years in the English language is *China, A Short Cultural History* by C. P. Fitzgerald (1902–). Published first in 1935, it has gone through many imprints and editions, mainly but not exclusively after World War II. Its primary influence was thus on the post-war generations but it certainly both reflected and helped create attitudes towards China's past in English-speaking countries in the decade of the 1930s as well.

Fitzgerald's account is in one volume only, albeit a large

one, and meant for the general reader. Though called a cultural history, it is actually fairly comprehensive, covering political and economic history as well as cultural. His main two approaches are spelled out in the preface. Firstly, he is concerned to focus attention not only on China's 'unhappy period of decline' where he believes 'undue emphasis' has hitherto been laid. Secondly, he hopes to correct the 'fallacious opinion' that the history of China 'is a monotonous record of three thousand years of stagnation ending in a disorderly collapse'.

Although Fitzgerald's book is mainly descriptive, it shines with enthusiasm for its subject. It brings Chinese history alive and conveys an image of vibrance. It is true that he opens the book with the observation that 'The history of every country is, to a great extent, determined by its geography' but this becomes a reason for beginning the study with an explanation of China's 'land and people'[30] not for denying social change and development. On the contrary, the overall image the book creates is of different characteristics in each period. Just as his statement of aims spells out, his emphasis is on change.

There was an enormous amount of other work done on ancient China, and on specific aspects of it. In *La Chine antique* (*Ancient China*), first published in 1927, Henri Maspero (1883–1945) covers the political, social, cultural, and philosophical history of China down to the Qin reunification of the third century BC; and had intended to follow it with a second volume on the period from Han (206 BC–AD 220) to Tang. Marcel Granet's (1884–1940) *La civilisation chinoise* (*Chinese Civilization*) was published in Paris in 1929 and focuses on the social history of China down to the end of the Han dynasty. Alfred Forke's (1867–1944) history of Chinese philosophy consists of three substantial volumes published in Hamburg in 1927, 1934, and 1938.[31] They cover respectively the ancient, medieval, and modern period and are probably still the most detailed treatment of the subject in any Western language.

The image of old China portrayed in works such as those above mentioned is reasonably positive. One contemporary Western scholar goes so far as to say that 'the spread of knowledge about the traditional China through the translation of Chinese works led after the first World War, especially in Germany, to a kind of renewal, within a limited framework, of the enthusiasm for China of the 17th and early 18th centuries'.[32]

Probably this enthusiasm continued to find its source in the sense of exoticism to which reference was made earlier.

For all their enthusiasm, some of the historians of the first half of the century retained a strong element of Eurocentrism. A good example comes in Maspero's treatment of 'the scientific movement and foreign influences' in ancient China. He writes:

> If the fourth and third centuries [BC] were marked by an intensity of life and an originality which China has hardly known since, they were owing in part to the influence of ideas brought by the first contacts, albeit distant and still tenuous, with the mediterranean civilizations, and which, gradually expanding, ended up by over-turning the scientific ideas of the Chinese.[33]

Maspero's assumption is that new ideas in China imply at least some input from Europe. He struggles to see such a partial European derivation even for China before the time of Christ. As we shall see in Chapter 8, Needham has shown such a suggestion to be false.

In company with Franke, these scholars were, in stark contrast to Hegel, prepared to see Chinese history as an important part of world history. Granet's *Chinese Civilization* is part of a series entitled 'The Evolution of Humanity, Collective Synthesis'. The general editor of the series, Henri Berr, opens Granet's work with the statement that 'it is only very recently that universal history has given its due share to that considerable part of humanity which occupies the Far East'. Oddly enough, Berr goes on to say that 'The Far East entered the great current of this universal history fairly late' because it was largely isolated.[34] Despite Berr's realization of the significance of placing the Chinese in the sweep of human history, he still assumes that isolation from Europe means being cut off from the great current of universal history.

Yet, Granet himself begins his work by refuting the motive of exoticism for his study: 'Chinese civilization deserves more than a curious interest'. Rather, it should be studied for itself, because of the 'great sum of human experience' which it enshrines.[35]

The historians of the first half of the twentieth century clearly thought of approaches which were new. A large-scale general history of China from the beginning down to the author's own time had never been accomplished before Cordier.

Fitzgerald's approach to China's cultural history was new in the 1930s. These works are descriptive and interpretative. Yet on the whole they lack 'big ideas', major new theoretical frameworks for the study of Chinese history.

Recent History

One final category of Western history-writing on China worth mentioning is the detailed and systematic analysis of the recent past, meaning not only the last decade but the fifty or sixty years leading up to the composition of the relevant book. The Western impact of the mid-nineteenth century resulted in such works being written early in the twentieth.

As with general histories, the leader was Henri Cordier, whose three-volumed *Histoire des relations de la Chine avec les puissances occidentales 1860–1900* appeared in 1901 and 1902 and represented a part of his ambition to produce a comprehensive study of Sino-Western relations. It is extremely detailed and factual, with numerous diplomatic documents. Like his general history, it is thus largely lacking in interpretation or commentary of the events he describes.

However, in the conclusion he does cast some judgements. He considers the impact of the West has been insufficient to produce change, at least under the Manchus. 'The lessons of the past will not help at all for the future,' he argues. The 1860 war, in which Beijing was occupied by British and French troops 'has remained unknown in most of the empire; I dare add in Beijing (Pé-King) itself'. Cordier expects the Chinese to forget the occupation of 1900 during the Boxer uprising as well, just as they have forgotten that of 1860. The implication that the Western impact was really no more than a pinprick is very striking indeed and prefigures some Western suggestions of the 1970s and 1980s. 'The first step the allies ought to have taken was to substitute a descendant of the Chinese dynasties for the degenerate heir of Kangxi and Qianlong.'[36] In other words, the Western powers and Japan should have effected a change of government in China by removing the Manchus. To be fair to Cordier, he is calling not for a colonialist government composed of Westerners but for an intrinsically Chinese one.

In the general history published two decades later Cordier

makes hardly any explicit judgements on these events. But his selection of material implies endorsement of Western actions, criticism of Chinese. He passes off the destruction of the Yuanmingyuan or Old Summer Palace in 1860 with one short sentence which gives no hint either of the extent of damage or of disapproval.[37] His treatment of the Boxer uprising and eight-power occupation likewise assumes the invading powers' actions to have been right and proper because of the Boxers' 'work of extermination against Christians'. He reserves detailed treatment of casualties to Western troops and representatives, even though he was well aware that most of the dying and suffering was in fact done by the Chinese.[38]

The best representative example from Britain of recent history writing in the early twentieth century is *The International Relations of the Chinese Empire* by H. B. Morse (1855–1934). It is in three volumes, the preface to the first dated October 1910 and that to the second and third October 1917. In accordance with its title this work is an extremely detailed political history of China from 1834 to 1911 with a strong emphasis on international relations.

Like Cordier's the tone of the work is generally scholarly. The author states in the 'prefatory note' to Volume I that he intends 'to give the events of the period such relative importance as they deserve' and will 'lay no undue stress on picturesque episodes'. He aims, moreover, 'to give an original authority or to cite a reference for every statement made'. Certainly the work fairly bristles with scholarly details and footnotes.

Yet it comes as no surprise that, just as with Cordier, the image of China which emerges from Morse's three volumes is a rather Eurocentric and 'Orientalist' one. Though with different conclusions, he shares Cordier's view that China is a corrupt and autocratic country which really needs foreigners to give it instructions in how to run itself. The Qing became 'abased and discredited' and bequeathed to the succeeding governments 'a heritage of corrupt administration and a status of subjection to the foreign powers'. Central to Morse's story is the Briton Sir Robert Hart and the 'great' British Customs Service which he organized.[39]

Morse implicitly, and often explicitly, justifies foreign intervention in China, especially British. Many illustrative examples could be found, but two suffice. Morse's comment on the destruction of the Old Summer Palace in 1860 is: 'Possibly a necessary act, possibly even a wise one; but there remained for many years in the minds of Chinese, who had forgotten the original offence or paid little attention to it, a vivid memory of the looting of the palace by the French and its destruction by the English.'[40] The assumption is that the Chinese were forgetful and lacking in understanding to be so resentful at having one of their most valuable palaces destroyed by foreigners. Again, Morse sums up the situation in 1894 by saying 'ample time had been given to China to set her house in order and to assert her equality with the nations which dominated her'. But China had done nothing, undertaken no reforms, nobody had offered leadership. So 'Chinese complacency still required some shocks to abate it, and one such shock was now to be given by Japan'.[41] Morse seems to be suggesting that China brought the war of 1894–95 upon itself and had mainly itself to blame for the invasion it suffered.

By the time Morse wrote, the Taiping uprising was a historical, not a contemporary, event. Morse justifies Western assistance to the Manchus against the Taipings, but is frank enough to give the reason: the foreigners intervened 'in defence of their own interests'. 'Trade was the principal, almost the only, Western interest; and for this the restoration of peace and order was essential.'[42] Of course the Taipings were a total disaster for which the rebels were to blame and from which it was foreigners who rescued the country.

The rebellion had devastated a dozen provinces, with an area equal to that of western and central Europe; it had directly killed, in battle, by outrage and massacre, and by famine, twenty millions of human beings; it had reduced the country to extreme poverty and brought the dynasty near to extinction; and from this, the candid historian must admit, China had been rescued mainly by foreign aid, given grudgingly in 1860, but with no sparing hand in the years 1862 and 1863 — an aid given because it served the interests of Western nations, but none the less helpful to the government and people of China.[43]

Morse was, of course, aware of the Chinese role in the suppression of the rebellion but to him it was Western aid that mattered, and especially the intervention of the 'Ever-victorious army' led by Major Charles Gordon.

The image which C. P. Fitzgerald projected some two decades later was much more understanding of the Taipings and, even though emphasizing their Western Christianity, more critical of the role of the Western powers. He argues that the Taipings could have brought China a 'new cultural outlook' in place of that of the 'effete' Manchus, one which would have been 'ready to accept the ideas of the west as a corollary of the new creed', namely Christianity. He attacks the way the British and French turned against the Taipings, and describes the alliance as 'one of the most remarkable, and certainly the most discreditable, episode in the history of Sino-European relations'.[44] He blames the West, and specifically the occupation of Beijing in 1860, for Chinese disasters in the late nineteenth century: 'For this tragic outcome the cynical policy of western imperialism in 1860 was mainly responsible.'[45] Unlike Cordier, he is not downplaying the significance of Western imperialism, even though he is more anxious than his French predecessor to discredit it.

Conclusion

In some periods from the sixteenth to the mid-twentieth centuries, Western images of China's past reflected quite clearly those of her present at the same time. The Jesuits and eighteenth-century philosophers who admired the China they knew saw merit also in its past achievements. In the first half of the twentieth century, renewed appreciation for China's current efforts went hand in hand with enthusiasm for her history. Yet, the strong sense of exoticism which persisted throughout all this period caused many in the imperialist nineteenth century and into the twentieth to hanker after 'discoveries' of China's past, even while they despised its present. Considering the extent of imperial China's decline at that time, their attitude is scarcely surprising.

It is equally to be expected that the level of analysis on Chinese history should have grown in the eighteenth century as the West learned more about it. What is striking is that analysis from about the middle of the nineteenth century failed to keep pace with the immense growth of knowledge of fact and detail, and the extremely impressive mastery of Chinese classical language found among Western sinologists. Two reasons go some way towards accounting for this. One is the enormity of the volume of material. Chinese history is so vast, and the Chinese-language sources so voluminous, that the process of digging out the facts is daunting, even without analysis. But the other reason is the unequal, even dependent, power relationship which had developed between the West and China. This tended to rob Chinese history of meaning in the eyes of the West, inhibiting analysis.

Two questions appear to dominate the period from the eighteenth to the mid-twentieth centuries: how great is the degree of essential social change in China's long history (see also Chapter 7), and to what extent is it part of world history. In response to the first, the historians of the twentieth century saw a far less stagnant China than had their counterparts of earlier times. As far as the second is concerned, Voltaire had seen China very much as part of world history, but many of his contemporaries and successors were far less broadminded than he. Only in the first half of the twentieth century could China's historical legacy as a valid part of world history become widely accepted in the West. The changes in Western approaches to both questions over the centuries reflected the progress of China's history itself. By the inter-war years social change was more obvious in China, and its role in world history more evident than had been the case two centuries or so earlier. At the same time, 'the power/knowledge' relationship remains relevant: the stronger the imperialism of the West, the more confident it was of its own exclusive role, the less inclined it was to admit the past of a country like China into the hallowed halls of 'world history'. Conversely, the decline of imperialism in the first half of the twentieth century, and especially after World War I, allowed for China's history to be promoted in significance in Western eyes.

7

The Lack of Change,
the Physical Environment,
and History

THE idea of China as an 'oriental despotism' dates back well before the nineteenth century. Montesquieu conceived it negatively, a reason for condemning China, but other thinkers, like Quesnay, held the same despotism as a reason for enthusiasm for China and its political system.

For Adam Smith, China may have been generally wealthy and populous, but it seemed also 'to have been long stationary'. Marco Polo, in the thirteenth century, had commented on 'its cultivation, industry, and populousness', almost in the same terms in which they are decribed by travellers in Smith's own times.[1]

The philosophers of history, who abounded in Europe in the late eighteenth and early nineteenth centuries, were on the whole not nearly so well disposed towards China as Adam Smith or his French Enlightenment contemporaries had been. They based their information on works such as that of de Mailla mentioned in Chapter 6, but interpreted this Confucianized Jesuit work according to their own schemas. J. G. von Herder (1744–1803), writing just after the publication of de Mailla's history, scoffed at the Chinese empire for its lack of change. 'Can one wonder', he asked, that such a nation 'should keep itself in the same place through thousands of years?' He denounced China as an 'embalmed mummy' with an 'inner cycle like the life of hibernating animals'.[2]

Georg Wilhelm Friedrich Hegel (1770–1831) saw history as a process of spiritual and moral progress. He criticized China for failing to distinguish between law and morality.

This was an 'oriental' peculiarity which marked China out as historically backward. He also shared Herder's view about changelessness. Indeed, in the sense that it cannot change, it has no real history at all.

Early do we see China advancing to the condition in which it is found at this day; for as the contrast between objective existence and subjective freedom of movement in it, is still wanting, every change is excluded, and the fixedness of a character which recurs perpetually, takes the place of what we should call the truly historical. China and India lie, as it were, still outside the World's History.[3]

For Hegel, the world appears to mean mainly Europe. Leopold von Ranke (1795–1886), the leading German historian of the nineteenth century, coined the famous phrase 'nations of eternal standstill' and counted China among them. It is of course true that at that time the rate of essential change was much slower in China than in Europe. Yet this does not alter the fact that philosophers of history such as Hegel and Ranke were simply using China as a construct against which to measure and revel in their own marvellous European progress.

Marx and China

Karl Marx (1818–83) took over the concept of 'oriental despotism' from earlier thinkers and developed it into a series of ideas which has gained great fame and influence as 'the Asiatic mode of production'. One of the key strands of China as an 'oriental despotism' is that the physical environment determines the nature of society, making change difficult if not impossible. It follows that those thinkers who have seen China as an oriental despotism have tended to apply their images both to their own day and the past.

Marx's primary aim was to critique the capitalism of his day. He lived almost his whole life in Western Europe and the overwhelming majority of examples he uses to illustrate his points derive from there. He was not interested in Asia, let alone China, despite the very high reputation he enjoys in that country. Comments he made on China are rarely central to his argumentation.

The core of Marx's ideas on the Asiatic mode of production

is the lack of private property. As the main point of a letter Marx wrote to his devoted friend and follower, Friedrich Engels (1820–95), on 2 June 1853, he stressed that 'the basic form of all phenomena in the East' was 'the *absence of private property in land*'.[4] Consequently the Asiatic mode is apparently characterized by a lack of classes and class struggle.

Because of the 'climate and territorial conditions, especially the vast tracts of desert', the despotic government must fulfil an 'economical function', namely public works. It must organize 'artificial irrigation by canals and waterworks' and these become 'the basis of Oriental agriculture'.[5] For Marx, oriental despotism was *not* a *political* phenomenon, but 'a non-progressive *economic* form marked by state intervention in the economy' through water control.[6]

Complementary to this centralized government was the self-sufficient and isolated village. To Marx the Asian village was backward, reactionary, and miserable, despite appearances to the contrary.

We must not forget that these idyllic village communities, inoffensive though they may appear, had always been the solid foundation of Oriental despotism, that they restrained the human mind within the smallest possible compass, making it the unresisting tool of super-stition, enslaving it beneath traditional rules, depriving it of all grandeur and historical energies.[7]

One of the main problems with these villages, and indeed of Oriental societies generally, was that they never changed. It followed for Marx that outside intervention was necessary to *force* change upon a resistant and miserable Asia. He saw the British 'mission' in India as both destructive and regen-erating in 'the annihilation of old Asiatic society, and the laying of the material foundations of Western society in Asia'.[8] The source of change was thus the West.

Marx recognized that the process of change would be painful. He likened the human progress which must follow intervention to 'that hideous pagan idol, who would not drink the nectar but from the skulls of the slain'.[9] But he nevertheless saw it as historically necessary and progressive.

Although Marx's main model of the Asiatic mode of production was India, he applied the concept also to a number of other countries, including China. He saw China as a despotism run by a vast machine-like bureaucracy which sustained the paternal authority of the emperor, the essential moral foundation on which the state depended.[10] The economy was based on a combination of small-scale intensive agriculture, carried on in isolated villages, and domestic manufacture.

Like so many European commentators before him, Marx was impressed by China's large and increasing population. But for him it was not a reason for admiration, but for concern and criticism. 'The increasing population of the country has long made social relations oppressive for the majority of the people', he wrote in 1850.[11] The year is striking. It stands at the end of at least two centuries of rapid population growth in China which had indeed contributed to miserable conditions among the masses. That very year saw the outbreak of the great Taiping rebellion caused, at least in part, by the misery of the people. The Taiping uprising thus followed population explosion but also for a while helped slow it down, because of the millions killed during or because of the rebellion.

Both Marx and Engels perceived China as having been stagnant and unchanging up to their own time. In August 1858 Marx called China 'a giant empire, containing almost one-third of the human race, vegetating to the teeth of time, insulated by the forced exclusion of general intercourse, and thus contriving to dupe itself with delusions of Celestial perfection'.[12] This self-satisfied stagnation, Marx believed, was assured in large part by China's isolation, which had made the country much like a 'mummy carefully preserved in a hermetically sealed coffin'.[13] The phraseology recalls Herder's likening China to an 'embalmed mummy'.

Marx and Engels saw China's isolation as approaching its end, and the agency of change was the West, which was forcing the door open. In the early 1850s Engels said of Austria that up to 1848 it had been 'sealed up to the eyes of foreign nations almost as much as China before the late war with England',[14] a clear reference to the first Sino-British War which had ended in the Treaty of Nanjing of 1842.

Although Marx and Engels appear to have considered the opening of China and the consequent unequal treaties to have been historically necessary and progressive, they were aware of the trauma involved and condemned the British for many of their actions. Marx denounced the British for the invasion of China which had followed the *Arrow* incident of October 1856; and just before the war which resulted in the occupation of Beijing in 1860 he wrote in the *New York Daily Tribune* (30 September 1859):

After a first Chinese war undertaken by the English in the interest of opium smuggling, and a second war carried on for the defense of the lorcha of a pirate, nothing was wanted for a climax but a war extemporized for the purpose of pestering China with the nuisance of permanent Embassies at its Capital.[15]

In numerous passages Marx and Engels comment on the impact of economic relations with Europe on the West itself. They both clearly hoped, and for a time expected, that such relations would hasten the revolution in Europe. The Chinese markets are one of the factors listed in *The Communist Manifesto* of 1848 which 'gave to commerce, to navigation, to industry, an impulse never before known, and thereby, to the revolutionary element in the tottering feudal society, a rapid development'.[16] For Marx and Engels this was a very positive function. Other passages show the two as expecting that China's economic role would precipitate a crisis in Europe. In his famous article of 14 June 1853 on China, Marx predicted that the Taiping rebellion would bring about an economic crisis in Britain because of the disruption of the Chinese market it must cause.[17]

Initially Marx was enthusiastic about the Taipings. He was impressed by what he had learned about their advocacy of a socialist ownership of land.[18] In his June 1853 article he gave the credit for the uprising to the British because they had forced open China's door: 'the occasion of this outbreak has unquestionably been afforded by the English cannon forcing upon China that soporific drug called opium'.[19] Still, his language suggests criticism of British intentions even while praising their historical role.

By the early 1860s Marx had changed his mind drastically about the Taipings. He no longer saw anything either revolutionary or socialist about them, and castigated them for their belief in religion.

From the start the movement had a religious coloration, but it shared this with all Oriental movements . . . Original in this Chinese revolution are only its protagonists. They are aware of no tasks, except the change of the dynasty. They have no slogans. Their goal seems to be only to assert, in contrast to the conservative marasmus, destruction in grosteque, repulsive forms, destruction without any germ of a new formation . . . After ten years of noisy pseudo-activity, they have destroyed everything and produced nothing.[20]

And what of the future? China appears to have been, with other oriental despotisms, an exception to the rules laid down in Marx's own principles of historical materialism. But now that change was being imposed on it by the advanced West, what progression would it follow? References in the later works of Marx and especially Engels suggest that they believed China would bypass the feudal mode of production but would then become capitalist and later undergo a socialist revolution. In this last prediction they were of course right, although the stages along the way are very much a matter of interpretation. But the comment of one contemporary scholar is surely apt: 'China's change would be a testimony to the dynamics of European capitalism, rather than the universality of historical materialism.'[21]

Clearly neither Marx nor Engels was well informed about China, or had any time for it. The images which emerge from their writings are based more on prejudice and Eurocentrism than on solid research. Most striking of all is that, while they did denounce particular actions of the imperialists of their day, they did not attack imperialism as a whole.

It was Lenin who abandoned the view of China as an unchanging 'oriental despotism', an example of the Asiatic mode of production. It was he who transformed the Marxist image of China from one of contempt to one of admiration and hope. One factor is the Leninist doctrine of anti-imperialism. Marx, the philosopher intent on a critique of European capitalism, could afford to see historical progress in colonialism, even while he condemned the aggression it involved. Lenin was a statesman whose aims were to resist aggression, to consolidate state power, and to build a backward country through socialism. So opposition to imperialism ranked at or near the top of his list of priorities.

Another factor in the changed Marxist image was that China was itself undergoing a transformation. It is hardly surprising that Marx in the nineteenth century perceived China differently from Lenin in his later years in the twentieth.

The Twentieth Century

Fascinating and significant as they are, Lenin's images of China do not warrant detailed treatment here, since under the definition given in Chapter 1 the Soviet Union does not fall into the category of a 'Western' country. Images based on the notion of an oriental despotism determined by China's physical environment and needing foreign intervention to bring about change, have persisted in the twentieth century, although with weakening influence. One geographer, writing during the Guomindang period, suggested that the Chinese 'had developed a culture pattern too rigid and inelastic to permit of progress beyond a certain point', because of the need to adjust to the environment. The result was a hardening 'into a routine from which escape was possible only through the aid of external stimuli'. This pattern, common enough in history, the author believed was 'being repeated today in China itself on an unprecedented scale',[22] presumably meaning either that Guomindang China was an unchanging society or that any changes were due to external, that is Western, stimuli.

The best known and most influential of the twentieth-century Western environmental determinists writing on China is Karl August Wittfogel. Explicitly deriving his ideas from the Asiatic mode of production, he was initially a Marxist. Of German origin, he later moved to the United States. Although he developed his main ideas in the German language in the 1930s, he continued to write prolifically in the United States, and his books appearing there include *Oriental Despotism, A Comparative Study of Total Power*, published in 1957, which gives the best summation of his analysis of China. Despite his Marxist beginnings, he moved very strongly to the right and his reaction to the People's Republic was extremely negative.

The core of Wittfogel's argument is that it was the control of the water supply on the semi-arid great northern Chinese plain which enabled the rise of Chinese civilization. Because water was not naturally available at the right time and place, it became necessary for a central authority to ensure its supply through control of great waterways, especially the Yellow River, and irrigation. This led to the rise of a centralized bureaucracy because no other mechanism could control water on the necessary scale. In one of his earliest and most detailed books on China,

Wittfogel begins the chapter called 'The State as Overarching Organ of Agricultural Production in China' as follows:

In our analysis of the role of water in the different regions of China we came across a set of facts which pointed beyond the scope of activity of individual producing 'primeval cells' (*Urzellen*). The control of water, which first made agriculture possible in the Northeast with its protective works, and which in the form of artificial irrigation is the basis of all intensive cultivation in North, Central and South China, requires for its implementation a scale of labour far larger than can usually be performed within local and communal frameworks. . . .[23]

Elsewhere Wittfogel articulates the obvious implication thus: 'Only planned, coordinated *mass* labour, *co-operation*, could lay the groundwork for the agricultural work process in the Chinese river regions.'[24]

Wittfogel calls the society which results from the bureaucracy 'hydraulic society' and the system of government 'oriental despotism'. It is not confined to China but is found in India, Mesoamerica, Egypt, and various other civilizations as well. Two points are in order, however. One is that in fact it is on China that Wittfogel has done most of his major work. The second is that although Wittfogel uses the term 'oriental', he appears to be including a large part, even most, of the civilizations of the past outside Europe. What he is doing is to find a dichotomy between the West, on the one hand, and, on the other, most other major civilizations, especially China's.

Although in the first instance the theory is designed to explain the *origin* of a civilization, it also functions as an interpretation for its survival and maintenance. The waterworks, the irrigation ditches, need constant upkeep and repair. Water control not only implants its stamp upon a civilization, it also helps maintain it more or less unchanged. So, even if the civilization spreads to areas which are not so dependent on water control, perhaps because of more plentiful or timely rainfall, the nature of the 'hydraulic society' does not change radically. China provides the most outstanding example. Its civilization originated in the Yellow River Valley where it was necessary to control water to survive. Confucianism thus derives from the hydraulic society. But later the south became more populous and a focus of civilization just as important as the north and economically more significant. The spread of Chinese civilization to a region of plentiful rainfall and numerous waterways does not exempt it from the tag of 'hydraulic society' because of the nature of government as established in the north survived in the south as well.

Wittfogel's 'hydraulic society' follows the Asiatic mode of production in that the state restricts the development of private property. Whereas in a number of stratified civilizations 'the representatives of private property and enterprise were sufficiently strong to check the power of the state', this was not so 'under hydraulic conditions'[25] because the state realized that a large class owning vast amounts of property constituted a challenge to itself. The bureaucracy gave it both the desire and the ability to keep total power for itself.

The way 'oriental despots' coped with the problem was by equal inheritance. If a property owner, small or large, must divide his land among his sons, the size of each one's plot will tend to get smaller over time. However, if only the oldest son inherits, as happened in feudal Europe, then the allocation to each family will remain the same. In China, the court was able to control the big families because these were never constant. They rose and fell according to the size of their landed estates. As for small property owners, they too suffered as their landholdings shrank. As the population rose, so the size of farms fell, food and consumables became scarcer, while what increased was toil and hardship.

Property ownership is but one of many mechanisms for the concentration of power in the hands of the state. Another, is ideology. For Wittfogel, Confucianism was an outgrowth of, and support for, the hydraulic state. He denies that such a state favours 'the rise of independent religious power'. 'Nowhere in hydraulic society did the dominant religion place itself outside the authority of the state as a nationally (or internationally) integrated autonomous church.' In the case of China the 'dominant religion' is of course Confucianism, and the contrast is with medieval Europe, where the kings of various countries struggled incessantly with the popes.

As for secondary religions, such as Daoism or Buddhism in traditional China, they 'usually originate and spread under relatively differentiated institutional conditions' and so do not constitute 'conspicuous competitors' to the dominant religion. The rulers 'tend with time to identify themselves with the dominant doctrine'.[26] This is a reference to the increasing strength of Confucianism, as against Buddhism, which occurred in the Chinese court and ruling classes from the Song dynasty onwards.

The theory of hydraulic society goes on to equate traditional China with a theocracy because of the dominance of Confucianism and because the ruler was 'the supreme authority both in secular and religious matters'. The overlords of the Zhou and later dynasties held the title of 'Son of Heaven' and occupied a quasi-theocratic position. As long as they were entrusted with the Mandate of Heaven, 'they controlled the magic relations with the forces of nature by elaborate sacrifices'. What all this means is that, even though the emperor and his high officials were occupied mainly with secular matters, they nevertheless 'fulfilled crucial priestly functions'. 'The government of traditional China therefore presents a consistent — and unusual — variant of theocracy.'[27] Wittfogel here maintains a Marxist analysis, for he sees religion as the servant of the hydraulic state, as part of the armoury of its power.

Another, and related, part is the family system, which in traditional China carried a significance even greater than in most other civilizations. But whereas many observers have seen the family as a competitor, even a threat, to the power of the traditional Chinese state, Wittfogel insists that it was a buttress, not a challenge to oriental despotism. It is correct to stress the family as a basic component of society, but misleading to see it as determining 'the quality and power of the institutional setting' of which it formed one part.

What is the evidence for this view? The authority of the father, argues Wittfogel, was much stronger than leadership within the family necessitated. The father 'owed his extraordinary power essentially to the backing of the despotic state', not to the family system. Disobedience to the father's orders 'was punished by the government', and if he was unable to prevent his own family members from infringing the law, local officials could have him punished. Wittfogel's conclusion is that 'acting as a liturgical (semi-official) policeman of his kin group, he can scarcely be considered the autonomous leader of an autonomous unit'.[28] Whereas many observers have seen the strong Chinese traditional family system as part of

Confucianism, the theory of oriental despotism sees both as related cogs in the wheel of the hydraulic state.

Even aspects of the family system are fitted into the schema. An example is polygamy, which becomes a 'factor of hydraulic demography'. How is it that not only society and the state, but even demography, can be described as 'hydraulic'? In such societies rich men have several wives and the richer the men the larger their harems tend to be. Consequently the number of their sons grows. This relates back to the point raised earlier about private property, because 'several heirs mean a quicker reduction of the original property through equal inheritance'.[29] What this idea implies is that concubinage and polygamy originated, or were at least maintained, as a device by the hydraulic state to prevent the growth of large property-ownership which might become a challenge to its power.

The general conclusion of Wittfogel's theory is well summed up in the following passage:

Living under the threat of total terror, the members of a hydraulic community must shape their behavior accordingly. If they want to survive, they must not provoke the uncontrollable monster. To the demands of total authority common sense recommends one answer: obedience. And ideology stereotypes what common sense recommends. Under a despotic regime, obedience becomes the basis of good citizenship.[30]

So traditional China, like all hydraulic societies, was unfree, cruel, and totalitarian. The citizens were like abject slaves with no recourse against the monster which oppressed them. Wittfogel is of course aware of peasant rebellions, but does not consider they rank high enough as a general phenomenon to alter the dominant image of a docile and helpless citizenry. It is a devastatingly negative and bleak picture; and while few would deny the accuracy of many of its brush strokes, it is also a very one-sided one.

The basic idea that the need for irrigation and large-scale water control determined the nature of traditional Chinese society has found a good deal of support among Western observers of China. Owen Lattimore is an good example. Andrew March is mainly correct in observing of Lattimore that 'although his rhetoric is less stringent than Wittfogel's, and he is certainly more concrete and sympathetic and less bemused by the power of government, still his China remains congruent with Wittfogel's'.[31] Yet it is necessary to point out another very signifigant difference between Wittfogel and Lattimore: whereas Wittfogel came to see communism in China as a force inflicting slavery on the people and merely another oriental despotism to be fought at all costs, Lattimore has been broadly sympathetic to it and reacted favourably to the establishment of the People's Republic.

Lattimore's most famous work is *Inner Asian Frontiers of China*, published originally in 1940. In his work he acknowledges considerable debt to Wittfogel. He writes that 'the formation of a centralized empire was inevitable', and the reason was that 'in no other way was it possible to maintain a state apparatus capable of initiating, operating, and supervising immense public works which transcended regions'. He goes on to stress the 'social coordination of a very high order' that was necessary to irrigate, dig long navigable canals, link natural waterways, and control flooding.[32]

Another sinologist to adopt a form of geographic determinism is the liberal American John King Fairbank. In a statement extremely reminiscent of Wittfogel and Lattimore he writes of old Chinese society:

Control of the water supply for agricultural production was a strategic factor in the growth of the government's economic function. It was typical of these societies that, unlike Western Europe, they were in regions of semi-aridity where the water supply of great rivers, if properly used, would supplement the insufficiency of rainfall. But irrigation and flood prevention to be effective must be centrally controlled. Both irrigation ditches and river dikes must be maintained throughout their length according to an overall program.[33]

Like Wittfogel, Fairbank starts from the semi-aridity of China's great northern plain and draws a contrast with Western Europe. The need for water control becomes a determinant of Chinese society.

Not surprisingly, Wittfogel's theories have also come under strong attack among Western observers of China. One of the grounds for criticism is the relationship with Marxism. One well-known review by the political sociologist S. N. Eisenstadt criticizes him for being too heavily influenced by Marxism, despite his strong opposition to Chinese communism: 'Although he has come to combat Marxism, it seems that his thinking has been too much rooted in it to enable him to do so effectively.'[34] There is some irony in this line since, as Eisenstadt points out,[35] *Oriental Despotism* specifically denies class struggle in Chinese history.[36]

On the other hand, Joseph Needham, the famous pro-China Cambridge sinologist, to whom we return in the next chapter, attacks Wittfogel from the left for the 'naïve assumption' that doctrines like Marxism are 'incapable of undergoing development' and for branding all Marxism as the same, a reasonable criticism. Needham also castigates Wittfogel for ignoring the development of science and technology in China, which were generally ahead of Europe's until about 1450.[37] So to put down China as oriental, despotic, and thus inferior to Europe is not only misleading but downright false.

Another line of attack is against the reductionism of the hydraulic society theory. The great, originally Hungarian, sinologist Etienne Balazs (1905–63) criticizes the concept as narrow and continues: 'it takes into account only one element in a complex whole, and from the many functions fulfilled by the mandarinate selects one only: that concerned with hydraulic constructions.'[38] Balazs focused his point on the bureaucracy which he, like Wittfogel, sees as central to traditional China. He also sees the old Chinese state as 'absolute and despotic' and believes the officials, even the highest ones, were at its mercy.[39] So despite his evident disagreement over the origins of Chinese civilization in the control of waterworks, his rejection of geographic determinism, there are areas of concord between Wittfogel and Balazs.

The most detailed critique of Wittfogel's theories, considered as a whole and not merely in the form of a review of *Oriental Despotism*, is that of Wolfram Eberhard. He rejects the term 'despotic' to describe the emperors of medieval China, allowing Qin Shihuang (reigned 246–210 BC) as the only exception. Han Wudi (reigned 140–87 BC), he claims, tried again to become an absolute ruler, but failed.[40]

Eberhard's main argument strikes at the root of geographic determinism. He contends that water control and irrigation were managed on a local or even private basis and so did not require the vast centralized bureaucracy so crucial to Wittfogel's theory. On the basis of what Eberhard admits as incomplete research he contends that what actually happened was very often that a private citizen spent his own money and took a personal initiative to organize labour necessary for waterworks or irrigation. He explains Chinese expansion into the south as follows:

Here we find the typical case that a Chinese settler acquired land from the natives or took possession of land. He then levelled the land and started irrigation. On the newly irrigated land he settled either his own family or clan or other immigrants. Thus a new Chinese colonial settlement was created; quickly it became much wealthier than the native settlements which had no irrigation or only simple slope-irrigation. With the growth of the 'colonial' settlement, an expansion of the irrigation system became necessary. Thus originally small systems developed into large-scale systems, all on the basis of private initiative.[41]

So a large bureaucracy did indeed grow, but it can in no way be explained through irrigation. Moreover, it was as likely to struggle within itself on a regional basis as to unite behind the court. Eberhard simply believes the giant, repressive, 'hydraulic', centralized bureaucracy to be a fantasy.

Just as with Marx, the twentieth-century theories of oriental despotism raise the recurring problem of stagnation versus change in traditional, and even contemporary, China. To be fair to Wittfogel, it must be pointed out that the opening paragraph of *Oriental Despotism* affirms the possibility of social change because 'man never stops affecting his natural environment'.[42] The formula retains the tight link between humankind and the physical environment, but it allows for interchange between them, not simply the total subordination of the first to the second.

· But earlier in his career Wittfogel had been very specific that geography did indeed determine history. Several passages could be quoted. The following concludes a long three-part article and is thus highlighted by its author.

Every step of active social labour must take place in dependence on the laws of motion of nature, the objective world external to humankind. All attempts of any kind whatsoever to transfer primacy into the movements of the social sphere lead back into the realm of free will, into the realm of a freedom of the will which detaches itself from the hard determinations of the real world surrounding us. The priest and mystic may take and eloquently recommend such a path for imitation, but real science cannot step along it.[43]

Andrew March has suggested that it is Wittfogel's self-perception as a fighter for freedom against the new hydraulic society of the People's Republic which caused the shift in his thinking on determinism.[44] Whatever the motivation behind the change, it appears to me to raise a serious, even fundamental, inconsistency in the theory. If the reaction of human beings and their environment is two-way, then the need for water control may explain the origins of Chinese civilization, but the features of its continuing nature do not follow logically, as Wittfogel appears to suggest.

Conclusion

To this writer the theories of oriental despotism, Asiatic mode of production, and hydraulic society need to be taken seriously, because of the fascinating and important issues they raise on social change and on the ways and extent to which a country's physical environment influences its history. Yet it is remarkable that a man as brilliant as Marx could devise a major general theory like the materialist conception of history, and then immediately exclude from it most of humanity, and in particular the overwhelming majority of non-European people.

The theory of the hydraulic society is ultimately flawed, mainly because it take insufficient account of regional and temporal variations in Chinese history. Its total negation of class war seems hard to substantiate, and extremely ironical for a theory which takes its origin from Marxism. The unrelievedly negative images of China, its people, and its history implied in the various ideas of the oriental despotism may show a portion of reality, but they are too one-sided and Eurocentric to carry conviction.

Part of the function of these images in Western intellectual history has been to show China as inferior. This is because the West has for several centuries regarded change as dynamic and good, and stagnation as undesirable. It follows that the image of the 'changeless China' sits very comfortably with Said's 'Orientalism'. For the late eighteenth and all of the nineteenth centuries, it also accords well with Foucault's 'regime of truth'. Even a man such as Marx, who devoted most of his life's work to the criticism of capitalism, could argue that

Western intervention in China was historically necessary and progressive. The doctrine of the stagnant oriental despotism had become part of the ideological justification for the power relationship which imperialist Europe imposed on China.

8

Post-War Western Views of China's Pre-Modern History

SINCE the end of World War II, there has been in the West an explosion of interest in China's pre-modern history. This has resulted in the writing and publication of more books on more issues than can possibly be touched on in this chapter. Perhaps more central from the point of view of 'images', this has been the period when the paperback and other kinds of popular book have caught the market, so that readership, even on history, has expanded greatly.

A few preliminary points are necessary. Firstly, the term 'pre-modern' is taken to apply to the period ending about 1800. The next chapter takes up the hotly debated issue of just when 'modern' history begins.

Secondly, Western writing about China before 1800 has been undertaken largely by academics working in universities. It is they who have been most influential in looking at primary sources, finding data, and establishing interpretations on an enormous range of broad or narrow issues. It must be added, however, that, in terms of the creation of popular images, other professions have contributed as much or more, especially those entrepreneurs, diplomats, journalists, and others who have helped the Chinese project themselves and their ancient arts to the West.

The tendency towards the internationalization of images has been strong, with three implications. First, most of the countries of Western Europe, North America, and Australasia have produced good or image-creating historical works about China, but not always by nationals of the relevant country. The second is that, despite continuing fine traditions of sinology in France, West Germany, and other countries of continental

Europe, most of the main work has been published in the United States or Britain, whatever the nationality of the author. Thirdly, English has been overwhelmingly the main language of communication, despite some good work in French, German, and Italian.

Finally, the post-war years have seen a change in the nature of the history written. For a start, scholars have been far more willing to venture into the medieval or late imperial periods, which include the Tang (618–907), Song (960–1279), Ming (1368–1644), and Qing (1644–1911) periods than was the case in the pre-war years. A related but distinct change has been the substantial growth of 'revisionist' history, as a result of which scholars have been eager not only to attack previously untouched topics but also to challenge and revise hitherto accepted interpretations, either on broad or narrow issues. What has been relatively lacking is the monumental, multi-volumed work on China's history or an aspect of it written by a single scholar. This is partly because the nature of academic life has changed, placing less emphasis on research, more on teaching and administration, than was the case in pre-war universities of the West.

Needham and Chinese Science

We begin with the main exception to this proposition. Though by many authors, it has been co-ordinated and supervised by one British scholar, who conceived the project and who certainly deserves the main credit for the work. It is Joseph Needham's extraordinarily influential and certainly image-creating *Science and Civilisaton in China*.

Originally Needham set out to cover the whole range of Chinese 'science and civilization' in seven volumes, but the project has grown in scale as it has proceeded. The first volume treats the background geography and history, and the 'conditions of travel of scientific ideas and techniques between China and Europe'; the second, the various systems of Chinese thought which have contributed to, or impeded, the growth of a scientific tradition in China. Volumes III to VI provide or will provide the core scientific data. In fact, there are already far more than seven volumes because Volumes IV to VII have expanded into numerous parts. Volume IV on 'physics and physical technology' contains three parts, each in its own large book. As of late 1987, fourteen parts were planned for Volume V on 'chemistry and chemical technology' of which seven were complete or published. Volume VII is planned in four parts, which will sum up the whole work and set Chinese achievements against their social background. The entire work is planned to include over thirty books, of which, as of late 1987, fourteen were published.

One of Needham's basic assumptions is that the Chinese were original, not merely imitators. 'There can be no doubt', he writes, 'that China was, among the ancient civilisations of the Old World, the one which was most isolated from the others. The originality of its characteristic cultural patterns was therefore greater.'[1]

It follows from this that cultural and scientific diffusion between China and other civilizations, and in particular the West, took place in both directions, not merely one, as implied in the Eurocentric views even of so fine a scholar as Henri Maspero, discussed in Chapter 6. Needham believes in fact that the Chinese succeeded in forestalling the Greeks in many important matters of scientific and technical discoveries, that between the third and thirteenth centuries, they had access to 'a level of scientific knowledge unapproached in the west', and that with the coming of the Jesuits to Beijing early in the seventeenth century 'Chinese science gradually fused into the universality of modern science'.[2]

Needham is thus highly appreciative of Chinese traditional scientific knowledge and techniques. The research carried out under his supervision has revolutionized the West's understanding of old China's science and dispelled a number of myths, such as that the Chinese were 'unscientific' and did not understand how to use tools and technology. Considering the importance of science and technology in the world today, this has raised the image of traditional China in the eyes of the West enormously.

However, it is in techniques where Needham considers China to have excelled, not theory. Their science was quasi-empirical and based on observation and experience. The element of scepticism was also in evidence. But the major element lacking was experiment. As a result, the 'old Chinese . . . were never

able to pass beyond' such 'relatively primitive and unquan-
tifiable theories' as the Five Elements (*wuxing*) or *yin-yang*.[3]

Needham analyses in great detail the ideas associated with
the development of science in old China. He sees concepts
conducive to science, and impeding it, in all the major systems
of traditional Chinese thought. Not surprisingly, attitudes
towards Nature and the natural world loom large in his analyses.
Thus he appears to hold the preoccupations of Confucianism
largely responsible for the lack of scientific theory, because
of its attitude to Nature:

Confucianism has little connection with the history of science. A
religion without theologians, it had no one to object to the intrusion
of a scientific view on its preserves, but in accordance with the ideas
of its founding fathers, it turned its face away from Nature and
the investigation of Nature, to concentrate on a millennial interest
on human society, and human society alone.[4]

In Daoism, however, Needham sees a scientific approach,
because the doctrine of *wuwei* (inaction) 'implied learning from
Nature by observation'.[5] Legalism was too authoritarian and
lacked the humanitarianism of Confucianism, but 'its tendency
to be quantitive, expressing things in numerical terms'[6] was
new in China and of assistance to scientific development. But
law in old China Needham sees as fundamentally inimical
to science because 'it was overwhelmingly social and ethical'
and thus 'made any extension of its sphere of influence to
non-human Nature impossible'. On the other hand, the Chinese
world-view was correct in seeing a 'harmonious co-operation
of all beings . . . because they were all parts in a hierarchy
that formed a cosmic pattern' and modern science has come
to share this viewpoint.[7]

Needham's approach is comparative as well as about China.
In one of his numerous works growing out of *Science and
Civilisation* he tries to compare, or 'titrate' as he terms it, the
great civilizations against one another. He thus makes an effort
to discover why it was that China far surpassed others during
the Middle Ages in Western Europe, but later on fell behind
so that it was eventually the West which could 'bring modern
science itself into existence'.[8]

And here is the nub of the problem. Needham recognizes

the faults of European science, especially negative aspects of Christianity in its development, and he rightly insists on the existence of a fine tradition in China. Early in the first volume he poses, as a central aim of the whole work and thus of his life, the problem thus:

What were the inhibiting factors in Chinese civilisation which prevented a rise of modern science in Asia analogous to that which took place in Europe from the 16th century onwards, and which proved one of the basic factors in the moulding of modern world order?[9]

It is a question of crucial historical significance which nobody has answered satisfactorily. Needham insists that the answer to such a question necessitates comprehending the Chinese tradition from the inside and is the first to organize the research required to reach such an understanding.

With his quite justified passion for 'titration', Needham also puts the question round the other way and asks why it was that '*modern* science, the tradition of Galileo, Harvey, Vesalius, Gesner, Newton, universally verifiable and commanding universal rational assent' developed 'round the shores of the Mediterranean and the Atlantic, and not in China or any other part of Asia'.[10]

It is Volume VII which will contain the fully worked out answers to this critically important historical problem. In the meantime he has offered tentative suggestions which he himself sums up thus:

Very likely the ultimate explanations will turn out to be highly paradoxical — aristocratic military feudalism seeming to be much stronger than bureaucratic feudalism but actually weaker because less rational — the monotheism of a personal creator God being able to generate modern scientific thought ... but not give it inspiration enduring into modern times — and so on. We do not yet know.[11]

It is already clear, however, that Needham sees the solution in the economic structures of society and in ideologies, rather than in science itself, let alone in chance, historical accident, or any theory which posits the inherent superiority of Europe. This thrust has won acceptance among most commentators on Needham's work.[12]

This does not mean that all Needham's conclusions so far have been approved by everybody. One reviewer criticizes him because he 'tends, at times, to over-stress the benevolent, pacific aspects of China's culture',[13] an interesting comment suggesting that Needham has elevated traditional China's image not only in its science but other areas as well. Another criticizes him for his ideological explanations for the early development of alchemy in China.[14]

One of the most interesting issues is the one arising from Needham's treatment of hydraulic engineering. He does not accept Wittfogel's interpretation and hardly refers to it at all except for an attack on 'subjective speculation about the "hydraulic foundations of oriental despotism"'; even there he does not mention his adversary by name.[15] Needham accepts the significance of waterworks. He describes the Chinese as 'outstanding among the nations of the world in their control and use of water'.[16] He even writes of the Qin dynasty of the third century BC that its power 'was largely built on extensive irrigation works'.[17] But that is quite different from explaining Chinese society on the basis of the organization of water, as Wittfogel does.

One reviewer expresses the dilemma of Needham's conflicting interpretations thus: 'On the one hand, his whole approach to Chinese science suggests that he believes a society's values radically affect its technological responses. On the other hand, he wishes to establish technology as a prime mover in human affairs.'[18] Should one establish any factor as decisive or attempt to balance them against each other? It is a critical issue with which many major historians have grappled.

Even those who believe they have found shortcomings in Needham's work agree on its enormous value. The same critic who expresses himself as dissatisfied by Needham's treatment of hydrology so far can call *Science and Civilisation* 'one of the major scholarly enterprises of the century'.[19] 'Needham's scholarship stands alone in its matchless range, thorough documentation, and human significance.'[20] Such strong, and well deserved, praise has been typical of the response to this monumental work.

Needham is a great admirer of Chinese civilization and, as is probably obvious from the foregoing account, left-wing in his views on history. He has always been very sympathetic towards the People's Republic. He has also received honours from China itself. In particular, in November 1983, he was given the National Award of Natural Science, First Class, the first time China had conferred this award on a foreign scholar.

Some Issues in 'Pre-Modern' History

Needham is the best known of hundreds of people who have worked on Chinese history in the West since World War II. He is among a small number who have tried and succeeded in devising quite new interpretations of the broad sweep of Chinese history. One major question which inevitably arises in conceiving Chinese history as a whole is how to periodize it. The normally accepted periodization is traditionally according to dynasties. In the West the three most influential concise general histories of 'pre-modern' China in the post-war years are probably those of C. P. Fitzgerald, already discussed in Chapter 6; Wolfram Eberhard, first published in 1948 in German and in 1950 in English,[21] and that contained in Edwin O. Reischauer and John K. Fairbank's *East Asia, the Great Tradition*, first published in 1958. All three, and above all the third, have been widely used as textbooks in university courses throughout the West and especially in the English-speaking world. All three are quite typical in periodizing Chinese history generally through single or pairs of dynasties. However, Fairbank makes a major exception by seeing 'the period of transition between late classic China and the "early modern" period centered around the eighth century', which, as he goes on to point out, fell 'right in the middle' of the Tang dynasty.[22] In addition to dynasties, Eberhard establishes some longer eras, each designated by a central characteristic, such as 'the period of absolutism' covering the Yuan, Ming, and Qing periods from 1280 to 1911, but the major imperial dynasties are still treated discretely, rather than as a continuum.

A partial break with the dynastic periodization was adopted by C. P. Fitzgerald in his pictorial 'Horizon' history of China, which uses a totally different schema from that of his much earlier cultural history and a much more sophisticated one. Here we find very broad periods such as 'the early empire (200 B.C. to A.D. 600)', 'the golden age (A.D. 600 to 1260)' and 'the later empire (1260 to 1912)' in which dynastic boundaries are only marginally relevant.[23] Charles Hucker's influential 'introduction to Chinese History and Culture', widely used as a textbook in the United States and elsewhere, likewise divides the history up into large slabs and designates each through short phrases such as 'the early empire, 206 B.C.–A.D. 960' and 'the later empire, 960–1850'. Hucker's designations are similar to Fitzgerald's, though his periodization is very different. While it is true that the boundaries of most of Hucker's eras coincide with a new dynasty's foundation, the subdivisions are topical, such as government, thought, society, and the economy, not chronological. Unlike Eberhard's, his treatment of particular topics crosses the boundaries of dynasties. His 'emphasis is on patterns and themes rather than factual data'.[24]

The dynastic periodization is still quite fashionable. One broad survey history of Chinese and Japanese civilizations justifies the 'standard dynastic framework' as the 'basic historical chronology' on the grounds that the text's basic aim is 'to serve as a work of orientation',[25] which implies a belief that convention is the best form of orientation, a view surely open to challenge. The dynastic framework is of course perfectly legitimate all the same, but may not be the most appropriate way to conceive or present Chinese history.

It is questionable that dynastic changes really brought about the most decisive new directions in Chinese history. One scholar to challenge the dynastic periodization totally is Bodo Wiethoff, whose *Introduction to Chinese History* was first published in German in 1971 and in English translation in 1975. His account is entirely topical with no separate divisions for individual dynasties at all. He discusses the issue of 'the periodization of Chinese history' and concludes that 'it must be clear already that the dynastic periodization of Chinese history, if anything, creates more problems than it solves'.[26]

One other influential scholar to withdraw altogether from periodizing Chinese history by dynasty is Mark Elvin. He has suggested a 'pattern' to imperial Chinese history, based on economic and social factors. He put forward his ideas in a highly scholarly book published in 1973 and later summarized them in a beautiful pictorial coffee-table book of the sort which conveys images to more people more forcefully than even a widely circulating academic work can hope to do. He posits a 'medieval economic revolution' which 'took place approximately half-way through the imperial age, in the centuries on either side of 1000 AD'[27] and made the Chinese economy after about 1100 the most advanced in the world. Revolutions took place in farming, water transport, money and credit, market structure and urbanization, and science and technology.[28] But then, between about 1300 and 1500, the Chinese economy fell into a depression from which it recovered only very slowly, and between 1500 and 1800 'invention was almost entirely absent'.[29] The trend that resulted was 'economic development without technological change'.[30] Social change never ceased, but it did become far less substantial than it had been earlier. China fell into a 'high-level equilibrium trap', meaning that 'the input–output relationships of the late traditional economy had assumed a pattern that was almost incapable of change through internally-generated forces'. Agricultural productivity reached the limits of what could be achieved without 'industrial–scientific inputs', while surplus product was eroded by population growth.[31]

Elvin has clearly made a contribution to the debate which has occupied Needham and others for so long. Otherwise, his main overall conclusion is 'that technological innovation and invention during the period 800 to 1300 produced changes so great that the result can only reasonably be described as a "revolution", and that Chinese growth thereafter slowed down not only relative to an accelerating Europe but also to its own earlier performance'.[32] The view that the mid-Tang represents a watershed in Chinese history is not new to Elvin, and has become conventional wisdom amounting to an 'image' largely through the work of Denis Twitchett,[33] but credit is due to him for his conception of an 'economic revolution' and for identifying not only when it began but also when it petered out.

The concept of a 'medieval economic revolution' raises again the issue of change in China. On the whole, the more scholars have examined the history of China, the more change they have seen in it. Certainly, historians are more conscious than formerly of the 'integrative factors' —geographical, intellectual, social, political, and so on — in China's past and their 'interaction' with each other.[34] Nevertheless, 'integration is not a constant and should not be confused with stagnation'.[35] It has often been repeated that China's is the oldest continuous civilization in the world, but it does not follow that it has not undergone deep change. It was the slowing down of change after the 'medieval economic revolution' had worked itself out, and the coincidence with the acceleration of transformation in Europe following the Reformation and especially the Industrial Revolution, which made observers see total stagnation in China. Such a view no longer has a major following.

The image of an integrated civilization is perhaps best summed up through the set of ideas which in the West bears the name of the most famous Chinese of any century before our own: Confucius. In view of its central role as an ideology, Confucianism may serve as a single example to illustrate Western images of pre-modern China.

This is like so much in traditional China in that it is not changeless. Confucianism developed in many ways and the existence of the revived Neo-Confucianism of the Song dynasty and later is well known. Post-war scholarship has established that the Neo-Confucianism of the early Ming 'underwent significant changes' and 'assumed a definite direction',[36] in contrast to the traditional view that the Ming period was one of 'general decline and aimless drifting'.[37] Yet, though there were still fine philosophers as late as the seventeenth century, it is probably the dominant view that Song Neo-Confucian 'orthodoxy remained the mainstream of Chinese philosophy' from the seventeenth century into the twentieth, and that Confucian intellectuals of the Qing period 'in general did not engage in speculative philosophizing but devoted themselves to politically safe scholarship in many realms'.[38] In other words Chinese thinking became stereotyped, just when European challenges to orthodoxy were gathering momentum.

Let us look at a few of the strands of Confucianism. Its humanitarianism, at least by comparison with Legalism, as well as its unscientific character, were mentioned by Needham and are largely accepted. It is a source and expression of 'harmony' rather than 'conflict' in the Chinese tradition. Mencius, Confucius's main early follower, stressed that in human nature 'there exists a natural tendency for goodness, as inevitable as the natural tendency of water to flow downward'.[39] Such an idea implants an optimistic stamp on Confucianism.

The core social image of Confucianism rests in the family. Many in the West see this strong influence of the family as a source of stability and harmony, and hence generally beneficial. On the other hand, the image is that the Confucian family system was not only male-centred but considerably more so than that of Christianity. Discrimination against the female sex is highlighted in many influential works, such as those of Fairbank.[40]

Confucianism is seen as having promoted serious inequalities, both between the sexes and more generally among classes and elsewhere in society. One of the leading and most influential American post-war historians of China has drawn attention to two main classes in the Confucian social order. They were 'the peasant masses, who produced food and cloth and provided soldiers and corvée laborers as the state needed them; and a numerically small elite, which had a monopoly of literacy, statecraft, and administrative skills'[41] and, he might have added, property.

Politically, Confucianism is seen as a conservative doctrine, one of support for the *status quo*. Its image is that of the ideological basis of an army of mandarins who entered the bureaucracy through a competitive and severe examination system, one which, though it delivered successful candidates great rewards, also 'drove many to nervous collapse, madness, or suicide'. The Confucian political culture was efficient and rational; one account describes the bureaucracy which the founder of the Ming dynasty assembled to run his empire as 'probably the most sophisticated administrative organization created anywhere up to that time'.[42]

To Westerners, one of the best known strands of Confucian political thought is the Mandate of Heaven. By this doctrine Heaven could withdraw the right to rule from any sovereign who was immoral or proved unworthy of the power he held. The main implication was 'the idea that the people had the right to rebel against oppressive rule'.[43] Many in the West have perceived here at least the hint that the will of the people held some significance, even if only slight.

Finally, what is the Western image of the Confucian attitude towards the outside world? It is widely known that *Zhongguo* means 'the middle kingdom', and for most people in the West China's name for itself holds a ring of strong ethnocentrism, or sinocentrism. John King Fairbank, undoubtedly the most influential post-war writer on traditional Chinese foreign relations, confirms that 'the relations of the Chinese with surrounding areas, and with non-Chinese peoples generally, were colored by this concept of Sinocentrism and an assumption of Chinese superiority'.[44] He has adopted the term 'culturalism' to express the Confucian attitude. It 'assumed that China was not only the largest and oldest among the states of the world but indeed their parent and the source of their civilization'.[45] Under China's system of foreign relations, which Fairbank terms 'the Chinese world order',[46] the emperor issued an official document of appointment to the rulers of certain nearby countries, and 'affected a paternal interest in the orderly government of the tributary state'. Some see in the growth of China's borders over the centuries an expansionism which gives grounds for fear even today. However, a more dominant image of China's behaviour towards neighbours in the past almost certainly follows Fairbank's: 'This was not an aggressive imperialism on China's part. Rather, it was a defensive expression of the "culturalism" we have already noted.'[47] The Chinese world order was based far more on ethical than military power. As with many other aspects of Confucianism, concepts underpinning China's traditional foreign relations would be resisted strongly if proposed today, but the West's main image of the system is that it suited the needs and requirements of the East Asian region of the past reasonably well.

Most of the works on which the perceptions discussed so far in this chapter rest have been designed or used as textbooks in tertiary colleges or universities, and thus contributed towards the formulation of images. However, one study of the problem of adapting scholarly work on China to the needs of secondary educators found that there was 'often a gap of a decade or more between the scholar's research and its reflection in the secondary school classroom'.[48] Other than a handful such as Needham, Fairbank, and Fitzgerald, very few individuals have exercised any influence on the popular view of China's premodern history. Most Western countries gave China's history in the classroom a low priority until the politics of the early 1970s forced them to understand its past as a door to coming to grips with events in its present.

Images through the Traditional Visual Arts

Other than through reading, images of a nation's past can be conveyed through pictures or other visual arts. Picture books are nothing new in the West, but there has been an enormous expansion in the post-war years of the glossy, beautifully and expensively produced coffee-table book with thick paper, abounding both in coloured and black-and-white illustrations and sometimes maps. In the case of China there is a wealth of surviving paintings, buildings, sculpture, pots, and other artefacts from the distant and more recent past to provide material for such books. There is a substantial Western literature on the history of the Chinese traditional visual arts, which themselves create images not only of China's artistic heritage but also of the country's history. However, a more appropriate set of examples in the present context is those works which specifically aim to present Chinese history through a combination of pictures and text, with the emphasis on the former and the text serving largely to explain the illustrations. A particularly well-known case in point is C. P. Fitzgerald's *Horizon History of China*.

Fitzgerald rightly begins by rejecting the 'mysterious' image of China. Of course it is true that Chinese culture 'was independent of Western influences'. The Chinese were indeed 'remote' from Europe, which makes them 'only alien' but 'not really mysterious'.[49]

Assuming the viewer is warned to try and look at the illustrations in their own terms, one strong impression to emerge from the pictures is how generally prosperous and developed China was at the time when Europe was still in its early Middle Ages. Zhang Zeduan's famous scroll of life in and near the Northern Song dynasty capital Kaifeng at the turn of the eleventh and twelfth centuries is featured in several books. It shows a thriving, bustling population, engaged in an enormous variety of commercial activities, entertainment, and so on, not only on land, but also on the river. A rainbow bridge is crowded with people, showing a high standard both of beauty and of technology. Near a vast and imposing city gate is a wineshop with the rich approaching in sedan chairs and on horseback. Camels walk through the gate, outside which peasants chat relaxedly.[50] (See Number 9 of the Plates in this book.)

The inequalities of society mentioned in the previous section are obvious in the pictorial accounts. Poor and shabby dwellings are numerous, though desperate poverty is not a particularly striking feature in the pictures presented. At the other end of society, the scholar–bureaucracy looms quite large. Many pictures show its life of leisure and devotion to literature or aesthetic beauty, waited on by servants, or dedication to the public good and the path of duty.[51] Perhaps even more striking is the magnificence of the life of the nobility and the emperors, as well as the grandeur of their buildings.[52]

One kind of inequality to come through with particular force is that between the sexes. Fitzgerald's book has a series of 'portfolios', one of which is called 'the second sex'. It describes the various forms of discrimination against women, while most of the pictures give the impression that women existed to serve or give pleasure to men, or perform the menial tasks. One of the few grim pictures shows an adultress being whipped.[53] The fact of foot-binding in traditional China is widely known and condemned among Westerners. A picture of the 'twisted and cramped bone structure' of a bound foot, set against that of a normal one, conveys a powerful image of the pain which this 'major curse' caused.[54]

Buddhism inevitably bulks fairly large in the historical pictures of China, simply because of the numerous surviving magnificent sculptures of the Buddha, some of stupendous size.[55] The love of nature which Needham rightly attributed to Daoism is conveyed beautifully through the landscape paintings which abound throughout Chinese history from the late Tang onwards. They show nature dwarfing people and even the most magnificent structures humankind has been able to build.[56]

The other side of the coin to the quietude this artistic love of nature implies is peasant revolt and war. Pictures show expeditionary forces sent to quell rebellion, pitched battles between two contending parties, or peasants burning their bonds of servitude in the very courtyard of the landlord's house.[57] However, the overall image to come through the picture books is rather positive, with stability, quietude, and beauty generally more in evidence than disturbances or war.

Even more influential for image-creation than picture books, however beautifully produced, is the presentation of actual cultural objects. In the mid to late 1970s a magnificent exhibition of Chinese archaeological artefacts toured many countries of the West, and elsewhere, and it was followed in the early 1980s by one of the entombed terracotta warriors of the first emperor of a unified China, Qin Shihuang (reigned 246–210 BC). There have been many other exhibitions of materials from China's distant past, but these two have exerted by far the greatest impact on images. China was using the opportunities of increased Western diplomatic acceptance to put forward a picture of its own past to the West. The numbers who visited these exhibitions was large. In London more than 750,000 people saw the first of the two exhibitions, while in Australia the total was about 600,000, or about 4 per cent of the people, as visitors to an artistic display a significant proportion of the national population. The terracotta warriors of the underground army proved even more popular: in Australia they attracted nearly 750,000 people, that being the record attendance for any art exhibition in the country's history.

Of course people filtered what they saw through their own experiences and biases, scholars and others were called upon to offer interpretations, but in general the exhibitions spoke for themselves. They 'enthralled' Westerners with an image of the 'exotic', of a past grandeur, and these responded 'with an interest and awe befitting such evocative relics'.[58] An immediate image to present itself was the weight of the past on the present. This was especially so in countries with short histories. Australia's first ambassador to the People's Republic of China, Stephen FitzGerald — no relation to C. P. Fitzgerald — commented: 'It may seem surprising that a modern socialist country should concern itself with the past in such a way, and yet the recognition that modern China has grown out of China of the past is not only indisputable fact but also an acknowledged feature of modern political ideology.'[59]

While any view of the Qin empire and of Chinese history as a whole are clearly two quite different things, some of the dominant images to emerge from the terracotta warriors do apply more widely in the minds of Westerners than simply to one narrow period. In other cases, the Qin may represent Legalism in a dichotomy another arm of which is represented by the Confucian tradition, it is the side of 'conflict' as against the 'harmony' of Confucianism.

The first image to mention is the 'monumental scale, grandiose conception and the sheer numbers' of the underground army.[60] The image of the Qin empire, and of Chinese emperors as a whole, is of men who did things in a big way, and were able to do so because they held enormous power and riches. Anyone who would spend so much money on so large a terracotta army, not only of life size but each member different from the others, must have been extraordinarily vain and interested in self-aggrandizement. A variant on the theme of extravagance and luxury was obvious in the premier exhibit of the 1970s archaeological display: the jade costume of Prince Liu Sheng's wife Princess Dou Wan, found in their tomb dating from the second century BC. It impressed people not only for its magnificence, but for what it showed about the life, and death, of the rich and the concomitant misery of the poor.

The power and self-importance of the Qin empire's founder, apparent from the underground army, strongly suggested an authoritarian government with a population lacking in freedom. The burning of the books and the suppression of all opposition, including among court scholars, reinforced this negative image. The much-vaunted unity of China achieved by this power-maniac was no doubt impressive because it lasted so long, but was bought at a frightful cost.

Another closely related image is of tyrannical cruelty against impoverished docile masses. If there is one fact very widely known about the man who ordered those entombed warriors be made, it is that he had the Great Wall completed, possibly the foremost image of China not only of pre-modern times but of any age.[61] Here is the gigantic scale epitomized, but also the oppression inflicted by the archetypal tyrant. 'Even to-day, after more than 2,000 years, the people repeat that a million men perished at the task, and every stone cost a human life.'[62] The image is of an efficient but savage slave-driver who cared naught for human life. His subjects were so numerous that it probably did not matter much anyway, and if those who did the dying cared they were mere cyphers whose opinion was utterly irrelevant.

Such images are probably not too different from those of today's Chinese about Qin Shihuang. Westerners are quite well aware of barbarities in their own past, although probably few would be willing to concede the history of Europe to be as replete with cruelty as China's. When the Campaign to Criticize Lin Biao and Confucius of 1973–4 rewrote the history of Qin China and extolled the First Emperor as the destroyer of the slave system and creator of feudalism, few of those in the West who were aware of the re-evaluation took it seriously. Not many of those who marvelled at the entombed warriors understood or had any clear image of Marxist categories like feudalism. While there are those in the West whose image of China during the Cultural Revolution is of its being like Qin dynasty times, the dominant view is that we can afford to be relaxed about the savageries of the past, because they are over and done with, and things are much better now.

One reason, perhaps the primary one, why judgements are unnecessary is the single overwhelmingly positive image to emerge from the entombed warriors, and indeed other exhibitions and pictorial histories: China certainly produced magnificent art, a superb culture. Moreover, though it may have been an emperor who issued the commands, the actual artists, the sculptors of the warriors, were unknown and quite likely ordinary artisans with a technical skill and sense of proportion and beauty difficult to rival anywhere. The thought of so many, so magnificent, and such large statues lying hidden underground for so long cannot fail to arouse awe and admiration. The obvious image to emerge from all examples mentioned in this section is of a highly cultured, highly intelligent, and extremely artistic people.

Fiction

Besides monumental exhibitions, another source of images reaching well beyond students and into the public at large is fiction. The overwhelming majority of novels and short stories written in the West since World War II take place in the West itself, and China is not a particularly popular setting for the remainder. However, there are some with Chinese background and, of special interest for this chapter, a few which show images of what China was like before the nineteenth century.

The most famous series of novels and short stories written by a Westerner and set in China's distant past is Robert Van

Gulik's Judge Dee detective stories. The earliest was *The Chinese Bell Murders*, published in Britain in 1958, but many others succeeded it, including *The Chinese Nail Murders*, *The Emperor's Pearl*, *The Lacquer Screen*, and *The Red Pavilion*. They have received universal acclaim in Western countries, hit the paperback market, and been made into a popular television series. They can most certainly claim to be image-formulating.

Van Gulik (1910–67) was Dutch and a career diplomat. An astonishingly brilliant man, he also mastered the Chinese language and achieved great distinction as a sinologist. Among his many works some are standard and acknowledged authoritative treatments of such topics as Chinese music and sexology.[63] Van Gulik was a great admirer of traditional Chinese civilization. He was much more than a mere thirster after the exotic, and really understood the society where he set his detective stories.

The central character in these novels and short stories is Di Renjie (630–700), a historical figure, a magistrate and judge, noted for his impartiality and justice, who rose to become a minister under the Empress Wu Zetian. The novels and short stories deal with the time before he went to court, when he was still a local official in such places as Penglai, Shandong province. He does occasionally need to deal with the high-ranking ministers in the capital, but to him they are men before whom one stands in awe and extreme respect.

It was after translating an anonymous eighteenth-century Chinese novel dealing with cases of Judge Dee that Van Gulik started to write his own stories on the same general theme.[64] However, while the Chinese story actually portrays a society closer to the anonymous author's own time than to that of the early Tang dynasty when Di Renjie actually lived, Van Gulik has been careful to make the social background details correct for the seventh century. The Chinese novel announces the criminals' identity at the beginning of the story, but Van Gulik has followed the practice more usual in Western detective literature of keeping the reader in suspense until near the end of the action.

The society depicted in Van Gulik's stories is a highly prosperous and sophisticated one, much better off in both respects than the Europe of a comparable period. Judge Dee is a lover of literature and music, who reads philosophy and history books in his spare time. The courtesans who feature in *The Red Pavilion* are also well educated, and the ability to play musical instruments, sing, and dance is part of their trade, while their patrons include poets and academicians.[65]

Though naturally Judge Dee lacks the technology of the recent period, his understanding of people is every bit as good as in modern Western detective stories, and it is this factor which enables him to solve the crimes and apprehend the criminals. It is very striking that the society depicted does not distinguish between judge and magistrate. Dee occupies both positions. He represents the imperial government equally as official, detective, and lawyer. It is the imperial authorities who are always in the right, since there is no concept of a private detective who competes with the police.

Judge Dee and his helpers hold immense power, and the image which emerges from the detective stories is of a strongly hierarchical society where ordinary people fear authority as much as they respect it. Nevertheless, Judge Dee himself is honest in the extreme, so though there are many references to less straight officials, the overall image is of a reasonably incorrupt officialdom, one which genuinely seeks the well-being of the people. Judge Dee himself carries out much of the investigative research which enables him to solve every crime fairly. Torture was indeed used very widely in the lawcourts, and its occurrence in the stories is associated both with crime and justice. Van Gulik does not gloss over the cruelty of the legal system, even including gruesome descriptions of court and public execution scenes.[66]

Society at large is both religious and superstitious, but Judge Dee himself adheres strongly to the humanist Confucianism of the official class. He is very hostile to Buddhism, which he considers an anti-social and dangerous doctrine. 'I don't mix much with the Buddhist crowd', he is quoted as saying.[67] In *The Chinese Bell Murders* the criminals include Buddhist monks who use their religious influence to carry out extortion and sexual crimes against married women.[68] A partial exception to this anti-Buddhist stricture is Zen Buddhism. In one story a Zen sexton co-operates with Judge Dee to catch a murderous poetess. Yet, he also is shown as obese and ugly, reminding one 'forcibly of a repulsive toad'.[69]

Judge Dee has several wives and concubines, in accordance

with the practice among men of his class. Women as sexual objects assume a dominating role in many of the stories. They are also cruelly treated or beaten sadistically for sexual purposes. Yet the status of females in general does not come over as particularly low in Van Gulik's stories, at least not by comparison with how he might have portrayed it in the later imperial period. A prostitute can behave towards Judge Dee very much as an equal, and even with slight disdain.[70] The custom of binding women's feet was not introduced until after the Tang dynasty, and none of Van Gulik's females suffer this artificial deformity.

A totally different sort of novel and set some thousand years later is *Manchu*, first published in 1980, by the American journalist and China specialist Robert Elegant. It is a long work, an adventure novel which describes vividly the China of the mid-seventeenth century, when the Ming dynasty gave place to the Manchu Qing. Though a fictional work, the main events of the plot and quite a few of the characters are historical.

The hero of *Manchu* is a Catholic English soldier called Francis Arrowsmith. He goes to China, where he fights at different times on both sides of the war between the Manchus and the Ming, marries or has a long-term affair with a Han Chinese, a Manchu, and a Portuguese, producing children by all three. He has dealings with both Ming and Manchu, emperors and nobility, and above all with the Jesuit missionaries of the Beijing court, in particular the famous Adam Schall von Bell, already mentioned as a historical figure in Chapter 3. In the end, Arrowsmith returns to Europe with his Portuguese wife and their son.

The back cover of the 1981 Penguin paperback edition claims that 'this great international bestseller will transport you back . . . to the savagery and the passion, to the magnificence, to the sensuality, to the great adventure of the last days of a dying dynasty'. Such a statement is obviously aimed at selling the book and sensationalizing rather than expressing the author's conception of his work. Yet this does not alter the fact that what a publisher writes on a paperback already conveys a lasting series of images not only of the book itself, but of the society where it is set.

At least to this reader, the China of this novel comes over not only as a very cruel place, but also as one much crueller than either the China of the Judge Dee novels or the Europe of the seventeenth century. Even a British adventurer was shocked at how cheap human life could be. Scenes of great savagery abound, creating an image of ugly yet fascinating exoticism. Among them is a description of a monk burning himself alive on a pyre to celebrate the emperor's birthday and to thus save the empire.[71] A particularly gruesome passage is a lurid description of a senior official's being publicly beaten to death at the command of the venal last Ming emperor for criticizing the corruption of the imperial family's relations.[72]

There is a great deal to confirm the image that Han Chinese women held a social status very much lower than their predecessors of the early Tang period, as described in the Judge Dee novels. It was also much lower either than their contemporary European or even Manchu sisters. The grotesqueness of foot-binding is frequently mentioned. On the day of his marriage, arranged in the traditional way, to a Chinese woman, Arrowsmith reacts to her as follows:

A painted puppet, a product of Chinese artifice, tottered interminably toward him through the chattering throng. He was to pledge himself to a creature of silk and metal and paint, not a living woman of blood and flesh and feeling.

Her gait revolted him. How could a Christian European live among a people who distorted God's handiwork by twisting their women's feet into hard little hoofs? How could he bind himself inalienably to a woman who had submitted to that torture?[73]

It was one of the aims of foot-binding to make women more passionate sexually, and this image emerges from the accounts in the novel. Though in the long term his marriage to his Han Chinese wife was not a particularly successful one, this was not through lack of satisfaction in bed, and the couple early 'attained a sexual Nirvana of utter abandon'.[74]

Francis Arrowsmith, and consequently the novel, convey many images of the Chinese, some positive, others negative. He sees them as 'supreme realists', but as basically conservative and unwilling to learn.[75] In particular the Chinese are antiforeign and, though willing to use foreigners, are reluctant to learn from them. All people from other nationalities — British or Manchu, it makes no difference — are dubbed 'barbarians'. Arrowsmith is impressed with the Chinese penchant for intrigue and insincerity: 'I'm stuffed with their villainy . . . their intrigues and their treachery. They are born to endless, smiling deceit.'[76]

Despite the criticisms, he becomes fascinated, even seduced, by China. Perhaps the major theme of the novel is the hold the country exercises over him. His Portuguese wife regards China as her 'deadly rival'.[77] Against his strong desire to live in and serve China, she wants to take him back to Europe. In the end she gets her way and it is Europe that wins over China, but only because he suffers from a severe illness made worse by the Chinese climate.

In terms of its historical background this novel is well researched, and its conception is a brilliant one. However, it is clearly designed to appeal to the lingering Western sense of exoticism. The idea of the gallant British soldier irresistible to Chinese, Manchu, and European women is itself heavy with exoticism. In contrast to Van Gulik's Judge Dee novels, *Manchu* left me with the strong impression that the demands of the market, of reaching the status of international bestseller, hold a higher priority than accuracy. By comparison with the Judge Dee novels it is Eurocentric. Not only are several of the main characters Europeans, but Christianity occupies a role out of proportion to its actual significance in the China of the seventeenth century. The aim of the novelist is to interest the reader more than to reflect accurate historical conditions. The images assume greater power when they are filtered through the eyes and experiences of a hero who can make comparisons with the more familiar Western culture.

Conclusion

Some of the controversies which loomed large before World War II have been apparently laid to rest. These include whether Chinese history should be seen as part of world history, and whether China was susceptible to change. Nobody would any longer suggest that it was not part of world history. Meanwhile, the processes and dynamics of change have been explored in considerable detail. Researchers have found that the rate of change has varied considerably in different periods of Chinese history. The issue of how to periodize China's history in a way which makes sense has become a lively one. Images have expanded enormously because of the fresh approaches which a great many Westerners have been prepared to take towards China's distant past.

More and more Westerners have been prepared to see originality and creativity in Chinese history. But the more creativity one is prepared to see, the stranger it becomes that China failed to make the breakthrough which resulted in the Industrial Revolution. The more vital the factors pointing towards rapid economic and technological development become, the more necessary becomes an explanation for China's relative lack of progress at just the time that Europe was beginning its rapid advance. It would not occur to anybody who looked down on China's technological capacities to ask why it was not the birthplace of modern industry. The fact that Needham and others are prepared to ask just that question is thus a compliment to Chinese scientific ingenuity, not the converse.

Although serious explorers into Chinese history have never overlooked what the Chinese themselves had to say about their own distant past, the opening to the West of the 1970s provided an excellent opportunity for Chinese art enthusiasts to put over a series of images about their national history through artefacts of various kinds. The way ordinary people reacted in the West showed the extent of enthusiasm for a magnificent cultural heritage.

Was this enthusiasm also an expression of hunger for the exotic? Is the past inherently 'nicer' than the present because one can revel in its grandeur without feeling its disadvantages, one can sympathize with those who suffered, in the full knowledge that they no longer experience the pain? There is a tinge of exoticism in the distant past of any people, and it becomes stronger in the case of very large and unfamiliar histories, such as China's. But it would be unfair to attribute the enthusiasm for China's pre-modern history only to a hankering after the exotic. Increasing numbers of people have come to see that an appreciation of the distant past is at least one door to an understanding of the present. It follows that an attraction towards China's pre-modern history is one concomitant of the expansion in relations between China and the West which began in the early 1970s and has on the whole gathered momentum since then.

Through the various exhibitions sent to the West by China,

the arts and fiction, and the enormous volume of material written by scholars and others about China's ancient and medieval history, more is known on this subject in the West now than at any time in the past. The images thus derived may still be inadequate, but they rest on a firmer basis than in former generations. This is not to say that Eurocentric or 'Orientalist' attitudes towards Chinese history have disappeared, and some images spread even by very influential people retain such ingredients. But Westerners appear more willing to judge China's past in its own terms than they used to be, less insistent on the exclusive correctness of their own values.

9

Post-War Images of Modern Chinese History

CHAPTERS 4 and 5 took a look at the 150 years or so before the victory of the Chinese Communist Party (CCP) through the eyes of Western writers living at the time. We now relook at the same period, but this time from the standpoint of those who have lived and worked since World War II. Despite quite strong influences remaining from the past, their views and images are somewhat different from the views and images of their predecessors.

Just as for China's pre-modern history, there has been for the recent era a veritable explosion of information, of print and other media, even greater for the period 1800–1950 than for before the nineteenth century. Chapter 8 made the role of contemporary politics in the study of ancient and medieval history obvious. However, probably the main difference between Western images of China's ancient and medieval history on the one hand, and of modern history on the other, is the far greater weight of politics as a prism through which to view the latter than the former. The relevance of the 'power/knowledge' relationship expounded by Michel Foucault becomes very clear. However, the aesthetic dimension which we saw as so significant in establishing images of ancient and medieval China is somewhat lacking for the recent period. On the whole, post-war Westerners have taken only little interest in China's modern pre-liberation art, and exhibitions of it in the West comparable to those mentioned earlier of artefacts from earlier times have been notable by their absence.

Despite the continuities it would be a mistake to consider the decades since the war as a unity. There are two broad periods. The dividing point is the late 1960s and early 1970s, and the events which contributed more than any other to the change were the Vietnam War and the visit of the then President of the United States, Richard M. Nixon, to China in February 1972. What the Vietnam War did was to raise crucial questions about the role of the West in Asia. The American youth and then the broader community turned against the war and against United States military involvement in Vietnam. But much wider questions followed, and they related to China as much as Vietnam, to the recent past as much as to the present.

Was the Western impact on China beneficial or necessary? How much real difference did it make — or was it merely a kind of scab affecting the treaty ports with little or no 'impact' on the vast hinterland? Is it possible that many of the processes which have brought about contemporary China were already in operation before the arrival of the Western armies, missionaries, and merchants? How does one balance tradition and modernity, and are these two really in opposition? When does 'modern' China begin anyway? Above all, America's experience in Vietnam and Nixon's coming to terms with the People's Republic necessitated a complete rethink and new evaluation of the role of the CCP in the history of the 1920s to the 1940s. These and many other questions have been debated endlessly. While most of the details of the arguments have been carried on among academics and specialists, broader Western images have been affected. It was by no means only specialists who took an interest in the Vietnam War, in the issues of Western involvement and the role of communism which it raised, and the extension of similar questions to the far bigger and internationally more influential country to Vietnam's north: China.

In the United States certainly, and possibly even in the Western world as a whole, the most influential figure since World War II in the field of modern China is John King Fairbank of Harvard University. He began as an instructor there in 1936 and some of his career thus belongs to the pre-war period. However, his main influence and works are in the post-war years. His own students claim, probably rightly, that he 'transformed the study of modern China'. His influence on public images as well as scholarship is evident from their comment in 1967 that 'the program of training which he developed now shows a multiplier effect as his former students assume responsibility for instruction in several dozen colleges and universities throughout the United States',[1] and from the fact that he is a multimedia personality as well as a scholar. However, since the early 1970s some of his main assumptions have come under strong challenge. The attack was led by the left-wing scholarly journal *Bulletin of Concerned Asian Scholars*,[2] itself spawned by the disillusionment among the new generation of Asian specialists over the role of the United States in the Vietnam War.

In the non-American English-speaking world perhaps the most distinguished historian of China in the post-war period is C. P. Fitzgerald, like Fairbank a man with an extraordinarily broad vision of Chinese history which encompasses both the pre-modern and recent periods. His *Revolution in China* was first published in 1952 and later in 1964 under the title *The Birth of Communist China* in a revised paperback which has enjoyed many imprints. This is but the first and probably most influential of his many works on the Chinese revolution. His views have unquestionably been image-formulating. He was also among the very earliest of the leading academics to place a positive interpretation on the rise of the Chinese Communist Party and to recognize the virtues of the revolution for the Chinese people.

The Nineteenth Century and 'Modern' China

One of Fairbank's most influential works, written with others, was a large-scale history of East Asia in two volumes, the first entitled *East Asia, The Great Tradition* discussed in Chapter 8, and *East Asia, The Modern Transformation*. He and his co-authors developed there a concept of 'change within tradition' to explain the limited change which characterized the millennia of East Asia's history before the coming of the Europeans or 'direct Western contact'. A second concept was that of 'challenge-and-response', meaning that East Asian countries responded to stimuli which came from the West. It was this which made possible 'the modern transformation' of East Asia.[3] 'Thus we discern two major factors that have shaped recent East Asian history', the authors conclude: 'the forces of modernization, originally introduced in large part from the West, and the native traditions'.[4]

Wolfram Eberhard's conception of 'modern times' placed their beginnings as early as the Song dynasty (960–1279). He defined the central criterion of such a concept as being 'the time of the emergence of a middle class',[5] and his suggested boundary for the beginning of 'modern' China has gained some following.[6] In his well known *Horizon History of China*, C. P. Fitzgerald distinguished between 'The impact of Europe', beginning in the sixteenth century, and 'Modern China (1912 to the present)',[7] but did not analyse the problem of when 'modern' China should commence. Fitzgerald's interpretation was consonant with Eberhard's in refusing to accept the conventional view which saw the 'modern' era as launched by the Western invasions.

One critic to analyse the implications of the term 'modern' in some detail was Philip Kuhn. His study of the social history of the Qing period had led him 'to doubt that the "modern" period of China's history can be demarcated by largely external events'. He believed instead that the deterioration was well under way before the Opium War and that 'the West was impinging, not just upon a dynasty in decline, but upon a civilization in decline: a civilization that would soon have had to generate fresh forms of social and political organization from within itself'.[8] It is thus misleading to view nineteenth-century Chinese history in terms of challenge and response. Moreover, if the idea of a 'modern' China beginning with the Opium War is thus attacked, so also is the association of 'modernization' with the Western 'impact'. Indeed, it may be unnecessary and ahistorical to designate a precise beginning of 'modern' China. It is striking that the view which undermines the centrality of the West's role in China also challenges the interpretation of when 'modern' China began held not only by Marx but also by Marxist historians in China.

Another ground for the onslaught on the Fairbank school is that it overlooks imperialism, and implies that really the West did much good for China, because it made 'modernization' possible. James Peck attacked the elder sinologists for refusing to take the role of imperialism seriously and thus for developing an elitist, reformist, and counter-revolutionary ideological construct by which to justify American political, military, and economic intervention in Asia since World War II.[9] This view sees Fairbank as an arch-reactionary serving American imperialist interests, but nevertheless agrees with him on the importance of the West as a mover of Chinese history. The great irony is that Fairbank's view is in a way closer to that of Karl Marx than is Peck's, for Marx had seen imperialism as historically necessary and even progressive.

Yet a third opinion is to challenge the significance both of the West and imperialism for China's economic development. Proponents of this view do not deny the impact of imperialism on China's political and intellectual history or the rise of nationalism, but argue that 'the Chinese economy as a whole was too gargantuan, too self-sufficient, and too poor to be substantially affected' by outside capital.[10] A proponent of this view is Rhoads Murphey who argues that the treaty ports were merely enclave economies of only marginal influence on the whole. He thus downgrades the impact of the West on China's economy, and by the same token clears it of blame for the deterioration of the countryside in the Republican period.[11] Nevertheless, though the influence of the treaty ports was 'slight in material terms', he does acknowledge that 'the intellectual and psychological impact was profound, in a way which became fully apparent only after 1949'.[12]

One of Fairbank's main concepts was that of 'change within tradition', until real 'transformation' came in the nineteenth century from the West. It was espoused by many influential historians in the 1950s and 1960s. Joseph Levenson, one of the leading interpretative sinologists of the time, could ask the rhetorical question whether 'the seemingly stable, traditionalistic Chinese society had the capacity to develop under its own power, without a catalytic intrusion of Western industrialism, into a society with a scientific temper'.[13] Immanuel Hsu's widely read account of 'the rise of modern China' asserts that between 1600 and 1800 'China's political system, social structure, economic institutions, and intellectual atmosphere remained substantially what they had been during the previous 2,000 years', and he goes on to give the credit for the more fundamental changes of the nineteenth century to the West.[14]

We saw in the previous chapter that an economic historian such as Mark Elvin could assert continuous change in China's history. Yet he still argues that the Chinese economy, political structure, thought, and art had 'reached a magnificent dead end' by the end of the eighteenth century[15] and that 'it was the historic contribution of the modern West to ease and then break the high-level equilibrium trap in China'.[16] It was this very trap which had prevented anything like an Industrial Revolution in China. It follows that Elvin is reasserting in very strong terms the role of the West in bringing about the changes of the nineteenth and twentieth centuries.

Yet, to emphasize change, to stress scientific and other development *before* the nineteenth century undoubtedly suggests that transformation was quite possible in China, without the West. A conference held in 1971 on local control and social protest during the Qing found that 'the entire period from the 1550s to the 1930s constituted a coherent whole'. It saw trends in the late Ming which 'set in motion administrative and political changes that continued to develop' over the course of the Qing.[17] The image is of a Chinese society changing through its own dynamic, not through any imposed from outside. 'The old picture of a stagnant, slumbering, unchanging China, waiting to be delivered from its unfortunate condition of historylessness by a dynamic, restlessly changing, historyful West'[18] has thus come under challenge.

One of the early reassessments concerning the Western impact came in interpretations of the Taiping uprising. The Eurocentric view of Morse who believed that the West had saved China from the Taipings had been a typical view before World War II. C. P. Fitzgerald had been much more sympathetic to the Taipings, though still focusing attention on their Christianity. He has retained this position in the post-war period. His view is that by rejecting the Taipings, Protestant missionaries 'may have given away the only serious possibility that ever existed for any form of Christianity to gain a dominant position in China'. Even in the 1960s the dominant view challenged the assumption that Western intervention was a crucial factor in the Taipings' defeat. According to Fitzgerald it was the Manchus who crushed them, though 'with considerable assistance from Britain and France'.[19] Fairbank and others saw the Western impact on the Taipings in terms of the aid it was giving the Confucian rulers of China, not in the military intervention of the Western powers.[20] But even this view does not go nearly as far as that of Mary Wright, who in 1965 'found nothing substantial in the newer literature to support the ever-recurrent thesis' that the Taiping Rebellion would have succeeded but for Western intervention on the Chinese imperial side.[21] She goes on to say that the struggles of the mid-nineteenth century were internal, and the Western impact 'was at the time still scarcely felt'. 'The foreign presence was seen as a local irritant, confined to five ports on the southeastern fringes of the Chinese Empire.'[22] Recent historians in the West point out that the Taipings did not direct their movement against the West in any meaningful sense. Nor were they an attempt to solve problems posed or created by the West. One terms the rebellion as 'a Western-influenced variation on a theme that was played in widely scattered parts of China from approximately 1850 to 1870 in response to conditions that by and large predated the impact of the West'.[23] 'The Taiping revolution reveals in essence the traditional character of Chinese peasant revolutions', says another.[24] Such views, showing the role of the West as relatively insignificant, are accepted widely enough nowadays among specialists in the West to be called images of China.

Yet the impact of such revisionist scholarship on overall popular images has been partial at best. Three examples of historical works, two of them broader in their coverage than the single country of China and designed for general readers and students, illustrate the point. One 'comparative history of civilizations in Asia' covering West, South, Southeast, and East Asia begins the 'early modern' period with the collapse of the Mongol empire,[25] but places the beginnings of 'modern Asia' in the middle of the nineteenth century with 'the emergence of a European-dominated international economic system'.[26] As for China specifically, the roots of modern change go back to the middle of the nineteenth century when the authorities 'initiated the first modest programs to introduce Western technology and industrial techniques into China'.[27] Though the authors are at pains to emphasize the actions also of the local regime, the crucial influences bringing about change are those which derive from the West.

The second example covers only China and Japan. Its last major section is entitled 'China and Japan in the Modern World' and opens with a chapter on 'The Intrusion of the West: China'.

The view put forward here is that it was Britain which 'initiated a new era in Chinese history by forcing China to . . . open her doors to the West'. The argument continues that 'the pivotal event was the Opium War (1839–42)'.[28] This simply restates the traditional view which puts the emphasis for developments in China on what the West did.

Finally, let us give Fairbank the last word. His introduction to the late Qing volume of the authoritative and certainly image-formulating *Cambridge History of China* stresses the enormous size, self-sufficiency, and regional variations of China, making it extremely difficult to influence. He does not analyse 'the boundaries of modern China'[29] and it is true that the 'late' Qing is defined in the work's title as beginning in 1800. Yet his earlier views on modernization, change, and the influence of the West are retained in the following statement:

China's modern history records two great dramas — first, the cultural confrontation between the expanding Western civilization of international trade and warfare, and the persistent Chinese civilization of agriculture and bureaucracy; and second, arising out of the first, the fundamental transformation of China in the greatest of all revolutions.[30]

Republican China, The Rise and Victory of the Chinese Communist Party

Fairbank here refers to the whole process which climaxed in the rise of the Chinese Communist Party and its victory in China, and to this we now turn. Just as in images of the nineteenth century, the trend is away from an emphasis on external factors and towards one on internal factors. The American and other Western governments were anxious to blame the Soviet Union and Japan for the Guomindang defeat. After all, Chiang Kaishek was insisting that it had been Soviet help which had enabled the CCP to gain a foothold in the first place and later to oust him. How else could he reach an explanation for his own fall that was not insulting to himself personally? Western scholars were initially inclined to view the CCP's victory in terms of the failure of Chiang Kaishek and his Nationalists rather than of the success of Mao and his Communists.

C. P. Fitzgerald was among the most perceptive to publish

soon after the liberation. He recognized the Communists' alliance with the peasantry as one of their greatest sources of strength. Their ability to carry out land reform was crucial to their success. He even believed that 'the Communist insurrection could have been contained, perhaps subdued' had the Nationalists 'put into effect a real policy of land reform'. Another source of strength for the CCP, and conversely weakness for the Nationalists, Fitzgerald believed lay in ideology. Unlike the CCP, the Nationalists had no 'real satisfying and inspiring ideology'. Their ideas 'repudiated the past, yet seemed to hanker after Confucianism'. There was no vision of the future.[31]

A rather similar view came at the same time from the French General Lionel Max Chassin, who commanded the French Air Forces in Indochina from 1951 to 1953 and thus had no reason for sympathy with the Communists. Indeed his preface to his book describes the victory of the CCP as a catastrophe. He writes that 'the cause of Mao's triumph lies in the fact that appealing as he did to ancient and deeply rooted reflexes, he gave a faith, a creed, to the peasants of China'.[32] Among the 'trumps' which Mao held, Chassin lists 'agrarian reform, xenophobia, the steadiness and discipline of the Red Army, the installation of honest officials'.[33]

The oft-quoted conventional wisdom of Fairbank and others describes the decline and fall of the Guomindang as 'a recent tragedy still hotly disputed among observers and still awaiting thorough research'.[34] Among the reasons offered for the débâcle was that American aid came too late. It should have begun in the early 1930s instead of a decade later, and in that case 'Chinese history might well have been changed', meaning presumably that the CCP might not have won. The argument in favour of this view is that 'American aid, in wartime, coming late to a hard-pressed government, served more as a crutch to lean on than a means to cure it ailments'.[35] But if Vietnam showed anything it was that American aid is not a medicine for all ills, however and in whatever quantities it is bestowed. The foregoing view would find fewer supporters in the late 1970s or 1980s than in the 1960s.

One issue which bears strongly on the allocation of credit to the CCP, and the role of foreign involvement, is the priority to give social revolution, as opposed to nationalist resistance to Japanese imperialism, as among the reasons for the victory of the CCP. In 1962, Chalmers Johnson advanced the thesis that what really gave the CCP the opportunity to win was its association with nationalism during the War of Resistance against Japan. Before 1937, he argues, 'the peasants were a passive element in politics', and the CCP's 'bid for power, based on an appeal to peasant economic interests, was a conspicuous failure'.[36] However, 'Japanese military activity in the rural areas compelled the Chinese peasant to join with other activated peasants for the common defense' and the 'resulting new environment was immensely favorable to the Communists' who were able to take advantage of the 'new situation' and win over the peasants.[37] Thus 'contemporary Communism in China may be understood as a particularly virulent form of nationalism'.[38]

Despite the use of words like 'virulent', Johnson regards himself as essentialy neutral 'with regard to the general merits of Communism in China'. He defends himself from attack from the right, fearing that he will be considered too sympathetic to the CCP, because he claims it was nationalist. 'There is an unfortunate tendency in Western educated circles to suppose that nationalism outside of Europe is axiomatically good, or at least "natural," and to condemn Communism as evil, regardless of its popular *bona fides*.'[39]

Johnson based himself mainly on Japanese sources and focused his attention partially on the years leading up to the war but principally on the war itself. A much broader and more general work, but one which also covers the issues raised by the CCP's victory, was that of Lucien Bianco. Originally in French, it was translated into English and published in that language in 1971. Bianco analyses the 'currents contributing to the revolution' and selects two as central, 'the social (or peasant) problem and the national problem'. Bianco finds 'a certain thinness in the thesis that the Chinese Revolution was entirely the work of imperialism and nationalism', in other words considers Johnson's idea too one-sided. He tries to balance the two most important factors and declares that 'it was the national problem, not the social problem that acted as a catalyst'. On the other hand, 'at the very heart of the decisive "national" stage of the revolution lay the social problem'.[40] Bianco agrees with Johnson that the CCP won over the peasants but portrays the reasons in a light reflecting more credit on it. 'In addition to being authentic patriots they [the Communists] were genuine revolutionaries, men who understood the needs of the people, knew what changes had to be made, and set about making them.'[41]

A third approach is that of Mark Selden, one of the early editors of the *Bulletin of Concerned Asian Scholars*, who, like Johnson, discusses the years leading up to the war and the war itself. His focus is on the Shaanxi-Gansu-Ningxia Soviet and Border Region. In his influential 1971 book, he declared that 'the hallmark of the Yenan period' was 'the ability of the Communist Party to transform its program of agrarian revolution in accordance with united front wartime imperatives while leading a bold and creative attack on problems of rural oppression and disintegration'.[42] In other words, the 'social revolution' was primary, the national secondary. His is a much more forthright view than Bianco's. His great admiration for the 'Yenan way' shines through the rhetorical opening to his preface: 'It is the central problem of our time. How can people break the shackles of oppression, poverty, and fear . . . ?'[43] The answer is that the Chinese revolution is a model which 'offers inspiration not only to those who would expel colonial oppressors'; it is even relevant to the rich West itself: 'it addresses men and women everywhere who seek to create a society free from stifling oppression, arbitrary state power, and enslaving technology'.[44]

These three views show varying degrees of sympathy for the CCP. They also raise the crucial historical question: would the CCP have won power but for the war against Japan? The Johnson view would imply definitely no; that of Bianco, maybe; but Selden's, yes, even if at a different time. His analysis suggests a genuine class struggle in which the Japanese were not the essential factor at all, not even necessarily a 'catalyst' to use Bianco's term. So another way of contrasting the three views would be to say that Johnson's places greatest weight on foreign intervention as a driving force in China's modern history, while Selden's strongest emphasis is on the internal factor of China's peasant revolution, and Bianco's juggles the two without a decisive verdict.

Although historians work principally at colleges and universities, the person whose writings and lectures have done more than any other since the war to shape popular images in the West of China's history over the century or so from 1850 to 1949 is probably Han Suyin. Some discussion of her works and the views she has conveyed is thus necessary.

Han Suyin's mother was Belgian, her father Chinese, one of China's early distinguished railway engineers. She was born and brought up in China and has had many dealings both with Chinese and foreigners there. She gained a good reputation as a novelist through her romance, *A Many-Splendoured Thing*, which was first published in 1952 and later made into a film. Her style everywhere retains a warmth and human sympathy which is always easy to read and cannot fail to make an impression. Her prose remains in the mind in a way that few academic historians can achieve.

Among historical works written after liberation about the pre-liberation period, three are pre-eminent. They are her famous trilogy *The Crippled Tree*, *A Mortal Flower*, and *Birdless Summer*, first published in 1965, 1966, and 1968. These are in essence an autobiography and general history of China, respectively from 1885 to 1928, 1928 to 1938, and 1938 to 1948. The passion of her novels is everywhere strongly in evidence, with much use of dialogue and quotation from letters.

The historical account is very broad. It includes not only commentary on specific events but also on society and culture. Being in effect part of the Chinese family system herself, she knows a great deal about it and it looms large in her coverage. *Birdless Summer* revolves partly around her unhappy marriage to a Guomindang soldier. Much space is given in all volumes to discussions of the shocking living conditions which prevailed for all but a few in China before 1949.

There is a very strong political line throughout the trilogy, and it is even stronger in the second and third volumes than in the first. It reflects everywhere the political line of the CCP current with the date of writing. *The Crippled Tree* emphasizes the desperation of the poor and the oppressed in the late nineteenth and early twentieth centuries, but *Birdless Summer* opens with an exaltation of revolution, including the Cultural Revolution.

For Han Suyin Chinese recent history is clearly a class struggle. It is also a story in which imperialism occupies a major, and very evil, place. There is no hierarchy among the various imperialists. 'The truth is, they were all the same.' Moreover, she believes that the core of imperialism was 'world-wide brigandage', not race, so that any Asian or African nation would have behaved as did those in Europe under similar historical circumstances.[45]

Her attitude to foreigners is ambivalent. She attacks any foreigner who might be aligned with imperialism and in the dialogues invariably takes the nationalist Chinese line against foreign activities. At the same time, she is at pains to find and praise progressive attitudes amongst foreigners, and they bulk large in her story. Above all, she is strongly anti-racist, whether this vice is directed against Chinese or anybody else. One of the factors which turned her against her Guomindang soldier husband was his self-righteous 'xenophobia in full spate, characteristic of the Whangpoo young officers, of Chiang Kaishek himself'. What he had said to her to draw such condemnation was: 'I don't care if you had affairs with ten ministers, twenty high officials, if they were Chinese. But a foreigner, a foreigner . . . '[46]

Han Suyin clearly considers her history to emphasize the strengths of progressive China, the ultimate weakness of the conservatives and the reactionaries. In particular, it is partly for this reason that she admires Mao and the CCP so much. 'From the very beginning Mao's strength was that he looked for China's salvation not *outside*, but *inside* China. And strength within China meant China of the peasantry.'[47] In her own eyes, hers is undoubtedly a history in which China and Chinese are always the focus, despite the role foreigners play in it and despite her own life, which is itself so central to her trilogy.

Pictorial Images, Television, Film

Pictures, almost all painted by Chinese artists, had contributed to images of pre-nineteenth-century China when available in sufficient numbers. What was new about the 'modern' period was the advent of photography. The earliest surviving photograph of China is attributed to Dr John McCosh in the early 1850s and shows the Five-Stories Pagoda in Guangzhou.[48] Since World War II, quite a few accounts of nineteenth-century China have featured pictures, especially photographs. One book collects photographs taken from the 1850s to the fall of the Qing dynasty.

While such photographs no doubt conveyed images in their own day, the collection is a fascinating pictorial history of the last few decades of Qing rule which puts over a strong set of images of that time to people living in the period when the book was published.

The subjects of the photographs are rather varied. Many show individuals or groups of people, some street or other urban scenes, others depict significant or interesting buildings, while a few, especially among the later pictures, are landscapes. For social images the most interesting are those of people. The circumstances are widely different, ranging from a group of men condemned to be executed to monks in a monastery, from an official sitting proudly in front of his house with his family standing on the floor above him to ten addicts lounging in an opium den.[49]

Reactions to pictures are even more personal than to the printed word, so the priority of images which come over to viewers in the post-war West will vary according to the individual. The following is no more than this writer's response to the collection.

The pictures convey the image of a strongly hierarchical and unequal society. The officials carry faces which suggest they are well aware of their power and very pleased with themselves. At the other end are the poor; for example, a crowd of ordinary Chinese gazing curiously through the gateway which barred Chinese from the Western legations in Guangzhou at the beginning of this century.[50] To be fair, however, no pictures show people starving. Several pictures show the luxury of the dress and life of the court and courtiers, another a general view of a wretchedly poor town in southern China.[51] Other than those pertaining to the court or high society, most buildings are run down.

The other kind of inequality is that between the sexes. The front cover has a rather self-satisfied official and his doll-like and expressionless wife with her tiny pointed shoes, both people luxuriously dressed, sitting either side of a table. The patriarchal family features as a social phenomenon in several other pictures, the children's faces being as joyless as those of their elders.

The photographs depict a cruel society. The back cover shows three expressionless or pained women standing together with their heads in a cangue. Another shows a man kneeling, while an executioner holds aloft a sword, about to behead him. A crowd watches, curious but seemingly unconcerned. A third shows decapitated corpses lying around an execution ground.[52] Not a single face among the many in this book wears a full smile. This reflects as much the photographic style of the day as the cruelty of Chinese society, a fact which does not affect the images the collectivity of the pictures conveys.

The final image relates to foreign influence. Leaving aside those pictures of the British colony Hong Kong, there are two of foreign occupation troops and one of a steam locomotive operated by Chinese drivers.[53] But the great majority of photographs suggest no foreign influence at all. China comes over as a traditional society with no more than the beginnings of foreign influence or 'modernization' here and there.

The overwhelming impression is of a strange, even exotic, society. No doubt the photographers selected the unusual as being most interesting. But the ordinary people too seem so different from those of the West in their expressions and their clothing as to be almost like aliens from another planet, one much worse than home.

In the twentieth century, photographers of China have been incomparably more numerous than in the nineteenth. One example is Hedda Morrison (daughter-in-law of the Australian journalist George Ernest Morrison), whose photographs of Beijing taken from 1933 to 1946 have been published. The volume includes very few photographs indeed in which the Japanese occupation of the city is obvious, in part because Morrison's stock of photographic materials was very low during the relevant years.

The emphasis of the photographs is very strongly on tradition. There are many of the beautiful old buildings and structures for which Beijing is justly famous. A few of the photographs show such modern phenomena as electric lines and lights or motor cars,[54] but on the whole even those are notable by their absence. Most of the people shown wear traditional clothing.

From a social point of view, the photographs present images suggesting that considerable improvement had taken place since the late Qing. There are still serious inequalities, but they are much less so than in the earlier period. At one end of the scale of occupations is a beggar woman, a blind fortune-teller, rickshaw pullers, or a collector of papers and rags. At the higher end is 'a quiet game of chess in a rich man's home', but the most luxurious buildings are palaces no longer inhabited by emperors and aristocrats but open to the public.[55]

A few photographs show poverty and degradation, such as one of an opium smoker with his pipe in his mouth and the beggar woman and her child whom the photographer often saw over the years, nearly always pregnant.[56] But on the whole, the impression is of comparative prosperity. Even the beggar woman and her child, though dirty and morose, are not starving or even barefooted. The book contains only one picture of a person wearing a full smile,[57] but none of the faces is particularly expressionless, even those of the women, certainly not when compared with those from the late-Qing collection. There are no pictures showing an execution ground, severed heads, or people wearing a cangue.

Still, many photographs exist which show the realities of war, foreign occupation, and misery during the Republican period. Pictures of boy coolies in Japanese mines, kneeling Chinese being searched by Japanese soldiers, and street fighting between Chinese and Japanese in Manchuria have been republished in pictorial history books since the war and contributed to images of the wartime years. In addition, photographs illustrating various aspects of the resistance to the Japanese by the Communists and others show an image of fierce opposition to foreign occupation.[58]

Even more image-formulating than simple photographs are documentary films, and this has been especially so since the advent of television as a mass medium. To absorb old still pictures into a more up-to-date film can create a vivid image. Among the American documentaries dating from the days before the Vietnam War and dealing with recent Chinese history is *The Fall of China*, about the civil war which resulted in the CCP's victory. The narration is by the well-known reporter Walter Cronkite, and there are interviews with Song Meiling (Chiang Kaishek's wife), American military leaders, and Pearl Buck. There is a great deal of emphasis on the American role in the civil war, with the reasons for the outcome being assigned to the military mistakes of the Guomindang and the ruthlessness of the Communists.

In striking contrast is a television documentary issued in 1986 called simply *China, The Long March*. Directed by Australians Chris Hooke and Peter Butt, it analyses the rise of the CCP to victory through a description of the Long March of 1934 and 1935. It uses footage which dates from the 1920s, 1930s, and 1940s but is focused around a retracing undertaken in 1985 to commemorate the fiftieth anniversary of the completion of the Long March. There are interview sections with the well known British journalist Tony Lawrence and a commentary written by Peter Butt. While the core of the documentary is the Long March, it also shows quite a bit of footage of other events which led to the CCP's victory, including harrowing shots of starvation, misery, and war. One American voice from the time describes China in the 1930s as 'a land of blood, revolution and war'. The contrast with Hedda Morrison's Beijing could not be greater.

One collective image which comes over from the documentary is that the victory of the CCP was both necessary and desirable. Even apart from the commentary, this view emerges from the juxtaposition, in black and white, of pictures of misery from the pre-1949 days with others, in colour, of scenes of comparative prosperity and cheerfulness from the 1980s. Other images which dominate the documentary are that the CCP performed heroically against the Guomindang, the Japanese and, above all, nature, and that the key to their success was their decent treatment of, and consequently support from, the peasantry. The summative evaluation of the Long March, given by the commentator near the end of the documentary, is as follows:

On the one hand, the Long March must be seen as a desperate retreat for survival, but on the other, it was a manifesto, announcing to hundreds of millions of peasants in eleven provinces that the road of the Red Army was their only road to liberation. The Long March was a seeding machine that yielded a rich harvest of political consciousness and class struggle, that helped secure final victory of the Communists.

The documentary does have shots of the Japanese. But the dominant image is that what mattered was what the Communists did. What was essential to their victory was the Long March, rather than resistance to Japan. Part of the quoted

1 Woman's natural foot, and another woman's feet bound to 4.5 inches. The practice of foot-binding was one of the most widespread and negative images of China in the nineteenth century, and, in general as an image of the past, remains so in the twentieth. This photograph comes from Mrs Archibald Little's *Intimate China, The Chinese as I have Seen Them* (Hutchinson, London, *c.* 1900), p. 95. Photographer Dr E. Garner.

2 An image of cruel China. Three women in the cangue, a photograph taken in Shanghai in 1907. From *Imperial China: Photographs 1850–1912* (Australian National University Press, Canberra, 1980), p. 61 and back cover. Photographer unknown.

3   An image of power and passive, soulless womanhood. A Cantonese mandarin and his wife, 1861–4. From *Imperial China: Photographs 1850–1912* (Australian National University Press, Canberra, 1980), front cover, and the same photograph on p. 29. Note the bound feet of the mandarin's wife. Photographer M. Miller.

4   An image of the harsh, uncaring legal system of nineteenth-century China. The execution ground in Guangzhou, 1870s. From *Imperial China: Photographs 1850–1912* (Australian National University Press, Canberra, 1980), p. 65. Photographer unknown.

5 A late-nineteenth-century German image of the 'yellow peril'. The Buddha's threat to the Christian West must be resisted by Christian angels and female fighters. From A. Diósy, *The New Far East* (London, 1898), and photographed, with permission, from Raymond Dawson, *The Chinese Chameleon, An Analysis of European Conceptions of Chinese Civilization* (Oxford University Press, London, 1967), opposite p. 143.

6 An image of poverty in Beijing in the 1930s or 1940s. Taken, with permission, from Hedda Morrison, *A Photographer in Old Peking* (Oxford University Press, Hong Kong, 1985), p. 101. Though the woman was 'nearly always pregnant', conditions had evidently improved since the Qing period. The beggars are not starving or even bare-footed, and the woman's feet are not bound. Photographer Hedda Morrison.

7 'A quiet game of chess in a rich man's house'; an image of tradition, relaxation, scholarly elegance, and prosperity. Taken, with permission, from Hedda Morrison, *A Photographer in Old Peking* (Oxford University Press, Hong Kong, 1985), p. 164. Photographer Hedda Morrison.

8 An image of ancient Chinese princely riches and aestheticism. Princess Dou Wan's jade burial suit, a centrepiece of the Chinese exhibition of archaeological artefacts which toured many Western countries in the mid-to-late 1970s. From *Historical Relics Unearthed in China* (Foreign Languages Press, Beijing, 1972), no. 96.

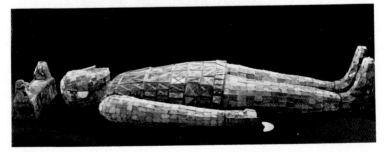

9 An image of the magnificence of old Chinese culture and its urban prosperity. The picture shows a section of Zhang Zeduan's scroll of life in the Chinese capital at the turn of the eleventh and twelfth centuries, which is featured in several Western books on Chinese history. Taken from *Social Sciences in China, A Quarterly Journal*, II, 4 (December 1981), between pp. 160 and 161.

10 An image of imperial splendour and beauty. A scene in the Imperial
Palaces, Beijing, with Coal Hill in the background. Taken by the author.

FAR EASTERN ☐ ECONOMIC
review
14

CHINA'S COMMUNISTS

THE MAOIST MOULD

A$ 50¢
Baht 9
HK$ 2.00
Kyats 2.00
M$ 1.30
Rs (I) 2.00
S$ 1.30
Sig 4/-
US$ 55¢
Yen 180
April 2
1 9 7 0

11   An image of soullessness during the Cultural Revolution. Puppets representing different groups in China, but with the military towering over all. The front cover of the *Far Eastern Economic Review*, LXVIII, 14 (2 April 1970).

12 An image of fun against grand and fierce surrroundings in contemporary China. A small girl hides from her father under an old stone lion. Taken, with permission, from the front cover of Leong Ka Tai and Frank Ching, *Beijing* (Hutchinson, Melbourne Sydney, London, 1986). Photographer Leong Ka Tai.

13 An image of a relaxed Westernized life-style in the China of the 1980s, where even the Public Security Bureau is 'swept up by the dance craze'. 'A uniformed woman security official dances with her boyfriend, clad in tight jeans, as the bureau's own band provides the music'. Taken, with permission, from Leong Ka Tai and Frank Ching, *Beijing* (Hutchinson, Melbourne, Sydney, London, 1986), p. 111. Photographer Leong Ka Tai.

evaluation is very close in wording to what Mao himself said at the end of 1935 about the Long March,[59] which suggests that the documentary adopts the basics of the Communists' interpretation of their own history and gives credit for their victory to the Communists themselves, not to any outside force.[60]

The last type of film to consider is features. As image-formulators, they are probably the most important of all, because of the mass audience they reach through both the cinema and television, and because of the role they play as leisure and entertainment, rather than as education. With the video revolution of the 1980s, the influence of those popular films which reach the video libraries has expanded still further.

Adventure novels and films set in the nineteenth century or pre-war period have been extremely popular since the war and remain so in the 1980s. Daryl Duke's spectacular *Tai-Pan* was released in 1986 and is based on the novel of the same name by James Clavell. It focuses on the adventures of a Scottish ruler of a powerful trading company or *tai-pan* against the background of the establishment of Hong Kong as a British colony, and most of it is set in Hong Kong or Macao. Yet a small portion is set in Guangzhou and there are certainly images both of China and Chinese.

There is plenty of sex, violence, cruelty, and profit in *Tai-Pan*, and while the sufferers are both Chinese and British, triumph goes almost entirely to the latter. The scenes set in Guangzhou feature a graphic execution and terrifying official power over individuals. The only major fully Chinese character in the film is the mistress, and later wife, of the *tai-pan*, and the image she presents of Chinese women and their relations with foreign men runs through the film as a central element. Her lust for him rests largely in her desire to be his slave; part of her attraction as a sexual partner is the masochistic thrill she derives from suffering pain at his hands. At the same time, the Scottish *tai-pan* hero is not anti-Chinese. He calls them 'a smart wise people', and regards them as cleaner personally than the British.

The image of the Chinese mistress in the film appears to this writer to emphasize the sexual domination of European men over Chinese women more than does the novel. The characterization in the film underplays her lust for power and the social status she believes she will gain by her attachment to the Scottish hero, especially as his wife or *taitai*, and exaggerates the exclusively sexual side of the relationship. In the novel she manipulates him more obviously and skilfully than in the film, and it is less clear who is whose slave. Yet there is plently of violence, sex, and masochism in the novel,[61] and the Chinese certainly come over as even crueller than the British.[62]

The Biggles-type pilot or Rambo-type hero, with his macho can-do triumphant contempt for lesser and uncivilized races, still retains a vast following. A recent example of such a film is Brian G. Hutton's *High Road to China*, issued in 1984, and based on a book by Jon Cleary. The story takes place in the inter-war period, about one-third being set in a very remote part of western China. All the central characters are Westerners, while the Chinese are shown as cruel and totally unable to govern themselves. Westerners play a crucial role in winning a petty war against a hoodlam who oppresses the masses and rapes the women. China is merely a playground for exciting adventures and thrills enjoyed by Westerners. The film is not a tragedy, but there is plenty of suffering in it, all done by the natives. The assumption of this film is that life is still cheap in China, as long as it is Chinese life, not Western.

Steven Spielberg's *Empire of the Sun* was released in 1987. It concerns a British boy who matures due to his war-time experiences in and near Shanghai from 1941 to 1945. From the point of view of Western images of China, the most striking feature of the film is that although it is set entirely in China, there is not a single major Chinese character in it. All the main characters are British or American, and there are one or two fairly minor Japanese. China becomes a background for wars fought out by others. Chinese people appear more or less only in enormous crowds, with images of a suffering mass humanity, or as servants to foreigners.

The film is based on the autobiographical novel by J. G. Ballard, published in 1984. An autobiographical novel is a perfectly legitimate undertaking and the book has been very well received. The novel is much more thoughtful and less sensationalized than the film. Yet the novel also relegates China to a background position. The picture of Shanghai shows, if anything, an even more desperate and poverty-striken city in the novel than in the film. It is a place where beggars abound and death is ever-present, and war is so commonplace that it becomes almost desirable: 'Wars always invigorated Shanghai, quickened the pulse of its congested streets. Even the corpses in the gutters seemed livelier.'[63]

A film of an entirely different type from any of these three, much grander, much more sensitive to China as important in itself, and much better generally, is Bernardo Bertolucci's *The Last Emperor*, released in 1987. This played to full houses in the West and excited many and enthusiastic reviews, as well as winning a record number of nine Academy Awards for a 'foreign' film, so it is certainly image-formulating. The film aims to describe accurately the history of China's last emperor, Puyi, from his coronation in 1908 until his death in 1967. The governor of the prison where Puyi spent the first ten years of the People's Republic is the most sympathetic character in the film and played by Ying Ruocheng, who became Deputy Minister of Culture the same year the film was released, so it is not surprising that the People's Republic comes off very well.

To this viewer the overwhelming images of China before 1949 to emerge from *The Last Emperor* are the grandeur of imperial life, the gaping chasm between the court and everybody else, and the horrors of Japanese invasion and occupation. The scenes within the court show intense colours, strangeness, and grandeur. Although there is much mention of eunuchs, there is not much dwelling on the cruelties of court life. The figure of Reginald Johnston, tutor to Puyi, looms quite large in the film, probably larger than historical accuracy would warrant, but in no way could one accuse this film of being merely the story of Europeans against a Chinese background. The West and Western influence are frequently mentioned, and usually positively as a modernizing agent, but there are no attempts to gloss over Western decadence and the problems which Western imperialism brought.

The real criminals of the film are the Japanese. Only in the segment showing Japanese occupation is there a dwelling on cruelty, especially the genuine documentary clips showing the Rape of Nanjing at the end of 1937 and the Japanese use of germ warfare in Manchuria. But the image to emerge from these scenes is that the cruel ones are the Japanese, not the

Chinese. Even as the Japanese puppet Emperor of Manchuria, Puyi is not portrayed either as evil or notably weak, but as the victim of circumstances engineered by the wicked Japanese and beyond his control.

Conclusion

The production of popular films such as *Tai-Pan* show the tenacity of the kind of view which sees 'modern' China as a place where heroic action was the preserve of Westerners. It remains quite fashionable to sensationalize that history and to emphasize its exoticism. The 'Orientalist' images which once dominated Western thinking on China still retain a substantial following.

Yet the images conveyed by a film such as *The Last Emperor* exemplify beautifully that the dominant trend in Western images of the Chinese history of the 150 years or so separating 1800 from liberation is towards a more sympathetic view of the miserable situation in which China found itself. More and more people, both specialists and others, have come to appreciate the internal dynamic of Chinese history, and given the Chinese credit for creating their own trends. One extremely important study of American historical writing on China's recent past entitles its concluding and main chapter 'Toward a China-Centered History of China', and lists and discusses many works its author believes heading in that direction.[64] The perception that Chinese people have made their own history extends to a willingness to recognize and even applaud the achievement of the Chinese Communist Party in winning a victory in the face of what seemed enormous odds.

Even though the main impulse for the trends was opposition to American intervention in Vietnam, it would be quite wrong to suppose that all the historical ideas spawned accord with those advocated by the historians of the People's Republic. It is true that both specialist and popular images of the 1920s to 1940s are much more sympathetic to the role of the CCP in the 1980s than they were in the 1950s. On the other hand, to downplay the role of the West can mean ignoring imperialism and thus absolving it from blame for China's ills, a view still not at all popular in China itself. The revisionist view of 'the boundaries of modern history' in China, which challenges the conventional opinion that it should start with the first manifestations of the Western impact, is diametrically opposed to the analysis which Marx himself advocated and historians in the People's Republic have hitherto accepted.

Nevertheless, it cannot escape notice that the heyday of opposition to Eurocentrism in the West corresponds, with a time lag of a few years always necessary for ideas to filter through and germinate, with the obsession with self-reliance in China itself. What is happening in the late 1980s is that China has itself reopened its doors to the West and by implication stressed that the West does indeed have a notable role to play in its future development. Perhaps there is a lesson for the interpretation of history as well as of the future. It may be that, in the next decade or so, there will be a trend back to Eurocentrism among history-writers in the West.

PART III

WESTERN IMAGES OF
THE PEOPLE'S REPUBLIC OF CHINA

10

Contemporary Images of
China, 1949–1966

THE seventeen years or so separating the birth of the People's Republic of China (PRC) from the beginning of the Cultural Revolution were the first time in history that a Chinese government had firmly, unequivocally, persistently, and successfully resisted the major interests of Western capitalism. Very early in the period, also, Chinese troops and those of several Western countries fought on opposite sides in the Korean War (1950–3). On the whole the image of China which Western governments tried to convey to their peoples was more negative during these years than at any preceding time.

The number of Westerners resident in China dropped sharply after 1949. The Americans can serve as the most spectacular example. In 1937 there were 13,300 American residents in China, but in 1957 the figure was about 100. Admittedly other countries were affected less drastically than the United States, but they, too, had far fewer residents in China after than before 1949. Virtually all the missionaries went home. The number of Western visitors to China of the kind who might contribute to creating images fell sharply after 1949. Americans were actually forbidden by their government to enter China. Among those Westerners who did go, most spoke to somewhat restricted audiences at home, such as peace groups, friendship societies, and left-wing associations.

In the United States especially, and to some extent in other Western countries, there was a strong and rather widespread feeling that the West had 'lost China', more or less as if China was a belonging, subject to losing and finding. The Chinese were 'ungrateful' to allow themselves to be lost; after all the West had done for them, how could they turn against it like

that? This feeling was especially pronounced among missionaries, who thought of themselves as bringing to the Chinese
the great gifts of their own beliefs, but was not confined to
them. Harold Isaacs quotes a public opinion analyst thus: 'I
would say that Americans are greatly disappointed. Their earlier
idea of the Chinese as friendly, honest people was wrong.
The Chinese bit the hand that fed them.'[1] The analyst's underlying
assumption was apparently that refusal to be grateful for
handouts from the United States was equivalent to dishonesty.

Yet there were certain variations and gradations. The peoples
of the United States and Australia accepted a more negative
image of China than those of most other Western countries.
One writer, noting that West Europeans began visiting China
in the 1950s some two decades before Americans, stated that
unlike Americans, European intellectuals travelled to China
without feeling the need 'to expiate the sins' their countries
had committed against China in the first years after liberation,
and 'with less of an expectation of an impending crisis in
their own society'.[2] Within each of the Western countries there
were differing views. In so far as they were concerned about
China, the trade unions and the left held, not surprisingly,
a far more positive view of China than conservative opinion.
Communist parties saw China as a model for the rapid development of a miserably poor country.

Although Westerners in general had only a dim knowledge
of events in China, there were in fact quite a few opportunities
to find out. Some journalists and others from the West did
visit or reside in China, and there was a whole army of observers
in Hong Kong, who carefully monitored what went on in
China through the press, radio broadcasts, and the accounts
of refugees. China became very much part of the academic
political science, economics, and anthropology trades.

Negative Images, 1949–1966

It was a common basic assumption among those holding hostile
images of China that the Communists had created a vast propaganda network which aimed to deceive everybody, especially
foreigners. To be taken in showed the observer to be naïve.
Guides selected excellent or exceptional sites or units to show
the visitor in an effort to demonstrate how happy the Chinese

were under the Chinese Communist Party (CCP). Everything ordinary was out of bounds and it was more or less impossible for a foreign visitor to establish a genuine or frank relationship with a Chinese.

The image of China which separates this period, or most of it, from any other was that of Soviet domination. The origin of this image was the American government. On 30 July 1949, even before formal establishment of the People's Republic, the United States' Secretary of State, Dean Acheson (1893–1971), made a statement on the rule of the Chinese Communist Party in a 'letter of transmittal' with the China White Paper entitled 'United States Relations with China', published on 5 August. In the letter Acheson declared, among other points, that 'The Communist leaders have foresworn their Chinese heritage and have publicly announced their subservience to a foreign power, Russia.'[3] This was Acheson's somewhat fanciful interpretation of Mao Zedong's declaration, put forward on 30 June in 'On the People's Democratic Dictatorship', that China would 'lean to one side', that of the Soviet Union.

The same image was taken up in journalistic, academic, and other quarters. In a long and scholarly treatment of Sino-Soviet relations published in 1956, Richard L. Walker wrote that between 1949 and 1954 there had been no important instances 'when the Mao regime failed to extend support and allegiance to the USSR'.[4] This 'allegiance' he considered was the factor which had made it possible for 'the top leaders in Red China' to achieve 'positions of power in their own country and abroad far beyond their probable expectations'.[5] However, Walker did go on to cast doubt on whether this allegiance would last. The 'unity, strength, and determined opposition of the world outside the iron curtain' had a chance of making the Chinese leaders change their policy.[6]

The French journalist Robert Guillain, who visited China in the mid-1950s, drew the conclusion that China was in the complete thrall of the Russians. 'China believes that the only way to go fast is blindly to copy the USSR.'[7] In contrast to Walker, he saw only 'a very remote possibility' of 'a revolt of the Chinese colossus against her Russian partner'. If it came at all, it would not be until the end of the century.[8]

The image of China as dominated by the Soviet Union and thus owing it allegiance was closely tied to the American government's policy of opposition to 'monolithic communism'. The Sino-Soviet dispute of the late 1950s proved that China was not dominated by the Soviet Union and that the monolith did not exist.

Nevertheless, there was one Western image of China which was related closely to that of Soviet domination for a few years from 1949 but which still survived the split, namely that of China as a threat. The American government in the 1950s and 1960s based much of its foreign policy on the proposition that China was a threat to its neighbours and the world. The Korean War was critical in hardening the United States' anti-China policy and in the creation of negative Western images of China. It was the Korean War that gave the American government the grounds it wanted to implant the verdict that China was a threat among the public. 'Aggressive China Becomes a Menace' headlined *Life* magazine on 20 November 1950, just after the intervention of Chinese troops. 'China's Red Army', it said, 'a guerrilla rabble 20 years ago, had been built into a menacingly Russianized fighting force'. On 23 January 1951 the United States Senate called on the United Nations to 'declare Communist China an aggressor in Korea', which the United Nations did nine days later. An American army colonel predicted to a Boston audience in February 1956 that the Chinese army would grow by 1970 to be 'the world's most dynamic fighting machine' and this process would place the survival of the United States itself in doubt.[9]

Ill-founded as his view was, there was one respect in which it constituted a kind of backhanded compliment. The idea of a backward country like China posing a military threat to American survival by 1970 is not only ludicrous but suggests extreme faith in China's technological growth. Already in 1951, many in official American circles were prepared to express surprise at China's military performance in Korea and were afraid that if the Chinese army became 'Russianized', then the 'Yellow Peril' would become a reality.[10]

In the United States, the government's image of China as a threat, as well as the view it put over of individual world events, was widely accepted among Americans. Moreover, China's threat image worsened with the Sino-Soviet split and its acquisition of nuclear weapons in 1964. Gallup Polls were taken on the question of whether the Soviet Union or China was seen as the 'greater threat to world peace'. In 1961, 49 per cent nominated the Soviet Union, and only 32 per cent China, but by 1963 the latter figure had risen to 47 per cent and the next year to 56.[11] Not just the government, but the people too, believed that 'the sleeping dragon had awakened'.

Another pervasive image in the West, exacerbated by the fact that China's government had embraced Marxism, was of China as a totalitarian society without any freedom. 'The communist regime, though it gives China strength, is a totalitarian one. It negates freedom absolutely.'[12] The West regarded itself as free and the American government considered as part of the 'free world' any country which supported American foreign policy objectives, no matter how it treated its own people. The way the Chinese Communist Party could neutralize opposition to its elimination of freedom was through 'brainwashing', a process which came to hold a quite high place in the West's hierarchy of images of China. Harold Isaacs remarks that 'for the Chinese there was a whole battery of relevant qualities to draw upon' to explain this dreadful practice, 'their inhuman cruelty, for one thing, and at its service, their inscrutability, their deviousness, their subtlety, and their devilish cleverness'.[13] On the other hand, one account from Britain explains brainwashing through the Chinese preference for trying 'to convert the intelligentsia' over the terror and killings practised by Stalin.[14]

In the period 1949–66, the Chinese Communist Party on a number of occasions initiated campaigns which depended on 'mobilizing the masses'. For many in the West this was part of a totalitarian system of government and conjured up an image of the 'faceless masses' with no individualism. French journalist Robert Guillain coined a phrase to describe the regimentation and total loss of individual freedom among the Chinese: 'An ant hill, yes, that is what they have become — ants, blue ants.'[15]

André Malraux, the author of La condition humaine discussed in Chapter 5, visited China in the summer of 1965 as the French Minister of Culture, the year after France established diplomatic relations with the People's Republic. Malraux devoted most of the account he wrote of his visit to meetings with state and CCP leaders, especially Mao Zedong, but does make some general comments on China as well. He found the sending of urban people to the countryside as 'boringly rigid as was compulsory military service in Europe' and was shocked to find the Party's slogans never questioned. His comments are thus still negative, though not nearly as caustic as Guillain's a few years earlier. He adds: 'But slogans are only followed if the masses remain mobilized. Mao can only build China with volunteers. He is more anxious to make China than to make war.'[16] Even though finding the result abhorrent himself, Malraux thus seemed quite willing to give Mao the benefit of reasonably good intentions in his efforts at mass mobilization.

It is true that the CCP regarded the mass line and individualism as in mutual contradiction and favoured the former. The relative lack of Western journalists and other writers did not help attach individual personalities to the 'blue ants', or faces to the masses. In a book about China's 'red masters', that is a selection of its CCP leaders, well known American journalist and novelist Robert Elegant praised them for being bold, but went on to argue that their 'very boldness may undo them when it strikes the bed-rock of integrity in Chinese society and the Chinese individual'.[17] His assumption seemed to be that anti-individualism was not only dishonest but also un-Chinese. It was an image shared by many in the West.

Fiction written and wholly or partly set in the period 1949 to 1966 provides a very similar set of images. Pearl Buck, author of *The Good Earth* discussed in Chapter 5, is certainly the most famous relevant author. She had continued writing voluminously after returning to live in the United States from the mid-1930s on and remained an image-formulator during the 1950s and 1960s. According to her own account it was the fact that she nearly lost her life at the hands of a Communist army that turned her against the Communists and made her realize she was American, despite being Chinese 'in education and feeling'.[18] In 1954, she published her autobiography and, although it does not have much to say about the Communist government, its attitudes are fiercely hostile, and show her quarrel with the Communists to have been much more deepseated than based on a single incident, however traumatic that may have been. In particular, she believes that China should never have overthrown the monarchy. 'The Throne should have been upheld, the system maintained, and within that framework reforms carried out.'[19] The British model is more appropriate for China than the American. She advocated gradualist reform, not revolution. 'It is dangerous to try to save people — very dangerous indeed!' Heaven may be 'an inspiring goal, but what if on the way the soul is lost in hell?'[20] The path she wanted for the China she loved so much was the direct antithesis of what the Communists had inflicted upon it.

One of Buck's later novels is *Letter from Peking*, which tells of an American woman's marriage to the son of a Chinese mother and American father. When the Communists come to power he decides to stay in China, but she returns home with their son to the United States, where her life is dominated by dreams that her husband will come to join her and their son. At first the husband is optimistic about the new order: 'I believe that a new day is coming in this old, old country of mine', he writes in his first letter to her.[21] However, with the passage of time, the situation deteriorates for him and eventually he tries to flee from China, but is shot and killed in the process.

The story personifies the main image of the People's Republic. It is a government so oppressive that people eventually attempt escape from it, so cruel that its representatives do not hesitate to shoot on sight. It is a regime which allows no freedom and censors letters, and the author goes to considerable pains to say how the various letters were smuggled out of China. Nevertheless, a strong image in the novel is that it was patriotism which had made the husband stay in China in the first place, and his choice thus expresses the initial Communist appeal to the Chinese intense love of their country. Yet, the virtue of patriotism has its bad side, namely hostility to America: 'The anti-American feeling in China is growing under the skilful Communist propaganda', the American woman tells her son.

Meanwhile, both mother and son find that society in the United States condemns them for their Chinese connections, regarding China under communism as so remote and awful as to be more or less equivalent to being on another planet. The son's first love is forced by her parents to reject him because he has a Chinese grandparent. She 'is not allowed' to love him. 'Her parents forbid it.'[22] The image is of an America both strongly anti-Communist and anti-Chinese.

Letter from Peking is more about the United States than China, but there were novels which presented a much more focused and scathing image of life in the PRC. One such concerns a man called Li Chi who, 'despite an unceasing effort in Communist China to stamp out individualism' succeeds in using the system favourably for himself.[23] The lesson comes in the last sentences of the novel.

He [Li Chi] has learned to *thrive* by exploiting the contradictions within the Chinese Communist ideology. He grows stronger and more secure as the contradictions increase and become more glaring. He probably represents the single most dangerous threat to China's present regime.

That threat, of course, is nothing more than the inherent and indestructible good sense of the Chinese people.[24]

The image is that few people in China take its Marxist ideology seriously, let alone believe in it. The system they have imposed is not only evil and oppressive, but inherently false.

A set of completely trivial adventure stories written in and referring to the period under review in this chapter is Captain W. E. Johns's Biggles books. Although by a man who knew virtually nothing about China these books were powerful image-formulators, at least among boys in several Western countries. Those with sections set in China show it as an oppressed country of fear, where those 'very fine men', the missionaries, are 'brutally murdered' and require saving by courageous airmen with a legal right to fly into China to get them, no matter what the government of the day may think.[25] The country is run by sadistic and wicked Communists, utterly subservient to the Russians. The army 'will kill anybody for the pleasure of it, including their own people if they're in the mood'.[26] One of these adventure novels is set at or near the famous Dunhuang Buddhist caves. 'The first man to see this amazing shrine', we are told, was Sir Aurel Stein, who was shown the secret library there 'by the guardian priest'.[27] Apparently Johns does not consider the priest a man and reserves that appellation for adult male persons from such civilized continents as Europe! Apart from its culture, this part of China is a place to avoid, because 'life is held cheaply, and death by violence a thing so commonplace that no one bothers much about it'.[28]

In economic terms, there was a tendency until the late 1950s to balance successes against the frightful human cost. Robert Guillain suggests the following formula to sum up his impressions of China: 'Material balance sheet remarkable — spiritual balance sheet terrifying.'[29] In 1956, Richard Walker was prepared to acknowledge that 'the Mao regime will accomplish further impressive feats' such as vast irrigation projects, flood control, road building, and defence works. But it is essentially brute force which makes any such achievements possible. 'Despite bureaucratic inefficiency, oppression which may increase passive resistance, and a population problem which grows more acute, it [the Mao regime] has the power to mobilize its great human resources'.[30]

In the late 1950s the Great Leap Forward, and the commune movement which was part of it, brought about an image of China's economic performance which was very much more negative than in the preceding years. The CCP was asking too much of the individualistic Chinese, especially the peasants, and was guilty not only of oppression, of trying to change human nature, but of incompetent planning. 'Great leap — great failure'[31] was a popular verdict among economists and ordinary people. Writing in one of the most prestigious American academic journals on Asia, one specialist made the typical statement that, as a result of the Great Leap Forward, 'the nation plunged rapidly into a deep economic quagmire' and was 'afflicted by a prolonged and serious agrarian crisis'.[32]

Its enormous population gave China an image of actual and potential economic backwardness, and made it loom large as a negative example among impoverished third world countries with serious population problems. Already the world's most populous country, China suffered from a population growth-rate which was excessive and unnecessary. The well known and highly regarded journalist and specialist on China, Dick Wilson, wrote in 1966 that 'this "Malthusian counter-revolution" blunts the successes of China's industrial revolution by providing more mouths to feed, more hands to employ, each year'.[33] His was a sober, and typical, view.

Positive Images

Up to this point we have considered what were probably the dominant images of the People's Republic in the West between 1949 and 1966. Most of them were heavily negative. There was, however, a whole range of rather more positive images, and it is to these we now turn.

In the first place, there were many who did not accept the image of China as a threat to world peace. Some saw China itself as under threat from the United States or other powers and explained China's actions in those terms. Others saw China as upholding the socialist principles to which she claimed to adhere. One opinion analysed China's foreign policy actions mainly in terms of the defence of its national interests. In this view China merely wanted to wipe out the humiliations of past encroachments against itself and desired respect in the world community. There was thus no need to see its actions as a threat. Professor C. P. Fitzgerald of the Australian National University was an influential exponent of this view.[34] The three particular examples of Chinese aggression before 1966 most often cited were intervention in the Korean War, the annexation of Tibet, and the Sino-Indian border war of 1962. Dick Wilson was among those who presented an alternate point of view on each of them, not so much to justify China's actions as to discredit the notion that they showed China to be bellicose, aggressive, or a threat to Asian or world peace.[35] On the basis of his own view Wilson not only favoured but also predicted détente between China and foreign countries. 'Communist China is not an impossible country, a nation condemned to perpetual mistrust and isolation', he said. Western policies had 'fed the pain and insecurity, rather than sought to overcome them' but still he believed that 'time is on the side of reconciliation'.[36] Read in the 1980s, Wilson's 1966 words come over as quite prophetic.

A very early and powerful positive image of the new communist China came from the hand of Han Suyin in her novel *A Many-Splendoured Thing*. Completed in July 1951, it was first published the following year by Jonathan Cape in London and has been through many impressions and editions, and has been made into a film. It is primarily a story of a love-affair between a Chinese–European woman and a British journalist who is eventually killed in the Korean War. Most of it is set either in Hong Kong or in China before the final victory of the CCP. Yet the spectre of the CCP looms very large in the story and comes over as a dominantly positive force, one which might well take away individual freedoms, but would at the same time make the Chinese people once more proud to be Chinese, and save the masses of poor and oppressed. Many of the best and most honest Westernized intellectuals chose to return home after the CCP's victory, suggests the author. 'They chose what might overwhelm them, not through cowardice, nor through opportunism, but because they had a social conscience, they loved their people, and they had a deep need to be whole again, unfrustrated in service to a land so much in need of them.'[37]

Among Americans it was Edgar Snow who most successfully told his countrymen that, for all its failings, China had benefitted from the revolution. The old China left behind was nothing to idealize, nothing to wish revived. As noted in Chapter 5, Snow had already worked in China as a journalist before 1949 and acquired a reputation for knowledge of the country and especially of the CCP. He revisited China in 1960 and on the basis of extensive travels and interviews, including two with Zhou Enlai, wrote *The Other Side of the River*. Because of its author's established credentials, its on-the-spot evidence, and its immense detail, it was probably not only the best but the most influential among books depicting a basically positive set of images of contemporary China between 1949 and 1966.

Snow covers an enormous range of subjects, both foreign policy and domestic conditions, religion, education, social life, and the minority nationalities. He is critical in the sense that he does not accept data at face value, but is definitely friendly both to China and its government. It is in his chapter on Shanghai that he most warmly praises the Communists for having rid China of the scourges that had afflicted the city before 1949. 'Gone the pompous wealth beside naked starvation . . . gone the island of Western civilization flourishing in the vast slum that was Shanghai. Good-by to all that.'[38] His is a long and rhetorical list. The point it brings through with crystal clarity and unrelenting force is that, though old Shanghai may have been very comfortable for foreigners and their few rich Chinese hangers-on, it was little better than hell for the poor people who constituted the overwhelming majority of the people. For them an image of communist rule much more appropriate than 'totalitarianism', 'brainwashing', 'disappointment', or 'dishonesty' was progress and dignity; nor was it obvious to them why they should be so grateful to the West in general or the Americans in particular.

Most of those Westerners with firsthand experience were not Americans. The Africa-specialist Basil Davidson, author of *Daybreak in China* (1953), was only one of a number of British writers sympathetic to the revolution. Sweden, which established full diplomatic relations with China as early as May 1950, produced several major firsthand accounts. Sven Lindqvist was a student of Chinese at Beijing University in 1961 and 1962. Journalist Jan Myrdal visited and made an intensive study of the village of Liu Ling in northern Shaanxi during the autumn of 1962. It was people such as these who helped create an ·image of the human face of China.

Sven Lindqvist's book details conversations with fellow Chinese students, enabling them to put forward their point of view. Lindqvist is critical of some aspects of Chinese policies, which is perhaps not surprising considering the period he was there. He criticizes the view of the outside world pushed in the Chinese media, and defends the many-sided images of China found in Sweden. However, he does convey an impression of improving conditions. 'During my time in China, Chinese society became more humane, more tolerant and more reasonable.'[39] He accepts the necessity of the revolution in China and urges the West to come to terms with it without prejudice or preconceived notions. Lindqvist stresses the need not merely to visit but to live in China and to know the Chinese language.

Jan Myrdal's approach was to interview as many people as possible in a single Chinese village, and find out as much as possible about their lives, what they thought about the world and each other.[40] The idea of such a project certainly emphasized both the importance of the peasants and their 'human faces'. Myrdal's overall impression — and the image he conveyed — was of a puritanical rural society. He considered this both natural and reasonable, and certainly did not portray the communes as a disastrous failure, nor did he appear to favour free enterprise as a solution to their problems. He suggested that 'Western experts on contemporary China gleefully report its failings' but, while he was not prepared to predict the eventual success of the Chinese rural economy, he was quite definite that a breakdown in China would be a catastrophe not only for China but for the world at large.[41]

Myrdal comments on the popular image of economic failure in the wake of the Great Leap Forward by referring to the precarious food situation existing when his wife and he arrived in China. 'That the peasants in this book do not speak about the famine and the agricultural catastrophe after the "Great Leap Forward", does not mean that the famine did not exist.'[42]

Edgar Snow's is a slightly, though not greatly, less grim picture. His experience in 1960 and researches from 1959 to 1962 led him to doubt 'Western press editorials and headlines' which 'continued to refer to "mass starvation" in China'. His conclusion challenged the prevailing image in the West, which accepted the press editorials and headlines. 'Isolated instances of starvation due to neglect or failure of the rationing system were possible. Considerable malnutrition undoubtedly existed. Mass starvation? No.'[43]

As a matter of fact, it should be pointed out that in this instance it was Snow who was wrong: there certainly was 'mass starvation'. Even the creators of negative images tended to underestimate the scope of the calamity. Figures issued in the 1980s by the economist Sun Yefang and officially by China's State Statistical Bureau suggest that this may have been twentieth-century China's most devastating famine. In 1960 the death rate reached 25.43 per thousand, as against 14.59 the previous year, while the birth rate declined somewhat and the overall population actually fell by about 10 million.[44] Although Snow is still regarded very highly in China today, nobody any longer defends the view he reached on this matter.

China's social revolution excited great praise from some in the West. Hewlett Johnson, Dean of Canterbury, was among the earlier and more fulsome admirers of China's 'new morality'. 'The moral change outweighed all other factors and lay at the root of all China's great successes', he declared, 'moral change which penetrated deep into the lives of the common people'.[45] Its main source he saw as 'the example of the whole-hearted self-sacrifice of the creative spirits who fashioned the

new China',[46] meaning the work of the CCP members, and
the similar labour of the People's Liberation Army. Johnson
was naturally concerned about the fate of Christianity in China;
he believed that despite the occurrence of attacks in isolated
places, the government itself had countenanced no persecution
of missionaries.[47]

One social issue Johnson considered was the treatment of
women, and the picture he paints of 'liberated womanhood'
is a very rosy one.[48] The French feminist Simone de Beauvoir
(1908–86) wrote a long book on her visit to China in 1955
and includes a highly detailed and well-researched chapter
on the family and the status of women.[49] She dwells at length
on the sufferings of women in the past and finds enormous
improvements under the current order. 'The family has been
preserved and respected in such a way that it is based on
free relations among individuals', she concludes. 'What has
been abolished is the alienation of the individual from an
oppressive and imperiously sanctified institution.' Marriage
and maternity have become free, while women have won their
'human dignity'.[50] Simone de Beauvoir's account is incomparably more sophisticated than Hewlett Johnson's, her
ideological assumptions very different from his, but her conclusions are actually rather similar.

The Issue of Change

We turn now to an issue which has bulked large and continued
to create controversy as a Western image of China despite
the revolution: the extent of change in China. Positions which
observers took up did not necessarily depend on their overall
ideological view of China nor on the value judgement they
made about the People's Republic.

A view which balances change and continuity is that of
Guy Wint. He sees change as substantial and as having come
about not merely as a result of the CCP revolution but over
a long period before that as well. He considers it 'likely that
the national character has changed radically' but goes on that
such an eventuality would not be extraordinary since 'national
character is seldom very stable'.[51] At the same time, he points
to many past features which have survived, such as authoritarian government and the 'contempt and suspicion' for private

trading and private fortunes made from commerce. Wint regards these 'surprising likenesses', which the Communists share with the old imperial order, as possibly the reason why the CCP 'proved acceptable' to the Chinese people.[52]

André Malraux takes a highly sophisticated view which acknowledges the power of the environment and thus stresses continuity, but does not thereby deny that change both has occurred and will continue to do so. On the side of continuity he sees a China 'strongly bound to its earth, its rivers, its mountains and its dead'. Using almost theological language which comes close to uniting change and its opposite he points to a China 'linked to its resurrection by another form of ancestor-worship, in which the history of the liberation is the gospel and Mao the son, in the sense in which the Emperor was the Son of Heaven'. But change gains the upper hand in the emphasis the new order places on the future. Malraux was struck by the posters seen in every Chinese city, in which 'a brave youth with flashing teeth joyously flourishes a rifle', together with a militia girl with a sub-machine-gun; they are looking not at each other but at the future. 'And this social-realist idealization symbolizes the dream of millions of Chinese.'[53] For Malraux, the image is not a pretty one, but he does at least appear to acknowledge youth's enthusiasm for the new Marxist–Leninist order.

An example of a differing interpretation — one which sees contemporary China as simply another phase in Chinese history in which the influences which matter most are traditional — is that of British journalist Dennis Bloodworth. He sees a sense of timelessness, of a China which absorbs and uses everybody and everything and rides essentially unchanged over them all. He simply does not take Marxism seriously, yet he is in no sense the dedicated anti-Communist and is in many ways well disposed towards the People's Republic. Of the Great Leap Forward he says: 'The attempt failed miserably. But nothing venture nothing gain. The Chinese did not die from it, they learned from it, and they recovered from it by their own unaided efforts.'[54] This is an interesting way of half-justifying a catastrophic mistake. In this unchanging China, Mao Zedong becomes a new emperor, a new superman, the People's Republic simply a new dynasty.[55] But that is all right. That is what the Chinese are used to, that is what they like.

Jan Myrdal's image of the Chinese countryside is to stress continuity with the past. He bases this attitude on the first-hand impressions he derived from village life in China and on his 'general belief in the continuity of cultural patterns'.[56] Like Bloodworth, he gives Marxist ideology a low priority among factors influencing rural life, but does not thereby attack China. There are numerous policy twists and turns, but beneath them, and more fundamental, he sees a texture of life which has survived essentially unchanged through the revolution.

The dedicated anti-Communist Richard Walker takes Marxism very seriously indeed, so much as to aver that 'specialists on Communism, not Sinologists, will be better qualified to analyze events' in China. He also concedes that real transformation of society was under way by 1954. It had 'already gone deep enough at least to modify such traditional patterns as remain' and would go much further in time. But Walker denounces both Marxism and the changes; they are evils which have subjected the people 'to a form of exploitation and oppression harsher than their country has ever known'.[57] One pre-eminent feature of the past has survived, namely the 'monopoly bureaucracy'. Walker sees the PRC in 1954 as having 'laid the foundations for a great new type of oriental despotism approaching "general slavery"'.[58] It turns out thus that he is a follower of the theories of Karl Wittfogel, discussed in Chapter 7, but this leads him, not to deny essential change from the past, as Wittfogel does, but to despair of China's being able to free itself of the Communists.

Robert Guillain bemoans 'the death of the ancient Chinese civilisation'. For him, China 'is launched upon an orgy of change in which there is no place for a resurrection of the past'. He sees the new ideology as extremely important: 'China is in the process of abandoning herself entirely to the Marxist–Leninist civilisation.'[59] Guillain takes a further step, one much stronger than Walker. The implication of Marxism is that China is becoming Western, it 'is no longer Asiatic'. He regards this 'Westernisation' as 'much more brutal and complete' than Japan underwent in the nineteenth century; at least the Japanese 'preserved their oriental souls, their Japanese heart', whereas China is making a 'clean sweep' in its surrender to Marxist–Leninist thought.[60]

Like Walker and Guillain, Han Suyin takes Marxism very

seriously, and sees radical social transformation in the People's Republic. But for her both are extremely beneficial and desirable, certainly not evil; they are causes not of despair but of rejoicing and hope. She likens the changes in progress early in 1966 to those 'which took place in Europe at the Renaissance and during the Industrial Revolution', but with a major difference. Whereas European change was haphazard, 'in China today the process of transformation is a conscious, aware, and deliberately wished for reshaping'.[61] It is consequently much better. She implies that whereas social change in Europe, though ultimately necessary and desirable, caused a great deal of misery, in China this was a necessary and desirable process bringing much more happiness and joy than suffering.

Conclusion

It is true that very few Westerners went to China, let alone lived there, in the period 1949 to 1966. Yet it appears from the above that what affected the West's images of China in those years was less ignorance than politics and ideology. Because of the severity of the Cold War split between the 'free world' and 'international communism', and the strains between left and right in politics in Western countries, attitudes towards China were a litmus test of one's ideological position on international issues.

For the United States, the leader of the 'free world' forces, a negative image of China was not only an ideological necessity but a weapon in international political rivalry, and thus the American government worked to reinforce these negative images of China. Given the status of the United States as the dominant Western superpower, its immense wealth, and its will and influence on Western governments and communications, it became the main determinant of the West's image of China from 1949 to 1966. In terms of Western images of China, the link between power and knowledge was very tight indeed.

Negative images of China were reinforced by Nationalist Chinese embassies, and other pro-Guomindang organizations, by church groups, especially among Catholics, and by other political organizations. On the other hand, positive images of China, from European sources, and on the left in Western countries, did exist, but made little headway in the Cold War climate of the 1950s and 1960s.

The response of the Chinese themselves to these developments was of course bitterly resentful and hostile. Statements and actions which to them seemed defence of their own national interests merely served to strengthen the dominance of the negative Western images over the positive. International events in Asia, such as the Korean War and the defeat of the French in Vietnam, merely proved how dangerous communism in Asia was, including or even especially that in China. The Great Leap Forward and its aftermath tarnished even the image of economic advance. The beginning of yet another war in Vietnam and the commitment of American troops against the 'Communist aggressors' early in 1965 did nothing to improve images of the northern Communist neighbour, China. And then the following year came the Cultural Revolution and with it new realities in China which, initially at least, merely served to confirm the West in its negative perceptions of Chinese communism.

11

Contemporary Images of the Cultural Revolution, 1966–1976

In 1966 the Cultural Revolution erupted on the streets of Beijing and other Chinese cities, while the year 1976 saw the deaths of the Premier of the State Council Zhou Enlai and Communist Party Chairman Mao Zedong, as well as the fall of the Cultural Revolution's main supporters, the 'gang of four'. In China the decade 1966 to 1976 has, since 1977, been officially considered the period of the 'cultural revolution'.

The same decade saw a change in the balance of power in the world and the East Asian region in particular. A war raged in Vietnam which weakened the strategic position of the United States in the region. Although both China and the Soviet Union supported the victors in Vietnam they were even more hostile to each other at the end of the decade than they had been at the beginning. Meanwhile China and the United States moved closer to each other, and from 21 to 28 February 1972 American President Richard M. Nixon visited the People's Republic.

There were enormous ramifications for Western images of China in the shifting balance of power and the Cultural Revolution. The Vietnam War changed the United States deeply and probably permanently. Doubts and then revulsion against the war caused Americans and other Westerners to rethink their attitudes and assumptions about Asia in general and Asian revolutions in particular. The Cultural Revolution also raised questions about the whole nature of the Chinese revolution.

Nixon's visit to China marked a major dividing point in Western images of that country. 'A week that changed the world' was Nixon's characterization of his own trip and his view, vain though it might have been, was shared by many Americans,[1] because it symbolized that the United States no longer regarded China as a major enemy, perhaps even not as an enemy at all.

In his typically colourful language Harold Isaacs has described the direct impact of the new American diplomacy and the Nixon visit on Americans' images of China.

When the American pendulum swings in such matters, it swings high and hard. The new medium of television lent all its enormously expanded scope and coverage to the event this time. When the president . . . announced his forthcoming trip to Peking, the passage from the China-minuses to the China-pluses became a mad and even gay rush. Pearl Buck reappeared . . . to remind everyone how great a time it was when Americans and Chinese were friends. The 'lo-the-wonder-of-the-wonderful-Chinese' reappeared in the country's print and on its screens.[2]

Isaacs goes on to comment on an expansion of interest in Chinese food, art, fashions, and acupuncture. The number of Americans going to China rose quickly. There was a 'mania for everything Chinese'.

To back up these generalizations Isaacs cites the results of Gallup Polls taken in 1966 and March 1972 showing the qualities, positive and negative, which Americans attributed to Chinese people. The following table shows the numbers who chose particular adjectives in the two years.[3]

Qualities	1966	1972
Hardworking	37	74
Honest	—	20
Brave	7	17
Religious	14	18
Intelligent	14	32
Practical	8	27
Ignorant	24	10
Artistic	13	26
Progressive	7	28
Sly	20	19
Treacherous	19	12
Warlike	23	13
Cruel	13	9

It will be seen that, when the Cultural Revolution began, the dominant images were hardworking, ignorant, warlike, and sly, three of them negative. But by the time Nixon had returned from China in 1972 the main images of Chinese among Americans had changed to hardworking, intelligent, progressive, practical, and artistic, all of them positive. Moreover, even though the sample was larger in 1972, the negative images such as ignorant, sly, treacherous, warlike, and cruel, had shrunk by 1972, in most cases substantially. At the same time, the positive images, like hardworking, brave, intelligent, practical, and artistic, had gone up.

These represent very great changes in public opinion in the United States.

Opinion in Education Circles on the Cultural Revolution

The most detailed public analysis of contemporary China from 1966 to 1976 was carried out in universities and colleges. Although some China specialists moved from profession to profession, especially in the United States, most were basically academics. Correspondingly, it has long been practice in the United States for government to seek advice from academics.

The Western academic world was split over China but initially mainly hostile to the Cultural Revolution. One of the best known and most outspoken purveyors of negative images was Pierre Ryckmans, and he is an appropriate representative example. A Belgian who at that time worked at the Australian National University in Canberra, Ryckmans writes his polemical works under the pen-name Simon Leys. There is, however, no secret about his identity and the copyright page of most of his books acknowledges both names, even though the title page still gives the author formally as Leys. He has aroused very great interest among those interested in China and has written for a variety of well known and influential journals.

His first book on the Cultural Revolution was published in 1971 in French and in 1977 in English translation. It is a chronological account of the Cultural Revolution, but its main analytical burden comes in the first sentences: 'The "Cultural Revolution" had nothing revolutionary about it except the name, and nothing cultural about it except the initial tactical pretext. It was a power struggle waged at the top between a handful of men and behind the smokescreen of a fictitious mass movement.'[4] It was thus not irrational, as others claimed, but it certainly was cruel and orchestrated by despots, first and foremost by Mao.

In later writings, Leys has expanded the scope of his condemnations, which became more intense in the early 1970s, when the general trend was in the opposite direction. China was totalitarian and its government bureaucratic with more hierarchy and less equality even than in the old days: 'In the sixth century BC . . . China's social hierarchy had only ten degrees. We have progressed since then: the Maoist bureaucracy today has thirty hierarchical classes, each with specific privileges and prerogatives.'[5] It was impossible for a foreigner to talk to a Chinese, because the latter were all too terrified. The Cultural Revolution and the Maoists destroyed a beautiful ancient and mass culture, replacing it with a narrow 'monstrous' nothingness. Ryckmans has almost nothing positive to say about the period 1966–76. It is true he does concede that the 'maoist regime . . . has very nearly succeeded in feeding and housing its people', but goes on: 'Yet if we stop and think about it, this is simply the minimum that any self-respecting stockbreeder would want to provide for his cattle.'[7] Even the ability to feed and house the people becomes an object of scorn.

The Vietnam War and the inability of the United States government to deal successfully with problems at home 'led a new generation of scholars to a more critically receptive approach to China'.[8] Not only in the United States but also in other Western countries, such scholars were willing to take a far more sympathetic attitude towards communism in China and to the Cultural Revolution than were those of the older school. In the United States a good symbol of the new approach was the foundation of the Committee of Concerned Asian Scholars in 1968 by students and academics, and while its primary aim was opposition to American intervention in Vietnam, most of its members were directly and vitally concerned with China. It should also be emphasized that there were in all the other countries of the West academics sympathetic to the aims of the Cultural Revolution from the mid–1960s.

Members of this Committee were among the first to visit

China as soon as it became possible for Americans to do so, and a group of fifteen of them stayed for a month in the summer of 1971, all students or teachers of China and all able to speak Chinese. They produced a highly laudatory book. Their 'overwhelming impression of China' was 'vitality — the enthusiasm, the humor, and the tremendous commitment of her people to their new China'.[9] They accepted the aims of the Cultural Revolution as desirable,[10] even if they did not express them in the same terms as the Chinese propaganda media were doing at the time. They were also impressed by developments in the arts and believed the main result of the new cultural movement was 'the enrichment of people's lives which the art and culture of China now has achieved'.[11]

A particularly influential American academic, one who has been mentioned many times in these pages, was the Harvard sinologist John Fairbank. When the Cultural Revolution first began he saw it as a movement both insane and anti-foreign. For him, the Red Guards of the Cultural Revolution held striking parallels with the Boxers of 1900.

A curious contradiction haunts Chairman Mao's revolution: the more he seeks to make China new, the more he seems to fall back on old Chinese ways of doing things. Two thirds of a century ago, in the midsummer madness of 1900, the Boxer bands who were officially commissioned to exterminate foreigners in North China were comprized largely of peasant youth — and they pursued their ends with the same zeal displayed today by Chairman Mao's officially commissioned 'Red Guards' in their attack on all things foreign.[12]

The irony for Fairbank was that the Red Guards, in trying to wipe out old ideas and habits, should use the same old methods as the Boxers.

When the worst excesses of the Cultural Revolution had settled down in the early 1970s and Nixon had made his visit, Fairbank also stayed in China for six weeks in mid-1972, at the invitation of Zhou Enlai. He was very favourably impressed, especially with the improvements in the situation in the villages of North China, where he had travelled widely in the early 1930s. 'Compared with 40 years ago the change in the countryside is miraculous, a revolution probably on the largest scale of all time.'[13] While he was still not enthusiastic about the Cultural Revolution, calling it a period of 'stress and even violence', he did believe it had produced some positive results and in

1972 sensed 'relaxation and euphoria' that made the year 'a happy time to be in China'.[14] Perhaps most significant of all, he was prepared to denounce the American policies which had kept China and the United States so hostile to each other for so long. They were based on false images and a misunderstanding of history.

> MacArthur's push for the Yalu in late 1950 was folly. Only Stalin, perhaps profited from the Sino-American war in Korea. The ensuing Dullesian cold war against Peking in the 1950s was fundamentally mistaken and unnecessary, based on an utter misconception of Chinese history and the Chinese revolution. Only the Nixon visit could get us beyond this quagmire of errors, and we still have a long way to go to reach firm ground.[15]

Another image-creating, favourable, general account of China was the book *800,000,000 The Real China* by Ross Terrill, an Australian academic then working at Harvard University. Based on the author's 1971 visit, it is a thorough account of his observations written in a highly personal style reminiscent of Edgar Snow's. Terrill outlines his general attitude to China, which is that he admires the cultural confidence of the Chinese and the social gains of the revolution but is harshly critical of many aspects of China, especially the position of intellectuals.[16] He warns against idealizing China and believes too many in the West are disposed to ignore the failings of the current order.[17] Terrill's position lies between those of the Committee of Concerned Asian Scholars and Pierre Ryckmans, but he certainly tilts much more heavily towards the former than the latter.

In addition to such general works based on personal observations, Western academics read the Chinese sources voluminously; they argued and wrote endlessly on what the Cultural Revolution was about, what its results were, and what had happened to the various aspects of Chinese society, education, health, industry, agriculture, communications, and so on. In addition, they argued about their own and their colleagues' underlying assumptions about China and revolution. A great deal was written and, although most works were not individually image-creating in their own time, the cumulative effect did help to alter popular images of China.

One such academic work may serve as an example, a collective volume called *China in Ferment*, edited by Richard Baum with Louise B. Bennett. It concerns the Cultural Revolution and devotes much space to analysing what that movement was 'really about'. Five schools of thought are put forward ranging from an acceptance of the Maoist view of the day to the 'classical Machiavellian struggle for political power among the organized supporters and opponents' of Mao Zedong.[18] The analyses imply sharply differing value judgements on the Cultural Revolution and on Mao himself. The conclusion identifies — and also questions — the main assumptions of social science writing on China. Ranking high among these is that 'human nature' makes certain political programmes, including the one pursued by Mao during the Cultural Revolution, impossible.[19] Such an assumption would maintain that, because of human nature, people could never be persuaded to work for the interests of the masses as a whole, rather than for themselves and their families.

In addition to works written by university and college academics, it is also worthwhile considering textbooks used at secondary level. Textbooks are primary formulators of images because there is a powerful tendency for nebulous visions of dirt, violence, and oppression gained in childhood or adolescence to persist into adulthood.

In 1969 two Americans published a long review of ten textbooks on China 'widely used, easily available, and especially designed for secondary school use' in the United States.[20] They appeal to numerous direct quotations to show assumptions, attitudes, and conclusions in the books which accord closely with the official policy of the day. As for the books themselves, these were 'a propagandistic not an educational exercise' and the overall image they were portraying at that time was that high school courses defined China as the Enemy.[21]

Specifically, the two scholars point to an overriding aim of American educators in the high school courses, namely to explain 'the loss of China'. To do this two points recur again and again. One is that China had the potential to modernize but this was thwarted by the victory of communism. The assumption is that only with Western, that is American, assistance and following the capitalist model, can a poor country like China develop and modernize. The other point is that Chinese communism poses a threat to the United States and the 'free world'. It is violent, aggressive, bent on conquest, and determined to snuff out individualism and thus freedom wherever it appears. The incipient liberties present under the Guomindang were cut off before they could flower properly.[22]

The question of violence loomed large in the image of China which high school courses conveyed. Here was a doctrine — Maoism — which explicitly called for the revolutionary and violent overthrow of the established order based on the Marxist notion of class struggle. Such an idea was flatly contrary to the traditional Confucian emphasis on social harmony and distrust of the military. This meant that communism, in addition to its other anti-individualist evils, was also destroying the best elements of Chinese traditional culture. A comparison was frequently drawn between the Legalists and Communists, between Qin Shihuang and Mao Zedong.[23] But there was hope. Just as the peasants had risen up and overthrown Qin Shihuang, so they would sweep away the despotic communist system in favour of freedom and democracy, American style.[24]

The courses under discussion were published in 1964 (two cases), 1967 (five), and 1968 (three), and thus refer generally to images of China prevalent during the early stages of the Cultural Revolution. On the whole these images were not entirely new. Certainly, however, the onset of the Cultural Revolution did strengthen them. Here was Mao behaving just as expected and stirring up a totalitarian and anti-modern madness. One course ends with a quotation from *Time* magazine drawing a parallel between the Cultural Revolution and the Legalists' overthrow of tradition,[25] and the function of *Time* as an image-creator was itself important.

In most other Western countries the tendency was to ignore China in the high schools. What there was represented images that supported the American government's stereotypes of China, rather than reality. American textbooks sometimes dominated the market even outside the United States itself. Two Austrian specialists on the relations of their country with China write that 'what school textbooks offered was sparse and deficient' in the 1950s and 'this situation improved only slightly later',[26] meaning the 1970s. Similar comments would describe how things stood in Australia and Britain, although they would perhaps underestimate the extent of change in the early 1970s.

Due in part to the outpourings by academics and journalists on China in the late 1960s and early 1970s, the variety of materials available was enormously greater in 1976 than 1966 and many of the best works were in paperback. The impact on the secondary schools throughout the Western world was that 'the teacher's dilemma became one of having too many books to read and evaluate for classroom use'.[27] There were drawbacks here for overworked teachers, for whom finding suitable books on China was only one part of their job, and various books were published as guides to the available materials.

Images from Journalists and Others

It goes without saying that the educational industry was not the only source of images of the Cultural Revolution. Among documentary films one to gain particular fame was *China*, by the distinguished Italian director Michelangelo Antonioni, which came out in 1973 based on a visit he had made to various parts of China the preceding year. The Chinese media attacked the film and Antonioni savagely and declared that he had used 'underhand and utterly despicable means' to find material 'that could be used to slander and attack China'.[28] This was nonsense, as the Chinese admitted not long after the death of Mao in 1976, but the campaign against the film certainly contributed to its fame and patronage in the West. Actually, the images it conveyed were rather sombre, depicting a backward, tradition-bound, and tenaciously poor country. There was none of the atmosphere of revolutionary vitality and enthusiasm which the Chinese were pushing to the world at the time and which shone through to the members of the Committee of Concerned Asian Scholars. But correspondingly, Antonioni certainly did not present China as the hell many in the West still accepted as its reality.

It was the job of journalists to gather what information they could, either from Hong Kong or China itself. A highly influential magazine based in Hong Kong but read widely both in Asia and the West is the *Far Eastern Economic Review*. One of its issues nicely summarizes two rather contradictory images, both negative, of China at the beginning of the 1970s.

The first was of the violence of the Cultural Revolution and resultant military rule: 'Murder, arson, rape and corruption, committed at the peak of the Cultural Revolution, and in the anarchic period since, are today meeting their just rewards at the hands of China's army.'[29] Among the most vivid images of China in the late 1960s in the West was of corpses floating from the mainland into Hong Kong harbour, their hands tied behind their backs. The violence and turmoil of the late 1960s are major themes of such books as Stanley Karnow's *Mao and China, From Revolution to Revolution*, which came out in 1972. Karnow is worth a special mention because of his status as one of the most influential American journalists writing on eastern Asia.

The other, supplementary, image comes forward from the front cover of the same issue of the *Far Eastern Economic Review* of 2 April 1970. It shows ten models of Chinese, apparently representing various groups but with the military towering over them. The headline is 'China's communists, the Maoist mould' and the image is of a passive, lifeless, long-suffering population, tired out through chaos, but too exhausted to resist further. In the minds of many in the West, a powerful image of the Cultural Revolution in its early stages was of hordes of young people waving little red books containing the thoughts of the pretended saviour Chairman Mao. But with the passage of time this enthusiasm had given way to a soulless uniformity, a mould.

One journalist and novelist to convey similarly negative images was the American Robert Elegant. Part of his popular and widely read novel *Dynasty* is set in the China of the late 1960s. The novel is about a distinguished part-Chinese, part-British family called Sekloong, one of whose members joins the Communists and rises to be a full general in the People's Liberation Army. Called James or in Chinese Shih Ai-Kuo, he opposes the Cultural Revolution on the grounds that it could consume the Communist Party and even lead to civil war and 'put China back a generation', a view which was, ironically, to become official policy in China only a few years after Elegant published his novel. Even Zhou Enlai, who is a friend of James's in the book, is quoted as saying 'we live in ridiculous times'. James does not dare to say too much even to his own wife and daughter, the latter an ardent supporter of the Cultural Revolution, because 'candor was not merely imprudent, but dangerous in a divided household'.[30]

The novelist clearly sides with James and the image he

portrays of the Cultural Revolution conforms quite well to what others were suggesting at the same time. It is an 'insane storm',[31] characterized by 'mindless violence', including even pitched battles one of which, as it turns out, causes severe and permanent injury to James's revolutionary daughter.[32] Another image is of public humiliation of leaders, especially that of the Chinese President's wife Wang Guangmei, an actual historical event which is described in some detail.[33]

Amid the confusion a very strong image to emerge from Elegant's novel is that the Cultural Revolution was a fraud. It did not seek equality, as it pretended to do. James's wife 'knew that her fate was directly linked to his, despite the Party's cant about "perfect equality between male and female"'.[34] His daughter, for all her revolutionary ardour, does not hesitate to accept privileges, even those emphasizing her sex: 'She deliberately suppressed her awareness that the cotton fabric was finer than that worn by others, while the skilful tailoring accentuated her rounded hips and full breasts.' She 'preferred to forget the external marks of the privilege she enjoyed because of her father's rank'.[35]

In the end James admits that 'absolute loyalty to any man or system is ultimately destructive, evil'.[36] The one constant power is the family. The strongest image to come out of the novel is that in China family loyalties in the end triumph over political or even nationalist ones. Beside the family, the Cultural Revolution is but a fleeting nightmare.

Another source of images condemning the Cultural Revolution was accounts by former Red Guards who had escaped the horrors of China and found help to relate their story to the West in a European language . A well-known case in point is a Chinese who under the pen-name Ken Ling wrote a book called *The Revenge of Heaven*. It describes how as a teenager he rose from being a schoolboy in Amoy to the leading position of all production for Amoy, a municipality of 700,000 people. His beloved, whom he met while working for the Cultural Revolution, is killed in a battle fought in Amoy University, and he blames himself. 'Was this fate? Was it because I offended the Lord of Heaven' through taking part in the Cultural Revolution so actively?[37] Another work relates the story of a schoolboy Red Guard, pseudonymed Dai Hsiao-ai, from June

1966 until he fled to Hong Kong late the next year. It takes the form of translated autobiography by Dai interspersed with extensive commentary by two Western authors.

The images of China Ken Ling presents are bleak in the extreme: children involuntarily turning against their teachers, pointless torture and cruelty, violence on a horrific scale, and public humiliations of individuals, especially Wang Guangmei. He also gives a picture of miserable backwardness and poverty. Describing the view from the window during a train journey in Anhui province, he writes: 'The trees had been stripped of their bark. From time to time we saw corpses by the tracks; once I glimpsed a child's leg. The stations were filled with ragged, starved people.'[38] Later he visits a village in the mountains west of Amoy where there was no primary school, no electricity, and no shops. He meets there a nineteen-year-old girl whose life has been so hard that she looks very much older. She is totally ignorant of anything outside her direct experience, and does not even know that the earth is round. She believes Mao Zedong a god 'in heaven, constantly watching over everybody', who 'would know whoever was not working hard and have him punished'.[39]

Dai Hsiao-ai is also highly critical of the Cultural Revolution. The final straw that made him turn against it was a visit to the countryside which convinced him of the peasants' feeling 'that communism had not helped them one bit'.[40] What finally persuaded him to leave China was his conclusion that 'China's Communist society was a lie' full of unfairness made worse by the fact that 'the leaders denied its existence' and even 'instituted policies which made the injustices worse'.[41] Still, despite this judgement, Dai Hsiao-ai was less bitter about his experiences than Ken Ling, and at the time he communicated them to his biographers, he still continued 'to question the soundness of his decision to leave' China.[42]

These generally negative images of the Cultural Revolution were most certainly the dominant ones in the first part of the decade 1966–76, no matter whether conveyed by educationalists, journalists, or anybody else. While it is true that they tended to lose popularity in the early 1970s, they remained widely held in the West until after 1976. They were not, however, the only views on China put to Westerners by people working outside the educational profession. Even in the late 1960s there were those prepared to put over to the West a line supportive of the Cultural Revolution and, even more, one sympathetic to the Chinese revolution as a whole. The idea of China as a bureaucratic yet chaotic hell was very much under challenge.

Among journalists working in the West, by far the most influential of the pro-China lobby was Edgar Snow, who has been mentioned in earlier chapters. Although he died on 15 February 1972, less than a week before Nixon arrived in Beijing, his 1970–1 visit to China, and in particular his 10 December 1970 interview with Mao Zedong, won widespread publicity and certainly facilitated and contributed to Nixon's visit to China. His last book, *The Long Revolution*, was published in 1971. Though still incomplete, it recorded his notes on his conversation with Mao, 'Breakfast with the Chairman', discussions with Zhou Enlai, 'A Night with the Premier', and many observations on China in 1970 and 1971.

Snow supported the aims of the Cultural Revolution and appears to have believed it successful by the time of his visit: 'Mao's Thought had by 1970 permeated the whole nation' with several aims, including the smashing of all bourgeois thought.[43] He also emphasized that one Cultural Revolution would lead on to many more. However, what distressed him most about the Cultural Revolution was the cult of personality. He even raised it over breakfast with Mao, who told him that certain ultra-leftist officials had successfully opposed Snow's return to China in 1967 and 1968 for writing about it. Snow reported Mao as acknowledging that the personality cult had been overdone but that most of the epithets like 'great leader' and 'great helmsman' would be eliminated sooner or later.[44] The point is worth making because Snow was not alone among those sympathetic to the Chinese revolution in finding the Mao cult an extremely negative image.

Snow also reported on life and conditions in China as he found them. The images he puts forward are of a well fed, healthy, and adequately clothed people. The average citizen 'is free from bank mortgages, debt, and the fear of starvation and beggary which plagued his parents'.[45] On the other hand, Snow is critical of the lack of variety in the cinema and the lack of foreign news which is 'scant and carefully screened'. His picture is generally positive and shines with enthusiasm for China and its people, although it also includes criticisms. His conclusion of life in China is half joking, half serious: 'In short, China is, as some wit has remarked before me, a veritable sink of morality.'[46]

There were quite a few Western admirers of the morality and simplicity of Chinese life. The lack of obsession with material possessions, greed, and sex attracted several Western authors on China. Other than Snow, these included the Italian journalist Maria Macciocchi, the American psychologist Carol Tavris, capitalist David Rockefeller, and actress Shirley MacLaine. Some senior Christian clergymen, like Hewlett Johnson, saw China's morality and purity as essentially religious, because it freed people from the slavery of acquisitiveness and covetousness. Many challenged the Leys view on inequality in China, claiming that while its society was in no way perfectly equal, it was much less hierarchical than before 1949.[47]

Another contributor to positive images of China during the Cultural Revolution was the Swede Jan Myrdal who, with his wife Gun Kessle, revisited the village of Liu Ling in the late autumn of 1969. By then he had moved considerably towards sympathy for the Cultural Revolution: 'The reader might say I am biased in favour of China and the cultural revolution. Of course I am. Nobody can read what I have written these last years without seeing this.'[48]

The picture Myrdal paints of the Shaanxi village is very rosy. The book is a sequel to *Report from a Chinese Village* and emphasizes how much the standard of living has risen since 1962. Myrdal says 'it is vital to point out that the standard of living in Liu Ling has risen during the cultural revolution' and thus gives the credit to that movement for the improvement. It is not enough to talk of the Cultural Revolution merely as a power struggle. 'The basis of Chinese policy . . . is that all of China's hundreds of millions shall attain a better life',[49] and Myrdal conveys the image of success in that aim. He was the only Westerner to visit a Chinese village remote from a provincial capital during the decade 1966–76, stay there over a period of more than a few hours — the two remained in the village for two weeks — and return home to write up his impressions and information in detail (his wife took the photographs). The resultant book thus carried the stamp of on-the-spot research which was rare at a time when few Westerners were being allowed to visit China, and was duly influential as an image creator. Moreover, there were quite a few others who conveyed to the West an image of reasonable material prosperity and progress in China, even though their impressions were not based on such a stay in a remote village.[50]

Other major non-academic writers putting forward views favourable to the Cultural Revolution and to the situation in China at that time included William Hinton and Han Suyin. Hinton's essay *Turning Point in China*, published in 1972 and based on lectures he had been giving before various American audiences during 1970 and 1971, follows more or less exactly the line being given out at the time by the CCP. His book *Hundred Day War*, which came out the same year, traces the history of the Cultural Revolution till 1971 at Qinghua University in Beijing. He makes no attempt to hide the violence involved, but still considers the Cultural Revolution to have been both necessary and successful.

Han Suyin's view, which she put forward in many lectures, articles, and books, was likewise more or less identical with the line advocated at the time by the CCP. She believed 1966 would 'probably become, in history, the Year of Decision for China', among other reasons because it was 'the year of a Cultural Revolution involving a massive psychological and political campaign to reshape the motivation and socialist morality of 700 million people'.[51] In a lecture given in October 1968 she declared the Cultural Revolution 'the greatest mass movement that has ever been seen in the world' and 'a herald of worldwide mass movements to come',[52] and while a single lecture may not be image-formulating, it was typical of the sort of view expressed by a person who most certainly could claim to be so at the time. She was tremendously optimistic about how China and the world would develop, since for her the China of the Cultural Revolution represented the wave of the future. The last words of her book on what China would be like at the beginning of the twenty-first century, *China in the Year 2001*, and thus the punch line of her views on the matter, are 'already the future has entered our present. The year 2001 has begun, in China, today.'[53]

Conclusion

The Cultural Revolution forced China specialists in the West to rethink their own assumptions about their own society. It created a model of development which was alternative to traditional capitalism. While the Chinese revolution in general had done both these things, the Cultural Revolution pinpointed the issues with even sharper clarity. Many came out of the re-examination of values more convinced than ever of the superiority of Western capitalism and the freedom it claims to entail. But others responded quite differently, and with greater interest in, and sympathy for, the alternative model. What is clear is that the process was associated with a decisive change of Western images of China between 1966 and 1976. Westerners were more aware of China in 1976 than they had been a decade earlier; and they were somewhat less hostile towards it.

Naturally the Chinese of the 1980s assess the main Western writers of the Cultural Revolution decade according to their current view — that the Cultural Revolution was a more or less total disaster which set China back by more than a decade. They give Ryckmans the full credit he deserves for having seen through the Cultural Revolution at a time when their own official policy was pushing it. Conversely, they are critical of Snow for having been deceived by it, despite the continuing high reputation he enjoys among them for his earlier work and for his role in the Sino-American rapprochement.

It is now clear that the Cultural Revolution was a failure and a mistake, and Ryckmans' judgement about it was well placed. Yet the greater and more sympathetic awareness of China in Western images which followed it has proved permanent and beneficial. In this sense the radical lobby played a very positive role in the decade 1966–76, even though its members misinterpreted much of what was happening in China at the time.

12

Western Post-1976 Images and the Past

BY comparison with the preceding decade the years 1976–87 were a period of convergence of China and the West towards each other. In China, following the death of Mao Zedong in September 1976 and the fall of his main followers the 'gang of four' the next month, a new leadership arose headed by Deng Xiaoping, which acted to demote Mao Zedong's status in China's recent history. China moved from the radical collectivism of the Cultural Revolution decade to a much more open market socialism called 'socialism with Chinese characteristics'. Along with condemning the Cultural Revolution, the new leaders abandoned and changed the great majority of its policies.

China and the West each followed a formal policy of openness to the other and communications burgeoned. In Western countries, television documentaries, radio commentaries, press reports, and books about China appeared in unprecedented numbers and interest was never higher. People from Western countries travelled to China or lived there in numbers far larger than at any other time since 1949. While it would be a mistake to suggest that 'average Westerners' were well informed about China, they certainly knew more than at any other time in history. In the early 1980s, about 10 per cent of Americans considered they knew 'a great deal' about China,[1] but it is uncertain if many of them really had a yardstick of comparison by which to make such a judgement.

It is the aim of this chapter to explore two quite different aspects of the past in post-1976 Western images of China. The first is how Westerners view China during the last ten years of Mao Zedong's life, 1966 to 1976, now that they have grown used to a country which is 'open' to the Western world and the Chinese Communist Party has itself denounced the Cultural Revolution in the strongest possible terms. The second is how Westerners view the role of the pre-revolutionary past, or tradition, in China's present, meaning the decade or so separating the death of Mao and the completion of the writing of this book, that is 1976 to 1987.

Post-1976 Western Images of the Cultural Revolution Decade

The dominant Western image of the Cultural Revolution has at all times been very negative. But images of those years have tended to be influenced by current Chinese interpretations, so that nearly all streams of thought have moved against the Cultural Revolution as the Chinese Communist Party itself has done so.

At the forefront of the attack on the Cultural Revolution were those observers who had never had any time for it anyway. A case in point is Pierre Ryckmans, who has been able, on the authority of the CCP itself, to point to the correctness of his own judgements and predictions. Others had been generally positive about the Cultural Revolution at the time, but also turned not only against that movement but against China as a whole. A third group comprises those who were sympathetic to the Cultural Revolution at the time, but were influenced by the revelations the Chinese themselves made about it in the late 1970s and early 1980s. With the passage of time condemnation of the Cultural Revolution and its impact on China has become the nearly universal Western image of the last ten years of Mao's rule.

A leading contributor to the image of the Cultural Revolution, as China correspondent of the widely read and extremely influential *Time* magazine, has been Richard Bernstein. He regards the Cultural Revolution as so extreme as to be unbelievable and 'one of the most irrational occurrences in modern history', destructive of art and education and also murderous. 'Nobody knows how many people died during the Cultural Revolution, but the Chinese now say hundreds of thousands, maybe more.'[2] Bernstein was horrified by the personality cult and was not alone in this view. 'The chairman had used his last remaining power-base . . . to build up a semi-magical cult of his own personality' write two historians, who go on to denounce the suffering meted out to intellectuals and others.[3] Just as Fairbank had done at the onset of the Cultural Revolution, they also draw a comparison between the Red Guards and the Boxers of 1900.

Roger Garside, a British diplomat who lived in China from 1976 to 1979, wrote a book called *Coming Alive, China after Mao*, 'the story of how life returned to a nation that had been half-dead'. He described the Cultural Revolution years as 'an Orwellian nightmare' and suggested that China's 'coming alive' proved the relevance of that mainly Western phenomenon, liberal democracy.[4] There is a certain irony in the contrast between the Committee of Concerned Asian Scholars' 'overwhelming impression' of 'vitality' in 1971, as noted in the previous chapter, and Garside's verdict that the Chinese were half-dead in 1976.

Television programmes and films on China invariably put forward the same images of the Cultural Revolution. Destruction, regression, and irrationality are the chief features, whether the programme concerns the arts, the minority nationalities, religion, or general conditions. The famous 1981 Academy Award-winning documentary feature film *From Mao to Mozart: Isaac Stern in China*, recording the violinist's experiences and impressions of China, and especially its musical life, leaves suppression of artistic talent as the major image of the Cultural Revolution. Musicians were forced to clean lavatories and undertake other such demeaning tasks, but were not allowed to practise their art.

The brilliant British television series *The Heart of the Dragon*, which was shown throughout the Western world and translated into several major European languages, describes the Cultural Revolution as 'an outburst of hysterical fanaticism', which suppressed religion. It likens the utopianism of the Cultural Revolution to the 'religiously-based popular uprisings of imperial times'. 'But unlike them', the programme goes on, the Cultural Revolution 'was deliberately instigated from the capital; it was promoted, like the Nazi excesses, by mass-communications'. One of the results was that the young urban students who were the main adherents 'decided that their idealism had been manipulated. They had lost their youth for nothing; they had lost hope for the future and trust in their leaders, or in nearly all of them.'[5] The comparison with Nazi excesses is a particularly telling one in terms of the associations of cruelty and evil.

Quite a large part of the magnificent feature film *The Last Emperor* is set in the People's Republic years and the clear image it conveys of them is that the Chinese Communist Party did indeed save China. The governor of the prison where the former emperor is an inmate invariably treats him humanely and kindly and thus wins his respect and even affection. The end of the film is set in 1967 at the height of the Cultural Revolution, and shows the governor with a dunce's cap accused of being a reactionary, while Puyi comes to plead unsuccessfully on his behalf. It thus suggests the late 1960s as the black period of the generally positive era of the PRC. On the other hand, no violence is shown, nor is the Cultural Revolution blamed for Puyi's death, which also occurred in 1967.

One highly influential category of indictments of the Maoist years, and especially of the Cultural Revolution, is books recording the experiences of individual Chinese, but actually written in large measure by Westerners. A well known and certainly image-formulating example is *Son of the Revolution* by Liang Heng and his American wife Judith Shapiro, first published in 1983. The 1984 Fontana paperback edition carries on its front cover an extract from a review saying that the book is 'a terrifying tale, so vividly written it almost makes you feel you were there . . . and thank God you were not'. The nature of the images conveyed by the book is summed up fairly accurately by the extract, for the major thrust of Liang Heng's experiences was of continual obeisance to political ideology, of corrupt bureaucrats interfering incessantly in his life and those of others, of witnessing violence and cruelty on a horrific scale. Asked in an examination to write a composition on 'the words I have in my heart to tell the Party', his private reaction, which naturally he did not write at the time, was 'what I had in my heart was bitterness, my life's accumulated bitterness, the accumulated bitterness of the lives of the people around me'.[6] And the concluding lesson from the narrative is 'the danger that lies in blind obedience'.[7] Although Liang Heng's life had not been entirely without bright spots, the overall impact of the book is savage and near total condemnation of the Cultural Revolution.

Son of the Revolution reads like a novel in many ways, but is in fact a record of actual events. Among novels published since 1976 which use the real happenings of the People's Republic, including the Cultural Revolution decade, as their background is the particularly popular *Till Morning Comes*, by Han Suyin, several of whose works have already come under discussion. *Till Morning Comes* is unquestionably image-formulating, even though Han Suyin's status as a commentator on China has declined in recent years because of her tendency to give full support to whatever regime happens to be in power in China.

The core of this very long novel is the love between a Chinese doctor called Jen Yong and an American, Stephanie Ryder, set against the history of China from the mid-1940s until the early 1970s. Stephanie remains in China until 1957 when both are attacked during the anti-rightist campaign, she as 'an agent of American cultural imperialism' and he as a rightist. She goes back to the United States to live, while he is sent to work in a remote region. Stephanie returns to China only at the very end of the novel when the forthcoming Nixon visit enables Americans to visit China. By that time, Jen Yong has been publicly humiliated and later beaten to death by young Red Guards during the Cultural Revolution. Stephanie learns of his fate only after her return to China.

Han Suyin had clearly changed her mind about the history of the People's Republic and in particular the Cultural Revolution. She had earlier declared the late 1950s as the time when the mass line and revolutionary enthusiasm would accelerate China's passage to socialism and transformation,[8] but now the anti-rightist campaign of 1957 had become an early stage in the rot of harmful revolutionary fanaticism. The Cultural Revolution no longer carried the image of immense progress and optimism we saw in her work in the previous chapter, but instead one of killing good people in cruel ways. She portrays the Cultural Revolution as the classic example of a movement which causes young people to carry out destructive and sadistic actions because they are misled by an excess of revolutionary enthusiasm. As had happened in the past, her thinking had changed to accord with the current official policy laid down by the CCP.

Since the Party must remain optimistic, it follows that the overall image of China and the Chinese to come from this novel is an optimistic one. The climax, or at least conclusion, is the reconciliation between China and the United States. The last sentence of the novel is 'Love had come to her, at last',[9] because as an American she was now able to go back to China. This is the 'morning' of the title, following the night the darkest hour of which was the Cultural Revolution.

For Robert Elegant in *Dynasty* the overriding Chinese phenomenon to endure against all political turmoil is the family, but for Han Suyin in *Till Morning Comes* it is China itself and patriotism. In an interview with American senators near the end of the novel, Stephanie is asked why her husband chose to remain in China. Her answer clearly reflects the view familiar from the author herself in *A Many-Splendoured Thing* and other works:

There are millions like him in China. The non-Communist intelligentsia. Who elected to remain in Communist China. Because 'China is China is China.' Immortal, forever. Not because of communism. . . .

They have seen the Communist Government at work. However abhorrent, authoritarian, crassly bureaucratic it is, it has also done an enormous amount of good for the ordinary people of China. For the ninety-five percent who were living in gross misery. . . .

My husband is Chinese. He loves his country and his people. He is a patriot, as are so many like him. Should we not understand, respect that patriotism?[10]

And when Stephanie is informed about her husband's death, the novelist adds that the gang who had murdered him had been caught, thus indicating that killing on the pretext of supporting revolution was no longer an approved action in China. Her father-in-law comments: 'There will be trouble still, but . . . I am hopeful, daughter. China is China. Is China. She has gone through so much tumult, so many centuries of upheaval. She endures. We shall endure.'[11]

Han Suyin can turn against the Cultural Revolution but retain faith in China and even its system. One novel set in the period beginning at the same time as *Till Morning Comes* ends is *The Chinese Assassin* by Anthony Grey, a journalist who was himself imprisoned in China for two years during

the Cultural Revolution. In view of this experience it comes
as no surprise that Grey does not share Han Suyin's optimism,
but gives a picture of bleak pessimism. The novel is about
the intrigue and counter-intrigue, both Chinese and international, of the last five years of Mao Zedong's life, that is from
1971 to 1976. The main images of China are of a country
ruled by a kind of imperial court, where the imperial tyrant,
Mao, has his torture chamber to keep control over his courtiers
and rival claimants to his throne. Socialist ideals are totally
irrelevant. Neither the revolution as a whole nor the Cultural Revolution has changed anything significant: 'The modern
scientific truths of Marxism have become the same empty
symbol to be hoisted aloft in the same vicious and unprin-
cipled personal intrigues that had racked the imperial courts.'
It was true that 'much had changed for the better in the lives
of the ordinary people. But it was a precarious change. The
great unknowing masses were still helpless prey to the caprices
of the secret court of the modern Son of Heaven, Mao.'[12] At
the time of the Cultural Revolution itself, fundamental change
was what many Westerners emphasized, even though some
saw in that a cause for praise, others for criticism or denunciation.
But such an image comes under strong challenge in Grey's
novel.

For Chinese people 'intimate contact with outsiders'[13] is
dangerous to the state and hence forbidden, except under
very special circumstances. Grey portrays Chinese power-
holders as both subtle and cruel. Their major talents include
the ability to persuade people to think in the correct, orthodox
way through 'thought reform'. A particularly powerful image,
not only about the last half of the Cultural Revolution decade
but about China in general, is expressed by the novel's main
character, a British journalist: 'I have learned, I think, above
all else, that nothing in China is what it seems to be at first
sight.'[14]

As usual, there were counter-images of the Cultural Revolution decade, mainly in the late 1970s, but even into the
1980s. In the first place, some observers writing at that time
could still see good in the basic aims of the Cultural Revolution,
even though they criticized its excesses. One influential
encyclopedia, completed in July 1978, considered that the
Cultural Revolution had brought about 'major reforms in

education, factory management, economic planning, medical care, and other areas of Chinese life', apparently all desirable. On the other hand, its authors believed the Cultural Revolution 'had been a traumatic event for China' and caused a great deal of harm and disruption. 'Not only were old wounds, both personal and political, reopened, but many new conflicts were created.' Moreover, 'the experiments to implement the egalitarian and participatory principles of the Cultural Revolution did not always progress smoothly'.[15] What is striking is that the authors still accepted the genuineness of the Cultural Revolution and did not even lay blame on the 'gang of four' for its failures. A guide-book which claims to be the 'world's best-selling guide to the People's Republic of China' and has an author common with the encyclopedia just cited, put forward a very similar view of the Cultural Revolution, even in its 1982–3 edition. The 'egalitarian spirit of that movement' was thwarted by 'unexpected chaos and violence', despite which 'the worst of the disruptions had ended' by the late 1960s allowing the 'major reforms in education, factory management, economic planning, and medical care' noted above to take shape.[16]

A textbook of the People's Republic general history, influential among tertiary students in the United Kingdom and Australia, followed a similar line. Completed in December 1979, its author conceded that 'many of the results of the Cultural Revolution were extremely negative'. Nevertheless, he saw some major social benefits. 'From whichever perspective one cares to look at them, one cannot deny that, for many people, the events of that time were a truly liberating experience. People began to ask questions which they had never considered before and came to a new understanding about the nature of power in Chinese society.' The author at that time believed the costs had been worthwhile. 'For all its excess, the achievements of the Chinese revolution have been immense.'[17]

Even in the mid-1980s there were observers who thought that particular experiments of the Cultural Revolution had some merit. Orville Schell considered it 'would be a distortion of fact' to write off the collective experience of agriculture as a total failure. 'Analysts of China's economy generally agree that collectivisation worked well in about a third of China's communes, had mixed results in a third, and was a disaster

in the last third.'[18] Schell acknowledged the short-term gains
in living standards that had been made when he wrote, but
believed the long-term costs had been underestimated. What
he perceived as total decollectivization he thus saw as a mistake
which ignored the possible advantages in the system advocated
during the Cultural Revolution.

Images of Tradition in Post-1976 China

We come now to images of China in the period 1976–87 itself,
as seen by Westerners contemporary with those years. But
the focus remains on the past, and the strength of its role
in present-day China.

The revival of tradition is a feature of post-1976 China which
receives attention from virtually all commentators. China is
a prisoner of its past in a way that other countries are not.
Journalist Fox Butterfield, in one of the more moderate passages
of a book savagely critical of contemporary Chinese realities,
writes that 'the longer I stayed in China the more I was struck
by the number of strong resonances to the past, if not exact
similarities'. In particular he was impressed by 'the specific
gravity of China's past' in 'the patterns of personal relations
in daily life, like *guan-xi* and the *li*, the importance of connections,
names, and face'.[19] Another author, Myra Roper, an academic
generally much more sympathetic to China and its political
system, opens her book by pointing out the inescapable
significance of the cliché 'the Past in China's Present'. The
lesson is that 'the beginning of our understanding of the People's
Republic is some acquaintance with China's long history'.[20]
An even stronger opinion comes from a well received and
influential encyclopedia of China. 'It is obvious that China
cannot free itself from traditional Chineseness overnight', says
the introduction, plausibly enough. It concludes that 'Despite
all efforts of the People's Republic to stress its new universalist
vision, the world will continue to find it hard to believe that
the new Chineseness can really be so different from the old
image which China says it has discarded.'[21]

Picture books readily give such images through their focus
on scenes showing the unreformed side of China, and the
magnificent coloured photography characteristic of contemporary coffee-table books merely accentuates the point. A

photograph of old-style junks on the front dust cover and a classical drama performer making up on the back cover create an image of a people among whom tradition remains strong. A photograph entitled 'The Imperial Grand Canal in the Suzhou suburbs' showing houses from long ago lining the ancient waterway with only little sign of modernity; and another of two peasants before and after a bullock-drawn plough, subtitled 'For 5000 years the Chinese peasant has endured hardships', reinforce the impression of a nation which sticks to its old ways, no matter how arduous or backward these may be.[22] A particularly well known picture book is *Chinese Encounters*, which includes extensive commentary by the playwright Arthur Miller. It places a strong emphasis on history, with pictures showing how the people blend with their surroundings, such as peasants working in the fields or elsewhere, or people enjoying the splendours of temples, palaces or other old places.[23] Miller himself sees the photographs as 'always drawn to the lasting, the beautiful, the evidences of history's grace'.[24]

Clearly there are many in the West who share the perception of a continuing and overwhelming tradition in China. The television series *The Heart of the Dragon* by its very title and structure makes the same point. Despite its focus on the People's Republic, it devotes as much space to the past as the present, and that means much less the recent history than the period of the great imperial dynasties. In numerous places a contemporary characteristic of China or the Chinese is explained by reference to its similarity with the past. An example follows from the question of how friends and even members of the same family could betray each other during the Cultural Revolution just for a belief.

In order to achieve the betrayal of friend by friend, the Chinese leaders had to attack the historical figure who represented the opposite principle, and who stood for hierarchy, order and relationships unshakeable by any difference of mere belief. Hence the slogan which amazed the West in the late stages of the Cultural Revolution, 'Criticize Lin Biao and Confucius'. Could one imagine a slogan like 'Criticize Richard Nixon and Aristotle' being carried on placards through the streets of Washington in 1973? China's is a very ancient culture, and two and a half thousand years after his death one man could still represent an entire way of thinking and living: one that has lasted through the Cultural Revolution in many ways and is still part of the texture of Chinese life today.[25]

The passage raises a few points. First, the emphasis is clearly on continuity in China, rather than change. Even the Cultural Revolution becomes part of a grand continuity. A second point is the contrast with the West. It is true that even had Aristotle been an American, few would have wished to denounce Nixon for being like him. Westerners, and especially Americans, perceive themselves as relatively free of their own history, of their own traditions.

The French scholar Marie-Claire Bergère places the question of change versus continuity in ideological terms. She considers that 'liberalism of Anglo-Saxon inspiration' in the first half of the twentieth century and Marxist revolution in the second half have both come up against the powerful barrier represented by a coherent and self-sufficient culture which continues to impede modernization. She raises the question whether with time 'the 1949 revolution will wane on our historical horizon just as mountains seem to lose their height as one moves further away from them'.[26] She implies the answer 'yes, to some extent', and thus places a strong emphasis on the power of tradition as opposed to the difficulties in the way of substantial and meaningful change.

Are we then back to the old stereotype about the unchanging Chinese? Certainly there are hints of it in some of the literature. One popular writer, Orville Schell, notes that 'the foundation of Chinese agriculture has always been the communally constructed waterworks that provided irrigation', transport of grain and protection from flood. He goes on to note that when the CCP came to power in 1949, 'like any dynasty it, too, turned its attention to the waterworks upon which the salvation of China depended'.[27] Is this an echo of the Wittfogelian theory?

The answer is that it is an echo, even a strong one, but only that. Neither Schell nor *The Heart of the Dragon* goes on to suggest that China cannot change, or that it has not done so. Bergère specifically allows for the possibility of change, and the overwhelming theme of Schell's book is the extent of Westernization. One could perhaps quote the introduction of an influential tourist guide-book, so popular that among some of the young backpackers so numerous in China in the

1980s it is known as 'the green bible': 'the outstanding feature of China is that, after what seems like several hundred years of utter stagnation, it is now making a determined effort to modernise itself and catch up with the west'.[28] My contacts with Western tourists, students, and others, suggest that such an opinion is widespread enough to be called a strong image.

Picture books convey a perception of change, even while affirming the weight of tradition. One coloured and glossy photographic treasure-house of China's capital city bears on its front cover a charming picture of a traditional stone lion between the two front paws of which a small girl hides in fun from her father. Both are completely unconcerned with the imperial significance of such a lion. Other pictures show groups of Chinese tourists within the former imperial palaces.[29] At one time it would have cost ordinary people their lives to enter this 'Forbidden City', but now only a few *fen*. Even more striking are two pictures of Chinese tourists in Zhongnanhai just near the imperial palaces.[30] This has been since 1949 the area where Mao Zedong and other senior members of the Chinese leadership have lived, and it is off limits to foreigners. But the very idea of Chinese or any other tourists visiting the home area of the imperial family or senior officials would have been anathema not so long ago.

Changelessness is not a dominant view. But there is an image that China changes less and more slowly than other places, in particular the West. As one character in a popular thriller about money and power observes: 'Things are changing, though one week in China is a day anywhere else.'[31] The slow pace of change is one reason why people should understand China's history. The negation of the Cultural Revolution has brought back all kinds of traditions many had considered eliminated by the revolution. So the image is widespread that the revolution was not as important for China's overall history as most observers once thought. There are some identifiable characteristics of the Chinese which have endured and which mark them out as distinct from any other people on earth.

On the whole this past is seen as something glorious which has benefited the Chinese of today. The attention given by Western tourists and picture books to palaces, old buildings, gardens, and temples[32] appears to bear this out. The Great Wall remains even now the single most vivid image of China in the West. Anybody who is anybody must climb it. It is an achievement so magnificent that 'Astronauts have said it is the only man-made object visible from space.'[33] The fact that the quoted astronauts have omitted to say how far out in space one would need to go before the Wall is no longer visible is neither here nor there as far as images are concerned. A small book on China for children, while applauding governmental changes, stresses that 'some basic concepts' of the Chinese have remained constant, for instance that 'the elderly are still respected and taken care of'. Happiness comes from being self-content. 'A person who always wants more than he has is never happy. Therefore, people are urged to compromise a little in their careers and business operations.' There follows the observation that 'In the United States everyone is urged to get to the top',[34] implying that perhaps Americans can learn something from China. The school of thought which marvels at the age of a tradition and wants to retain it is strong in the West where some people still hanker after certain lost traditions.

A Westerner who exults in the combination of Chinese traditional social and aesthetic values, a man who makes no pretence to expertise on China but by the deservedly high esteem in which he is held both in the West and in China is certainly an image-formulator, is the playwright Arthur Miller. After visiting China in 1978, he wrote:

China surprised us in a hundred ways, perhaps most of all by her pervasive beauty. There is an instinct for aesthetic harmony among the Chinese, even in the thoughtless way a woman will arrange a handful of leeks she is washing by a brook, setting them down in a fan shape. The Chinese child is a triumph of humanity, and in the aged there is a sort of dignity that can come only from social respect and a decent tradition. There is also a certain rightness of proportion, a native taste in objects held in the hand. And a poetic tradition inconceivable in the West — where else in the world is a leader's calligraphy of importance, and where could it evoke pride that it is elegant? Indeed, the use of imagery in political discourse threatens to turn China into a fairyland for the unwary foreigner. And what people so profoundly understands food?[35]

One of those images to revive together with the emphasis on tradition is the 'exoticism' of China. This was a dominant image before 1949, but appeared to decline after that, especially during the Cultural Revolution. However, less well-informed television programmes and other media clearly retain it even in the 1980s. An example is an American television documentary called *Cycling through China*. Released in 1982 it describes the journey through parts of southern China by a group of American entertainers. Although it is supposed to be about the present, there is also a good deal of focus on China's great past and traditional arts. The 'hostess', actress Kate Jackson, begins by telling us her own view: the very word 'China' evokes images of mystery and a forbidden land. In other words, this is an exotic, strange and 'mysterious' country remote from our consciousness, but perhaps mainly because of that still attractive and desirable.

An alternative image, especially among strongly anti-communist observers, is to view the revival of tradition as fraudulent. 'China is in the process of putting together a cultural and historic monster, a kind of archeological Frankenstein, for the exclusive benefit of foreign consumers', says Tiziano Terzani,[36] the well known Italian journalist who was expelled from China in 1984 for his critical reporting. He was responding to a visit to an ancient Daoist temple in Shanxi province. He sees the past as something desirable, which still lingers in the minds of people 'left disoriented and insecure by the policies of the past 35 years',[37] but, in opposition to such ordinary people, Chinese traditional culture is under strong attack from its enemy communism.[38] He is especially shocked by 'the destruction of old Peking'. Once a 'wonderful' city, it is now 'dying'. Its walls, gates, arches and most of its temples, palaces, and gardens are gone. 'More and more of centuries-old Peking vanishes every day under the blows of hammers and the crushing of bulldozers.'[39]

Conclusion

There are thus major exceptions to the proposition that the strength of China's tradition is a reason why the West should admire China. The revival of female infanticide and some sexist aspects of the treatment of women point in precisely the opposite direction and will be considered in the next two chapters. Terzani's view has enough support in the West to rate as an image. A moving story about how a young man tried to make amends to the teacher he ill-treated during the late 1960s links the traditional and recent past and portrays both as negative. 'The traditional obedience to authority and the tight political controls that had brought the nightmare' of the Cultural Revolution upon China in the first place 'still remained' in the post-Mao period.[40] The story is reprinted in a magazine which calls itself 'the world's most-read' and can consequently claim to be both a reflector and formulator of images.[41]

Yet this writer's reading of the literature, audio-visual media, and other evidence suggests that overall the retention of the past in China's present is indeed not only a strong but a positive image for Westerners. One sign is the apparent preference for the distant over the very recent past. There is something beautiful about the ancient traditions and culture, whereas the Cultural Revolution is redolent with ugliness. What is most visible to Westerners about the distant past are the fine, positive, or magnificent features. But they see or hear very little indeed which suggests that the Cultural Revolution caused anything but suffering and destruction. Both the distant past and the Cultural Revolution had their cruel features, but at least the former did not suppress creative talent or artistic imagination, and has left behind visible monuments of which every Chinese can be proud.

Perhaps the key phrase in the images discussed in this chapter is the one cited from Han Suyin's novel: 'China is China is China'. Not a very profound or original statement, it is nevertheless open to some interesting interpretations. One is that China is unique and hence totally different from all other nations. Another is that China is unchangeable or nearly so. A third, closely related to the second suggestion, is that history weighs more heavily on China than on Western, or other, countries.

The first of these interpretations, the image of China's uniqueness, would be borne out by the material in this chapter. China's past is so extensive, so varied and so long, that it could hardly avoid rendering the country unique. While it is true that all countries are in a sense unique, an argument could probably be sustained that in the long haul of history, China has been subjected less to outside influence than most other civilizations.

The discussion of the issue of how strong is the past in

the present led to the conclusion that while Westerners may perceive China as less suceptible to change than other, principally Western, countries, few any longer accept the stereotype of unchangeability. Still, history certainly weighs upon China. But surely it weighs upon every country, since nobody can fully escape the past. Yet the vastness of China's still backward countryside, the enormous peasant population, lend credence to the image which binds China more closely to its traditions, to its past, than is familiar to the peoples of the West.

Karl Marx believed that 'the tradition of all the dead generations weighs like a nightmare on the brain of the living'.[42] Though he had more Europe in mind than Asia, let alone China, his dictum is obviously applicable also to that country. But there could be wide disagreement over the extent to which the negative value judgement which likens tradition to a nightmare requires revision.

13

Images of Post-1976 China, I: Politics and the Economy

IN this writer's perception, China has changed and is changing very rapidly since 1976. It is legitimate to date the last period of images from that time. The range of images presented to the West continues to be vast and even to expand, especially since the formal establishment of diplomatic relations between the United States and the People's Republic at the beginning of 1979. Because of the enormous scope of Western images since 1976 it is appropriate to focus attention on a few major topics, most of them selected not only for their importance but also to give a clear idea of how Western images have changed or remained the same over time. In this chapter we deal with a few political and economic aspects, including population policy and foreign relations.

Government

Western observers are still fascinated with leadership. Generally their image of the 1976–87 leadership was extremely positive and in the case of Deng Xiaoping, in the West overwhelmingly the most famous living Chinese, quite surprisingly so. The American magazine *Success!* selected him as the 'success story of the year' for 1985. Harrison Salisbury, who wrote the feature article on him, claimed that he had 'put China on a new and successful fast track, and he has not hesitated to borrow from the West'. No praise could be higher than that. 'The whole Chinese economy has surged forward', he continued, because Deng had 'introduced free enterprise, entrepreneurship, price competition, stock offerings, and even toyed with reopening the wild and woolly Shanghai Stock Exchange', in other words behaved rather like a capitalist.[1] In 1985 *Time* magazine also selected Deng as 'man of the year' for the second time, the first being in 1978.[2]

Perhaps just as striking, and in some ways even more so, is the extremely positive image which Derek Davies, the British editor of the influential *Far Eastern Economic Review*, cast about Deng. Davies's view was that 'for my money Deng Xiaoping is carving out a sizable claim for the title Man of the Last Quarter of the 20th century'. Davies was impressed by the changes and progress Deng had wrought in a country 'once thought of as a giant buried inertly under its party and the bureaucracy'. But whereas Salisbury emphasized turning to the West, Davies's focus was on Chinese tradition. Deng's 'fabled pragmatism sits comfortably within the Confucian tradition of moderation'. Above all he admired the Chinese leader's optimism, his belief that problems 'can be solved as long as common sense prevails'.[3]

Davies praised Deng for his resilience in repairing a career which seemed to lie in ruins 'within a totalitarian Maoist society', and the image of Mao's China as a totalitarian or police state was widespread. Much of the right wing and even some of the extreme left in the West continue to draw similar conclusions about China. One magazine sums up Fox Butterfield's lengthy account of China's 'control apparatus' as describing a 'horrifying police state'.[4] This is a correct understanding of Butterfield's chapter 'The Control Apparatus', which dwells at length on restrictions placed on the people's lives, including their most private affairs, and quotes one Chinese as complaining 'we are like caged animals'.[5] Although Butterfield does not actually call China a police state, he does use the word totalitarianism to designate that country in the 1980s.[6]

The other extreme is perhaps represented by the view, put forward in a much used guide-book, which sees the Chinese government as 'promoting citizens' rights and democratic processes in its continuing effort to modernize by the end of this century'. The image is of a 'historic breakthrough', by which the PRC is introducing freedom and democracy through 'legal codification'. Marxism is an appropriate combination of tradition and modernity. It resembles the tenets of Daoism in stressing the interconnections of human experience and knowledge, and

Confucianism in placing social relationships at the core of its political theory.[7]

Few Westerners hold an image of China as being as free as their own society. However, a widespread image of contemporary China is to point out the totalitarian and authoritarian traditions within which the present government operates and the immense problems it faces. As 'the green bible' puts it: 'for China to have come even as far as it has today [in the area of democracy] is extraordinary. So far the Communists have not delivered all that they promised, yet it seems unlikely that anyone else could have done a better job.'[8] A scholarly French account conveys an image of 'supervized liberty' (*liberté surveillée*), in which Deng Xiaoping confronts the difficulty of 'granting more freedom but refusing complete freedom'. He faces dangers in such an approach because he risks 'alienating the old élites without winnning new supporters'.[9] The television series *The Heart of the Dragon* draws attention to the Confucian tradition of 'rites' (*li*), signifying 'all behaviour in accordance with the requirements of the moral order'. It sees in this concept 'one of the chief reasons why the Chinese have been able to live in large family groups or modern collectives, apparently with less friction than other peoples'.[10] The image is not so much that no 'control apparatus' exists, but that the main basis of social order is not fear or compulsion but moral suasion.

The 'totalitarian model' of Chinese politics is not the dominant image nowadays. According to *Asiaweek* in 1983, 'most observers agree' that China 'is less of a dictatorship now than it was ten years ago', a correct perception of American opinion. It goes on to suggest, again rightly, that 'the current fad of writing off China', an allusion to works like Butterfield's, is due more to American trends than to Chinese. Specifically, because of the heightened nationalism associated with the Reagan administration's accession to power, 'some academics and mediamen have apparently felt a new desire (or need) to assert the superiority of American values and institutions worldwide'.[11]

Another widespread image of Chinese administration is inefficiency and bureaucratism. John Fraser, who was for two years in the late 1970s the *Toronto Globe and Mail* reporter in China, claims that there was no central control and that 'the primitive communication system plus the size of the bureaucracy enables local officials to carry on much as they want to'. Such a view is at variance with the 'police state' model, which would normally presuppose efficiency. Fraser appears aware of this even though the chaos he describes 'does not necessarily work for benefit of the people',[12] and his overall picture of Chinese governance is sharply negative.

A question of great importance for a socialist society is equality. Here again images vary greatly. Both Bernstein and Butterfield paint a shockingly unequal society in which rank, power, and privileges are rampant and ubiquitous.[13] Neither, it is true, goes quite as far as Pierre Ryckmans, whose views on this subject were discussed in Chapter 11. Butterfield concedes that 'in purely monetary terms . . . the Communists still maintain the appearance of their old egalitarianism' but goes on to argue that money is not what matters; 'the real differences are the hidden privileges, prerogatives, and perquisites that go with political status'.[14]

At the other extreme are those whose image is of a China where the ideals and reality of egalitarianism more or less correspond. One such is Clyde Cameron, a minister in the Australian Labor government of Gough Whitlam. He visited China in 1977, 1978, and 1979 and drew an extremely favourable impression of social equality in China. He saw 'no evidence of either opulence or abject poverty'. 'No-one dies of gluttony or of starvation.' 'Housing is not luxurious but it is cheap and no-one goes without shelter.' 'Privately-owned motor cars are not permitted but in China that rule applies to the leaders as well as to the led.'[15] Cameron makes no claims to great learning on China, but he does speak for a body of opinion and certainly both represents and helps formulate images.

Numerous contacts with Westerners on the subject lead this writer to the view that the dominant image on the question of equality lies somewhere in between these two extremes. Such an image recognizes the widespread existence of privilege and corruption, and the continuation of a hierarchy among Party and government workers. The CCP is an élite in political and power terms, not surprising since in Leninist theory 'the party is *supposed* to be an élite of sorts'.[16] On the other hand, such a view gives the CCP credit for some degree of sincerity in creating a society much less unequal than that of the past. It sees China as far less unequal than other societies of a comparable level of economic development. According to a widely used scholarly textbook on China's political system, 'in general, contemporary Chinese society is not marked by powerful class distinctions'. The authors do indeed see 'differences in income, social status, and political influence among different strata of the population', but consider 'they have a relatively moderate character'.[17]

Many see inequalities as having widened in the years 1976–87 as a result of the new policies followed by the government. One widely used general history of the People's Republic, and generally quite sympathetic to it, claims that such growing inequalities have spawned resentment in some quarters and could 'conceivably nourish a backlash of opposition'.[18] The context of this image is of the strong, even 'revolutionary',[19] economic growth and reform on which China has recently embarked.

The Economy

Over the period 1976–7, the open-door policy became a major part of the government blueprint for China's economic development. Although 'openness to the outside' (*duiwai kaifang*), as the Chinese term literally means, did not apply only to Western countries, they did occupy a major section of foreign dealings with China under the policy. Moreover, Westerners saw themselves as paramount in economic dealings with China and the new policy designed, in a sense, especially for them. Western business and government circles were particularly positive about the new economic policies, because these opened the possibilities of investment and more customers. The overriding image such people held of China from 1976 to 1987 from an economic point of view was of being a potential source of large-scale profits.

China's large population has made it a market attractive to the West for a long time. However, there appears to be a better prospect of this than on previous occasions, because the large population is not only larger than ever but also better able to buy the sorts of goods Westerners might sell. 'For foreign investors', writes one reporter, 'the prospect of having access to a market of 1 billion consumers no longer seems like a pipedream.' The reason she gives is that 'the Chinese — in particular the rural population — are getting richer and now want visible improvements to their standard of living: they aspire to their own colour TV sets, refrigerators, trucks, washing machines and better radios, bicycles and clothing'.[20] One popular novel, which its publisher presents as a 'shattering superthriller of ultimate high-finance global warfare', ends with the central character, an American, leasing an islet from the City of Shanghai for 50 years in order to live and do business there. He intends 'to build trade between China and the rest of the world' because he believes that 'in several years, maybe less, this will be the largest trading city in the world'.[21]

Despite such surprisingly positive and optimistic images, the realities do not appear, as of the mid-1980s, to be matching expectations, let alone hopes. Western (and Japanese) business people actually living in China were sending out expressions if not of desperation then certainly of strong disappointment. Late in 1985 the University of Manchester's Nigel Campbell directed a survey among 115 of the more than 500 foreign companies in Beijing. Out of a scale of one to five measuring satisfaction with financial relations, American companies registered only 2.9. Foreign business people considered that the Chinese drove far too hard a bargain in their transactions. As many as 86 per cent of respondents, including those from Western Europe, the United States, and Japan, believed the Chinese treated foreign business in a way tailored 'to exact the maximum amount of money in the shortest possible time'. The majority considered that charges for offices and local staff were unreasonable. Campbell's summation of present and prediction of future images was: 'People are lining up because China is overselling. But sooner or later, the message will get through' that China is not a particularly attractive market. As if to back up his view, the Chinese Ministry of Foreign Economic Relations and Trade issued figures on 30 July 1986 which showed that contracted foreign investment had fallen by 20 per cent in the first half of 1986 as compared to the same period the year before. The Chinese government responded by trying to take measures to improve the economic environment for foreign companies, with what success was unclear as of the end of 1987. Nevertheless, even Campbell's survey had shown that a small majority of foreign firms believed that negotiation with Chinese officials had speeded up, providing hope for improvement in economic relations and greater profits over time. But there may need to be fairly rapid results. Forty-one per cent of European but only 21 per cent of American companies had told Campbell's survey that they would be willing to subsidize their Chinese operations for more than 11 years.[22]

The prevailing image of the current state and future prospects of the Chinese economy in the mid-1980s is probably not too far from the reports of the World Bank. These are examples of works which both reflect and also formulate Western economic thinking. The first major World Bank study of the Chinese economy was completed in 1981 and published in 1983; it 'broadly endorsed China's economic reforms and was widely influential as the most comprehensive study of the Chinese economy yet undertaken'.[23] Its successor was completed in May 1985 and published in October that year by the Johns Hopkins University Press; and is worth some discussion as an economic image of China in the 1980s.

The 1985 World Bank report quotes the Chinese government's stated aim of quadrupling the gross value of industrial and agricultural output, and increasing national income per person from about US$300 to US$800 between 1980 and 2000. This aim 'seems feasible' because of, and assuming, two factors: China's 'unusually slow' population growth, about 1 per cent per year, and its consistently and 'unusually high' investment rate.[24] It calls for more efficient use of available resources, including labour, and regards them as the key to modernization, outweighing in importance even availability of energy or access to advanced foreign technology. The report states that, in these terms, the 'conditions for rapid, sustained growth are at present far from fully met in China, except in agriculture, where outstanding progress has been made in recent years with the introduction of the production responsibility system'.[25] It advocates greater use of market regulation to stimulate innovation and efficiency, and expansion of the service sector, which in 1985 occupied less than 20 per cent of the gross national product, far less than its share of gross national product in India, Indonesia, South Korea, or Japan.

The World Bank report supports China's open-door policy and suggests that greater involvement in the world economy is necessary to introduce modern technology, 'but also — more importantly — to increase the efficiency with which all resources are used'. Although this policy is essential 'to achieve rapid, sustained growth', the report acknowledges certain risks in it, such as exposing China to inflation and fluctuations in world demands for industrial products and increased regional inequalities.[26] Despite criticisms, the report is essentially optimistic about China's economic future and strongly in support of the basics of present policy. The conclusion of the section entitled 'Overview' is that 'China's long-term development objectives seem attainable in principle, and if recent experience is any guide, there is a good chance that they will be attained in practice'.[27] The thrust of the report will most certainly promote a positive image of the Chinese economy in Western business communities, as well as encouraging them to continue investing in and trading with China.

The singling out of the agricultural sector for special praise due to the production responsibility system has become a persistent feature of Western images of the Chinese economy. An American report of 1983 on China the previous year stated that 'agriculture remained a relative bright spot in the Chinese economic picture'. The new system had 'succeeded in unleashing latent productivity and quickly improving peasant incomes'. The report also expressed worry that the system would 'widen inequality in the countryside'.[28] The British Granada television series *Inside China*, first screened in 1983, includes a programme called 'The Newest Revolution' on Chinese agriculture in the 1980s; it portrays an image of rising prosperity in a village near Wuxi, Jiangsu province.

This emphasis on the countryside brings the question of images to the realm of food consumption and the standard of living of some four-fifths of the Chinese people. These are matters which do not merely interest economists and business people but others as well.

Extremely negative views about the state of the rural diet down to the late 1970s were pushed not only by the representatives of the 'current fad of writing off China',[29] to whom reference was made earlier, but others as well. Thus *The Heart of the Dragon* quoted the State Statistical Bureau in 1978 as estimating average food consumption in China at 2,311 calories a day, as against a record by John L. Buck that it stood at 2,280 calories a day in the 1920s. What this implied was that 'in the supposedly evil days of "warlord rule", there had been a level of food consumption possibly not attained until the very end of the half century of war, civil war and central planning that followed'.[30] The programme does go on to say that food consumption grew spectacularly between 1978 and 1982, reaching an average of 2,666 calories a day in the latter year. The situation was still precarious, however, due to the 'inherited problems' and 'slender reserves' of the Chinese. In particular, it points out an inherent contradiction between the need to keep population growth down, in order to push consumption up, and the fact that the return of family farming which results from the production responsibility system encourages peasants to want more labour units, that is, sons.[31] This 'paradox' emerges also from the programme 'The Newest Revolution' in the series *Inside China*, and elsewhere; it is discussed not only by China specialists but others as well so often that it must be regarded as an 'image' of contemporary rural China. However, conversations with numerous Western tourists and residents in China from various countries have convinced this writer that another, and much stronger, image sees the people, both urban and rural, as well fed and clothed with no starvation and hardly any malnutrition. The World Bank report came to the conclusion that 'despite its long history of food problems, China's per capita consumption of calories and protein is currently similar to the average for middle-income countries'.[32]

To illustrate the dominant image of good and improving diet and standard of living some discussions of markets can be cited. The first refers to Chongqing in the autumn of 1979 and comes from the acid pen of Richard Bernstein. He describes the principal meat and vegetable market in the city as 'truly abysmal, unprosperous, empty, depressing, even shocking. There were people in large numbers but there was, almost literally, nothing for them to buy.' His only concession to an alternative point of view is an afterthought: 'Perhaps an afternoon in fall was a bad time to judge.'[33]

There could hardly be a more spectacular contrast than a description of rural markets in Guangdong by Orville Schell, published in 1984. He quotes a Western anthropologist friend as saying that in one brigade in 1979, 'there was virtually nothing in the market', echoes of Bernstein and Chongqing. He goes on that in 1981, 'things had started to pick up', but in 1983 he couldn't believe what he saw. 'There were hundreds of people selling things. There were tanks of live fish, and piles of fruit and vegetables heaped up everywhere. Lots of pigs were being slaughtered for meat — something you rarely would have seen in the past. You could buy Coca-Cola, Budweiser beer, and foreign cigarettes at private shops. The prosperity was impressive.'[34] Schell visited a rural market town in Guangdong himself in January 1984 and was also much impressed by the prosperity shown in the markets. Even on normal non-market days, he writes, the main streets 'were lined with hundreds of booths and peddlers selling everything from clothing, household goods, and hardware to produce and wild animals. But at official market times — every fifth day — the number of private merchants swelled into the thousands.'[35] During extensive travelling in China's south-west, Sichuan, Yunnan, and Tibet, in the autumn of 1985, this writer found that Western tourists invariably placed great weight on visiting the free markets and were always struck by their bustling activity, the range of goods on sale, and their general air of prosperity.

In terms of images of China's economy the most obvious question to flow from these discussions seems to be, Is China going capitalist? There is a degree of concensus that the reforms undertaken in China go beyond precedents in other socialist countries, causing some people to 'see China as giving up on socialism and copying capitalism'.[36] Few outside the radical supporters of the Cultural Revolution believe China's economy to be capitalist today, but the direction in which things are moving is a debate among those in the West interested in China, and ordinary people do hold an image on this question.

Three views predominate. The first is that what matters is modernization and prosperity, not whether China is 'going capitalist'. Derek Davies writes that it is 'sterile' to discuss whether China is merely making use of 'the tools of capitalism and decentralisation' in order to 'promote progress along the road to eventual socialism and communism or whether it is moving inexorably towards an open-market system, with all that implies socially and politically as well'.[37]

A second view recognizes trends in the direction of private enterprise and the ability of entrepreneurs to hire and fire, but does not believe they will or are likely to lead to capitalism. Among the people who hold this image are those who accept the assurance of Chinese foreign-language publications that China not only is, but will remain, a socialist country; and those who have always wanted China to abandon socialism but believe it cannot possibly do so under a communist party. A much more moderate expression of this second view comes in an influential textbook which interprets the reforms 'as innovative attempts within the Chinese socialist tradition to cope with the problem of modernization', not as a drift towards capitalism. Its authors think it unlikely that China has 'embarked on a smooth convergence with capitalism'.[38]

The dominant image is that while China is still a socialist country, its direction is towards capitalism. The 'dominant image' is evident in the comments of numerous Westerners in all sorts of contexts, most of whom favour what they perceive as the trend, because they see it as part and parcel of China's opening to the West. One expression of this view comes from a French scholar who draws an analogy between China's reforms and the Meiji Restoration in Japan, which began that country's opening to the West and its strong and successful capitalist drive towards modernization in the nineteenth century. She adds that the Chinese reforms are both more radical and less reversible than comparable developments in other socialist countries and 'risk putting in question the functioning of the regime and perhaps even its nature',[39] a clear implication that it might not remain socialist indefinitely.

It is perhaps necessary to add that few people in the West define precisely what they mean by capitalism, despite the term's critical importance in a country like China. But in a discussion of 'images' what matters is attitudes and mindsets, not whether people define the features of the terms they use.

Population Policy

Whether seen as in a capitalist direction or not, it is widely acknowledged in the West that China's economy can modernize only if the population growth rate is kept low. As we saw, the World Bank report, based on already established Chinese policy, specified 1 per cent per year. However, China's one-child-per-couple policy has aroused much heated controversy in the West and a number of different images and views.

The first point to make is a widely held admiration for China's having dared to take serious action to come to grips with an extremely serious problem. The United Nations undoubtedly expressed a view shared by most people in Western countries when in September 1983 its Secretary-General, Javier Perez de Cuellar, presented one of its two first annual population awards to Qian Xinzhong, Chinese minister in charge of the State Family Planning Commission, for his outstanding contribution to family planning. In August 1984 the United Nations held an international population conference in Mexico City. One report states that amid the airing of many problems the conference heard some good news, including that developing countries as a whole had slowed their birth rates by 11 per cent in 15 years. 'Much of the credit for this goes to Asian countries. The most startling example is China: the country's one-child-family programme has resulted in a 33% drop in the population growth rate in 15 years.' Indeed, China's achievement is so great as to cover up failures elsewhere, 'since China's statistics affect the world average so heavily'.[40]

The alternative image of China's relative failure in population control also has its supporters, especially when considering the vast countryside in the late 1980s. The 'draconian' birth-control policy 'does not work' is the flat verdict of the influential Italian journalist Tiziano Terzani.[41] When in 1987 Chinese statistics recorded a substantial rise in the population growth rate the preceding year over 1985, some in the West declared that China's birth-control campaign had lost its impact. 'Population experts say the emphasis on limiting couples to one child has been somewhat misleading, except for urban residents',[42] wrote one international newspaper, meaning that many peasants were both able and willing to defy the prohibition on a plurality of children. Such reductions as occurred to the mid-1980s still fell short of the authorities' targets. The conclusion of one general history of the People's Republic that 'the whole problem proved both insistent and intractable' would certainly find enough supporters in the West to be described as an image.[43]

To attain a drop in population growth rate, it has been necessary to carry out intensive organization and surveillance. If there is one paramount Western value it is that the state should not interfere in the private lives of the people directly. Most have been prepared to concede that China's values may be different and the problem it faces is grave enough to warrant the necessity of the one-child policy. An example is a fifty-minute British Broadcasting Corporation 'Horizon' television documentary of 1983 entitled *China's Child*, which focused attention on the city of Changzhou in Jiangsu province. It explained in some detail the quota system and the women who went round keeping an eye on younger women, persuading them to sign pledges and to undergo abortions if they became pregnant by mistake. The programme concluded by supporting the policy as necessary, whatever the disadvantages for the individual person. 'It *is* harsh, but is there an alternative?' was the final rhetorical question.

An essentially similar verdict resulted from an International Workshop held in England in 1983. In particular, the discussion of the problems in the countryside found the achievements to that time remarkable but recognized the great human cost: 'A whole generation is being asked to give up the children it wants. Millions of women undergo abortions which they would prefer not to have.' But 'against all this must be balanced the potential cost of inaction', the implication being that failure of the programme would bring disasters very much greater than long-term persistence in it.[44]

The reference to abortions, partly or fully forced, has been perennial in the discussion of China's population policy and aroused very negative images. Bergère refers to 'the brutality of this family planning policy'. She cites an example of 'terrorism' in one part of Guangdong province in 1981, when the official press reported that the public security had forcibly taken pregnant women to the local hospital for abortions. She does not claim such cases as necessarily representative but does conclude that coercive methods are in widespread use to procure abortions to end pregnancies which are not permitted in China by the relevant authorities.[45]

Steven Mosher lived and travelled in southern China from September 1979 to April 1980 as a graduate student of Stanford University. He had the opportunity of studying intensively a commune in Shunde county near Guangzhou and reported frequent forced abortions, including in the third trimester.[46] He also photographed a woman undergoing an abortion, and published the resultant picture; both actions were undertaken without her permission. For this and other breaches of anthropological and academic ethics he was expelled from Stanford University in February 1983,[47] but became a *cause célèbre* throughout the Western world, many supporters arguing that freedom of speech should have prevented his dismissal from Stanford's graduate programme. The extent of support for Mosher's position in the academic community in general is far from clear. However, right-wing anti-abortion groups in the United States and elsewhere lobbied against China's population policy as contravening the right to life of the unborn baby.

The Reagan administration, quite apart from its attitude towards China, introduced anti-abortion and other similar anti-feminist measures in the United States and enjoyed much popular support for so doing. Despite strenuous protests from China, the US International Development Agency in 1985 and 1986 actually withheld substantial pledged contributions to the United Nations Fund for Population Activities, arguing that it was not prepared to contribute money towards a programme like China's which involved forced abortions. There is no doubt that such action enjoyed support from a rather substantial number of people in the United States and elsewhere, whose image of China's population policy was that it seriously violated human rights because it involved forced abortions, even in the third trimester, and unwarranted interference by the state in the private affairs of the people.

Not only the methods but also several by-products of the population policy have become very widely known and discussed in the West, even among people not normally interested in China. These include the problem of an aging population and the only-child syndrome. Terzani's belief is that the population policy is producing a generation of 'lonely, pampered, overprotected, overfed' children, of 'spoiled people'.[48] But the one to arouse the greatest interest and concern is the 'tragic problem' of female infanticide,[49] which has been widely discussed in academic, journalistic, and other circles. The 'green bible' probably reflects the views and images of many ordinary non-China-specialists in the West who believe that the population policy is both necessary and at least partly effective. Its commentary on the problem of infanticide is as follows:

If the Chinese can be convinced or cajoled or persuaded or pressured into accepting birth control, the one thing they cannot agree to accept is the sex of their only child. The desire for male children is deeply ingrained in the Chinese mentality, and the ancient custom of female infanticide continues to this day — as the Chinese government and press will freely admit.[50]

The desire for sons, as well as female infanticide, are thus seen as part of a return to tradition. Terzani is more outright in his condemnation. His account of the population policy is headed 'The Best Baby is a Dead Baby', a title giving the impression that infanticide is more or less official policy, and begins with horrific stories of female infanticide and forced abortions so late as to be hardly different from murder.[51]

It is obvious from earlier chapters that the image of China as a country with an enormous population is nothing new. But whereas in dynastic times it was usually a positive image, a feature appropriate to China's prosperity, grandeur, or power, it is now dominantly a negative one. For the majority it is an obstacle to modernization. David Bonavia (1940–88), well known British journalist and correspondent of two influential image-formulators, *The Times* and *Far Eastern Economic Review*, expressed a thoroughly typical view when he said that 'The solution of many of China's most pressing problems has created a new monster, population growth.' What he meant is as follows: 'Improved medical services, an end to protracted civil war, and reasonably stable food supplies have led the country into a demographic crisis which must be solved in the near future if past achievements are not to be wiped out.'[52] That is a view essentially similar to current Chinese policy. It is true that for some people in the West, the chances of modernization do not balance out the negative features of the birth control policy. But few still see China's large population as a reason for admiration, certainly not as a source of prosperity.

Foreign Relations

There was a time, not so long ago, when China's large population was seen in some influential quarters as a reason why China was about to attempt conquest of other countries. The nightmare of the millions spilling over borders does still exist, but it is weak now, certainly not dominant. In the West, China is seen by most people as peace-loving and not expansionist. 'China needs a peaceful environment to modernize' is a typical comment which shows how obviously it is in China's interests to support stability and peace. *Time* magazine writes that 'The motto under Deng seems to be: try to get along with everyone so that the nation's energies can be concentrated on economic development.'[53] The China threat image which dominated the 1950s and 1960s has receded to the back seat in the 1980s. Indeed, China is seen in many quarters as itself under threat, from the Soviet Union. A rather typical article in the 'world's most-read magazine' relates how 'Moscow hopes to chip away at American influence' in the Pacific through such mechanisms as 'military buildup and economic aid', with China remaining 'subject to Soviet enmity and suspicion'.[54]

At the same time, the Chinese have long been, and remain, renowned in the West for their patriotism and its modern-day equivalent, nationalism. The well known American political science specialist Tom Bernstein — not to be confused with namesake Richard — asks, 'What values will bind China together now that Maoism, and indeed socialism, have lost their attractiveness?' He replies: 'The answer, of course, is nationalism, but it is not an expansionist nationalism.'[55]

It is a typical view among well-informed people in the West that Chinese foreign policy reflects and is determined by 'the country's unique culture, history, its domestic politics and the geopolitical calculus'.[56] Few believe that China will do other than pursue what it sees as its own national interest, or perceive it as different in that respect from any other country.

From much of what has been said it is clear that Westerners see China as a country appropriately compared and contrasted with those of the Third World. There are also very many who compare and contrast China with Western countries, usually to say how different are the values of the Chinese or how much lower are the standard of living and the economic level in general. Certainly, most people in the West see China as a superpower or near superpower which likes to compare itself with the West and finds no psychological problem in dealing with the superpowers. China may still be within the Third World, but its main foreign policy concerns are its relations with the superpowers, the United States and the Soviet Union, and with two Asian neighbours, Japan, with which it is friendly, and its number one enemy, Vietnam. Leaving aside its obsession with the evils of Vietnam, a typical Western perception would see China as relatively little concerned with the developing countries, its own public statements to the contrary notwithstanding.[57]

Of the United States, the Soviet Union, and Japan, the overwhelming image in the West is that it is the United States which is the most significant, not only for the West itself, but also for China. This view is particularly prevalent among Americans — even one of their own China historians criticizes 'the myth of American exceptionalism' as 'still widely accepted today with important consequences for our vision of our foreign relations'[58] — but is widespread in other Western countries.[59] David Bonavia writes that China's friendship with the United States and other capitalist countries, pursued 'doggedly' by China throughout the 1970s and into the 1980s, 'has been perhaps the most important single factor' in the development of international relations throughout the world down to the end of the twentieth century.[60] Strategic concerns pull great weight. Many in the West, especially in government circles, perceive China as 'a balance' against the Soviet Union, and thus helpful to Western interests.

Looking at the other side of the picture, the dominant Western image of why China should tend so heavily towards the United States and other capitalist countries can be summed up in one word: modernization. As noted earlier, the World Bank report emphasized the need for foreign technology, management know-how, and efficiency. It was the Western nations and Japan which could supply not only 'badly needed goods and technologies', but also markets for exports, tourism, and the 'capital necessary for industrial development'. It follows that a prevailing image of Chinese foreign policy in the Deng era was of characterization 'by the "open door" to the West' and at the same time 'a cold posture toward the Soviet Union'.[61] Very few would concede the possibility that the Soviet Union could contribute to China's modernization remotely as well as the West or Japan.

A particular event which symbolized just how far China had moved towards the capitalist world and away from the socialist in strategic terms was the Sino-Vietnamese war of February–March 1979. It also showed the irony of the enormous change in Western images of China's external behaviour which had emerged since the death of Mao. It can serve as one example to illustrate Western views of Chinese foreign relations in the years 1976–87.

The deterioration in Sino-Vietnamese relations, which became public from May 1978 on, and the war of early 1979, came as a tremendous shock to the generation mentioned earlier, which had been led by opposition to American intervention in Vietnam in the 1960s to rethink its own attitude towards China. They had consistently opposed the threat image and denied that China would ever invade another country. Yet here was China publicly acting, in imperial fashion, to 'teach Vietnam a lesson', as Deng Xiaoping put it, for having invaded Kampuchea a few weeks earlier. They were used to seeing China and Vietnam as revolutionary allies, and the Marxist wing of the generation had believed both countries to be sincere advocates of proletarian internationalism. Yet here were two socialist countries actually at war with each other and behaving in a way which ignored all methods but the use of raw power and any ideology but nationalism.

The reaction of Western governments and those who supported them had also done something of a turn about. Whereas a border war with India in October and November 1962 had brought accusations of aggression from the Western powers against China, this time what was striking was the restraint and low key of their official comments. The US State Department spokesman who commented on China's action immediately after it was announced declared the Administration of President Jimmy Carter to be opposed to both the Vietnamese invasion of Kampuchea and the Chinese invasion of Vietnam. He called for the immediate withdrawal both of Vietnamese troops from Kampuchea and Chinese troops from Vietnam. Other Western governments issued rather similar statements which, although

not exactly justifying what China had done, did not criticize
it very sharply either.[62]

When the war broke out, Deng Xiaoping had just, amid
enormous fanfare, made a highly successful visit to the United
States. The American press was generally very impressed with
him and was not keen to denounce him for his decision to
punish Vietnam. Media reaction tended to follow governments
in deflecting outright condemnation from China by linking
its action with Vietnam's invasion of Kampuchea. One of the
country's most influential newspapers, in an editorial entitled
'The Red Brotherhood at War', listed the various acts of
ruthlessness, aggression, and invasion which had led to China's
attack on Vietnam and concluded 'none of them are justified'.[63]
In Western Europe, one major weekly thought the Chinese
invasion 'maladroit' and ill-judged but, 'based on strategic
thinking or on human rights', refused to 'express a preference'
between it and Vietnam's invasion of Kampuchea.[64] In its editorial
of 19 February, London's *Daily Telegraph* sided clearly with
China; Vietnam was the aggressor by invading Kampuchea,
while China's 'failure to react would have led to intolerable
loss of face and to further reverses'.

When the war was over, *Asiaweek* declared that it 'must
be considered a successful military campaign',[65] a highly questionable assessment. Another evaluation of the overall results
of the war which showed China in a positive light suggested
that it had 'gained some credibility as a power seriously taking
on the challenge of Moscow and its expansionist ally Vietnam'.[66]
Views diametrically opposed to these and less favourable to
China were put forward perhaps even more frequently. A
political scientist writing very soon after the war in the most
influential English-language academic journal on contemporary China declared that the war had been 'costly and
unsuccessful' and was leading the country to an 'agonizing
reappraisal' of its foreign policy which would take a more
cautious approach to the Americans and a slow opening to
Moscow.[67] A French historian reached a very similar conclusion, declaring that the cost of the war had been high enough
to 'compromise the realization of the Four Modernizations';
rather than 'teaching Vietnam a lesson', the war 'seems above
all to have taught China that its army was not in a fit state
to undertake a modern offensive war'.[68] Journalist David

Bonavia's condemnation of the whole venture was strong and unequivocal: 'The invasion of Vietnam in February 1979 was infused with a spirit of vengefulness and hate which barely sought to cover itself with a political apologia.'[69]

On one point closely related to the war, Western opinion is if not unanimously then certainly strongly hostile to China's position, namely the continuing support for the Khmer Rouge regime headed by Pol Pot which the Vietnamese had ousted by invading Kampuchea. Although Western governments have not openly criticized China for backing the ousted Pol Pot, they have all condemned the barbarities his regime perpetrated while in power. In Australia, for instance, this was the crucial factor in the government's withdrawal of recognition from the Khmer Rouge regime early in 1981. Michael Yahuda, one of the leading academic authorities on China's foreign policy, writes of the 'price' Beijing is paying 'for the bestial if not genocidal policies' of the former Pol Pot regime; however much the Vietnamese occupation may be disliked in Kampuchea, he believes that the return of the Khmer Rouge is feared even more.[70] David Bonavia put the matter more strongly and sardonically. 'In international terms', he wrote, 'China has gained no kudos for winking at the appalling atrocities of the Khmer Rouge which have turned that once lovely and peaceable country into a vast mass grave.'[71] In this writer's impression, even those Westerners with little interest in China hold an image of its attitude to Pol Pot and his regime similar to that articulated by Bonavia.

Conclusion

The change in the realities of China in the decade and more under discussion in this chapter is probably more substantial than in the Western images of them. The reason for this is that the major change in the policy of the United States and several other Western countries towards China came in the early 1970s, whereas the change-over period in China itself was not until the late 1970s. By then the images of Westerners were on the whole towards a friendly nation, at times even nearly an ally.

Although China remained under the rule of a Communist Party which still claimed to adhere to Marxism–Leninism, there was much to be gained through friendship with the capitalist West. Most Westerners saw absolutely no reason why the West and China should not trade and hold other economic dealings with each other, deriving extensive and mutual profits. At times, China even seemed to exult in the rejection of socialist notions and in the adoption of economic and governmental patterns usually associated with capitalism. It was quite possible for Westerners to appreciate China without too much need to come to grips with unfamiliar or challenging values.

14

Images of Post-1976 China, II:
Society, Overall Views

THE term 'society' covers an enormous range of subtopics. Images of a society might include those of its religion, education, rural or urban daily life, or a host of others, all of which would be both interesting and relevant for Western images of China from 1976 to 1987. In view of the enormity of the subject, it is necessary in this, as in the previous, chapter, to narrow down coverage to just a few areas. Those chosen are life-style, Westernization, family, and the status of women.

Life-Style, Westernization

We begin with the background, an image of China's capital before the onset of the new life-style. In an image-formulating Time-Life picture book published in 1978, David Bonavia noted the transformation Beijing underwent after 1949, 'changing more rapidly and profoundly than any other capital city on earth'.[1] He praises the absence of malnutrition, poverty, brothels, opium dens, beggars, and drug pedlars. 'More extraordinary, it is a city without privately owned cars, without churches (excluding two relics, one Catholic and one Protestant), without commercial advertising, and without any night-life (even most restaurants are closed by 8.30 p.m.).' He also noted the lack of birds and flies.[2] The prevailing image of the Chinese life-style, even that of the main cities, was that it was puritanical and insufferably virtuous, stark, drab, colourless, and downright boring. Clothing was far too uniform, with too many Mao suits; women tried to avoid their sexual attraction to men by wearing dull garb and no make-up. Social dancing, which to most Westerners meant that in the Western style, was banned as bourgeois.

In his visit to China in 1978, playwright Arthur Miller had been horrified by the 'nearly total ignorance of the West's culture' he found in China, even among the intelligentsia. He had assumed that, even in a totalitarian state such as China, the leaders and intellectuals would 'not be foolishly bound by the isolation imposed on the people', but had found this belief quite wrong.[3] Miller's commentary on China is frank, provocative and insightful, but generally sympathetic to the Chinese and defensive of what they do. His comment on their ignorance of Western culture is among the more trenchant sections in its criticism.

But in the 1980s, things are vastly different in China's urban life-style and in its knowledge of, and influence from, the West. 'New new China, a stunning change in lifestyle', gloated the American Hong Kong-based *Asiaweek* on its front cover.[4] The feature article on China's life-style emphasized enthusiasm for Westernized pop music and social dancing. 'In the wake of unprecedented sales of hi-fi equipment and leather shoes has sprouted a new generation of dancebugs, who have been tangoing and discoing since late 1984.'[5] The 'chart-topping British duo, "Wham!" made it to China', even though its concert did encounter some harassment. 'The quasi-bourgeoisification of everyday life in China has progressed dramatically. Big spending and the indulgence of personal tastes are not only sanctioned but in many instances encouraged by the Communist Party!'[6] But of course it is still fashionable to point out how out of date most of the pop music is: 'Back in the late 70s', says the 'green bible', 'Saturday Night Fever (1940s style) hit Beijing.' 'Discos popped up in various hotels', it adds, and even attracted locals for a time despite the high price.[7]

Photographs of China convey similar images of China in the 1980s. A specific example is a glossy coffee-table book which categorizes the coloured photographs, devoting an entire section to 'signs of modernization'. One of the photographs shows a dance class and another a uniformed public security woman dancing with her boy-friend, who is dressed in tight jeans, while the Public Security Bureau's own band provides the music. 'Even the Public Security Bureau has been swept up by the dance craze', says the caption.[8]

Another aspect of the change in life-style is in the use of cosmetics and in personal appearance generally. Academic Beverley Hooper's paperback on youth, based on material from the early 1980s, gives a fairly staid impression. The range of cosmetics is growing and so is that of available clothing. Denim jeans are a symbol of growing material prosperity. Young people like smart but generally conservative clothing and carefully arranged hairstyles. They are in this respect similar to youth 'in many other developing countries — and in the West in the 1940s and 1950s'.[9] Asiaweek's account is much more exuberant, partly because more recent. 'The concern for the pampering of the self is most evident in newfangled ways to deck oneself out', it exults. Beauty parlours opened in Beijing, Shanghai, and Guangzhou late in 1984, while Max Factor, Shiseido, and other imported cosmetics it claimed to be 'the rage among the swelling ranks of the fashion-conscious'.[10] The coffee-table picture book cited includes coloured photographs of a fashion show, a fashionably dressed woman, a young woman wincing with pain as her ears are pierced, and women undergoing a 'facial' and other such treatment in a beauty saloon which uses Japanese equipment and has pictures of Japanese and Western beauties on the wall.[11] It is only very recently that beauty saloons were possible in China, or that Han Chinese women wore earrings.

There are pictures also of Maxim's French restaurant, where 'many of the ingredients are imported from France' and the waiters are trained in Paris; of a French bread shop, and of a French chef at the Great Wall Hotel instructing a smiling female Chinese trainee.[12] A fast-food store sells pastries, buns, hamburgers, hot dogs, and colas, and uses American equipment. A supermarket has an electronic adding machine at the check-out stand, a symbol of Western influence and an example of advanced technology, while just to check that the wonder of the modern age does its job correctly, two traditional abacuses lie on the counter.[13]

Luxury wedding feasts, another feature of the new prosperity, are back again with a vengeance. Of course we here confront not a new but a revived phenomenon, for the image of the Chinese as lovers of banquets is as old as the culture itself. 'Whether the occasion is a business deal or a family gathering, a birthday or a New Year festival, the Chinese love to celebrate it at the table',[14] declares the British television series *The Heart of the Dragon*, referring to all periods of Chinese history, including the present.

This is representative of a more general image which emphasizes social stability as a Chinese virtue, and which tends to place a high priority on the Chineseness of life-style in China at all times. A good exponent of this view was David Bonavia, who saw China as 'a genuinely ancient polity which has set up social cohesion and stability as the most important goal of human life'. In this view, the Chinese are marked out as superior to the Russians who are deeply insecure, obvious from the incidence of alcoholism: very high in Russia, but vanishingly low in China. Life there 'is geared to make everyone feel wanted — the surest defence against personal insecurity'. His conclusion about the Chinese people was that they are 'of a fundamentally stable temperament — industrious when properly motivated, unambitious of conquest or expansion, good-humoured in the main, appreciative of all the pleasures of life, and inventive' in coping with problems.[15] He explained the exceptions as a result of misgovernment and by implication the revulsion of the Chinese against the political instability of the present era.

Yet what is most striking about Western images of the new life-style of the 1980s is the extent to which it is seen as nearly synonymous with Westernization. *Asiaweek* calls the change 'the modernisation and Westernisation of lifestyle' and sees it as a central element in an official 'effort to bring China into the ranks of the world's most advanced nations'.[16] It is the experience of the West and other advanced capitalist countries that modernization, advancement, and economic power have gone hand in hand with luxury cosmetics and beauty parlours, with ever-changing styles of social dancing and Western or Westernized pop music, in short with that originally Western phenomenon, consumerism. So obviously the Western image is that China's experience is presently following this well-tried model.

Probably the great majority in the West see this new consumerism as highly desirable both for the West and the Chinese themselves. It certainly cannot do any harm to trade and other economic relations between China and Western countries. There is, however, another side to the picture: people who are worried about the short- and long-term effects of Western consumerism on China.

Perhaps the dominant symbol of American capitalistic consumerism, in terms of popular images, is Coca-Cola. Its introduction into China is something of a joke among Western tourists in China, most of whom love to drink it themselves. Among those who definitely disapprove is Clyde Cameron, the former Australian Labor government minister mentioned in Chapter 13. He writes that the announcement of the Chinese deal with Coca-Cola 'gave me the sinking feeling which comes when one hears that a plane on which a close relative might possibly have been a passenger has crashed'. He complains that 'anti-Maoists were quick to taunt me about revisionists and "capitalist roaders"' and that 'the shafts found their mark'. Drawing a strong and amusing parallel, he carps that 'The idea of the Coca-Cola banner over China left me feeling much the same as I guess a good Catholic would feel at seeing the hammer and sickle hoisted over St Peter's Basilica.' Still, he does see 'the need to cater for foreign tourists' and ends up with the belief, and hope, 'that Coca-Cola will earn more foreign currency for the Chinese people than it does for its own shareholders'.[18]

A more broad-ranging though less hard-hitting attack on the excessive Westernization some perceive to have reached China comes from Orville Schell. On a visit to China in the mid-1980s he was very struck by the rapid growth of large and magnificent luxury hotels, Western restaurants such as Maxim's, fashion parades and a thriving cosmetics industry, and other such manifestations of consumerism and Westernization. 'Once again China is looking westward.' In some ways, this is well and good since China is now 'unified and stronger' than in the past! Schell continues:

But as Westerners flood back into China, reviving foreign enclaves of privilege in the old coastal cities that once comprised the ignominious 'treaty ports', one cannot help but wonder what has become of that very tender place in China's collective psyche which in the past had felt so humiliated in the face of Western wealth, power, and technological superiority. At least in those areas through which I travelled in 1983 and 1984, the Chinese appeared to have at least temporarily lost touch with this current in their recent history.[19]

Such comments probably spring from surprise at the speed, extent, and manner of Westernization in China. Among the Vietnam War generation were many who saw good in those prepared to resist the consumerism of their own society, and China was a model. Even though the great majority would be prepared to admit that they misread the nature of the anti-consumerist society they admired, they still feel let down by many of the manifestations of the 'open door'.

Family, Women

It is a dominant image of China to suppose that the key social unit has always been, and remains, the family. 'So Chinese . . . Bred for loyalty, the family always coming first',[20] thinks the main character in a popular 'superthriller' about a Chinese male friend. Of course there was a time, in the 1950s, when some image-creators claimed that the Chinese Communist Party was trying to break down and destroy the family but, though some Westerners may have believed it then, very few indeed still do so in the 1980s. The general revival of tradition already noted as one image of the 1980s means that the family as an institution is seen as stronger now than at any other time since 1949. 'Since the death of Mao the family has been given an increasingly positive role, especially in the economic sphere', says an influential television programme.[21]

One persistent image is thus of comparatively little change, especially in the countryside. 'The patrilineal family remains strong. The state, in a sense, has been preempted by the family both in authority over individuals and even in economic organization', states academic specialist Margery Wolf. 'Social and kin relationships persist to this day, retarding and sometimes deflecting ideological change.' In the cities 'changes have been greater and less superficial. Ideological education has been more persuasive and more pervasive.' Thus authority over individuals has been transferred from family to state in a much more thoroughgoing way in the cities than has been the case in the countryside.[22]

One area to show some change in the 1980s, for the first

time in the People's Republic, is 'the new infatuation with romantic love'.[23] The image is not of a sexual revolution, or anything even remotely approaching it. On the contrary, it is closer to the Hollywood era of the 1930s and 1940s with 'tender but chaste embraces in the moonlight, and couples living happily ever after'.[24] This 'falling in love with love', as Hooper entitles her chapter on the subject, is thus seen as another example of Western influence, albeit very, even absurdly, old-fashioned.

It does not necessarily follow from the image of the discovery of romantic love that arranged marriages are seen as having disappeared. One very well informed coffee-table book claims that 'the choice of marriage partners still lies mainly with the parents' in the Chinese countryside, 'but the young people have a right of veto', so there is some improvement on the past. In the cities, 'choice of partners tends to be initiated by the young themselves, but is subject to a degree of veto by the parents and cadres in the unit in which they work'.[25] Beverley Hooper's research confirms not only the image that marriages arranged with the agreement of the spouses concerned are still normal in the countryside, but also the 'considerable parental influence' in marriage in the cities.[26] This has become a popular image found both in academic and journalistic literature. It suggests some change from pre-1949 patterns, but not nearly as much as observers of the Vietnam War generation believed in the late 1960s and early 1970s.

So marriage remains essentially a partnership between two families, rather than two individuals. It is certainly the popular Western perception that this system works to the disadvantage of women. British academic Elisabeth Croll is among those who cite 'the persistence of the betrothal gift' as one of the reasons why arranged marriages are still so numerous in the countryside. The betrothal gift from the groom's family makes the marriage its 'thinly disguised purchase' of a bride from another family.[27]

The role and status of women in Chinese society since Mao has been examined by quite a few people in the West, especially feminist academics, and images are being formulated on these subjects. Possibly the leading one is Margery Wolf, whose book *Revolution Postponed: Women in Contemporary China* in some ways represents fairly general opinion in well-informed circles in the West. Her view is that though women have always been part of the revolution, they have not benefitted from it to an extent even slightly approaching their commitment to it. Life for the average person in China 'has been raised to standards beyond the hope of the previous generation', but whenever a crisis has occurred the CCP has sacrificed the interests of women first. Today, under the policies of the Four Modernizations, 'women are being told to step aside in the interests of the nation' yet again. 'Though the revolution for women has never been repudiated, it has been postponed all too many times.'[28] It may be added that Wolf's view contrasts on this point with the even stronger image presented by Judith Stacey, who argues that the Party has not postponed the women's revolution but, despite its numerous statements to the contrary, never wanted or encouraged it in the first place. What the Party has always wanted for women is a stable family life in the traditional patriarchal style.[29] In this image, socialism is the enemy of feminism, not its friend.

The scholars researching women include many who at one time admired what they perceived as China's leading role in the liberation of women, especially as a result of the Cultural Revolution. But whereas Western feminist women once looked to China for guidance, they no longer do so. One scholar, taking part in a seminar discussion on the position of women in China since 1978, was moved to ask, what do Chinese women 'have to teach us now?' What 'vision' did anyone find in China? And the answer: 'There was a collective sigh . . . Neither the speakers nor anyone else in the room could cite recent lessons from the Chinese women's movement.'[30] The collective sigh was perhaps a rather patronizing way of expressing disappointment of a sort encountered before in these pages, among those who saw good in the Cultural Revolution and felt let down when China denounced it as a fraud. But whatever one thinks about the feminist stand, it is striking to find anybody expecting to draw a lesson for the West in China, not the usual converse.

The reasons for the 'postponed revolution', in the view of Western observers, are various. One writer in an influential British encyclopedia on China selects three. One is 'the lack of sustained commitment by leaders', in other words it is the fault of the authorities. But a second, more important, reason is that structural change in rural life has not been on a scale large enough to force a greater rise in women's status. Finally, there are not enough 'social settings in which informal contacts between boys and girls occur'. So what alternative is there but to retain arranged marriages, including 'the payment of a substantial bride price to the girl's family'?[31] In focusing on rural society as a whole for his reasons, the author again raises the familiar issue of how to balance change and continuity in China; his judgements show that he tends towards the continuity side of the spectrum. Limitations on improvements in the status of women result from the failure to change rural society as a whole.

One of the persistent Western images relating to Chinese women is of the 'double bind', meaning that women are doubly burdened if they take on work outside the home without being relieved of household chores. Margery Wolf sees the double bind as a primary reason why women rarely advance to senior positions. People of both sexes regard women as less committed to their jobs than men because of greater household and family responsibilities. Wolf believes that 'the acceptance of the double burden as women's lot by both Party and populace is the virtual acceptance of women's second-class status'.[32] David Bonavia put a different, though also negative, perspective: 'As in all socialist countries, it is a moot point in China whether the employment of women in low-paid industrial jobs (especially neighbourhood cooperative workshops) is a liberating measure or a new form of subjugation.'[33] Steven Mosher also dwells on the double bind to suggest that while inequalities among rural women have indeed been reduced, this process has left the 'more fundamental inequality' between males and females largely untouched.[34] In other words, he argues that the double bind has prevented any substantial rise in women's status since 1949.

On the issue of the double bind, as on so many others, it appears to me that it is the West which has changed as well as China. Since the 1960s women in the West have moved into the workforce in a big way. Childminding facilities and the technology of help in the home (washing-up machines and so on) have got much better, but most men still contribute much less home labour than women. The improvements have been slight by comparison with what women require if they are to fulfil two jobs properly when men still do only one. Bonavia introduces his comment on the 'double bind' by including 'all socialist countries'. But surely it is their own experience, more than those of their counterparts in socialist countries, which affects the images many Western women hold about the double bind in China.

Is it possible to draw any general conclusions on images of the status of women in contemporary China? The dominant image seems to be that, for all the many shortcomings, they have indeed come a long way since 1949. David Bonavia wrote that 'there can be no question that women have immensely improved their social and economic position since 1949, and if they have sacrificed certain cultural and political freedoms in doing so, the men have sacrificed them too'.[35] A husband-and-wife team of journalists attached to two influential American newspapers has written of 'an ironic aspect of how important women have become' in the fact that it is nearly always the woman who sues for divorce in China. They are also struck by the fact that the age-old deference and strict obedience women once had to pay their husbands have to some extent declined, even in the countryside.[36]

Elisabeth Croll retains a degree of optimism about the future when she ends her book on Chinese women since Mao by writing that 'they may yet become equal with the men of their household, their community and their society'.[37] By contrast, Margery Wolf's image of the future is somewhat grim. She concludes her 'none too cheerful book'[38] by speculating that if a revolution for women is ever to occur, 'they must be allowed to do as Mao did, to gather together like-minded people who see the shortcomings of the present social order and want to change it'. The positive reference to Mao is highly ambiguous, and could be taken as support for the policies of the Cultural Revolution as they affected women or as a call for violent overthrow of the social system. She believes a revolution is desirable and in accordance with the wishes of at least a section of Chinese women, but nevertheless unlikely in the short term. 'Everything I read and hear suggests that those people are out there, but thus far they are isolated souls only partially aware of their shared oppression. Until they join together, they are not a movement, let alone a revolution.'[39]

Overall Contemporary Views, Prospects for the Future

Do all these images on various particular aspects of China since 1976 and especially in the 1980s add up to any general images about the present and future of China? The answer is that most accounts of contemporary China include some overall assessment of conditions in the country. And if they do not spell out a general evaluation of present and future patterns they certainly imply one.

A German study, which could easily have issued from any Western country, advocates and expects more 'dialogue' between China and the West. The author is optimistic that both the West and China 'will keep those values that they can offer one another in mind while preserving their cultural individuality and independence'. Such a development, he believes, would be 'in the interest of China, in the interest of the West, and to the advantage of the whole world'.[40]

This image would find a great deal of support, though probably most people would imagine the West's influence on China to be greater than *vice versa*. One of the dominant images Westerners hold of China is that, while retaining its essential Chineseness, it is progressively and willingly becoming more like the West. The great majority of people in Western countries are convinced that, for all its faults, theirs is by far the world's finest civilization. Consequently, Westernization in China means that China is moving in the right direction. The overall Western image of China is thus a broadly positive one. In the United States in 1979 a Gallup Poll took a survey on China which asked respondents to place China on a scale ranging from +5 to -5. Only 29 per cent put China in the plus categories, but the next year the proportion had leapt to 42 per cent. In 1980, another surveying body, Potomac Associates, found 53 per cent of people 'mildly favourable' and 17 per cent 'highly favourable' in their feelings about China.[41] The range of views about China's present may best be shown through a few specific examples.

Fox Butterfield represents an extreme negative position. He concludes his book by quoting a conversation with a Chinese woman at the beginning of his flight home to the United States. She informed him she was going to study in the United States and did not intend to return home, despite her love for China and pride in being Chinese. 'If China ever opened its doors', she said, 'everybody would go. To the United States.'[42] Clearly Butterfield agrees with her, or he would not allow her statement to close his book without comment.

Images such as this one are familiar still, but certainly no longer dominant. The expressions of public opinion, as shown in the surveys quoted earlier, would suggest that another more positive image would find much more support. David Bonavia articulated it well.

The Chinese are beginning to enjoy a richer and more satisfying cultural life, greater political freedom, and the prospect of an easier, more comfortable existence. The country's international prestige has never been higher, and the rich nations are all keen to lend China money for development.[43]

Bonavia later had some quite trenchant criticisms to make, but his overall views were quite positive about China. And the last words of his book call for a greater attempt to understand China: 'The other two superpowers have made gross mis-calculations in their past dealings with China. To do so in the future will be dangerous for all.'[44]

A third view agrees with Bonavia in demanding under-standing of China and in seeing its experience as extremely significant. Roger Garside quotes a Chinese approvingly as saying: 'Always remember two things about our country . . . One billion people and three thousand years of feudalism.' The large population and the tradition recur again and again as Western images of contemporary China. Garside goes on to make out a case for Chinese uniqueness, a country which 'fits none of our ready-made categories for classify-ing the world'.[45] He sees China as trying to steer clear of the worst of its own tradition, and the Soviet and Western models, to find its own path. China, he believes, is engaged in a 'movement from totalitarian tyranny to a system more humane', in a 'struggle . . . to free itself from a straitjacket woven of feudalism, Marxism–Leninism, and twentieth-century technology.' His conclusion: 'There is no true precedent for this, and there is no country that will be unaffected by its outcome.'[46]

A highly enthusiastic and laudatory view emerges from

the 1982 American television documentary *Cycling through China*. The 'hostess' Kate Jackson is clearly and rightly exuberant over what was then something most unusual — permission given for famous American entertainers to go cycling through much of China. The dominant images that come across from the show are of a wise, happy, and hardworking people with a magnificent body of traditional arts. Unlike the other examples, this one comes from people who make no pretence to knowing anything about China. Yet they are probably just as or more important as image-formulators.

One problem in overall images of contemporary China is how observers project the past or the present into the future. Specifically, will China's modernization drive succeed or not?

As usual, views are rather diverse. Naturally, the strong supporters of China and its social system tend to be highly optimistic, and there are also observers who believe China has failed in whatever it has attempted, and is bound to do so in the future as well. Prevailing informed opinion would fall between these two extremes, but vere more strongly towards optimism than pessimism.

An example of a rather bleak view is that of French historian Marie-Claire Bergère. She contrasts the Chinese against the French and Soviet revolutions. Whereas the European revolutions affected 'the world or part of the world', China's never spread outside its own borders, and its main social and economic measures, in particular the people's communes, proved only temporary. Unlike the Soviet, the Chinese revolution 'assured neither the country's industrialization nor its technological evolution'. For all China's experimentation with foreign ideologies, modernization remains elusive. Bergère concedes the possibility that the strength of tradition can make for powerful changes, as has been shown in Japan and other East Asian countries, but believes such a factor 'remains to be demonstrated in China'. She concludes her general history of the People's Republic by 'wondering if, once realized, socialism with Chinese characteristics (*le socialisme à la chinoise*) will be very different from capitalism with Confucian characteristics (*capitalisme à la confucéenne*)'.[47] The implication is that Confucianism, the core of traditional Chinese culture, is indestructible and will continue to dominate China for ever, despite its socialism. So the likelihood is that any modernization will be essentially traditional, even if successful, which means that China faces an inherent contradiction, an insoluble dilemma.

An American historian of the People's Republic concludes his account with an overall evaluation of the Chinese revolution, which leads him to an expressed hope and implied assessment of the future.

Finally, a certain humility is called for in evaluating this great Revolution. It has exhibited excesses and imperfections in abundance. But excesses and imperfections are not unique to China, as any review of Western history will show. Moreover, China's difficulties have been very serious. Even as legitimate complaints abound over one or another aspect of the system, one cannot but be impressed by what has been accomplished and hope that Mao's dictum of 1959 is rather more appropriate now than it was then:

The achievements are tremendous, the problems are numerous, the experience is rich, and the future is bright.[48]

Unlike Bergère, the author of this statement is very positive about the Chinese revolution. A quotation from the revolutionary Mao remains an appropriate way to end a book. The revolution has its failings, but it is essentially a cause for optimism, not just another in the long series of failures to bring a better future to the Chinese people.

Time magazine suggests that 'the relatively free economy' of China will lead to greater political liberty and reduction of Party power, which would presumably be a desirable development. The magazine raises the possibilities of a reinterpretation of Lenin as well as Marx but adds 'That may be too much to hope for, at least anytime soon'. Its conclusion, however, is optimistic. It sees a good chance that China's economy will continue to work well and that China will 'enter the modern world on its own terms rather than on any dictated by Western capitalists, Soviet Marxists or anyone else'.[49]

A particularly optimistic prediction of the future of China's modernization in an international context comes from an influential textbook on Chinese politics. The authors predict a 'global shift of power from the Atlantic to the Pacific'. As China modernizes it will occupy a major place in the 'Pacific-centred order' which is likely to emerge in the twenty-first century, rightly dubbed the 'Pacific century'. And the final words of the book offer a strong defence of Chinese nationalism: 'Chinese may once again look upon their country as at least one of the world's central kingdoms.'[50]

The last example emphasizes the possibility of change, the rise in the standard of living, and Western influence, but also China's ability to absorb and transform foreign creeds of all kinds. The final programme of *The Heart of the Dragon*, entitled 'Trading — Into the Four Seas', speculates that 'with Western products displayed in the shop windows and with Western images flooding people's imaginations through films and television', expectations are likely to rise. The CCP is, in addition, anxious to bring about change and greater material progress and thus differs from the old imperial governments which were 'concerned with maintaining a status quo'.

What the outcome will be cannot be predicted. Only one thing is reasonably certain. Just as the Chinese transformed the Buddhism they imported from India by fusing it with their native beliefs to form Chan Buddhism, so, to the extent that they import consumerism from the West, they are likely to transform that also. Will Chan Consumerism be the next teaching to 'flow into one' with the others?[51]

This passage exemplifies Western images of China perfectly for several reasons. In terms of form, it comes from a television programme and thus reaches more people than any book could do. In terms of content, it assumes Western importance, but not to an inordinate or absurd degree. It focuses on the economy and the standard of living. Most striking of all, it mentions an event of well over a thousand years ago as an appropriate analogy to the present and the future in the same breath as it predicts vital change. As aware of history as Bergère, its author is nevertheless much more sanguine about China's ability to handle the contradictions between tradition and modernity. The message seems to be a corroboration of an image encountered earlier several times: the uniqueness of China.

Conclusion

There have been numerous images presented of post-1976 China to the West and those offered in this and the preceding two chapters are but examples both of topics and of images within them. In general, however, the views are reasonably typical of those given in literature and media presentations about China of the sort which could count either as representers or creators of images.

On the whole, Western images of China have been fairly positive since 1976. There are of course major exceptions to this suggestion. For example, we noted the 'fad of writing off China' in some quarters in the early 1980s. Images of Chinese society, especially its treatment of women, are in many ways decidedly critical, and the reaction of the American government to China's population policy has been condemnatory. Westerners generally hold very negative images of China's human rights record and treatment of Tibetans. Yet prevailing views on China's economy and standard of living, government, foreign relations, and other topics, and especially overall images of the present and prospects for the future, are definitely sympathetic to, and even admiring of, China's performance.

In line with Foucault's 'power/knowledge' correlationship, Western images of China since the 1970s have fitted the strategic and economic interests of Western government and ruling groups nicely. Strategic interests are notoriously transitory, and could change if China were to realign itself with the Soviet Union. In the economic sphere, Western interests have been leading over the last few years towards the expectations of major profits deriving from dealings with China and thus towards more positive images. However, to this writer it appears doubtful whether China either can or whether its decision-makers really want to integrate its economy closely enough with those of the West to yield anywhere near the profits many Western business people hope for or even expect. If this is the case, then the current phase of dominantly positive Western images of China may not be permanent, any more than any other preceding phase either of positive or negative views has been so.

15

Conclusion

DESPITE their variety, Western images of China have tended to follow fashions and it is legitimate to see certain types of views as dominant at any particular time. Over the centuries a pendulum can be perceived of positive and negative images, though it is not one which swings regularly or smoothly. At times China has been seen as a 'model'. In the eighteenth century Voltaire was prepared to hold up China's marvels as a way of criticizing the politics, customs, and ideas of his own day, and quite a few of his contemporary countrymen shared his views. During the 1970s, China represented one 'model' of development which found favour in some circles, though certainly not among anything like a majority of Westerners. On the other hand, China's image has at times been extremely negative. One thinks of the nineteenth and early twentieth centuries and the 'heathen Chinee', the 'yellow peril', hideously cruel tortures and the murder of infant girls.

The 'pendulum' metaphor does not demand that each swing be equal in size. Moreover, it takes account of alternative views. There has not for centuries been a time when a dominant positive or negative image has not been at least partly balanced by dissenting opinion. Montesquieu, who was very negative about China, was roughly contemporary with Quesnay and Voltaire, who praised it so highly. Augustus Lindley was able to write a strong defence of the Taipings of the mid-nineteenth century during a period when the great weight of Western opinion was hostile to them. The 1950s produced some works highly sceptical of the condemnatory view the United States government was pushing, while in the late 1960s the hostility of many Westerners to the American intervention in Vietnam caused appreciation of Asian revolutions in general to gather momentum. At most times since then, certainly in the 1980s, academic and journalistic opinion has been more critical than popular opinion in general. The images of China put forward by specialists in the 1980s have tended strongly to be more restrained and sceptical than those by people, like actress Kate Jackson, discovering China for the first time.

The Introduction discussed two theories and posed the question whether they could appropriately be applied to Western images of China. The first of these is Michel Foucault's 'power/knowledge' concept. Can one validly argue that the main determinant of Western images of China at any particular time is power, and not Chinese reality, or a combination of any number of China's myriad realities?

It appears to this writer that the dominant images of most periods have tended to accord with, rather than oppose, the interests of the main Western authorities or governments of the day. There has indeed been a 'regime of truth' concerning China, which has affected and raised 'the status of those who are charged with saying what counts as true' about that country.

We may perhaps exempt the first period of Sino-European contact in the thirteenth and fourteenth centuries because it is unlikely that China loomed large enough in the European mind to warrant anything approaching a meaningful 'regime of truth'. However, from the sixteenth century on, the wish of the Catholic Church in general and the Jesuits in particular to convert the Chinese to Christianity influenced the images which spread to Europe about China. Mendoza's great work was written at the command of the Pope and with the aim of beginning the conversion of the Chinese to Catholicism. When the Jesuits thought they could convert China to Christianity by praising it, they were for well over two centuries active in disseminating extremely positive images about it. But as this hope dwindled and then vanished, so the perceptions became tarnished. Moreover, it was the Jesuits' defeat in the power struggle, climaxing in their suppression by Pope Clement XIV in 1773, which spelled the end of Jesuit activity in China and of the favourable images they sent back to Europe.

Although the Western images in these centuries did suit Europe's Christian interests, it is necessary to point out that secular governments were only marginally involved. In fact, quite a few of them were bitterly hostile to the Jesuits, and it was pressure from the governments of Catholic Portugal, France, and Spain which eventually resulted in their suppression by the Pope. Even within the Catholic Church there was bitter division over how to interpret and Christianize China. The 'regime of truth' was primarily a Jesuit phenomenon.

It was in the nineteenth century that Europe 'colonized' images of China. The three main types of European activity in China from about the middle of the nineteenth century until after the fall of the Qing dynasty were imperialism, profit, and conversion to Christianity, all of them connected with a power relationship. The prevailing Western images, decisively more negative than in the preceding period, made these activities easier, not more difficult. The idea of China as a stagnant oriental despotism, which even a strong opponent of the capitalist system such as Karl Marx advocated, was used to justify Western intervention to force change upon a reluctant China.

It suited American, and later on other Western, interests to regard China as a friend during the first half of the twentieth century, and as an ally during World War II. For the first time, Chinese authors, able to write in a European language, became· major conveyors of images to the West. The most prominent examples are Chiang Kaishek's wife, Song Meiling, and Lin Yutang, a strong supporter of the modernized traditional system of Chinese government represented by Chiang Kaishek. Through her novels, and in particular the moving and best-selling *The Good Earth*, Pearl Buck promoted essentially conservative and positive images about China and its countryside which accorded well with the power relationship emerging between the West and China in the 1930s. The dominant Western images of China improved dramatically, especially during World War II.

The 1950s and 1960s saw a China strongly opposed to Western interests, and in particular most Western governments. It consciously strove to change the unequal power relationship which it believed had existed between China and the West in the preceding century. The United States denounced the People's Republic as aggressive and a 'threat' to itself and the world. American opposition to the People's Republic spawned many authorities eager to create and foster a public opinion which would back up the American government's policy. At least in the United States, and to some extent also elsewhere, it became possible for educational authorities to push a line on China in the schools which was designed to accord with the American government policy of the day. The dominant Western images of China meshed nicely with the most powerful Western interests.

But the most spectacular example supporting the point about the 'regime of truth' is the Nixon visit of 1972. The American government changed its policy at a time when China was still in the throes of the Cultural Revolution. It is true that the seeds of a change in public opinion had been sown beforehand, but the strength of enthusiasm for Nixon's action suggests most strongly that popular images sat beautifully with American interests as they were being perceived by the government of the day. It was the American government that changed the images much more than the other way round. It was a calculation of interests that counted much more than a perception of right and wrong.

Images of recent history have been influenced quite heavily by the politics of the day since World War II, and constitute a part of the 'regime of truth'. In the 1950s and 1960s, the result was a strong tendency for the West to continue to see its own role in pre-1949 China, and that of those it supported, as important and broadly positive, but that of the Communists as negative. The challenge to the American role in Vietnam brought with it new ways of thinking about recent East Asian history in general, and Chinese history in particular. Many Western historians were led to a greater appreciation of the internal dynamic of recent Chinese history, to rethink and downgrade the high priority they had formerly attached to the Western impact of the nineteenth century. The Communist role in China's pre-1949 history received far greater attention, and in general more positive images.

The suggestion that Foucault's 'power/knowledge' theory is indeed applicable to a study of Western images of China does not imply either bad motives or incompetence on the part of any but a small minority of image-formulators. Even less does it imply that alternatives to the dominant opinions or images cannot exist. Foucault's idea can be supported irrespective of any conspiracy theory. Particular power relations do not necessarily exercise a decisive impact on individuals, but they certainly do so on groups, on societies in general. The operation of power is often invisible, but in some cases quite overt. The American authorities of the 1950s and 1960s did not reveal all they were doing to influence public opinion in the West and elsewhere against China, but there was no secret that they were indeed expending an enormous amount of money and effort to achieve precisely that objective.

The second and related theory raised in the Introduction is Edward Said's 'Orientalism'. Have Western images of China been distorted by ethnocentric biases, by a failure to judge China in its own terms?

The answer depends on the period. I see very little of the 'Orientalist' in Marco Polo, despite the threat to Europe the Mongols had appeared to present not long before his time. What is striking is how fair he was, the extent to which he was prepared to see and judge China in its own terms, especially as far as its emperor and political system were concerned.

Moving into the sixteenth to eighteenth centuries, it is necessary to remember the aim of most observers, which was a frankly ethnocentric one, namely to replace Chinese religions with a European one on the grounds that only the latter was true. However, most observers tried to be fair according to their own criteria and they were not prejudiced against China. One can hardly charge a man like Joseph de Mailla with 'Orientalism' when his great history of China was a translation of Confucian works. It is true that Montesquieu's views on despotism in China were both hostile and 'Orientalist', but Voltaire and Quesnay praised China in order to criticize their own country, the precise antithesis of 'Orientalism'.

By the nineteenth century Europe had begun its Industrial Revolution and its confidence of its own superiority was at a peak, just at the time when China's civilization was in sharp decline. So it is not surprising that the overwhelming majority of images presented reflect that feeling of superiority in a sharply 'Orientalist' way. Even those who believed they were sympathetic to China assumed their superiority explicitly or implicitly. An example is Thomas Meadows, who was prepared to defend the Chinese as highly intelligent and to attack racism, but was still a strong and active supporter of British imperialism in China.

'Orientalism' remained very strong, indeed dominant, in

the first half of the twentieth century. Yet there was arising a quite clear trend willing to analyse China in its own terms, to challenge unarticulated assumptions of Western superiority. Social science notions of cultural diversity were applied to China more frequently. More and more people saw its history as worth studying, even if so great a scholar as Maspero among others retained a strong sense of Eurocentrism in his work. The fact that Pearl Buck could write a popular novel about China in which *all* the main characters are Chinese was a clear sign of the times. China was itself undergoing a revolutionary process with the growth of the CCP. A few Westerners, such as Edgar Snow, reported on it in a manner at odds with the prevailing 'regime of truth', making a successful attempt to judge it in its own terms despite the opposition of their own society.

The rise of the CCP to power in 1949 brought a new wave of 'Orientalism' to the West's images of contemporary China. Few commentators were really prepared to judge China on its own terms. A serious challenge was mounted to this 'Orientalism' because of the opposition to American intervention in Vietnam, which brought with it calls to reassess socialist revolutions in Asia. With the Nixon visit in 1972 it was once again fashionable to see good in and even admire China, including its political system. As a result more people tried to use criteria set by the Chinese themselves, including both the government and apparently the people, to comment on China.

Since the primary distinguishing feature of the People's Republic until the 1970s was its adherence to Marxism–Leninism, the new wave of 'Orientalism' did not extend to images of China before the nineteenth century. The Judge Dee novels of Robert Van Gulik are masterpieces of social commentary on the period in which they are set, as well as exciting detective stories. They have certainly reconstructed the seventh-century setting in its own terms. Joseph Needham's monumental research has discovered a magnificent and independent scientific tradition which, though it did not yield anything comparable to the Industrial Revolution in Europe, was for most of its history both progressive and productive, and ahead of the Europe of its day.

The 'opening up' of China since the late 1970s has resulted

in more Westerners visiting the country, more serious and better study of it in the West, and more attempts by more Western people to learn the Chinese language. The result has been a gradual decline in 'Orientalism' as more people have been forced to confront Chinese values and aims. It would be difficult to impute 'Orientalism' to a film such as *The Last Emperor,* which brims with appreciation for China's problems in the twentieth century. Yet it appears to me that commentaries and statements laden with Western values and regarding China as an inferior civilization which should expect only to learn from the West are still very easy to find, especially in items aimed at reaching mass audiences such as the film *High Road to China.* The assumption that China exists largely for the triumphs, profits, and sexual gratifications of Westerners is widespread and strong, as shown in a film like *Tai-Pan.* 'Orientalism' may be in decline in the West, but it is very far from dead.

Even today, despite the changes which have occurred since the early 1970s, there is more than a grain of truth in Said's statement that a European or American studying the Orient 'comes up against the Orient as a European or American first, as an individual second'. His warning against 'Orientalism', against refusing to judge the peoples of other cultures in their own terms, remains a valid and worthwhile one.

What is it that makes images as they are?

The main determinant of Western images of China is the West itself. In this book the subject has been the West, China but the object. The conclusion which follows from the material presented in this book is that the major power-concentrations have exercised a determining influence over Western images of China at any particular time, not the other way about. An application of Foucault's 'power/knowledge' theory yields the same conclusion.

A good illustrative example comes from the United States. Public opinion no doubt affects American foreign policy to some extent, but my suggestion is that the impact on Western images of China as a whole is not decisive. The American government has only to feed information into a giant international mass media machinery to put its own views over to the Western world. On occasions, such as during the Korean

[handwritten margin notes: "which China?", "is too like ROC in 1948, why not in 1980s?"]

War of 1950 to 1953, or at the time of the visit of President Nixon to China in 1972, it also has the wish to influence the images people hold.

Yet if American government policies were the only determinant, we should be unable to explain the series of widely known and bitterly anti-China books published in the United States in the early 1980s just after the United States and the People's Republic of China established full diplomatic relations at ambassadorial level. In this case it was President Jimmy Carter who made the break in China's favour. Ronald Reagan was explicitly unwilling to retain Carter's China policy but did so for pragmatic reasons. By the time the main image-formulating anti-China material appeared Reagan was in power. In this case it is not suggested that Reagan or any in his government orchestrated the publication of the material, but rather that the same conservative trend in American public opinion which brought Reagan to power also resulted in a backlash against positive images about China. This fashion enabled books like Fox Butterfield's *China, Alive in the Bitter Sea*, with its one-sided and black-and-white negative approach to China, to gain a large and continuing popularity in the United States.

If the application of Foucault's theory suggests one determinant of Western images of China, that of Said's yields another: simple prejudice. Ethnocentrism usually results in negative images, because anyone who judges China with the standards and value systems of the West will find it deficient and backward. There is, however, an alternative kind of ethnocentrism, that which trivializes through excessive praise but still keeps the observer centre stage. An example is the glowing television programme *Cycling through China*, in which the Americans, not the Chinese, are usually the focus of attention and many shots show Chinese people looking at the American guests with wonderment, admiration, or curiosity.

A third determinant of Western views of China is how well the Chinese treat the potential image-formulator, how effectively they project images to the West. The good treatment Marco Polo and the early Jesuits received in China was one factor encouraging them to transmit favourable images to the West. The 'open door' policy currently in operation is more likely to result in positive images than the tight restrictions on the entry, movements, and activities of Western foreigners which characterized the late 1960s.

A variant on the same theme lies in the degree to which the Chinese themselves accept the West and its influence. Ever since the sixteenth century, but especially since the nineteenth, the West has tended strongly to assume a right to influence China. On the whole, Chinese receptiveness to this influence has resulted in favourable images in the West, and resistance to it in negative. After China signalled in unmistakable terms in the eighteenth century that it had no intention of accepting Christianity, the positive images the Jesuits had been pushing began to wear off. China's initial resistance to the Western impact strengthened the harsh images prevalent in the nineteenth century. On the other hand, the Republican period saw a somewhat greater receptiveness to Western ways in China and a corresponding improvement in images. Perhaps the best example of all is the 1980s, which have seen, in Chinese terms, a high degree of receptiveness to Western influence, in some sectors of society even great enthusiasm for it. At the same time, Western images have been dominantly positive.

And finally, a major determinant of Western images of China is the realities of China itself. Clearly much of what Western image-formulators say, write, or depict of China reflects some of the many realities accurately. This is especially so at times when the Chinese themselves present Westerners with the opportunities to research on or find out about Chinese realities. For instance, the obstacles in the way of a researcher doing field work in China in the 1980s are minimal by comparison with what they were in the late 1960s and early 1970s, when it was virtually impossible to undertake any serious field research in China.

But, as noted in the Introduction, the relationship between images and realities is an enormously complex and problematic one. In fact, China has been over the centuries and remains a country so diverse that misery and joy, poverty and prosperity have been and are all completely real. Moreover, different observers of China attach distinct scales of importance to the same phenomena because each may differ sharply from the others in knowledge, experience, skills, and assumptions. And so even for specialists the fit between images and realities is highly imperfect. How much more is this so for the great majority who make no pretence to knowledge about China and who, if interested, seek guidance in the formulation of their own images!

The China about which the West has devised images is large and the period here covered extensive. Both the West and China have changed greatly over the centuries and not always in the same direction. Is there any conceivable unity between a Mendoza who looks at the China of the sixteenth century and an Edgar Snow who observes the same country in the twentieth? Are there any observable patterns in the images created which may be worth comment?

Possibly the most persistent of all issues in Western images of China has been change versus continuity, and related questions such as whether China was a despotism or was/is totalitarian. Naturally the creators of images in the early centuries ignored such problems since Europe itself was not yet obsessed with its own spectacular transformations. Early observers to focus attention on Chinese despotism were the eighteenth-century French thinkers Quesnay and Montesquieu, the first seeing this political system as benign, the second as oppressive because based on fear. Montesquieu held that China's climate and terrain were the main factors shaping its society and political order. J. G. von Herder, writing late in the eighteenth century, and basing himself on de Mailla's history, poured scorn on China for its changelessness and likened it to an 'embalmed mummy'. Hegel saw no historical development in China, and Ranke included it among his 'nations of eternal standstill'.

In one major interpretation of Karl Marx, he perceived China as an example of the Asiatic mode of production, and that meant he regarded it as despotic, reactionary, and without history until outside intervention forced change. It was Lenin and Stalin who broke away from this view, seeing China as a country where a revolution could and should oppose imperialism and create a new society.

In the twentieth century Karl Wittfogel, basing himself on some of Marx's writings and on an intensive reading of Chinese-language sources, posited an unchanging and repressive 'oriental despotism', shaped and maintained by the need for waterworks managed by a centralized bureaucracy. He called this the 'hydraulic' society because of the large-scale irrigation and water control which were its determining factors. Wittfogel found some support for his views but also serious opposition, in particular from Wolfram Eberhard and Joseph Needham.

Since World War II, Western historians have tended to discover greater change in Chinese history, especially in the period before about AD 1300. A significant and image-formulating example of such work is Mark Elvin's theory of the 'medieval economic revolution'. This posits economic and social change in the centuries on either side of AD 1000 amounting to radical transformation. The Chinese were quite capable of social change, even revolution, centuries before the age of European industrialization and colonialism.

The People's Republic was initially for some a new but essentially unchanged version of the oriental despotism. However, others, such as Robert Guillain, expressed shock at *too much* change. China was renouncing its own tradition by adopting Marxism–Leninism and was thus in a way casting aside its own Chineseness. Those sympathetic to the CCP argued that China had indeed changed radically but retained its Chineseness, and that both developments were desirable.

The doctrine of the changeless China underwent drastic decline during the Cultural Revolution. However, more observers than ever castigated it as totalitarian. Supporters admired the attempts to overthrow a regressive and feudal tradition, to force desirable change even on a reluctant people. Opponents saw only repression, and total disappearance of freedom. They saw change all right, but in an evil direction.

With the fall of the 'gang of four' and the revival of tradition, popular and specialist images have once again emphasized the impact of its past on China's present. While the dominant image would continue to see China as more heavily influenced by its past than Western countries are by theirs, there is a major difference between the present and past analyses of continuity and change in China. Very few people indeed would any longer regard China as *incapable* of change.

The dominant school of thought welcomes the return of tradition, regarding it as a reassertion of Chineseness. The prevailing image undoubtedly sees China as moving *away* from totalitarianism. It is true that most people in the West give their own influence much credit for this trend, but most recognize that it is China which has freely chosen this direction. Neither the Marxist theory of the Asiatic mode of production nor Wittfogel's environmentally determinist hydraulic society any longer have many adherents, either among specialists or in the popular image.

Apart from political system, already discussed as part of the issue of change versus continuity, one of the main subjects of Western images has been the family. Despite some extremely negative views, including those of such diverse people as Robert Fortune and Agnes Smedley, the West's perception of the traditional Chinese family system has in general been remarkably positive. Marco Polo made no mention of one of its more horrible features, foot-binding, while Mendoza was not at all shocked by that practice. Montesquieu was impressed by the Confucian family system, despite his generally critical view of China. In her *The Good Earth*, Pearl Buck could remain extremely positive about Chinese society, despite the suffering she knew the Confucian family system caused the poor, especially women. It was probably consistent with such an attitude that many in the West took the CCP's onslaught on the Confucian family system in the 1950s as an attack on family life altogether and hence cause for a negative image. Robert Elegant's novel *Dynasty* could put over the image that during the Cultural Revolution the family was the main surviving bastion of sanity in Chinese society. Western images of the revival of family power in the 1980s, though not of the sexism of the traditional Chinese family system, have on the whole tended to be enthusiastic.

Various other subjects have recurred throughout this book. For Mendoza China's large population was a source of wonderment. But Du Halde saw it as a cause of poverty and Marx as a source of oppressive social relations. Since 1949 it has most often held the image of an obstacle to economic progress or modernization. The one-child policy of the 1980s may have aroused great controversy and various images in the West, but very few people anywhere would welcome another population explosion in China.

On the whole, the West has viewed China as peace-loving. In the seventeenth century, Ricci remarked on its lack of ambition for conquest, which he contrasted with the peoples of Europe. Fairbank in the twentieth century has promoted a similar image of traditional China. During the Guomindang years and since the mid-1970s, the prevailing Western view has been that China wants peace and constitutes no threat to the world. Yet the 'yellow peril' image has also had its day. The German Kaiser Wilhelm II coined the phrase at the same time Europe indeed posed a threat to China. And the American policy of the 1950s and 1960s revived the image as part of its anti-communism. It castigated China as a threat to world peace, bent on the conquest of neighbouring countries.

Finally, what significance is it possible to find in the study of Western images of China? One can answer this question on both a practical and theoretical level.

One of my points has been that a general correlation exists between the images one country holds of another and state-to-state relations between the two at any given time. I have argued that government impact on popular images is greater than the converse, but both play a role. It follows that well-informed images can contribute to an intelligent policy one country adopts towards another. Thus for any government to formulate policies for dealing with the people or government of another state, it should not only understand that nation but also the various levels of popular images about it. I believe that relations between China and Western nations would have been smoother if each had held a clearer idea of precisely what the people of the other country thought. It may be comfortable to be shielded from hostile images but it serves no useful purpose.

The study of one civilization's images of another raises the whole issue of how to handle relations between peoples of totally different cultures. To understand another people's culture one should immerse oneself in it, but that does not mean that it is either possible or desirable to become part of it or abandon one's own culture. I see the core of the problem in attitudes and mindsets. In other words, to understand another people one should know so clearly what their attitudes, views, and practices are, and why, that one becomes able not only to see the world from their point of view but also able to relate to them on their own terms, and to make judgements based on their criteria. This means that understanding another culture involves overcoming all prejudices. This is not as easy as it sounds. All cultures bring up their members with a whole series of unarticulated assumptions, of which the people who hold them are often unaware. To remain ignorant of these assumptions often leads to prejudices against others, or to untested attitudes of superiority towards other cultures, based on criteria and priorities which may be quite different in such other cultures.

It does not follow from this that a fair interaction between Westerners and Chinese necessarily means agreement between them, though this will often occur. Even less does it mean that a Western individual or government should necessarily support any particular Chinese government or set of policies. New and critical interpretations by Westerners both of China's past and its present are highly desirable, whether or not they find agreement from Chinese counterparts. Thus, debate among Western historians over when 'modern China' began is healthy, no matter what priority such a controversy might take in China itself. Western observers who denounced the Cultural Revolution at the time are not thereby 'Orientalist' just because they disagreed with the Chinese official policy of the day. It is perfectly possible for a Western observer to understand China's population problem in the 1980s to the extent of seeing it in Chinese terms and according to Chinese criteria, and still disagree with the particular solutions adopted by the Chinese government to solve it.

Ethnocentrism and prejudice are not exclusive to the West, and have never been so. It is not only the study of Western images of China which offers the potential of moving against these twin evils. An equally valid and useful, but entirely different, topic of research from the one attacked in this book would be 'Chinese images of the West'.

Notes

Notes to Chapter 1

1. Colin Gordon, 'Afterword', in Colin Gordon (ed.), Colin Gordon, Leo Marshall, John Mepham, Kate Soper, trans., *Power/Knowledge, Selected Interviews and Other Writings 1972–1977, Michel Foucault* (The Harvester Press, Brighton, 1980), p. 233.

2. Michel Foucault, 'Truth and Power', in Gordon (ed.), *Power/Knowledge*, p. 131.

3. Foucault, 'Truth and Power', in Gordon (ed.), *Power/Knowledge*, p. 133.

4. Edward W. Said, *Orientalism* (Random House, Vintage Books, New York, 1978; 1979), p. 23.

5. Said, *Orientalism*, p. 11.

6. Said, *Orientalism*. This phrase occurs on p. 326, and refers to the positive example of Clifford Geertz, whom Said ranks among the select Western scholars not infected by 'Orientalism'.

7. Said, *Orientalism*, p. 326.

8. Said, *Orientalism*, pp. 325–6.

9. See Louis Althusser and Étienne Balibar, Ben Brewster (trans.), *Reading Capital* (New Left Books, London, 1970), especially pp. 14–15.

10. Two particularly good examples from the post-war period are Raymond Dawson, *The Chinese Chameleon, An Analysis of European Conceptions of Chinese Civilization* (Oxford University Press, London, 1967) and Harold R. Isaacs, *Scratches on our Minds, American Images of China and India* (John Day, New York, 1958), updated and republished as *Images of Asia, American Views of China and India* (Harper Torchbooks, New York, 1972 ed.).

Notes to Chapter 2

1. See Henry Yule and Henri Cordier, *Cathay and the Way Thither, Being a Collection of Medieval Notices of China* (4 vols.; The Hakluyt Society, London, 1913–16), I, p. 197.

2. Yule and Cordier, *Cathay and the Way Thither*, I, pp. 20–1.

3. Yule and Cordier, *Cathay and the Way Thither*, I, p. 198.

4. Yule and Cordier, *Cathay and the Way Thither*, I, pp. 29–32, 232–3.

5. Donald F. Lach, *Asia in the Making of Europe Volume I, The Century of Discovery Book One* (University of Chicago Press, Chicago and London, 1965), p. 22.

6. Igor de Rachewiltz, *Papal Envoys to the Great Khans* (Faber and Faber, London, 1971), p. 81.

7. Lach, *Asia in the Making of Europe*, I, One, p. 32.

8. Yule and Cordier, *Cathay and the Way Thither*, I, pp. 157–8.
9. Yule and Cordier, *Cathay and the Way Thither*, I, pp. 159, 161.
10. Lach, *Asia in the Making of Europe*, I, One, p. 32.
11. Richard Humble, *Marco Polo* (G. P. Putnam's Sons, New York, 1975), p. 35.
12. Ronald Latham (trans. and introduced), *The Travels of Marco Polo* (Penguin, Harmondsworth, 1958), p. 155.
13. Latham, *The Travels of Marco Polo*, p. 213.
14. Latham, *The Travels of Marco Polo*, p. 218.
15. Latham, *The Travels of Marco Polo*, pp. 128–9.
16. Latham, *The Travels of Marco Polo*, pp. 156–7.
17. Latham, *The Travels of Marco Polo*, p. 158.
18. Latham, *The Travels of Marco Polo*, p. 111.
19. Latham, *The Travels of Marco Polo*, p. 133.
20. Latham, *The Travels of Marco Polo*, pp. 134, 101.
21. Yule and Cordier, *Cathay and the Way Thither*, II, pp. 192–3.
22. See the lengthy description in Yule and Cordier, *Cathay and the Way Thither*, II, pp. 215–26.
23. Yule and Cordier, *Cathay and the Way Thither*, II, p. 256.
24. de Rachewiltz, *Papal Envoys*, p. 18.
25. See J. M. Braga, 'The Western Pioneers and Their Discovery of Macao', *Instituto Português de Hongkong, Boletim*, No. 2 (September 1949), p. 60, quoted in Donald F. Lach, *Asia in the Making of Europe Volume I, The Century of Discovery Book Two* (University of Chicago Press, Chicago and London, 1965), p. 731.
26. C. R. Boxer (ed.), *South China in the Sixteenth Century* (The Hakluyt Society, London, 1953), pp. 13, 15.
27. Boxer, *South China in the Sixteenth Century*, p. 18.
28. Boxer, *South China in the Sixteenth Century*, p. 17.
29. Boxer, *South China in the Sixteenth Century*, p. lxii.
30. Boxer, *South China in the Sixteenth Century*, p. 115.
31. Boxer, *South China in the Sixteenth Century*, p. 118.
32. Boxer, *South China in the Sixteenth Century*, p. 175.
33. Boxer, *South China in the Sixteenth Century*, p. 146.
34. The original Spanish title was *Historia de la cosas mas notables, ritos y costumbres del gran Reyno de la China*, which means literally 'history of the most notable things, rites, and customs, of the great kingdom of China'.
35. Boxer, *South China in the Sixteenth Century*, p. xvii.
36. Lach, *Asia in the Making of Europe*, I, Two, p. 744.
37. Juan Gonzales de Mendoza, R. Parke (trans.), George T. Staunton (ed.), *The History of the Great and Mighty Kingdom of China and the Situation Thereof* (2 vols.; The Hakluyt Society, London, 1853–4), I, p. 20. This edition is reprinted from the English translation from Spanish of R. Parke, published first in 1588. I have retained the original words in quotations, but changed the spelling to conform to contemporary, not sixteenth-century, usage.
38. Mendoza, *History of the Great and Mighty Kingdom*, I, p. 25.
39. Mendoza, *History of the Great and Mighty Kingdom*, I, p. 27.
40. Mendoza, *History of the Great and Mighty Kingdom*, I, p. 103.
41. Mendoza, *History of the Great and Mighty Kingdom*, I, pp. 124–8.
42. Mendoza, *History of the Great and Mighty Kingdom*, I, p. 111.
43. Mendoza, *History of the Great and Mighty Kingdom*, I, p. 116.
44. Mendoza, *History of the Great and Mighty Kingdom*, I, p. 32.
45. Mendoza, *History of the Great and Mighty Kingdom*, I, p. 31.
46. Mendoza, *History of the Great and Mighty Kingdom*, I, p. 53.
47. See Lach, *Asia in the Making of Europe*, I, Two, pp. 791–2.

Notes to Chapter 3

1. H. J. Coleridge (ed.), *The Life and Letters of St. Francis Xavier* (2 vols.; Burns and Oates, London, 1872, 1902), II, p. 347.

2. Coleridge, *Life and Letters of St. Francis Xavier*, II, pp. 300–1.

3. John D. Young, *Confucianism and Christianity The First Encounter* (Hong Kong University Press, Hong Kong, 1983), p. 23.

4. Paul Rule, 'Jesuit Sources', in Donald D. Leslie, Colin Mackerras, and Wang Gungwu (edd.), *Essays on the Sources for Chinese History* (Australian National University Press, Canberra, 1973), p. 185.

5. Otto Berkelbach van der Sprenkel, 'Western Sources', in Leslie, Mackerras, and Wang (edd.), *Essays on the Sources*, p. 156.

6. The full title is 'Lettres édifiantes et curieuses écrites des missions étrangères par quelques missionaires de la Compagnie de Jésus', and an English edition was published after 1707 under the title 'Edifying and Curious Letters of Some Missioners, of the Society of Jesus, from Foreign Missions'.

7. The full title is 'Mémoires concernant l'histoire, les sciences, les arts, les mœurs, les usages, etc., des chinois, par les missionaires de Pékin' ('Memoirs on the History, Sciences, Arts, Manners, and Customs, etc. of the Chinese, by the Missionaries of Beijing').

8. The Latin title was *De Christiana Expeditione apud Sinas Suscepta ab Societate Jesu* (*On the Christian Expedition of the Society of Jesus among the Chinese*). For a translation into English see Louis J. Gallagher, S.J., *China in the Sixteenth Century: The Journals of Matthew Ricci: 1583–1610* (Random House, New York, 1942, 1953).

9. Paul A. Rule, *K'ung-tzu or Confucius? The Jesuit Interpretation of Confucianism* (Allen & Unwin, Sydney, 1986), p. 27.

10. Donald Lach claims in his *Asia in the Making of Europe Volume I, The Century of Discovery Book Two* (University of Chicago Press, Chicago and London, 1965), p. 804 that 'the first European writer to make clear that the examinations were written exercises' was the Jesuit Giovanni Pietro Maffei, who published a history of the Society of Jesus in 1588; the section on China was based largely on Ricci, who had been providing information to his order since earlier in the decade.

11. Rule, *K'ung-tzu or Confucius?*, p. 1.

12. Gallagher, *China in the Sixteenth Century*, p. 85.

13. Rule, *K'ung-tzu or Confucius?*, p. 28.

14. Gallagher, *China in the Sixteenth Century*, p. 30.

15. Rule, *K'ung-tzu or Confucius?*, p. 27.

16. Gallagher, *China in the Sixteenth Century*, p. 10.

17. Gallagher, *China in the Sixteenth Century*, p. 55.

18. Gallagher, *China in the Sixteenth Century*, pp. 85–8.

19. Paul Rule, 'Jesuit Sources', in Leslie, Mackerras, and Wang (edd.), *Essays on the Sources*, p. 182.

20. Rule, *K'ung-tzu or Confucius?*, p. 120.

21. Louis Daniel Le Comte, *Nouveaux mémoires sur l'etat present de la Chine* (2 vols.; Desbordes & Schelte, Amsterdam, 1698), II, pp. 2–3.

22. Le Comte, *Nouveaux mémoires*, I, p. 129.

23. J. B. Du Halde, *Description géographique, historique, chronologique, politique, et physique de l'empire de la Chine et de la Tartarie chinoise* (4 vols.; Henri Scheurleer, The Hague, 1736), II, p. 37. The translation is that of R. Brookes in *The General History of China* (4 vols.; J. Watts, London, 1741), II, p. 49.

24. Du Halde, *Description*, II, p. 163, as translated in *The General History*, II, p. 236.

25. Du Halde, *Description*, II, p. 89. The translation is my own.

26. Du Halde, *Description*, II, p. 90, as translated in *The General History*, II, p. 131.

27. Du Halde, *Description*, II, p. 95, as translated in *The General History*, II, p. 139. Note that Du Halde's original French says 'désagréable à nos yeux Européans' (disagreeable to our European eyes). 'Disagreeable to foreigners' is a loose translation.

28. Du Halde, *Description*, II, p. 87, as translated in *The General History*, II, p. 126.

29. Du Halde, *Description*, II, p. 154, as translated in *The General History*, II, p. 224.

30. Du Halde, *Description*, II, p. 162, as translated in *The General History*, II, p. 235.

31. Quoted from Wolfgang Franke, R. A. Wilson (trans.), *China and the West* (University of South Carolina Press, Columbia, South Carolina, 1968), p. 62.

32. Voltaire, *Essai sur les mœurs et l'esprit des nations et sur les principaux faits de l'histoire depuis Charlemagne jusqu'à Louis XIII Tome 1* (Éditions Garnier Frères, Paris, 1963 ed.), pp. 215–16.

33. Voltaire, *Essai sur les moeurs*, pp. 69–71.

34. Voltaire, *Essai sur les moeurs*, pp. 209–13.

35. François Quesnay, *Depotism in China*, translated by Lewis A. Maverick in *China, A Model for Europe* (Paul Anderson, San Antonio, 1946), pp. 141–2. This work was originally published in two volumes, the second of which is a translation of Quesnay's work.

36. Quesnay, *Despotism in China*, p. 170.

37. Quesnay, *Despotism in China*, p. 168.

38. Adam Smith, Edwin Cannan (ed.), *An Inquiry into the Nature and Causes of the Wealth of Nations* (2 vols.; Methuen, London, 1904; 1961), I, p. 80.

39. Smith, *An Inquiry*, I, pp. 80–1.

40. Smith, *An Inquiry*, II, p. 202.

41. Baron de Montesquieu, trans. Thomas Nugent, *The Spirit of the Laws* (Hafner, New York, 1949), pp. 303–4.

Notes to Chapter 4

1. Raymond Dawson, *The Chinese Chameleon, An Analysis of European Conceptions of Chinese Civilization* (Oxford University Press, London, 1967), p. 132.

2. J. L. Cranmer-Byng (ed.), *An Embassy to China, Being the Journal Kept by Lord Macartney During his Embassy to the Emperor Ch'ien-lung 1793–1794* (Longmans, London, 1962), p. 226.

3. Macartney (in Cranmer-Byng, *An Embassy to China*, p. 239) actually predicted the 'dislocation or dismemberment' of the Qing empire would occur before his own 'dissolution'. He died in 1806 but the Qing empire lasted until 1912.

4. Cranmer-Byng, *An Embassy to China*, p. 219.

5. Sir George Leonard Staunton, *An Authentic Account of an Embassy from the King of Great Britain to the Emperor of China* (2 vols.; G. Nicol, London, 1797).

6. Dawson, *The Chinese Chameleon*, p. 33.

7. John Barrow, *Travels in China, Containing Descriptions, Observations, and Comparisons, Made and Collected in the Course of a Short Residence at the Imperial Palace of Yuen-min-yuen, and on a Subsequent Journey through the Country from Peking to Canton* (T. Cadell and W. Davies, London, 2nd edition 1806), p. *xii.*

8. Barrow, *Travels in China*, p. 360.

9. Barrow, *Travels in China*, p. 179.

10. Barrow, *Travels in China*, p. 173.

11. Barrow, *Travels in China*, p. 77.

12. Barrow, *Travels in China*, p. 187.

13. Barrow, *Travels in China*, p. 183.

14. Dawson, *The Chinese Chameleon*, p. 134.

15. Dawson, *The Chinese Chameleon*, p. 135.

16. S. Wells Williams, *The Middle Kingdom, A Survey of the Geography, Government, Education, Social Life, Arts, Religion, &c., of the Chinese Empire and its Inhabitants* (2 vols.; John Wiley, New York, 1851), I, pp. 500–1.

17. Williams, *The Middle Kingdom*, I, pp. *xiv–xv.*

18. Williams, *The Middle Kingdom*, I, p. 297.

19. Williams, *The Middle Kingdom*, I, p. 458.

20. Williams, *The Middle Kingdom*, II, pp. 95–9.

21. Jerome Ch'en, *China and the West, Society and Culture 1815–1937* (Hutchinson, London, 1979), p. 43.

22. A. H. Smith, *Chinese Characteristics* (Oliphant Anderson and Ferrier, Edinburgh and London, 5th revised edition 1900), p. 12.

23. Smith, *Chinese Characteristics*, p. 94.

24. Smith, *Chinese Characteristics*, pp. 206–7.

25. Smith, *Chinese Characteristics*, p. 202.

26. Smith, *Chinese Characteristics*, p. 213.

27. Smith, *Chinese Characteristics*, p. 214.

28. Smith, *Chinese Characteristics*, p. 320.

29. Smith, *Chinese Characteristics*, p. 324.

30. Smith, *Chinese Characteristics*, p. 330.

31. John K. Fairbank, *The United States and China* (Harvard University Press, Cambridge, Mass., 3rd edition 1971), p. 294.

32. Dawson, *The Chinese Chameleon*, pp. 137–8.

33. S. Wells Williams, *The Middle Kingdom, A Survey of the Geography, Government, Literature, Social Life, Arts, and History of the Chinese Empire and its Inhabitants* (2 vols.; Charles Scribner's Sons, New York, 1883), I, pp. *ix*, *xiv.*

34. Williams, *The Middle Kingdom*, I, p. 578.

35. Williams, *The Middle Kingdom*, I, p. 836.

36. J. J. M. de Groot, *The Religious System of China, Its Ancient Forms, Evolution, History and Present Aspect, Manners, Custom and Social Institutions Connected Therewith* (6 vols.; Brill, Leiden, 1892–1910), I, p. 1.

37. Thomas Taylor Meadows, *The Chinese and their Rebellions, Viewed in Connection with their National Philosophy, Ethics, Legislation, and Administration to which is Added, An Essay on Civilization and its Present State in the East and West* (Smith, Elder & Co., London, 1856), p. 64.

38. Meadows, *The Chinese and their Rebellions*, pp. 72–3.

39. Robert Fortune, *Three Years' Wanderings in the Northern Provinces of China* (John Murray, London, 1847), p. 9.

40. Fortune, *Three Years' Wanderings*, p. 7.

41. Fortune, *Three Years' Wanderings*, pp. 10–11.

42. George Ernest Morrison, *An Australian in China, Being the Narrative of a Quiet Journey across China to Burma* (Horace Cox, London, 2nd edition 1895), p. 2.

43. Isabella L. Bird Bishop, *The Golden Chersonese and the Way Thither* (G. P. Putnam's Sons, New York, 1883), p. 64.

44. Fortune, *Three Years' Wanderings*, pp. 7–8.

45. Morrison, *An Australian in China*, p. 104.

46. Bishop, *The Golden Chersonese*, p. 87.

47. Fortune, *Three Years' Wanderings*, p. 319.

48. Bishop, *The Golden Chersonese*, p. 83.

49. Morrison, *An Australian in China*, p. 129.

50. Morrison, *An Australian in China*, p. 13.

51. Morrison, *An Australian in China*, p. 90.

52. Morrison, *An Australian in China*, p. 105.

53. *Chambers's Encyclopædia, A Dictionary of Universal Knowledge for the People, Illustrated with Maps and Numerous Wood Engravings* (10 vols.; W. and R. Chambers, London, Edinburgh, 1874), II, p. 819.

54. Robert K. Douglas, 'China', *Encyclopædia Britannica* (25 vols.; Adam and Charles Black, Edinburgh, 1875–89), V, p. 669. Vol. V appeared in 1876.

55. *Allgemeine deutsche Real-Encyklopädie für die gebildeten Stände. Conversations-Lexicon* (15 vols.; Brockhaus, Leipzig, 1852), IV, p. 107.

56. *Chambers's Encyclopædia*, II, p. 818.

57. Douglas, 'China', *Encyclopædia Britannica*, V, p. 670.

58. Douglas, 'China', *Encyclopædia Britannica*, V, p. 671.

59. *Conversations-Lexicon* , IV, p. 107.

60. Quoted in Prescott Clarke and J. S. Gregory, *Western Reports on the Taiping, A Selection of Documents* (Australian National University Press, Canberra, 1982), p. 56.

61. Quoted Clarke and Gregory, *Western Reports*, pp. 89–90.

62. Quoted Clarke and Gregory, *Western Reports*, p. 131.

63. Meadows, *The Chinese and their Rebellions*, p. 324.

64. Quoted Clarke and Gregory, *Western Reports*, p. 399.

65. *Chambers's Encyclopædia*, II, p. 822.

66. A. F. Lindley (Lin-Le), *Ti-Ping Tien-Kwoh: The History of the Ti-ping Revolution* (2 vols.; Day & Son, London, 1866), I, p. 248.

67. Quoted Lindley, *Ti-Ping Tien-Kwoh*, II, p. 693.

68. Quoted Lindley, *Ti-Ping Tien-Kwoh*, I, p. 300–1.

69. For instance, see two such cartoons from *Punch* of 10 April 1858 and 22 December 1860 reprinted in Dawson, *The Chinese Chameleon*, pp. 133 and 151. The former also carries the following stanza which includes several racist stereotypes:

> John Chinaman a rogue is born,
> The laws of truth he holds in scorn;
> About as great a brute as can
> Encumber the Earth is John Chinaman.
> Sing Yeh, my cruel John Chinaman,
> Sing Yeo, my stubborn John Chinaman,
> Not Cobden himself can take off the ban
> By humanity laid on John Chinaman.

70. Edward W. Said, *Orientalism* (Random House, Vintage Books, New York, 1979), p. 204.

Notes to Chapter 5

1. Pearl S. Buck, *My Several Worlds, A Personal Record* (John Day, New York, 1954), p. 10.

2. Sarah Pike Conger, *Letters from China, with Particular Reference to the Empress Dowager and the Women of China* (A. C. McClurg & Co., Chicago, 1909), p. 168.

3. Conger, *Letters from China*, p. *viii*.

4. A. Henry Savage-Landor, *China and the Allies* (2 vols.; William Heinemann, London, 1901), I, p. 257.

5. Conger, *Letters from China*, p. 168.

6. Conger, *Letters from China*, p. 188.

7. L. R. Marchant (ed.), *The Siege of the Peking Legations, A Diary Lancelot Giles* (University of Western Australia Press, Nedlands, 1970), p. 148.

8. Gerd Kaminski and Else Unterrieder, *Von Österreichern und Chinesen* (Europaverlag, Vienna, Munich, Zürich, 1980), p. 335.

9. Quoted in Kaminski and Unterrieder, *Von Österreichern*, pp. 405–6.

10. From an unpublished manuscript this section of which is quoted in Kaminski and Unterrieder, *Von Österreichern*, p. 405.

11. Harold R. Isaacs, *Images of Asia, American Views of China and India* (Harper Torchbooks, New York, 1972), pp. 142–3.

12. Kaminski and Unterrieder, *Von Österreichern*, p. 336.

13. Quoted by R. H. Scott, 'Foreword', in Marchant, ed., *The Siege*, p. *xx*.

14. Scott, 'Foreword', in Marchant, ed., *The Siege*, pp. *xxiv–xxv*.

15. Herbert A. Giles, *The Civilization of China* (Williams and Norgate, London, no date, preface dated 12 May 1911), p. 249.

16. Daniel Harrison Kulp II, *Country Life in South China, The Sociology of Familism* (Teachers College, Columbia University, New York, 1925), p. 346.

17. Edwin D. Harvey, *The Mind of China* (Yale University Press, New Haven, 1933), p. 287.

18. Harvey, *The Mind of China*, p. 294.

19. Harvey, *The Mind of China*, p. 295.

20. Lin Yutang, *My Country and my People* (Heinemann, London, Toronto, 1936), p. 11.

21. Rodney Gilbert, *What's Wrong with China* (John Murray, London, 1926), p. 14.

22. Gilbert, *What's Wrong with China*, p. 49. Lin Yutang believed Rodney Gilbert's to be a commonplace view in the West. One may cite also the example of A. F. Legendre, a French doctor who had been Director of the Imperial School of Medicine at Chengdu and Commissioner for Scientific Research. He wrote a book in which he claimed that the Chinese suffered from a lack of cerebral activity by comparison with Westerners. His conclusion was that the great powers of the day were making 'a fatal mistake' by refusing to intervene in China's affairs 'for there is no other solution to the Chinese problem'. See A. F. Legendre, Elsie Martin Jones (trans.), *Modern Chinese Civilization* (Jonathan Cape, London, 1928), pp. 168–9.

23. Lin, *My Country*, p. *xiv*.

24. Lin, *My Country*, pp. 40–1.

25. Lin, *My Country*, pp. 168–70.

26. Lin, *My Country*, p. 196.

27. Lin, *My Country*, p. 326.

28. See Isaacs, *Images of Asia*, p. 79.

29. 'The Spirit that Is China' is the title, and also the last and decisive

words of the first chapter of May-ling Soong Chiang, *China Shall Rise Again* (Harper, New York and London, 1940), pp. 3–7.

30. 'Seven Deadly Sins', in *China Shall Rise Again*, p. 38.

31. 'Seven Deadly Sins', in *China Shall Rise Again*, pp. 42–3.

32. Isaacs, *Images of Asia*, p. 150.

33. Carl Crow, *Four Hundred Million Customers* (Hamish Hamilton, London, 1937), p. 11.

34. Carl Crow, *Foreign Devils in the Flowery Kingdom* (Hamish Hamilton, London, 1941), p. 326.

35. Crow, *Foreign Devils*, p. 340.

36. Isaacs, *Images of Asia*, p. 147.

37. Earl Herbert Cressy, 'Converting the Missionary', *Asia* (June 1919), quoted by Isaacs in *Images of Asia*, p. 148.

38. See E. R. Hughes, *The Invasion of China by the Western World* (Adam and Charles Black, London, 1937; 1968), p. 101.

39. See Paul Varg, *Missionaries, Chinese, and Diplomats, The American Protestant Missionary Movement in China, 1870–1952* (Princeton University Press, Princeton, 1958), pp. 198–211.

40. Osbert Sitwell, *Escape with Me! An Oriental Sketch-Book* (Macmillan, London, 1939), p. *vii.*

41. Sitwell, *Escape with Me!*, p. 204.

42. Sitwell, *Escape with Me!*, p. 331.

43. For a full-length biography of Strong, see Tracy B. Strong and Helene Keyssar, *Right in her Soul: The Life of Anna Louise Strong* (Random House, New York, 1983).

44. Agnes Smedley, *The Great Road, The Life and Times of Chu Teh* (Monthly Review Press, New York, 1956), p. 3.

45. Agnes Smedley, *China's Red Army Marches* (Lawrence and Wishart, London, 1936), p. *xx.*

46. Israel Epstein, 'Smedley, Strong, Snow — Bridge Builders from People to People', *Beijing Review*, XXVIII, 28 (15 July 1985), p. 23.

47. For a bibliography of her books and pamphlets see Strong and Keyssar, *Right in her Soul*, pp. 377–8.

48. Anna Louise Strong, *The Chinese Conquer China* (Doubleday, New York, 1949), p. 59.

49. Strong, *The Chinese Conquer China*, p. 275.

50. Edgar Snow, 'Preface to the Revised Edition', *Red Star over China* (Victor Gollancz, London, 1937; Penguin, Harmondsworth, 1972 ed.), p. 20.

51. Jerome Ch'en, *China and the West, Society and Culture 1815-1937* (Hutchinson, London, 1979), p. 55.

52. Ch'en, *China and the West*, p. 55. According to A. T. Steele, *The American People and China* (McGraw–Hill, New York, 1966), pp. 171–2, Snow's book sold about 125,000 copies in the UK edition, but only some 15,000 in the initial Random House edition in the US.

53. See Michael H. Hunt, 'Pearl Buck — Popular Expert on China, 1931–1949', *Modern China, An International Quarterly*, III, 1 (January 1977), p. 59.

54. Dorothy B. Jones, *The Portrayal of China and India on the American Screen 1896–1955* (MIT Center for International Affairs, Cambridge, Mass., 1955), p. 47.

55. Hunt, 'Pearl Buck', p. 34.

56. Pearl S. Buck, *The Good Earth* (John Day, New York, 1931; edition of April 1965), p. 308.

57. Hunt, 'Pearl Buck', p. 56.

58. Buck, *The Good Earth*, p. 303.

59. Hunt, 'Pearl Buck', p. 52.

60. Quoted in Axel Madsen, *Malraux, A Biography* (William Morrow, New York, 1976), p. 128.

61. André Malraux, trans. Haakon M. Chevalier, *Man's Fate (La condition humaine)* (Random House, New York, 1961), p. 246.

62. Malraux, *Man's Fate*, p. 359.

63. Malraux, *Man's Fate*, p. 167.

64. Malraux, *Man's Fate*, p. 155.

65. W. Somerset Maugham, *The Painted Veil* (William Heinemann, London, 1925; Pan Books, London, 1978), pp. 140, 149.

66. Maugham, *The Painted Veil*, p. 117.

67. Maugham, *The Painted Veil*, p. 103.

68. Ted Morgan, *Somerset Maugham* (Jonathan Cape, London, 1980), p. 244.

69. W. Somerset Maugham, 'On a Chinese Screen', in *The Travel Books of W. Somerset Maugham* (Heinemann, London, 1955), p. 48.

70. Maugham may exaggerate. Even Rodney Gilbert does not equate the Chinese with animals or half animals, though he does make the comparison: 'Like children and animals, they [the Chinese] squirm under ridicule, find everything most amusing but themselves, and simply abhor the person who refuses to take them seriously' (*What's Wrong with China*, p. 47).

71. Steele, *The American People and China*, p. 22.

72. Isaacs, *Images of Asia*, p. xix.

73. Hunt, 'Pearl Buck', p. 52.

Notes to Chapter 6

1. C. R. Boxer, (ed.), *South China in the Sixteenth Century* (The Hakluyt Society, London, 1953), pp. 278–82.

2. See Juan Gonzalez de Mendoza, R. Parke (trans.), George T. Staunton (ed.), *The History of the Great and Mighty Kingdom of China and the Situation Thereof* (2 vols.; The Hakluyt Society, London, 1853–4), I, pp. 69–76.

3. Mendoza, *History of the Great and Mighty Kingdom*, I, p. 74.

4. Donald F. Lach, *Asia in the Making of Europe, Volume II, A Century of Wonder Book Two. The Literary Arts* (University of Chicago Press, Chicago and London, 1977), p. 220.

5. The phrase occurs in Arrivabene's preliminary note to his work and is quoted in Lach, *Asia in the Making of Europe*, II, Two, p. 220.

6. Paul A. Rule, *K'ung-tzu or Confucius? The Jesuit Interpretation of Confucianism* (Allen & Unwin, Sydney, 1986), p. 187.

7. J. B. Du Halde, *Description géographique, historique, chronologique, politique, et physique de l'empire de la Chine et de la Tartarie chinoise* (4 vols.; Henri Scheurleer, The Hague, 1736), I, pp. 257–488.

8. Du Halde, *Description*, I, pp. 259–65.

9. Du Halde, *Description*, I, p. 266.

10. Du Halde, *Description*, I, p. 259.

11. Du Halde, *Description*, I, p. 260.

12. Du Halde, *Description*, I, p. 399.

13. Du Halde, *Description*, I, p. 473.

14. See Rule, *K'ung-tzu or Confucius?*, p. 189, citing an article of 1885 by J. Brucker.

15. See Henri Cordier, *Histoire générale de la Chine et de ses relations avec les pays étrangers depuis les temps les plus anciens jusqu'à la chute de la dynastie mandchoue* (4 vols.; Librairie Paul Geuthner, Paris, 1920–1), I, pp. 15–19. The passage from Voltaire is quoted p. 19.

16. Theodore Besterman, *Voltaire* (Longman, London, 2nd revised edition, 1970), p. 408.

17. Voltaire, *Essai sur les mœurs et l'esprit des nations et sur les principaux faits de l'histoire depuis Charlemagne jusqu'à Louis XIII Tome I* (Éditions Garnier Frères, Paris, 1963 ed.), p. 67.

18. Voltaire, *Essai sur les moeurs*, pp. 69–70.

19. Paul A. Rule, 'Jesuit Sources', in Donald D. Leslie, Colin Mackerras, and Wang Gungwu (edd.), *Essays on the Sources for Chinese History* (Australian National University Press, Canberra, 1973), p. 184.

20. S. Wells Williams, *The Middle Kingdom, A Survey of the Geography, Government, Education, Social Life, Arts, Religion &c. of the Chinese Empire and its Inhabitants* (2 vols.; John Wiley, New York, 1851), II, pp. 193–4.

21. *Allgemeine deutsche Real-Encyklopädie für die gebildeten Stände. Conversations-Lexicon* (15 vols.; Brockhaus, Leipzig, 1852), IV, p. 110.

22. The French title is *Le Tcheou-li ou Rites des Tcheou, traduit pour la première fois du chinois* and the work was a French government publication.

23. Osbert Sitwell, *Escape with Me! An Oriental Sketch-Book* (Macmillan, London, 1939), p. 257.

24. Sitwell, *Escape with Me!*, pp. 315–19.

25. Otto Berkelbach van der Sprenkel, 'Western Sources', in Leslie, Mackerras, and Wang (edd.), *Essays on the Sources for Chinese History*, p. 171.

26. Zoe Zwecker, 'Henri Cordier and the Meeting of East and West', in Cyriac K. Pullapilly and Edwin J. Van Kley (edd.), *Asia and the West, Encounters and Exchanges from the Age of Explorations, Essays in Honor of Donald F. Lach* (Cross Cultural Publications, Notre Dame, Indiana, 1986), p. 319.

27. Zwecker, in *Asia and the West*, p. 323.

28. O. Franke, *Geschichte des chinesischen Reiches, Eine Darstellung seiner Entstehung, seines Wesens und seiner Entwicklung bis zur neuesten Zeit* (5 vols.; W. de Gruyter, Berlin, 1930–52), I, p. *xxii.*

29. Franke, *Geschichte des chinesischen Reiches*, I, p. *xvii.*

30. C. P. Fitzgerald, *China, A Short Cultural History* (Cresset Press, London, 1935), p. 1.

31. The titles of the three volumes are, respectively, *Geschichte der alten chinesischen Philosophie, Geschichte der mittelalterlichen chinesischen Philosophie,* and *Geschichte der neueren chinesischen Philosophie.*

32. Wolfgang Franke, R. A. Wilson (trans.), *China and the West* (Basil Blackwell, Oxford, 1967), p. 148.

33. Henri Maspero, *La Chine antique* (Presses Universitaires de France, Paris, 1965 ed.), pp. 504–5.

34. Henri Berr, 'Avant-Propos', in Marcel Granet, *La civilisation chinoise, La vie publique et la vie privée* (La Renaissance du Livre, Paris, 1929), p. *v.*

35. Granet, *La civilisation chinoise*, p. 1.

36. See Henri Cordier, *Histoire des relations de la Chine aves les puissances occidentales 1860–1902* (3 vols.; Ancienne Librairie Germer Baillière, Paris, 1901–2), III, pp. 552–4.

37. Cordier, *Histoire générale*, IV, p. 68.

38. Cordier, *Histoire générale*, II, pp. 219–42, especially pp. 233, 238–9, 235.

39. Hosea Ballou Morse, *The International Relations of the Chinese Empire* (3 vols.; Longmans, Green and Co., London, 1910–18), II, p. *vi.*

40. Morse, *International Relations*, I, pp. 611–12.
41. Morse, *International Relations*, II, p. 415.
42. Morse, *International Relations*, II, pp. 64–5.
43. Morse, *International Relations*, II, p. 111.
44. Fitzgerald, *China*, p. 576.
45. Fitzgerald, *China*, pp. 584–5.

Notes to Chapter 7

1. Adam Smith, Edwin Cannan (ed.), *An Inquiry into the Nature and Causes of the Wealth of Nations* (2 vols.; Methuen, London, 1904; 1961), I, p. 80.

2. See J. G. von Herder, 'Ideen zur Geschichte der Menschheit', in *Ausgewählte Werke in einem Bande* (J. G. Cotta, Stuttgart, 1844), p. 833.

3. Georg Wilhelm Friedrich Hegel, J. Sibree (trans.), *The Philosophy of History* (Dover Publications, New York, 1956), p. 116.

4. See Shlomo Avineri (ed.), *Karl Marx on Colonialism and Modernization, His Despatches and Other Writings on China, India, Mexico, The Middle East and North Africa* (Doubleday, New York, 1968), p. 427. Italics in original.

5. Karl Marx, 'The British Rule in India', *Karl Marx and Frederick Engels Selected Works* (3 vols.; Progress Publishers, Moscow, 1969–70), I, p. 489.

6. See Marian Sawer, *Marxism and the Question of the Asiatic Mode of Production* (Martinus Nijhoff, The Hague, 1977), pp. 46–7.

7. Marx, 'The British Rule in India', *Selected Works*, I, p. 492.

8. Marx, 'The Future Results of British Rule in India', *Selected Works*, I, p. 494.

9. Marx, 'The Future Results of British Rule in India', *Selected Works*, I, p. 499.

10. Marx, 'Revolution in China and in Europe', *New York Daily Tribune*, 14 June 1853. See *Karl Marx Frederick Engels Collected Works Volume 12 Marx and Engels 1853–1854* (Lawrence and Wishart, London, 1979), p. 94. It was in the *New York Daily Tribune* that Marx published much of what he wrote on China in the 1850s.

11. Quoted in Donald M. Lowe, *The Function of 'China' in Marx, Lenin, and Mao* (University of California Press, Berkeley and Los Angeles, 1966), p. 19.

12. Marx, 'History of the Opium Trade', *Karl Marx Frederick Engels Collected Works Volume 16 Marx and Engels 1858–60* (Lawrence and Wishart, London, 1980), p. 16.

13. Marx, 'Revolution in China and in Europe', *Collected Works*, XII, p. 95.

14. Frederick Engels, 'Revolution and Counter-Revolution in Germany', *Selected Works*, I, p. 320.

15. Marx, 'The New Chinese War IV', *Collected Works*, XVI, p. 524.

16. Marx, 'Manifesto of the Communist Party', *Selected Works*, I, p. 109.

17. Marx, 'Revolution in China and in Europe', *Collected Works*, XII, p. 96.

18. See Lowe, *The Function of 'China'*, p. 20.

19. Marx, 'Revolution in China and in Europe', *Collected Works*, XII, p. 93.

20. *Die Presse*, Vienna, 7 July 1862. I have followed the translation in Karl A. Wittfogel, 'The Marxist View of China (Part 1)', *The China Quarterly*, 11 (July–September 1962), pp. 6–7.

21. Lowe, *The Function of 'China'*, p. 25.

22. C. W. Bishop, 'The Rise of Civilization in China with Reference to its Geographical Aspects', *Geographical Review*, 22 (1932), p. 619.

23. K. A. Wittfogel, *Wirtschaft und Gesellschaft Chinas: Versuch der wissenschaftlichen Analyse einer grossen asiatischen Agrargesellschaft; Erster Teil: Produktivkräfte, Produktions- und Zirkulationsprozess* (C. L. Hirschfeld, Leipzig, 1931), p. 410.

24. Wittfogel, *Wirtschaft und Gesellschaft Chinas*, p. 126. The translation of this sentence is that of Andrew L. March in *The Idea of China, Myth and Theory in Geographic Thought* (Wren, Melbourne, 1974), p. 80.

25. K. A. Wittfogel, *Oriental Despotism: A Comparative Study of Total Power* (Yale University Press, New Haven, 1957), p. 78.

26. Wittfogel, *Oriental Despotism*, p. 87.

27. Wittfogel, *Oriental Despotism*, pp. 95–6.

28. Wittfogel, *Oriental Despotism*, p. 116.

29. Wittfogel, *Oriental Despotism*, p. 80.

30. Wittfogel, *Oriental Despotism*, p. 149.

31. March, *The Idea of China*, p. 98.

32. Owen Lattimore, *Inner Asian Frontiers of China* (American Geographical Society, New York, 1940), pp. 373–4.

33. John King Fairbank, *The United States and China* (Harvard University Press, Cambridge, Mass., 1971 ed.), p. 44.

34. S. N. Eisenstadt, 'The Study of Oriental Despotisms as Systems of Total Power', *The Journal of Asian Studies*, XVII, 3 (May 1958), p. 446. The whole review extends pp. 435–46.

35. Eisenstadt, 'The Study of Oriental Despotisms', p. 437.

36. Wittfogel, *Oriental Despotism*, pp. 327–9.

37. See Joseph Needham's review of *Oriental Despotism* in *Science and Society*, XXIII, 1 (1959), p. 58–65. The direct quotation is on p. 60.

38. Etienne Balazs, H. M. Wright (trans.), *Chinese Civilization and Bureaucracy, Variations on a Theme* (Yale University Press, New Haven and London, 1964), p. 20.

39. Balazs, *Chinese Civilization*, p. 6.

40. Wolfram Eberhard, *Conquerors and Rulers, Social Forces in Medieval China* (Brill, Leiden, 1965 ed.), p. 61. This is the 2nd revised edition of a work originally published in 1952.

41. Eberhard, *Conquerors and Rulers*, p. 85.

42. Wittfogel, *Oriental Despotism*, p. 11.

43. K. A. Wittfogel, 'Die natürlichen Ursachen der Wirtschaftsgeschichte', *Archiv für Sozialwissenschaft und Sozialpolitik*, LXVII, 6 (August–September 1932), p. 731. See also the translation by March in *The Idea of China*, p. 71.

44. March, *The Idea of China*, pp. 94–5.

Notes to Chapter 8

1. Joseph Needham, with the research assistance of Wang Ling, *Science and Civilisation in China, Volume I, Introductory Orientations* (Cambrige University Press, Cambridge, 1954), p. 156.

2. Needham, *Science and Civilisation*, I, p. 3.

3. See Colin A. Ronan's 'abridgement of Joseph Needham's original text' in *The Shorter Science and Civilisation in China Volume I* (Cambridge University Press, Cambridge, 1978), p. 191.

4. Ronan, *The Shorter Science and Civilisation*, I, p. 84.

5. Ronan, *The Shorter Science and Civilisation*, I, p. 98.

6. Ronan, *The Shorter Science and Civilisation*, I, p. 275.

7. Ronan, *The Shorter Science and Civilisation*, I, p. 306.

8. Joseph Needham, *The Grand Titration, Science and Society in East and West* (University of Toronto Press, Toronto, 1969), p. 12.

9. Needham, *Science and Civilisation*, I, p. 4.

10. Needham, *Science and Civilisation*, I, p. 19.

11. See, for example, the Author's Note in Joseph Needham with the collaboration of Lu Gwei-djen, *Science and Civilisation in China, Volume V, Chemistry and Chemical Technology, Part II: Spagyrical Discovery and Invention: Magisteries of Gold and Immortality* (Cambridge University Press, Cambridge, 1974), pp. *xxiii–iv*.

12. See, for example, the review by N. Sivin, himself a historian of Chinese science, of *The Grand Titration* in *Journal of Asian Studies*, XXX, 4 (August 1971), pp. 870–3, especially p. 872.

13. David N. Keightley, '"Benefit of Water": The Approach of Joseph Needham', *Journal of Asian Studies*, XXXI, 2 (February 1972), p. 370.

14. Derk Bodde, reviewing Needham's *Science and Civilisation, Volume V, Part II* in *Journal of Asian Studies*, XXXV, 3 (May 1976), pp. 489–90.

15. Joseph Needham and others, *Science and Civilisation in China, Volume IV, Physics and Physical Technology, Part 3: Civil Engineering and Nautics* (Cambridge University Press, Cambridge, 1971), p. 214.

16. Needham, *Science and Civilisation*, IV, 3, p. 212.

17. Needham, *Science and Civilisation*, IV, 3, p. 227.

18. Keightley, 'Benefit of Water', p. 369.

19. Keightley, 'Benefit of Water', p. 367.

20. Keightley, 'Benefit of Water', p. 370.

21. The original German edition, published in Switzerland, is called *Chinas Geschichte*. The English translation, by E. W. Dickes, is entitled *A History of China*. The work has been through many editions and reprints and became a paperback in 1977. The fourth revised edition was published by the University of California Press, Berkeley and Los Angeles, in 1977.

22. Edwin O. Reischauer and John K. Fairbank, *East Asia, The Great Tradition* (George Allen & Unwin, London, 1958), p. 184. The work has been through many reprints and editions.

23. C. P. Fitzgerald, *The Horizon History of China* (Heritage, New York, 1969), p. 5.

24. Charles O. Hucker, *China's Imperial Past, An Introduction to Chinese History and Culture* (Duckworth, London, 1975), p. *vii*.

25. Conrad Schirokauer, *A Brief History of Chinese and Japanese Civilizations* (Harcourt Brace Jovanovich, New York, 1978), pp. *v–vi*.

26. Bodo Wiethoff, Mary Whittall (trans.), *Introduction to Chinese History From Ancient Times to 1912* (Thames and Hudson, London, 1975), p. 31. The original title is *Grundzüge der älteren chinesischen Geschichte*.

27. Caroline Blunden and Mark Elvin, *Cultural Atlas of China* (Phaidon, Oxford, 1983), p. 120.

28. See Part Two, entitled 'The medieval economic revolution', of Mark Elvin, *The Pattern of the Chinese Past, A Social and Economic Interpretation* (Stanford University Press, Stanford; Eyre Methuen, London, 1973), pp. 111–99.

29. Elvin, *Pattern of the Chinese Past*, p. 203.

30. The title of Part Three, which extends in Elvin, *Pattern of the Chinese Past*, pp. 201–316.

31. Elvin, *Pattern of the Chinese Past*, p. 312.

32. Elvin, *Pattern of the Chinese Past*, p. 318.

33. See, among many other places, Denis C. Twitchett, *Land Tenure and Social Order in T'ang and Sung China* (Oxford University Press, New York, 1962), pp. 28–32, reprinted as 'Economic and Social Changes in T'ang and Sung China', in James T. C. Liu and Wei-ming Tu (edd.), *Traditional China* (Prentice-Hall, Englewood Cliffs, 1970), pp. 38–41.

34. See James T. C. Liu, 'Integrative Factors through Chinese History: Their Interaction', in Liu and Tu (edd.),*Traditional China*, pp. 10–23.

35. James T. C. Liu and Wei-ming Tu, 'Introduction', in Liu and Tu (edd.), *Traditional China*, p. 3.

36. Wing-tsit Chan, 'The Ch'eng-Chu School of Early Ming', in Wm. Theodore de Bary and the Conference on Ming Thought, *Self and Society in Ming Thought* (Columbia University Press, New York and London, 1970), p. 29.

37. Wm. Theodore de Bary, 'Introduction', in de Bary, *Self and Society*, p. 1.

38. Hucker, *China's Imperial Past*, pp. 375, 376.

39. See the influential article of Derk Bodde, 'Harmony and Conflict in Chinese Philosophy', in Arthur F. Wright (ed.), *Studies in Chinese Thought* (University of Chicago Press, Chicago, 1953 and many impressions), p. 37.

40. For instance John King Fairbank, *The United States and China* (Harvard University Press, Cambridge, Mass., 1948; third edition 1971), pp. 19–20. This influential book has been through numerous editions and reprints.

41. Arthur F. Wright, 'Introduction', in Arthur F. Wright (ed.), *Confucianism and Chinese Civilization* (Atheneum, New York, 1964), p. *vi*.

42. See Edward L. Farmer and others, *Comparative History of Civilizations in Asia Volume I: 10,000 B.C. to 1850* (Addison-Wesley, Reading, Mass., 1977), p. 446.

43. Richard J. Smith, *China's Cultural Heritage, the Ch'ing Dynasty, 1644–1912* (Westview, Boulder, 1983), p. 120.

44. John K. Fairbank, 'A Preliminary Framework', in John K. Fairbank (ed.), *The Chinese World Order, Traditional China's Foreign Relations* (Harvard University Press, Cambridge, Mass., 1968), p. 2.

45. Reischauer and Fairbank, *East Asia, The Great Tradition*, p. 317.

46. See Fairbank, 'A Preliminary Framework', in Fairbank, (ed.), *The Chinese World Order*, p. 1.

47. Reischauer and Fairbank, *East Asia, The Great Tradition*, p. 319.

48. Jonathan Spence, 'Adapting Scholarly Work to the Needs of Educators', in Arlene Posner and Arne J. de Keijzer (edd.), *China a Resource and Curriculum Guide* (University of Chicago Press, Chicago, 2nd revised edition 1976), p. 9.

49. Fitzgerald, *The Horizon History of China*, pp. 10–11.

50. See sections of Zhang Zeduan's 'Going on the River at the Qingming Festival' reproduced in Fitzgerald, *The Horizon History of China*, pp. 266–79, Bradley Smith and Wan-go Weng, *China, A History in Art* (Studio Vista, London, 1973), pp. 162–9, and Blunden and Elvin, *Cultural Atlas*, pp. 120–1.

51. See, for example, Fitzgerald, *The Horizon History*, pp. 40–1, 182, 186–7, 192, and Smith and Weng, *China*, pp. 138–9, 173, 179.

52. See, for example, Fitzgerald, *The Horizon History*, pp. 97, 162, 250–3, 262, and Smith and Weng, *China*, pp. 114–15, 156–7, 158, 214, 250, 254–5.

53. Fitzgerald, *The Horizon History*, pp. 100–11, 185.

54. See Reischauer and Fairbank, *East Asia, The Great Tradition*, p. 225.

55. See, for example, Smith and Weng, *China*, pp. 93–6, Fitzgerald, *The Horizon History*, pp. 138, 139, and Blunden and Elvin, *Cultural Atlas*, pp. 112,

113. The last mentioned page depicts the famous stone sitting Buddha at Leshan in Sichuan, which is about 70 metres high.

56. See, for example, Smith and Weng, *China*, pp. 160–1, 222, 242–3, Blunden and Elvin, *Cultural Atlas*, pp. 116–17, Fitzgerald, *The Horizon History*, pp.132, 304–5.

57. See, for example, Fitzgerald, *The Horizon History*, pp. 258–9, 346–7, Blunden and Elvin, *Cultural Atlas*, pp. 68–9, 100–1, 132–3.

58. Edmund Capon, *Art and Archaeology in China* (Macmillan, Melbourne and Sydney, 1977), p. 7.

59. S. FitzGerald in Capon, *Art and Archaeology*, p. 8.

60. Blunden and Elvin, *Cultural Atlas of China*, p. 87. See pp. 84–7 for an account, with photographs, of 'the underground army'.

61. Pictorial histories usually include a picture of the Great Wall. For example, see Blundern and Elvin, *Cultural Atlas of China*, front dustcover; Fitzgerald, *The Horizon History*, pp. 18–19; and Smith and Weng, *China*, pp. 58–9. In fact much of the present Great Wall dates from Ming times.

62. C. P. Fitzgerald, *China, A Short Cultural History* (Cresset Press, London, 3rd revised edition 1961), p. 140.

63. His best known academic treatises include *The Lore of the Chinese Lute, An Essay in Ch'in Ideology* (Sophia University, Tokyo, 1940) and *Sexual Life in Ancient China, A Preliminary Survey of Chinese Sex and Society from ca. 1500 B.C. till 1644 A.D.* (E. J. Brill, Leiden, 1961).

64. Van Gulik did this translation during the Pacific War, and published it privately in 1949 in Tokyo. A wider-circulation edition was published in the US much later: *Celebrated Cases of Judge Dee (Dee Goong An), An Authentic Eighteenth-Century Chinese Detective Novel* (Dover Publications, New York, 1976).

65. See, for example, *The Red Pavilion, A Chinese Detective Story* (Heinemann, London, 1964), pp. 25–8.

66. See, for example, Robert Van Gulik, *The Chinese Bell Murders, Three Cases Solved by Judge Dee* (Lythway Press, Bath, 1973 ed.), pp. 253–73.

67. Robert Van Gulik, *Poets and Murder, A Chinese Detective Story* (Heinemann, London, 1968), p. 13; republished as *The Fox-Magic Murders* (Panther, Frogmore, St Albans, 1973), p. 17.

68. Van Gulik, *The Chinese Bell Murders*, p. 189.

69. Van Gulik, *Poets and Murder*, p. 1 or *The Fox-Magic Murders*, p. 1.

70. See, for example, Robert Van Gulik, *The Lacquer Screen, A Chinese Detective Story* (Penguin, Harmondsworth, 1968), pp. 93–101.

71. Robert Elegant, *Manchu* (McGraw-Hill, New York, 1980; Penguin, Harmondsworth, 1981), pp. 400–2.

72. Elegant, *Manchu*, pp. 413–7. See scenes of great cruelty described also pp. 53, 260, 340, 445–6.

73. Elegant, *Manchu*, pp. 172–3.

74. Elegant, *Manchu*, p. 181.

75. Elegant, *Manchu*, p. 333.

76. Elegant, *Manchu*, p. 226.

77. Elegant, *Manchu*, p. 606.

Notes to Chapter 9

1. Albert Feuerwerker, Rhoads Murphey, and Mary C. Wright (edd.), *Approaches to Modern Chinese History* (University of California Press, Berkeley and Los Angeles, 1967), p. 6.

2. Paul A. Cohen claims in his book *Discovering History in China, American Historical Writing on the Recent Chinese Past* (Columbia University Press, New York, 1984), p. 98 that 'the opening salvo was fired by James Peck'. His reference is to Peck's article 'The Roots of Rhetoric: The Professional Ideology of America's China Watchers', *Bulletin of Concerned Asian Scholars*, II, 1 (October 1969), pp. 59–69.

3. John K. Fairbank, Edwin O. Reischauer, and Albert M. Craig, *East Asia, The Modern Transformation* (Houghton Mifflin, Boston, 1965), p. 5. The book appeared originally in 1960 and with its forerunner has been through many editions and versions.

4. Fairbank, Reischauer, and Craig, *East Asia, The Modern Transformation*, pp. 9–10.

5. Wolfram Eberhard, E. W. Dickes (trans.), *A History of China* (University of California Press, Berkeley and Los Angeles, 4th revised edition 1977), p. 205.

6. In the 'China' entry of the *Encyclopædia Britannica Volume 5* (Encyclopædia Britannica, Chicago, London, 1971), p. 581, L. Carrington Goodrich writes that the establishment of the Song dynasty 'inaugurates the period that has been described rightly as early modern' and goes on to list some features which make it 'modern'.

7. See Chapters 13 and 14 of C. P. Fitzgerald, *The Horizon History of China* (Heritage, New York, 1969).

8. Philip A. Kuhn, *Rebellion and its Enemies in Late Imperial China, Militarization and Social Structure, 1795–1864* (Harvard University Press, Cambridge, Mass., 1970), pp. 5–6.

9. See Peck, 'The Roots of Rhetoric', pp. 59–69.

10. Cohen, *Discovering History in China*, p. 125.

11. Rhoads Murphey, *The Outsiders: The Western Experience in India and China* (University of Michigan Press, Ann Arbor, 1977), pp. 104–8, 128–9, 159.

12. Murphy, *The Outsiders*, p. 129.

13. Joseph Levenson, *Confucian China and Its Modern Fate Volume One, The Problem of Intellectual Continuity* (University of California Press, Berkeley, 1958), p. 3.

14. Immanuel C. Y. Hsu, *The Rise of Modern China* (Oxford University Press, New York, London, 1970), p. 6.

15. Caroline Blunden and Mark Elvin, *Cultural Atlas of China* (Phaidon, Oxford, 1983), p. 144.

16. Mark Elvin, *The Pattern of the Chinese Past, A Social and Economic Interpretation* (Stanford University Press, Stanford, 1973), p. 315.

17. Frederic Wakeman, Jr., 'Introduction: The Evolution of Local Control in Late Imperial China', in Frederic Wakeman, Jr. and Carolyn Grant (edd.), *Conflict and Control in Late Imperial China* (University of California Press, Berkeley, 1975), p. 2.

18. Cohen, *Discovering History in China*, p. 57.

19. C. P. Fitzgerald, *The Horizon History of China*, p. 125. See also *The Birth of Communist China* (Penguin, Harmondsworth, 1964), p. 124, where Fitzgerald writes that the defeat of the Taipings 'ended, in effect, the Protestant offensive to convert China to Christianity'.

20. Fairbank, Reischauer, and Craig, *East Asia, The Modern Transformation*, p. 177.

21. Mary Clabaugh Wright, *The Last Stand of Chinese Conservatism The T'ung-chih Restoration, 1862–1874* (Atheneum, New York, 1966), p. viii. The preface, containing the cited passage, is dated September 1965 and is not

in the original edition of the book, published in 1957 by Stanford University Press.

22. Wright, *The Last Stand of Chinese Conservatism*, p. *ix*.

23. Cohen, *Discovering History in China*, p. 20.

24. Wolfgang Franke, Stanley Rudman (trans.), *A Century of Chinese Revolution 1851–1949* (Basil Blackwell, Oxford, 1970), p. 19.

25. Edward L. Farmer and others, *Comparative History of Civilizations in Asia, Volume II: 1350 to Present* (Addison-Wesley Publishing Company, Reading, Mass., 1977), p. 409.

26. Farmer, *Comparative History of Civilizations*, p. 730. See also pp. 732–3.

27. Farmer, *Comparative History of Civilizations*, p. 770.

28. Conrad Schirokauer, *A Brief History of Chinese and Japanese Civilizations* (Harcourt Brace Jovanovich, New York, 1978), p. 380.

29. The title of the first section of Kuhn's *Rebellion and Its Enemies in Late Imperial China*, pp. 1–10.

30. John K. Fairbank, 'Introduction: The Old Order', in Denis C. Twitchett and John K. Fairbank (edd.), *The Cambridge History of China, Volume 10, Late Ch'ing, 1800–1911, Part 1* (Cambridge University Press, Cambridge, 1978), pp. 1–2.

31. Fitzgerald, *The Birth of Communist China*, p. 77.

32. Lionel Max Chassin, Timothy Osato and Louis Gelas (trans.), *The Communist Conquest of China* (Harvard University Press, Cambridge, Mass., 1965), pp. 248–9. Chassin's book was first published in France in 1952 under the title *La conquête de la Chine par Mao Tse-tung*.

33. Chassin, *The Communist Conquest of China*, p. 251.

34. Fairbank, Reischauer, and Craig, *East Asia, The Modern Transformation*, p. 716.

35. Fairbank, Reischauer, and Craig, *East Asia, The Modern Transformation*, p. 717.

36. Chalmers A. Johnson, *Peasant Nationalism and Communist Power, The Emergence of Revolutionary China 1937–1945* (Stanford University Press, Stanford, 1962), p. 69.

37. Johnson, *Peasant Nationalism and Communist Power*, p. 70.

38. Johnson, *Peasant Nationalism and Communist Power*, p. *xi*. The preface is dated 1 October 1962.

39. Johnson, *Peasant Nationalism and Communist Power*, p. *xi*.

40. Lucien Bianco, Muriel Bell (trans.), *The Origins of the Chinese Revolution, 1915–1949* (Stanford University Press, Stanford; Oxford University Press, London, 1971), p. 202. The French original was published in 1967 by Éditions Gallimard under the title *Les origines de la révolution chinoise, 1915–1949*.

41. Bianco, *Origins of the Chinese Revolution*, p. 159.

42. Mark Selden, *The Yenan Way in Revolutionary China* (Harvard University Press, Cambridge, Mass., 1971), p. 120.

43. Seldon, *The Yenan Way*, p. *vii*.

44. Seldon, *The Yenan Way*, p. *viii*.

45. Han Suyin, *The Crippled Tree* (Jonathan Cape, London, 1965; Panther, St Albans, 1972), p. 116.

46. Han Suyin, *Birdless Summer* (Jonathan Cape, London, 1968), p. 50.

47. Han Suyin, *A Mortal Flower* (Jonathan Cape, London, 1966), pp. 94–5.

48. Reproduced in *Imperial China Photographs 1850–1912* (Pennwick Publishing, USA, 1978; Scolar Press, London and Australian National University Press, Canberra, 1980), p. 55. The book contains historical texts on 'Photography in Imperial China' by Clark Worswick and on 'Imperial China: A Chinese View' by Jonathan Spence.

49. The photographs referred to are shown respectively in *Imperial China Photographs*, pp. 64, 60, 56, 86.

50. *Imperial China Photographs*, p. 87.

51. *Imperial China Photographs*, pp. 18–19.

52. *Imperial China Photographs*, pp. 63, 65.

53. *Imperial China Photographs*, pp. 84, 85, 120–1.

54. Examples are in Hedda Morrison, *A Photographer in Old Peking* (Oxford University Press, Hong Kong, Oxford, New York, 1985), pp. 24, 86, 87.

55. Morrison, *A Photographer in Old Peking*, pp. 101, 119, 106–7, 100, 164, 30–9.

56. Morrison, *A Photographer in Old Peking*, pp. 111, 101.

57. Morrison, *A Photographer in Old Peking*, p. 220.

58. For example, see the pictorial history of C. P. Fitzgerald and Myra Roper, *China: A World So Changed* (Nelson, Melbourne, London, 1972), especially pp. 103–112.

59. See Mao Zedong, 'On Tactics against Japanese Imperialism', *Selected Works of Mao Tse-tung [Mao Zedong] Volume I* (Foreign Languages Press, Peking, 1965), p. 160.

60. The producer and distributor of the documentary was Independent Productions of Sydney, which co-published the corresponding book of the same name with China National Publishing Industry Trading Corp, and China Photographic Publishing House.

61. The scene in the film where the mistress exults in being beaten by the *tai-pan* comes straight from the novel, but in the latter the thrashing is specified as 'hard enough to hurt, but not to damage'. See James Clavell, *Tai-Pan* (Michael Joseph, London, 1966; Coronet Books, Hodder and Stoughton, London, 1975, 22nd impression 1987), p. 429.

62. Clavell, *Tai-Pan*, p. 436.

63. J. G. Ballard, *Empire of the Sun* (Victor Gollancz, London, 1984), p. 39.

64. Cohen, *Discovering History in China*, pp. 149–98.

Notes to Chapter 10

1. Harold R. Isaacs, *Images of Asia, American Views of China and India* (Harper Torchbooks, New York, 1972 ed.), p. 194.

2. Paul Hollander, *Political Pilgrims, Travels of Western Intellectuals to the Soviet Union, China and Cuba 1928–1978* (Oxford University Press, New York, 1981), p. 279.

3. Quoted from Roderick MacFarquhar (ed.), *Sino-American Relations, 1949–71* (Wren, Melbourne, 1972), p. 68. Extracts from the 'Letter of Transmittal' are given pp. 67–9.

4. Richard L. Walker, *China under Communism, The First Five Years* (George Allen and Unwin, London, 1956), p. 271.

5. Walker, *China under Communism*, p. 297.

6. Walker, *China under Communism*, p. 300.

7. Robert Guillain, Mervin Savill (trans.), *The Blue Ants, 600 Million Chinese under the Red Flag* (Secker and Warburg, London, 1957), p. 225. The French original was published in France by René Julliard in 1956 under the title *600 Millions de Chinois*.

8. Guillain, *The Blue Ants*, p. 66.

9. See Isaacs, *Images of Asia*, pp. 237–8.

10. For example, see Hanson W. Baldwin, 'China as a Military Power', *Foreign Affairs*, XXX, 1 (October 1951), pp. 51–2, 62.

11. See Isaacs, *Images of Asia*, p. *xvii*.

12. Guy Wint, *Common Sense about China* (Victor Gollancz, London, 1960), p. 155.

13. Isaacs, *Images of Asia*, p. 218.

14. Wint, *Common Sense*, p. 156.

15. Guillain, *The Blue Ants*, p. 107.

16. André Malraux, Terence Kilmartin (trans.), *Antimemoirs* (Hamish Hamilton, London, 1968), p. 390.

17. Robert Elegant, *China's Red Masters, Political Biographies of Chinese Communist Leaders* (Twayne, New York, 1951), p. 254.

18. Pearl S. Buck, Theodore F. Harris (comp. and ed.), *China as I See It* (Methuen, London, 1971), p. *xi*.

19. Pearl S. Buck, *My Several Worlds, A Personal Record* (John Day, New York, 1954), p. 381.

20. Buck, *My Several Worlds*, p. 382.

21. Pearl S. Buck, *Letter from Peking* (Methuen, London, 1957; 1984), p. 110. The novel has been through numerous paperback and other editions.

22. Buck, *Letter from Peking*, p. 97.

23. Humphrey Evans, *The Adventures of Li Chi, A Modern Chinese Legend* (E. P. Dutton, New York, 1967), p. 10. Although the novel was not actually published until 1967, it was written before the Cultural Revolution began and the story ends in 1965.

24. Evans, *The Adventures of Li Chi*, p. 222.

25. For example, Captain W. E. Johns, *Biggles in the Gobi* (Hodder & Stoughton, London, 1953), p. 13.

26. Johns, *Biggles in the Gobi*, p. 50.

27. Johns, *Biggles in the Gobi*, p. 8.

28. Johns, *Biggles in the Gobi*, p. 51.

29. Guillain, *The Blue Ants*, p. 233.

30. Walker, *China under Communism*, p. 325.

31. For example, such was the heading of the relevant section in Robert F. Dernberger, 'Economic Realities', in Ruth Adams (ed.), *Contemporary China* (Peter Owen, London, 1969), p. 135. Dernberger was in the Department of Economics, University of Chicago, and was one of 35 panelists at a seminar on contemporary China held in Chicago in February 1966 reflecting images just before the Cultural Revolution.

32. Kang Chao, 'Economic Aftermath of the Great Leap in Communist China', *Asian Survey*, IV, 5 (May 1964), p. 851.

33. Dick Wilson, *A Quarter of Mankind, An Anatomy of China Today* (Weidenfeld and Nicolson, London, 1966; Pelican, Harmondsworth, 1968), p. 155.

34. See, for example, C. P. Fitzgerald, 'Chinese Foreign Policy', in Adams (ed.), *Contemporary China*, pp. 7–25.

35. Wilson, *A Quarter of Mankind*, pp. 211–34.

36. Wilson, *A Quarter of Mankind*, p. 275.

37. Han Suyin, *A Many-Splendoured Thing* (Jonathan Cape, London, 1952; Little, Brown and Co., Boston, 1952), p. 282.

38. Edgar Snow, *The Other Side of the River, Red China Today* (Random House, New York, 1961; 1962), p. 529.

39. Sven Lindqvist, *China in Crisis* (Faber and Faber, London, 1963), p. 104.

40. The resultant book was first published in 1963 in Swedish under the title *Rapport från kinesisk*. It was translated into English by Maurice Michael and entitled *Report from a Chinese Village* and published by William Heinemann in 1965.

41. Jan Myrdal, 'The Reshaping of Chinese Society', in Adams (ed.), *Contemporary China*, pp. 90–1.

42. Myrdal, *Report from a Chinese Village* (Pan Books, London, 1975 ed.), p. xxxiii.

43. Snow, *The Other Side of the River*, p. 620.

44. See *Zhongguo tongji nianjian 1983* (*Chinese Statistical Yearbook 1983*) (Chinese Statistical Press, Beijing, 1983), pp. 105, 103.

45. Hewlett Johnson, *China's New Creative Age* (Lawrence and Wishart, London, 1953), p. 175.

46. Johnson, *China's New Creative Age*, p. 185.

47. Johnson, *China's New Creative Age*, p. 110.

48. Johnson, *China's New Creative Age*, pp. 32–40.

49. Simone de Beauvoir, *La longue marche, essai sur la Chine* (Gallimard, Paris, 1957), pp. 123–59.

50. de Beauvoir, *La longue marche*, p. 159.

51. Wint, *Common Sense*, p. 166.

52. Wint, *Common Sense*, p. 164.

53. Malraux, *Antimemoirs*, pp. 371–2.

54. Dennis Bloodworth, *The Chinese Looking Glass* (Farrar, Strauss and Giroux, New York, 1966), p. 399.

55. Bloodworth, *The Chinese Looking Glass*, pp. 403–4.

56. Myrdal, 'The Reshaping of Chinese Society', p. 71.

57. Walker, *China under Communism*, pp. xi–xii.

58. Walker, *China under Communism*, p. 324.

59. Guillain, *The Blue Ants*, p. 221.

60. Guillain, *The Blue Ants*, p. 223–4.

61. Han Suyin, 'Social Transformation in China', in Adams (ed.), *Contemporary China*, p. 93.

Notes to Chapter 11

1. The influential American journalist Joseph Kraft was one of those who accompanied Nixon to China. He wrote a short book called *The Chinese Difference* (Saturday Review Press, New York, 1973), the first section of which, pp. 3–43, deals with the Nixon visit and is called 'the week that changed the world'.

2. Harold Isaacs, *Images of Asia, American Views of China and India* (Harper Torchbooks, New York, 1972 ed.), p. xv.

3. Isaacs, *Images of Asia*, p. xviii.

4. Simon Leys, Carol Appleyard and Patrick Goode (trans.), *The Chairman's New Clothes* (Allison and Busby, London, 1981 ed.), p. 13. The French original was entitled *Les habits neufs du président Mao* and published by Éditions Champs Libres in Paris in 1971. For the quoted passage see p. 23.

5. Simon Leys, *Chinese Shadows* (The Viking Press, New York, 1977), p. 113. The French original *Ombres chinoises*, came out in 1974. For further examples of the inequality image see Paul Hollander, *Political Pilgrims, Travels of Western Intellectuals to the Soviet Union, China and Cuba 1928–1978* (Oxford University Press, New York, 1981), pp. 303–7.

6. Leys, *Chinese Shadows*, pp. 30–1.

7. Simon Leys, Steve Cox (trans.), *Broken Images, Essays on Chinese Culture and Politics* (St Martin's Press, New York, 1979), p. 107. The essay from which the passage comes, also called 'Broken Images', was originally published in *Contrepoint* in 1975.

8. Edward Friedman, 'Teaching Materials on Contemporary China: a Critical Evaluation', in Arlene Posner and Arne J. de Keijzer (edd.), *China, A Resource and Curriculum Guide* (University of Chicago Press, Chicago, 2nd revised ed. 1976), p. 6.

9. Committee of Concerned Asian Scholars, *China! Inside the People's Republic* (Bantam Books, New York, 1972), p. 2

10. Committee of Concerned Asian Scholars, *China!*, pp. 102–3.

11. Committee of Concerned Asian Scholars, *China!*, p. 265.

12. John K. Fairbank, 'A Nation Imprisoned by Her History', *Life International*, XLI, 11 (28 November 1966), p. 60.

13. John K. Fairbank, '1972, The New China and the American Connection', in *China Perceived: Images and Policies in Chinese-American Relations* (Random House, New York, 1976 ed.), pp. 21–2. This article first appeared in *Foreign Affairs* in October 1972.

14. Fairbank, *China Perceived*, p. 31.

15. Fairbank, *China Perceived* pp. 29–30.

16. For a strong attack on the favourable image of the position and treatment of intellectuals in China conveyed by some writers see Hollander, *Political Pilgrims*, pp. 331–5.

17. Ross Terrill, *800,000,000 The Real China* (Penguin, Harmondsworth, 1975 ed.), pp. 20–1.

18. Richard Baum with Louise B. Bennett (edd.), *China in Ferment, Perspectives on the Cultural Revolution* (Prentice-Hall, Englewood Cliffs, 1971), p. 49.

19. Louise B. Bennett, 'Conclusion', in Baum with Bennett (edd.), *China in Ferment*, p. 229.

20. Leigh Kagan and Richard Kagan, 'Oh Say, Can You See? American Cultural Blinders on China', in Edward Friedman and Mark Selden (edd.),*America's Asia: Dissenting Essays on Asian–American Relations* (Random House, New York, 1969), p. 35.

21. Kagan and Kagan, 'Oh Say, Can You See?', in *America's Asia*, p. 3.

22. Kagan and Kagan, 'Oh Say, Can You See?', in *America's Asia*, p. 4.

23. For example, see Edwin Fenton, 'Totalitarian Government in China', in *Tradition and Change in Four Societies: An Inquiry Approach* (Holt, Rinehart and Winston, New York, 1968), p. 338.

24. For example see Fenton, 'Totalitarian Government', and John P. Armstrong, *Chinese Dilemma* (Laidlaw Brothers, River Forest, 1967), p. 27.

25. Fenton, 'Totalitarian Government', p. 338.

26. Gerd Kaminski and Else Unterrieder, *Von Österreichern und Chinesen* (Europaverlag, Vienna, Munich, Zürich, 1980), p. 913.

27. David L. Weitzman, 'Teaching about China in the Classroom: What We Look for beyond Seeing', in Posner and Keijzer (edd.), *China, A Resource and Curriculum Guide*, p. 15.

28. See 'A Vicious Motive, Despicable Tricks', *Peking Review*, XVII, 5 (1 February 1984), p. 7. The article originally appeared in Chinese in *Renmin ribao* (*People's Daily*), 30 January 1974.

29. Colina MacDougall, 'The Maoist Mould', *Far Eastern Economic Review*, LXVIII, 14 (2 April 1970), p. 17.

30. Robert S. Elegant, *Dynasty, A Novel* (McGraw-Hill, New York, 1977), pp. 571–2. Although this novel came out the year after the death of Mao,

the last section was written during the Cultural Revolution years and the finale is set in 1970. It certainly reflects contemporary images of the Cultural Revolution.

31. Elegant, *Dynasty*, p. 579.

32. Elegant, *Dynasty*, pp. 583, 584–8.

33. Elegant, *Dynasty*, pp. 567–70, 581–2.

34. Elegant, *Dynasty*, p. 585.

35. Elegant, *Dynasty*, p. 566.

36. Elegant, *Dynasty*, p. 618.

37. Ken Ling, Miriam London, and others, *The Revenge of Heaven: Journal of a Young Chinese* (G. P. Putnam's Sons, New York, 1972), p. 368.

38. Ling, *The Revenge of Heaven*, p. 148.

39. Ling, *The Revenge of Heaven*, p. 301

40. Gordon A. Bennett and Ronald Montaperto, *Red Guard, The Political Biography of Dai Hsiao-ai* (Anchor Books, Doubleday, Garden City, 1972), p. 215.

41. Bennett and Montaperto, *Red Guard*, p. 218.

42. Bennett and Montaperto, *Red Guard*, p. 226.

43. Edgar Snow, *China's Long Revolution* (Penguin, Harmondsworth, 1974 ed.), p. 29.

44. Snow, *China's Long Revolution*, p. 114.

45. Snow, *China's Long Revolution*, p. 31.

46. Snow, *China's Long Revolution*, p. 32.

47. See Hollander, *Political Pilgrims*, pp. 291–308.

48. Jan Myrdal and Gun Kessle, Paul Britten Austin (trans.), *China: The Revolution Continued* (Penguin, Harmondsworth, 1973 ed.), p. 13. This book was originally published in Swedish in 1970 and first published in English by Chatto and Windus in 1971.

49. Myrdal and Kessle, *China: The Revolution Continued*, pp. 24, 25.

50. See Hollander, *Political Pilgrims*, pp. 315–25.

51 Han Suyin, *China in the Year 2001* (Penguin, Harmondsworth, 1967), p. 162.

52. Han Suyin, *Asia Today, Two Outlooks, Beatty Memorial Lectures* (McGill-Queen's University Press, Montreal, London, 1969), p. 71.

53. Han Suyin, *China in the Year 2001*, p. 232.

Notes to Chapter 12

1. 'A Romance Turns Sour', *Asiaweek*, IX, 13 (1 April 1983), p. 44.

2. Richard Bernstein, *From the Center of the Earth, The Search for the Truth about China* (Little, Brown and Company, Boston, 1982), pp. 65–6.

3. Caroline Blunden and Mark Elvin, *Cultural Atlas of China* (Phaidon, Oxford, 1983), p. 169.

4. Roger Garside, *Coming Alive, China After Mao* (McGraw-Hill, New York, 1981), p. *vii*.

5. Alasdair Clayre, *The Heart of the Dragon* (Collins/Harvill, London, 1984), pp. 30–1.

6. Liang Heng and Judith Shapiro, *Son of the Revolution* (Chatto and Windus, London, 1983; Fontana Paperbacks, London, 1984), p. 266.

7. Liang and Shapiro, *Son of the Revolution*, p. 292.

8. Han Suyin, *Asia Today, Two Outlooks, Beatty Memorial Lectures* (McGill-Queen's University Press, Montreal, London, 1969), p. 54.

9. Han Suyin, *Till Morning Comes* (Bantam Books, New York, 1982), p. 620.

10. Han Suyin, *Till Morning Comes*, pp. 598–9.

11. Han Suyin, *Till Morning Comes*, pp. 618–19.

12. Anthony Grey, *The Chinese Assassin* (Michael Joseph, London, 1978; Futura, London, 1979), p. 73.

13. Grey, *The Chinese Assassin*, p. 220.

14. Grey, *The Chinese Assassin*, p. 239.

15. Frederic M. Kaplan, Julian M. Sobin, and Stephen Andors, *Encyclopedia of China Today* (Macmillan, London, 1979), p. 52.

16. Fredric M. Kaplan and Arne J. de Keijzer, *The China Guidebook* (Eurasia Press, New York, 3rd edition 1982), p. 27.

17. Bill Brugger, *China: Radicalism to Revisionism 1962–1979* (Croom Helm, London, 1981), pp. 251–2.

18. Orville Schell, *To Get Rich is Glorious, China in the Eighties* (Robin Clark, London, 1985), p. 73.

19. Fox Butterfield, *China, Alive in the Bitter Sea* (Hodder and Stoughton, London, 1982), pp. 61–2.

20. Myra Roper, *Emperor's China, People's China* (Heinemann, Melbourne, 1981), p. *xviii*.

21. Wang Gungwu, 'The Chineseness of China', in Brian Hook (ed.), *The Cambridge Encyclopedia of China* (Cambridge University Press, Cambridge, 1982), p. 34.

22. Charles Meyer, Jean Joss (trans.), *China Observed* (Kaye & Ward, London, 1980; Gallery Books, New York, 1986), pp. 72–3, 142-3. The original French version was published by Hachette in 1980.

23. Inge Morath and Arthur Miller, *Chinese Encounters* (Secker & Warburg, London, 1979), for example, pp. 115, 116–17, 119, 121, 138, 152–3, 162, 185, 206–7, 220–1, 237–8, and many more. The photographs were taken by Inge Morath.

24. Morath and Miller, *Chinese Encounters*, p. 9.

25. Clayre, *The Heart of the Dragon*, p. 40.

26. Marie-Claire Bergère, *La République populaire de Chine de 1949 à nos jours* (Armand Colin, Paris, 1987), pp. 222–3.

27. Schell, *To Get Rich is Glorious*, pp. 72–3.

28. Alan Samagalski and Michael Buckley, *China — A Travel Survival Kit* (Lonely Planet Publications, Melbourne, Berkeley, 1984), p. 7.

29. Leong Ka Tai and Frank Ching, *Beijing* (Hutchinson, Melbourne, Sydney, London, 1986), pp. 12–13.

30. Leong and Ching, *Beijing*, pp. 16–17.

31. David R. Cudlip, *Comprador* (Secker & Warburg, London, 1984; Grafton Books, London, 1987), p. 316.

32. For example, Meyer, *China Observed*, pp. 79, 86–7, 114–37.

33. Leong and Ching, *Beijing*, p. 24.

34. Jean Burchfield, *China: Geography, History, Customs, Festivals, Food* (Youth Publications, Indianapolis, 1979), p. 23.

35. Morath and Miller, *Chinese Encounters*, p. 111.

36. Tiziano Terzani, *Behind the Forbidden Door, Travels in China* (Allen & Unwin, London, 1986), p. 158. The book was first published by Rowohlt in Hamburg, 1984, under the title *Fremder unter Chinesen*.

37. Terzani, *Behind the Forbidden Door*, p. 174.

38. One chapter of Terzani's book is subtitled 'Communism against Chinese traditional culture', *Behind the Forbidden Door*, p. 157.

39. Terzani, *Behind the Forbidden Door*, p. 22.

40. Liang Heng and Judith Shapiro, 'The Loving Penance of Hu Bo', *Reader's Digest* (Australian edition), CXXX, 787 (November 1987), p. 40.

41. The story ends Liang Heng's and Judith Shapiro's *After the Nightmare, a Survivor of the Cultural Revolution Reports on China Today* (Alfred A. Knopf, New York, 1986). The passage where the quoted words occurs is a revision of the phraseology, though not the sense, of the last paragraph in the book (p. 240).

42. 'The Eighteenth Brumaire of Louis Bonaparte', in *Karl Marx and Frederick Engels Selected Works* (3 vols; Progress Publishers, Moscow, 1969-70), I, p. 398.

Notes to Chapter 13

1. Harrison E. Salisbury, 'China's CEO', *Success!*, XXXIII, 1 (January/February 1986), p. 72.

2. See the several articles in *Time*, CXXVII, 1 (6 January 1986), pp. 6–37.

3. Derek Davies, 'Traveller's Tales', *Far Eastern Economic Review* (hereafter *FEER*), CXXX, 40 (10 October 1985), p. 35.

4. 'A Romance Turns Sour', *Asiaweek*, IX, 13 (1 April 1983), p. 40.

5. Fox Butterfield, *China, Alive in the Bitter Sea* (Hodder and Stoughton, London, 1982), p. 325.

6. See, for example, Butterfield, *China*, p. 329.

7. Fredric M. Kaplan and Arne J. de Keijzer, *The China Guidebook* (Eurasia Press, New York, 1982), pp. 29–31.

8. Alan Samagalski and Michael Buckley, *China — A Travel Survival Kit* (Lonely Planet Publications, Melbourne, Berkeley, 1984), p. 51.

9. Marie-Claire Bergère, *La République populaire de Chine de 1949 à nos jours* (Armand Colin, Paris, 1987), p. 192.

10. Alasdair Clayre, *The Heart of the Dragon* (Collins/Harvill, London, 1984), p. 93.

11. 'A Romance Turns Sour', pp. 42–3.

12. John Fraser, *The Chinese, Portrait of a People* (Collins, Toronto, 1980), p. 87. On p. 158 Fraser says 'totalitarianism in China is more pervasive than it is in Vietnam, but curiously, it is less repressive'.

13. See especially Richard Bernstein, *From the Center of the Earth, The Search for the Truth about China* (Little, Brown and Company, Boston, 1982), pp. 127–40, and Butterfield, *China*, pp. 64–88.

14. Butterfield, *China*, p. 88.

15. Clyde Cameron, *China, Communism and Coca-Cola* (Hill of Content, Melbourne, 1980), p. 2.

16. Leslie Holmes, *Politics in the Communist World* (Clarendon Press, Oxford, 1986), pp. 141–5.

17. James R. Townsend and Brantly Womack, *Politics in China* (Little, Brown and Company, Boston, Toronto, 3rd edition 1986), p. 413.

18. Craig Dietrich, *People's China, A Brief History* (Oxford University Press, New York, Oxford, 1986), p. 278.

19. Dietrich, *People's China*, p. 273. The opening sentence of the segment on 'The Economy' from 1981 to 1985 is: 'Revolutionary is a word that could legitimately be applied to China's economic policies in the 1980s'.

20. Mary Lee, 'The Curtain Goes Up', *FEER*, CXXVII, 4 (31 January 1985), p. 50.

21. David R. Cudlip, *Comprador* (Secker & Warburg, London, 1984; Grafton Books, London, 1987), p. 468.

22. See 'Why Are We Here?', *FEER*, CXXXIII, 33 (14 August 1986), p. 103.

23. Robert Delfs, 'Economic Marathon', *FEER*, CXXIX, 34 (29 August 1985), p. 50.

24. Ian Porter, and others, *China, Long-term Development Issues and Options* (Johns Hopkins University Press, Baltimore and London, 1985), pp. 1–2.

25. Porter, *China, Long-term Development Issues*, p. 8.

26. Porter, *China, Long-term Development Issues*, p. 98–9.

27. Porter, *China, Long-term Development Issues*, p. 20.

28. Richard C. Bush, 'Introduction', in Richard C. Bush (ed.), *China Briefing, 1982* (Westview, Boulder, 1983), pp. 3–4.

29. For example, Bernstein, *From the Center of the Earth*, p. 50.

30. Clayre, *The Heart of the Dragon*, p. 146.

31. Clayre, *The Heart of the Dragon*, p. 148.

32. Porter, *China, Long-term Development Issues*, p. 3.

33. Bernstein, *From the Center of the Earth*, p. 52.

34. Schell, *To Get Rich is Glorious*, p. 50.

35. Schell, *To Get Rich is Glorious*, p. 51.

36. Womack and Townsend, *Politics in China*, p. 194.

37. Derek Davies, 'Traveller's Tales', *FEER*, CXXX, 40 (10 October 1985), p. 35.

38. Womack and Townsend, *Politics in China*, p. 195.

39. Bergère, *La République populaire de Chine*, p. 160.

40. *Far Eastern Economic Review Asia 1985 Yearbook* (Far Eastern Economic Review, Hong Kong, 1985), pp. 38, 40.

41. Tiziano Terzani, *Behind the Forbidden Door, Travels in China* (Allen & Unwin, London, 1986), p. 189.

42. *International Herald Tribune*, Paris, quoted in *Asian Recorder*, XXXIII, 20 (14–20 May 1987), pp. 19456–7.

43. Dietrich, *People's China*, p. 291.

44. Delia Davin, 'The Single-child Family Policy in the Countryside', in Elisabeth Croll, Delia Davin and Penny Kane (edd.), *China's One-Child Family Policy* (Macmillan, London, 1985), p. 74.

45. Bergère, *La République populaire de Chine*, p. 187.

46. Steven Mosher wrote a book on his findings entitled *Broken Earth: The Rural Chinese* (The Free Press, New York, 1983). On forced abortions see pp. 256–61.

47. Following extensive internal reviews, Mosher's termination was upheld by the Stanford University President, Donald Kennedy, in September 1985. Mosher was appointed Director of the Asian Studies Center at the Claremont Institute in Montclair, California. In September 1986 he sued Stanford University in the San Francisco Superior Court for slander, breach of contract, and violation of his civil rights. See 'Mosher Sues', *Stanford Observer*, XXI, 1 (October 1986), p. 13.

48. Terzani, *Behind the Forbidden Door*, p. 196.

49. Davin, 'The Single-child Family Policy', in Croll, Davin and Kane (edd.), *China's One-Child Family Policy*, p. 62.

50. Samagalski and Buckley, *China*, p. 56.

51. Terzani, *Behind the Forbidden Door*, p. 189.

52. David Bonavia, *The Chinese* (Penguin, Harmondsworth, 1982 ed.), p. 91.

53. George J. Church, and others, 'China, Deng Xiaoping Leads a Far-

Reaching, Audacious but Risky Second Revolution', *Time*, CXXVII, 1 (6 January 1986), p. 17.

54. Clyde Haberman, 'Russia's Reach for the Pacific', *Reader's Digest*, CXXX, 786 (October 1987), pp. 22, 25.

55. For example, Thomas P. Bernstein, 'China in 1984, The Year of Hong Kong', *Asian Survey*, XXV, 1 (January 1985), p. 50.

56. Wo-Lap Lam, 'Peking Pursues Its Own Path', *Asiaweek*, XI, 7 (15 February 1985), p. 48. Lam is reviewing and summarizing the views put forward in a book by six American sinologists: Harry Harding (ed.), *China's Foreign Relations in the 1980s* (Yale University Press, New Haven, 1984).

57. For example, see David Bonavia, 'Superpower Links are the Prime Concern', *FEER*, CXXVII, 11 (21 March 1985), p. 92.

58. Michael Hunt, 'Chinese Foreign Relations in Historical Perspective', in Harding (ed.), *China's Foreign Relations*, p. 3.

59. In her section on 'The Rapprochement with the United States and the West', Bergère does not mention any Western country specifically, other than the US. See *La République populaire de Chine*, pp. 209–11.

60. Bonavia, *The Chinese*, p. 279.

61. Dietrich, *People's China*, p. 284.

62. See *Keesing's Contemporary Archives*, XXV (12 October 1979), pp. 29872–73.

63. *New York Times*, 19 February 1979, p. A14.

64. *Guardian Weekly*, CXX, 9 (week ending 25 February 1979), p. 1.

65. *Asiaweek*, V, 11 (23 March 1979), p. 9.

66. *Far Eastern Economic Review Asia 1980 Yearbook* (Far Eastern Economic Review, Hong Kong, 1980), p. 301.

67. Daniel Tretiak, 'China's Vietnam War and its Consequences', *The China Quarterly*, 80 (December 1979), pp. 755–6.

68. Bergère, *La République populaire de Chine*, p. 214.

69. Bonavia, *The Chinese*, p. 301.

70. Michael Yahuda, *Towards the End of Isolationism: China's Foreign Policy after Mao* (St Martin's Press, New York, 1983), p. 234.

71. Bonavia, *The Chinese*, p. 290.

Notes to Chapter 14

1. David Bonavia, *Peking* (Time-Life Books, Amsterdam, 1978), p. 5.

2. Bonavia, *Peking*, p. 7.

3. Inge Morath and Arthur Miller, *Chinese Encounters* (Secker & Warburg, London, 1979), p. 14.

4. *Asiaweek*, XI, 16 (19 April 1985), p. 30.

5. 'Enjoying Life', *Asiaweek*, XI, 16 (19 April 1985), p. 30.

6. 'Enjoying Life', p. 29.

7. Alan Samagalski and Michael Buckley, *China — A Travel Survival Kit* (Lonely Planet Publications, Melbourne, Berkeley, 1984), p. 568.

8. Leong Ka Tai and Frank Ching, *Beijing* (Hutchinson, Melbourne, Sydney, London, 1986), pp. 110–11.

9. Beverley Hooper, *Youth in China* (Penguin, Ringwood, Harmondsworth, 1985), p. 18.

10. 'Enjoying Life', p. 30.

11. Leong and Ching, *Beijing*, pp. 112–19.

12. Leong and Ching, *Beijing*, pp. 124–5, 106–7.

13. Leong and Ching, *Beijing*, pp. 108–9.

14. Alasdair Clayre, *The Heart of the Dragon* (Collins/Harvill, London, 1984), p. 122.

15. David Bonavia, *The Chinese* (Penguin, Harmondsworth, 1982 ed.), pp. 300–1.

16. 'Enjoying Life', p. 30.

17. Clyde Cameron, *China, Communism and Coca-Cola* (Hill of Content, Melbourne, 1980), p. 252.

18. Cameron, *China, Communism and Coca-Cola*, p. 253.

19. Orville Schell, *To Get Rich is Glorious, China in the Eighties* (Robin Clark, London, 1985), pp. 209–10.

20. David R. Cudlip, *Comprador* (Secker & Warburg, London, 1984; Grafton Books, London, 1987), p. 335.

21. Clayre, *The Heart of the Dragon*, p. 81.

22. Margery Wolf, 'Marriage, Family, and the State in Contemporary China', *Pacific Affairs*, LVII, 2 (Summer 1984), p. 235.

23. Hooper, *Youth in China*, p. 176.

24. Hopper, *Youth in China*, p. 177.

25. Caroline Blunden and Mark Elvin, *Cultural Atlas of China* (Phaidon, Oxford, 1983), p. 217.

26. Hooper, *Youth in China*, pp. 190–2.

27. Elisabeth Croll, *Chinese Women Since Mao* (Zed Books, London, 1983), p. 79.

28. Margery Wolf, *Revolution Postponed: Women in Contemporary China* (Stanford University Press, Stanford, 1985), p. 26.

29. Judith Stacey, *Patriarchy and Socialist Revolution in China* (University of California Press, Berkeley, 1983), pp. 155–7.

30. Marilyn B. Young, 'Introduction', *Pacific Affairs*, LVII, 2 (Summer 1984), p. 209.

31. Gilbert Rozman, 'The Status of Women', in Brian Hook (ed.), *The Cambridge Encyclopedia of China* (Cambridge University Press, Cambridge, 1982), p. 116.

32. Wolf, *Revolution Postponed*, pp. 70–3.

33. Bonavia, *The Chinese*, p. 80.

34. Steven Mosher, *Broken Earth: The Rural Chinese* (The Free Press, New York, 1983), p. 221.

35. Bonavia, *The Chinese*, p. 80.

36. Jay Mathews and Linda Mathews, *One Billion, A China Chronicle* (Random House, New York, 1983), pp. 118–19. Jay Mathews was attached to the *Washington Post*, his wife Linda to the *Los Angeles Times*.

37. Croll, *Chinese Women*, p. 129.

38. Wolf, *Revolution Postponed*, p. 261.

39. Wolf, *Revolution Postponed*, pp. 272–3.

40. Willy Kraus, E. M. Holz (trans.), *Economic Development and Social Change in the People's Republic of China* (Springer-Verlag, New York, Heidelberg, Berlin, 1982), p. 323. The original German edition was published in 1979 under the title *Wirtschaftliche Entwicklung und sozialer Wandel in der Volksrepublik China*, but the American edition has been updated.

41. 'A Romance Turns Sour', *Asiaweek*, IX, 13 (1 April 1983), p. 44.

42. Fox Butterfield, *China, Alive in the Bitter Sea* (Hodder & Stoughton, London, 1982), p. 457.

43. Bonavia, *The Chinese*, pp. 292–3.

44. Bonavia, *The Chinese*, p. 305.

45. Roger Garside, *Coming Alive, China after Mao* (McGraw-Hill, New York, 1981), p. 426.

46. Garside, *Coming Alive*, p. 427.

47. Marie-Claire Bergère, *La République populaire de Chine de 1949 à nos jours* (Armand Colin, Paris, 1987), pp. 222–3.

48. Craig Dietrich, *People's China, A Brief History* (Oxford University Press, New York, Oxford, 1986), p. 278.

49. George J. Church, and others, 'China, Deng Xiaoping Leads a Far-Reaching, Audacious but Risky Second Revolution', *Time*, CXXVII, 1 (6 January 1986), p. 21.

50. James R. Townsend and Brantly Womack, *Politics in China* (Little, Brown and Company, Boston, Toronto, 3rd edition 1986), p. 425.

51. Clayre, *The Heart of the Dragon*, p. 264.

Works Cited

Primary Sources*

Printed Works

Adams, Ruth (ed.), *Contemporary China* (Peter Owen, London, 1969).

Allgemeine deutsche Real-Encyklopädie für die gebildeten Stände. Conversations-Lexicon, 10th edition (15 vols.; Brockhaus, Leipzig, 1852).

Armstrong, John P., *Chinese Dilemma* (Laidlaw Brothers, River Forest, 1967).

Arrivabene, Ludovico, *Il magno Vitei*, late sixteenth century.

Avineri, Shlomo (ed.), *Karl Marx on Colonialism and Modernization, His Despatches and Other Writings on China, India, Mexico, The Middle East and North Africa* (Doubleday, New York, 1968).

Balazs, Etienne, *Chinese Civilization and Bureaucracy, Variations on a Theme*, trans. H. M. Wright (Yale University Press, New Haven and London, 1964).

Baldwin, Hanson W., 'China as a Military Power', *Foreign Affairs*, XXX, 1 (October 1951) pp. 51–2, 62.

Ballard, J. G., *Empire of the Sun* (Victor Gollancz, London, 1984).

Barrow, John, *Travels in China, Containing Descriptions, Observations, and Comparisons, Made and Collected in the Course of a Short Residence at the Imperial Palace of Yuen-min-yuen, and on a Subsequent Journey through the Country from Peking to Canton* (T. Cadell and W. Davies, London, 2nd edition 1806).

Baum, Richard, with Bennett, Louise B. (edd.), *China in Ferment, Perspectives on the Cultural Revolution* (Prentice-Hall, Englewood Cliffs, 1971).

Bennett, Gordon A., and Montaperto, Ronald, *Red Guard, The Political Biography of Dai Hsiao-ai* (Anchor Books, Doubleday, Garden City, 1972).

---

* Primary sources are all those works used to illustrate or exemplify the images discussed, including those which contain in addition cited commentaries on such works.

Bergère, Marie-Claire, *La Répulique populaire de Chine de 1949 à nos jours* (Armand Colin, Paris, 1987).

Bernstein, Richard, *From the Center of the Earth, The Search for the Truth about China* (Little, Brown and Company, Boston, 1982).

Bernstein, Thomas P., 'China in 1984, The Year of Hong Kong', *Asian Survey*, XXV, 1 (January 1985), pp. 33–50.

Bianco, Lucien, *Les origines de la révolution chinoise, 1915–1949* (Gallimard, Paris, 1967); *The Origins of the Chinese Revolution, 1915–1949*, trans. Muriel Bell (Stanford University Press, Stanford; Oxford University Press, London, 1971).

Bishop, C. W., 'The Rise of Civilization in China with Reference to its Geographical Aspects', *Geographical Review*, 22 (1932), pp. 617–31.

Bishop, Isabella L. Bird, *The Golden Chersonese and the Way Thither* (G. P. Putnam's Sons, New York, 1883).

Bloodworth, Dennis, *The Chinese Looking Glass* (Farrar, Strauss and Giroux, New York, 1966).

Blunden, Caroline and Elvin, Mark, *Cultural Atlas of China* (Phaidon, Oxford, 1983).

Bodde, Derk, Review of Joseph Needham's *Science and Civilisation, Volume V, Part 2* in *Journal of Asian Studies*, XXXV, 3 (May 1976), pp. 488–91.

Bonavia, David, *Peking* (Time-Life Books, Amsterdam, 1978).

—— *The Chinese* (Penguin, Harmondsworth, 1982 ed.).

—— 'Superpower Links are the Prime Concern', *Far Eastern Economic Review*, CXXVII, 11 (21 March 1985), pp. 92–4.

Boxer, C. R. (ed.), *South China in the Sixteenth Century* (The Hakluyt Society, London, 1953).

Brugger, Bill, *China: Radicalism to Revisionism 1962–1979* (Croom Helm, London, 1981).

Buck, Pearl S., *The Good Earth* (John Day, New York, 1931; edition of April 1965).

—— *My Several Worlds, A Personal Record* (John Day, New York, 1954).

—— *Letter from Peking* (Methuen, London, 1957; 1984).

—— *China as I See It*, comp. and ed. Theodore F. Harris (Methuen, London, 1971).

Burchfield, Jean, *China: Geography, History, Customs, Festivals, Food* (Youth Publications, Indianapolis, 1979).

Bush, Richard C. (ed.), *China Briefing, 1982* (Westview, Boulder, 1983).

Butterfield, Fox, *China, Alive in the Bitter Sea* (Hodder and Stoughton, London, 1982).

Cameron, Clyde, *China, Communism and Coca-Cola* (Hill of Content, Melbourne, 1980).

Chambers's Encyclopædia, A Dictionary of Universal Knowledge for the

People, Illustrated with Maps and Numerous Wood Engravings (10 vols.; W. and R. Chambers, London, Edinburgh, 1874).

Chao, Kang, 'Economic Aftermath of the Great Leap in Communist China', *Asian Survey*, IV, 5 (May 1964), pp. 851–8.

Chassin, Lionel Max, *The Communist Conquest of China*, trans. Timothy Osato and Louis Gelas (Harvard University Press, Cambridge, Mass., 1965).

Chavannes, Édouard, *Documents sur les Tou-kiue (Turcs) Occidentaux* (Adrien-Maisonneuve, Paris, 1942).

Chiang, May-ling Soong, *China Shall Rise Again* (Harper, New York and London, 1940).

Chinese Classics, The, trans. James Legge (2nd revised ed., 5 vols.; Clarendon Press, Oxford, 1893–5).

Church, George J., and others, 'China, Deng Xiaoping Leads a Far-Reaching, Audacious but Risky Second Revolution, *Time*, CXXVII, 1 (6 January 1986), pp. 6–21.

Clarke, Prescott, and Gregory, J. S., *Western Reports on the Taiping, A Selection of Documents* (Australian National University Press, Canberra, 1982).

Clavell, James, *Tai-Pan, A Novel of Hong Kong* (Michael Joseph, London, 1966; Coronet Books, Hodder and Stoughton, London, 1975; 22nd impression 1987).

Clayre, Alasdair, *The Heart of the Dragon* (Collins/Harvill, London, 1984).

Coleridge, H. J. (ed.), *The Life and Letters of St. Francis Xavier* (2 vols.; Burns and Oates, London, 1872, 1902).

Committee of Concerned Asian Scholars, *China! Inside the People's Republic* (Bantam Books, New York, 1972).

Conger, Sarah Pike, *Letters from China, with Particular Reference to the Empress Dowager and the Women of China* (A. C. McClurg & Co., Chicago, 1909).

Cordier, Henri, *Histoire des relations de la Chine avec les puissances occidentales 1860–1902* (3 vols.; Ancienne Librairie Germer Baillière, Paris, 1901–2).

—— *Histoire générale de la Chine et de ses relations avec les pays étrangers depuis les temps les plus anciens jusqúà la chute de la dynastie mandchoue* (4 vols.; Librairie Paul Geuthner, Paris, 1920–1).

Cranmer-Byng, J. L. (ed.), *An Embassy to China, Being the Journal Kept by Lord Macartney During his Embassy to the Emperor Ch'ien-lung 1793–1794* (Longmans, London, 1962).

Croll, Elisabeth, *Chinese Women Since Mao* (Zed Books, London, 1983).

—— Davin, Delia, and Kane, Penny (edd.), *China's One-Child Family Policy* (Macmillan, London, 1985).

Crow, Carl, *Four Hundred Million Customers* (Hamish Hamilton, London, 1937).

—— *Foreign Devils in the Flowery Kingdom* (Hamish Hamilton, London, 1941).

Cudlip, David R., *Comprador* (Secker & Warburg, London, 1984; Grafton Books, London, 1987).

Daily Telegraph, London.

Davidson, Basil, *Daybreak in China* (Jonathan Cape, London, 1953).

Davies, Derek, 'Traveller's Tales', *Far Eastern Economic Review*, CXXX, 40 (10 October 1985), p. 35.

de Bary, Wm. Theodore, and the Conference on Ming Thought, *Self and Society in Ming Thought* (Columbia University Press, New York and London, 1970).

de Beauvoir, Simone, *La longue marche, essai sur la Chine* (Gallimard, Paris, 1957).

de Groot, J. J. M., *The Religious System of China, Its Ancient Forms, Evolution, History and Present Aspect, Manners, Custom and Social Institutions Connected Therewith* (6 vols.; Brill, Leiden, 1892–1910).

Dietrich, Craig, *People's China, A Brief History* (Oxford University Press, New York, Oxford, 1986).

Du Halde, J. B., *Description géographique, historique, chronologique, politique, et physique de l'empire de la Chine et de la Tartarie chinoise* (4 vols.; Henri Scheurleer, The Hague, 1736).

—— *The General History of China*, trans. R. Brookes (4 vols.; J. Watts, London, 1741).

Eberhard, Wolfram, *Conquerors and Rulers, Social Forces in Medieval China* (Brill, Leiden, 1965 ed.).

—— *A History of China*, trans. E. W. Dickes (University of California Press, Berkeley and Los Angeles, 4th revised edition 1977).

Eisenstadt, S. N., 'The Study of Oriental Despotisms as Systems of Total Power', *The Journal of Asian Studies*, XVII, 3 (May 1958), pp. 435–46.

Elegant, Robert, *China's Red Masters, Political Biographies of Chinese Communist Leaders* (Twayne, New York, 1951).

—— *Dynasty, A Novel* (McGraw-Hill, New York, 1977).

—— *Manchu* (McGraw-Hill, New York, 1980; Penguin, Harmondsworth, 1981).

Elvin, Mark, *The Pattern of the Chinese Past, A Social and Economic Interpretation* (Stanford University Press, Stanford; Eyre Methuen, London, 1973).

Encyclopædia Britannica, 9th edition (25 vols.; Adam and Charles Black, Edinburgh, 1875–89).

Encyclopædia Britannica (24 vols.; Encyclopædia Britannica, Chicago, London, 1971).

'Enjoying Life', *Asiaweek*, XI, 16 (19 April 1985), pp. 28–37.

Evans, Humphrey, *The Adventures of Li Chi, A Modern Chinese Legend* (E. P. Dutton, New York, 1967).

Fairbank, John King, *The United States and China* (Harvard University Press, Cambridge, Mass., 1948; 3rd ed. 1971).

—— 'A Nation Imprisoned by Her History', *Life International*, XLI, 11 (28 November 1966).

—— (ed.), *The Chinese World Order, Traditional China's Foreign Relations* (Harvard University Press, Cambridge, Mass., 1968).

—— *China Perceived: Images and Policies in Chinese–American Relations* (Random House, New York, 1976 ed.).

—— Reischauer, Edwin O., and Craig, Albert M., *East Asia, The Modern Transformation* (Houghton Mifflin, Boston, 1965).

Far Eastern Economic Review Asia 1980 Yearbook (Far Eastern Economic Review, Hong Kong, 1980).

Far Eastern Economic Review Asia 1985 Yearbook (Far Eastern Economic Review, Hong Kong, 1985).

Farmer, Edward L., and others, *Comparative History of Civilizations in Asia* (2 vols.; Addison-Wesley, Reading, Mass., 1977).

Fenton, Edwin, *Tradition and Change in Four Societies: An Inquiry Approach* (Holt, Rinehart and Winston, New York, 1968).

Feuerwerker, Albert, Murphey, Rhoads, and Wright, Mary C. (edd.), *Approaches to Modern Chinese History* (University of California Press, Berkeley and Los Angeles, 1967).

Fitzgerald, C. P., *China, A Short Cultural History* (Cresset Press, London, 1935; 3rd revised edition 1961).

—— *The Birth of Communist China* (Penguin, Harmondsworth, 1964).

—— *The Horizon History of China* (Heritage, New York, 1969).

—— and Roper, Myra, *China: A World So Changed* (Nelson, Melbourne, London, 1972).

Fortune, Robert, *Three Years' Wanderings in the Northern Provinces of China* (John Murray, London, 1847).

Franke, O., *Geschichte des chinesischen Reiches, Eine Darstellung seiner Entstehung, seines Wesens und seiner Entwicklung bis zur neuesten Zeit* (5 vols.; W. de Gruyter, Berlin, 1930–52).

Franke, Wolfgang, *A Century of Chinese Revolution 1851–1949*, trans. Stanley Rudman (Basil Blackwell, Oxford, 1970).

Fraser, John, *The Chinese, Portrait of a People* (Collins, Toronto, 1980).

Garside, Roger, *Coming Alive, China After Mao* (McGraw–Hill, New York, 1981).

Gilbert, Rodney, *What's Wrong with China* (John Murray, London, 1926).

Giles, Herbert A., *The Civilization of China* (Williams and Norgate, London, no date, preface dated 12 May 1911).

Granet, Marcel, *La civilisation chinoise, La vie publique et la vie privée* (La Renaissance du Livre, Paris, 1929).

Grey, Anthony, *The Chinese Assassin* (Michael Joseph, London, 1978; Futura, London, 1979).

Guardian Weekly, London.

Guillain, Robert, *600 Millions de Chinois* (René Julliard, Paris, 1956); *The Blue Ants, 600 Million Chinese under the Red Flag*, trans. Mervin Savill (Secker and Warburg, London, 1957).

Haberman, Clyde, 'Russia's Reach for the Pacific', *Reader's Digest*, CXXX, 786 (October 1987), pp. 22–6.

Han Suyin, *A Many-Splendoured Thing* (Jonathan Cape, London, 1952; Little, Brown and Co., Boston, 1952).

—— *The Crippled Tree* (Jonathan Cape, London, 1965; Panther, St Albans, 1972).

—— *A Mortal Flower* (Jonathan Cape, London, 1966).

—— *China in the Year 2001* (Penguin, Harmondsworth, 1967).

—— *Birdless Summer* (Jonathan Cape, London, 1968).

—— *Asia Today, Two Outlooks, Beatty Memorial Lectures* (McGill–Queen's University Press, Montreal, London, 1969).

—— *Till Morning Comes* (Bantam Books, New York, 1982).

Harding, Harry (ed.), *China's Foreign Relations in the 1980s* (Yale University Press, New Haven, 1984).

Harvey, Edwin D., *The Mind of China* (Yale University Press, New Haven, 1933).

Hegel, Georg Wilhelm Friedrich, *The Philosophy of History*, trans. J. Sibree (Dover Publications, New York, 1956).

Herder, J. G. von, *Ausgewählte Werke in einem Bande* (J. G. Cotta, Stuttgart, 1844).

Hook, Brian (ed.), *The Cambridge Encyclopedia of China* (Cambridge University Press, Cambridge, 1982).

Hooper, Beverley, *Youth in China* (Penguin, Ringwood, Harmondsworth, 1985).

Hsu, Immanuel C. Y., *The Rise of Modern China* (Oxford University Press, New York, London, 1970).

Hucker, Charles O., *China's Imperial Past, An Introduction to Chinese History and Culture* (Duckworth, London, 1975).

Imperial China Photographs 1850–1912 (Pennwick Publishing, USA, 1978; Scolar Press, London and Australian National University Press, Canberra, 1980).

International Herald Tribune, Paris.

Johns, Captain W. E., *Biggles in the Gobi* (Hodder & Stoughton, London, 1953).

Johnson, Chalmers A., *Peasant Nationalism and Communist Power, The Emergence of Revolutionary China 1937–1945* (Stanford University Press, Stanford, 1962).

Johnson, Hewlett, *China's New Creative Age* (Lawrence and Wishart, London, 1953).

Kaplan, Fredric M., and de Keijzer, Arne J., *The China Guidebook* (Eurasia Press, New York, 3rd edition 1982).

Kaplan, Frederic M., Sobin, Julian M., and Andors, Stephen, *Encyclopedia of China Today* (Macmillan, London, 1979).

Keesing's Contemporary Archives, London.

Keightley, David N., '"Benefit of Water": The Approach of Joseph Needham', *Journal of Asian Studies*, XXXI, 2 (February 1972), pp. 367–71.

Kraft, Joseph, *The Chinese Difference* (Saturday Review Press, New York, 1973).

Kraus, Willy, *Economic Development and Social Change in the People's Republic of China*, trans. E. M. Holz (Springer-Verlag, New York, Heidelberg, Berlin, 1982).

Kuhn, Philip A., *Rebellion and its Enemies in Late Imperial China, Militarization and Social Structure, 1795–1864* (Harvard University Press, Cambridge, Mass., 1970).

Kulp, Daniel Harrison II, *Country Life in South China, The Sociology of Familism* (Teachers College, Columbia University, New York, 1925).

Lach, Donald F., *Asia in the Making of Europe Volume I, The Century of Discovery* (2 Books; University of Chicago Press, Chicago and London, 1965).

—— *Asia in the Making of Europe Volume II, A Century of Wonder Book Two: The Literary Arts* (University of Chicago Press, Chicago and London, 1977).

Lam, Wo-Lap, 'Peking Pursues Its Own Path', *Asiaweek*, XI, 7 (15 February 1985), p. 48.

Lattimore, Owen, *Inner Asian Frontiers of China* (American Geographical Society, New York, 1940).

Le Comte, Louis Daniel, *Nouveaux mémoires sur l'etat present de la Chine* (2 vols.; Desbordes & Schelte, Amsterdam, 1698).

Le Tcheou-li ou Rites des Tcheou, traduit pour la première fois du chinois, trans. Édouard Biot (2 vols.; French government, Paris, 1851).

Lee, Mary, 'The Curtain Goes Up', *Far Eastern Economic Review*, CXXVII, 4 (31 January 1985), pp. 50–1.

Legendre, A. F., *Modern Chinese Civilization*, trans. Elsie Martin Jones (Jonathan Cape, London, 1928).

Leong Ka Tai, and Ching, Frank, *Beijing* (Hutchinson, Melbourne, Sydney, London, 1986).

Les mémoires historiques de Se-ma Ts'ien, trans. Édouard Chavannes (5 vols.; E. Leroux, Paris, 1895–1905).

Levenson, Joseph, *Confucian China and Its Modern Fate Volume One, The Problem of Intellectual Continuity* (University of California Press, Berkeley, 1958).

Leys, Simon, *Les habits neufs du président Mao* (Éditions Champs Libres, Paris, 1971); *The Chairman's New Clothes*, trans. Carol Appleyard and Patrick Goode (Allison and Busby, London, 1981 ed.).

—— *Chinese Shadows* (The Viking Press, New York, 1977).

—— *Broken Images, Essays on Chinese Culture and Politics*, trans. Steve Cox (St Martin's Press, New York, 1979).

Liang Heng, and Shapiro, Judith, *Son of the Revolution* (Chatto and Windus, London 1983; Fontana Paperbacks, London, 1984).

—— *After the Nightmare, a Survivor of the Cultural Revolution Reports on China Today* (Alfred A. Knopf, New York, 1986).

—— 'The Loving Penance of Hu Bo', *Reader's Digest* (Australian edition) CXXX, 787 (November 1987), pp. 36–42.

Lin Yutang, *My Country and my People* (Heinemann, London, Toronto, 1936).

Lindley, A. F. (Lin-Le), *Ti-Ping Tien-Kwoh: The History of the Ti-ping Revolution* (2 vols.; Day & Son, London, 1866).

Lindqvist, Sven, *China in Crisis* (Faber and Faber, London, 1963).

Ling, Ken, London, Miriam, and others, *The Revenge of Heaven: Journal of a Young Chinese* (G. P. Putnam's Sons, New York, 1972).

Liu, James T. C., and Tu Wei-ming (edd.), *Traditional China* (Prentice-Hall, Englewood Cliffs, 1970).

MacDougall, Colina, 'The Maoist Mould', *Far Eastern Economic Review*, LXVIII, 14 (2 April 1970), pp. 17–21.

MacFarquhar, Roderick (ed.), *Sino-American Relations, 1949–71* (Wren, Melbourne, 1972).

Malraux, André, *Les conquérants* (Grasset, Paris, 1928).

—— *La condition humaine* (Gallimard, Paris, 1933); *Man's Fate (La condition humaine)*, trans. Haakon M. Chevalier (Random House, New York, 1961).

—— *Le miroir des limbes. Tome I, Antimémoires* (Gallimard, Paris, 1967); *Antimemoirs*, trans. Terence Kilmartin (Hamish Hamilton, London, 1968).

Marchant, L. R. (ed.), *The Siege of the Peking Legations, A*

Diary Lancelot Giles (University of Western Australia Press, Nedlands, 1970).

Marx, Karl, and Engels, Frederick, *Selected Works* (3 vols.; Progress Publishers, Moscow, 1969–70).

—— *Collected Works Volume 12 Marx and Engels 1853–1854* (Lawrence and Wishart, London, 1979).

—— *Collected Works Volume 16 Marx and Engels 1858–60* (Lawrence and Wishart, London, 1980).

Maspero, Henri, *La Chine antique* (Presses Universitaires de France, Paris, 1965 ed.).

Mathews, Jay, and Mathews, Linda, *One Billion, A China Chronicle* (Random House, New York, 1983).

Maugham, W. Somerset, *The Painted Veil* (William Heinemann, London, 1925; Pan Books, London, 1978).

—— *The Travel Books of W. Somerset Maugham* (Heinemann, London, 1955).

Maverick, Lewis A., *China, A Model for Europe* (Paul Anderson, San Antonio, 1946). This work was originally published in two volumes, of which the second is a translation of François Quesnay's *Le despotisme de la Chine* (*Despotism in China*), originally published in Paris in 1767:

Meadows, Thomas Taylor, *The Chinese and their Rebellions, Viewed in Connection with their National Philosophy, Ethics, Legislation, and Administration to which is Added, An Essay on Civilization and its Present State in the East and West* (Smith, Elder & Co., London, 1856).

Mendoza, Juan Gonzales de, *The History of the Great and Mighty Kingdom of China and the Situation Thereof*, trans. R. Parke, ed. George T. Staunton (2 vols.; The Hakluyt Society, London, 1853–4). The original was published under the title *Historia de la cosas mas notables, ritos y costumbres del gran Reyno de la China* in Spanish in Rome in 1585.

Meyer, Charles, *China Observed*, trans. Jean Joss (Kaye & Ward, London, 1980; Gallery Books, New York, 1986).

Montesquieu, Charles Louis de Secondat, *The Spirit of the Laws*, trans. Thomas Nugent (Hafner, New York, 1949).

Morath, Inge, and Miller, Arthur, *Chinese Encounters* (Secker & Warburg, London, 1979).

Morrison, George Ernest, *An Australian in China, Being the Narrative of a Quiet Journey across China to Burma* (Horace Cox, London, 2nd edition 1895).

Morrison, Hedda, *A Photographer in Old Peking* (Oxford University Press, Hong Kong, Oxford, New York, 1985).

Morse, Hosea Ballou, *The International Relations of the Chinese Empire* (3 vols.; Longmans, Green and Co., London, 1910–18).

Mosher, Steven, *Broken Earth: The Rural Chinese* (The Free Press, New York, 1983).

Murphey, Rhoads, *The Outsiders: The Western Experience in India and China* (University of Michigan Press, Ann Arbor, 1977).

Myrdal, Jan, *Report from a Chinese Village*, trans. Maurice Michael (William Heinemann, London, 1965; Pan Books, London, 1975 ed.).

—— and Kessle, Gun, *China: The Revolution Continued*, trans. Paul Britten Austin (Chatto and Windus, London, 1971; Penguin, Harmondsworth, 1973 ed.).

Needham, Joseph, Review of K. A. Wittfogel's *Oriental Despotism* in *Science and Society*, XXIII, 1 (1959), pp. 58–65.

—— *The Grand Titration, Science and Society in East and West* (University of Toronto Press, Toronto, 1969).

—— with the research assistance of Wang Ling, *Science and Civilisation in China, Volume I, Introductory Orientations* (Cambrige University Press, Cambridge, 1954).

—— and others, *Science and Civilisation in China, Volume IV, Physics and Physical Technology, Part 3: Civil Engineering and Nautics* (Cambridge University Press, Cambridge, 1971).

—— with the collaboration of Lu Gwei-djen, *Science and Civilisation in China,Volume V, Chemistry and Chemical Technology, Part II: Spagyrical Discovery and Invention: Magisteries of Gold and Immortality* (Cambridge University Press, Cambridge, 1974).

New York Times, New York.

Peck, James, 'The Roots of Rhetoric: The Professional Ideology of America's China Watchers', *Bulletin of Concerned Asian Scholars*, II, 1 (October 1969), pp. 59–69.

Polo, Marco, *The Travels of Marco Polo*, trans. and introduced Ronald Latham (Penguin, Harmondsworth, 1958).

Porter, Ian, and others, *China, Long-term Development Issues and Options* (Johns Hopkins University Press, Baltimore and London, 1985).

Reischauer, Edwin O., and Fairbank, John K., *East Asia, The Great Tradition* (George Allen & Unwin, London, 1958).

Ricci, Matteo, *China in the Sixteenth Century: The Journals of Matthew Ricci: 1583–1610*, trans. and ed. Louis J. Gallagher S. J. (Random House, New York, 1942; 1953). This is a translation of an adaptation of Ricci's diaries by Nicholas Trigault S. J., published in Augsburg in 1615 under the title *De Christiana Expeditione apud Sinas Suscepta ab Societate Jesu*.

Ronan, Colin A., *The Shorter Science and Civilisation in China Volume I* (Cambridge University Press, Cambridge, 1978).

Roper, Myra, *Emperor's China, People's China* (Heinemann, Melbourne, 1981).

Salisbury, Harrison E., 'China's CEO', *Success!*, XXXIII, 1 (January/February 1986), pp. 72–5.

Samagalski, Alan, and Buckley, Michael, *China — A Travel Survival Kit* (Lonely Planet Publications, Melbourne, Berkeley, 1984).

Savage-Landor, A. Henry, *China and the Allies* (2 vols.; William Heinemann, London, 1901).

Schell, Orville, *To Get Rich is Glorious, China in the Eighties* (Robin Clark, London, 1985).

Schirokauer, Conrad, *A Brief History of Chinese and Japanese Civilizations* (Harcourt Brace Jovanovich, New York, 1978).

Selden, Mark, *The Yenan Way in Revolutionary China* (Harvard University Press, Cambridge, Mass., 1971).

Sitwell, Osbert, *Escape with Me! An Oriental Sketch-Book* (Macmillan, London, 1939; Oxford University Press, Hong Kong, 1983).

Sivin, N., Review of Joseph Needham's *The Grand Titration* in *Journal of Asian Studies*, XXX, 4 (August 1971), pp. 870–3.

Smedley, Agnes, *China's Red Army Marches* (Lawrence and Wishart, London, 1936).

—— *The Great Road, The Life and Times of Chu Teh* (Monthly Review Press, New York, 1956).

Smith, Adam, *An Inquiry into the Nature and Causes of the Wealth of Nations*, ed. Edwin Cannan (2 vols.; Methuen, London, 1904; 1961).

Smith, A. H., *Chinese Characteristics* (Oliphant Anderson and Ferrier, Edinburgh and London, 5th revised edition 1900).

Smith, Bradley and Weng Wan-go, *China, A History in Art* (Studio Vista, London, 1973).

Snow, Edgar, *Red Star over China* (Victor Gollancz, London, 1937; Penguin, Harmondsworth, 1972 ed.).

—— *The Other Side of the River, Red China Today* (Random House, New York, 1961, 1962).

—— *China's Long Revolution* (Penguin, Harmondsworth, 1974 ed.).

Stacey, Judith, *Patriarchy and Socialist Revolution in China* (University of California Press, Berkeley, 1983).

Staunton, Sir George Leonard, *An Authentic Account of an Embassy from the King of Great Britain to the Emperor of China* (2 vols.; G. Nicol, London, 1797).

Strong, Anna Louise, *China's Millions: The Revolutionary Struggles from 1925–1935* (Knight Publishing Company, New York, 1935; Foreign Languages Publishing House, Beijing, 1965).

—— *The Chinese Conquer China* (Doubleday, New York, 1949).

Terrill, Ross, *800,000,000 The Real China* (Penguin, Harmondsworth, 1975 ed).

Terzani, Tiziano, *Behind the Forbidden Door, Travels in China* (Allen & Unwin, London, 1986).

Townsend, James R. and Womack, Brantly, *Politics in China* (Little, Brown and Company, Boston, Toronto, 3rd edition 1986).

Tretiak, Daniel, 'China's Vietnam War and its Consequences', *The China Quarterly*, 80 (December 1979), pp. 740–67.

Twitchett, Denis C., *Land Tenure and Social Order in T'ang and Sung China* (Oxford University Press, New York, 1962).

—— and Fairbank, John K. (edd.), *The Cambridge History of China, Volume 10 Late Ch'ing, 1800–1911, Part 1* (Cambridge University Press, Cambridge, 1978).

Van Gulik, Robert H., *The Lore of the Chinese Lute, An Essay in Ch'in Ideology* (Sophia University, Tokyo, 1940).

—— *Sexual Life in Ancient China, A Preliminary Survey of Chinese Sex and Society from ca. 1500 B.C. till 1644 A.D.* (E. J. Brill, Leiden, 1961).

—— *The Red Pavilion, A Chinese Detective Story* (Heinemann, London, 1964).

—— *The Lacquer Screen, A Chinese Detective Story* (Penguin, Harmondsworth, 1968).

—— *Poets and Murder, A Chinese Detective Story* (Heinemann, London, 1968).

—— *The Chinese Bell Murders, Three Cases Solved by Judge Dee* (Lythway Press, Bath, 1973 ed.).

—— *The Fox-Magic Murders* (Panther, Frogmore, St Albans, 1973).

—— (trans. and ed.), *Celebrated Cases of Judge Dee (Dee Goong An), An Authentic Eighteenth-Century Chinese Detective Novel* (Dover Publications, New York, 1976).

Voltaire, François-Marie Arouet, *Essai sur les mœurs et l'esprit des nations et sur les principaux faits de l'histoire depuis Charlemagne jusqu'à Louis XIII Tome 1* (Éditions Garnier Frères, Paris, 1963 ed.).

Wakeman, Frederic, Jr., and Grant, Carolyn (edd.), *Conflict and Control in Late Imperial China* (University of California Press, Berkeley, 1975).

Walker, Richard L., *China under Communism, The First Five Years* (George Allen and Unwin, London, 1956).

Wiethoff, Bodo, *Introduction to Chinese History From Ancient Times to 1912*, trans. Mary Whittall (Thames and Hudson, London, 1975).

Williams, S. Wells, *The Middle Kingdom, A Survey of the Geography,*

Government, Education, Social Life, Arts, Religion, &c., of the Chinese Empire and its Inhabitants (2 vols.; John Wiley, New York, 1848, 1851).

—— The Middle Kingdom, A Survey of the Geography, Government, Literature, Social Life, Arts, and History of the Chinese Empire and its Inhabitants (2 vols.; Charles Scribner's Sons, New York, 1883). This is an updated edition of the previous item.)

Wilson, Dick, A Quarter of Mankind, An Anatomy of China Today (Weidenfeld and Nicolson, London, 1966; Pelican, Harmondsworth, 1968).

Wint, Guy, Common Sense about China (Victor Gollancz, London, 1960).

Wittfogel, K. A., Wirtschaft und Gesellschaft Chinas: Versuch der wissenschaftlichen Analyse einer grossen asiatischen Agrargesellschaft; Erster Teil: Produktivkräfte, Produktions- und Zirkulationsprozess (C. L. Hirschfeld, Leipzig, 1931).

—— 'Die natürlichen Ursachen der Wirtschaftsgeschichte', Archiv für Sozialwissenschaft und Sozialpolitik, LXVII, 4 (1932), pp. 466–92; 5 (1932), pp. 579–609; 6 (August–September 1932), pp. 711–31.

—— Oriental Despotism: A Comparative Study of Total Power (Yale University Press, New Haven, 1957).

Wolf, Margery, 'Marriage, Family, and the State in Contemporary China', Pacific Affairs, LVII, 2 (Summer 1984), pp. 213–36.

—— Revolution Postponed: Women in Contemporary China (Stanford University Press, Stanford, 1985).

Wright, Arthur F. (ed.), Studies in Chinese Thought (University of Chicago Press, Chicago, 1953 and many other impressions).

—— (ed.), Confucianism and Chinese Civilization (Atheneum, New York, 1964).

Wright, Mary Clabaugh, The Last Stand of Chinese Conservatism The T'ung-chih Restoration, 1862–1874 (Stanford University Press, Stanford, 1957; Atheneum, New York, 1966).

Yahuda, Michael, Towards the End of Isolationism: China's Foreign Policy after Mao (St Martin's Press, New York, 1983).

Young, Marilyn B., 'Introduction', Pacific Affairs, LVII, 2 (Summer 1984), pp. 209–12.

Yule, Henry, and Cordier, Henri, Cathay and the Way Thither, Being a Collection of Medieval Notices of China (4 vols.; The Hakluyt Society, London, 1913–16).

Films

China, The Long March, documentary, directed by Chris Hooke and Peter Butt, Independent Productions, Sydney, 1986.

China's Child, documentary, written and produced by Edward Goldwyn, British Broadcasting Corporation, Horizon, 1983.

Chung-kuo: Cina, documentary, directed by Michelangelo Antonioni, RAI (Italian state television), 1973.

Cycling through China, documentary, hosted by Kate Jackson, directed by John Ripper, A World Pacific Pictures Production, 1982.

Empire of the Sun, feature, directed by Steven Spielberg, Warner Bros., 1987.

Fall of China, The, documentary, narrated by Walter Cronkite, Columbia Broadcasting System, 1961.

From Mao to Mozart, Isaac Stern in China, documentary, produced by Murray Lerner, Hopewell Foundation production, 1981.

Good Earth, The, feature, directed by Sidney Franklin, Metro-Goldwyn-Mayer, 1937.

Heart of the Dragon, The, documentary series, produced by Alasdair Clayre, Antelope-Sino-Hawkshead Films Ltd., 1985.

High Road to China, feature, directed by Brian G. Hutton, Golden Harvest/Jadran Films, 1984.

Inside China, documentary series, produced by André Singer and Leslie Woodhead, Granada Television, 1983.

Last Emperor, The, feature, directed by Bernardo Bertolucci, Fox Columbia, 1987.

Love is a Many-Splendored Thing, feature, directed by H. King, Fox, 1955.

Tai-Pan, feature, directed by Daryl Duke, De Laurentiis Entertainment Group, 1986.

Operas

Turandot, music by Giacomo Puccini, libretto by G. Adami and others, based on Carlo Gozzi, premiered at La Scala, Milan, April 1926.

Secondary Sources

'A Romance Turns Sour', *Asiaweek*, IX, 13 (1 April 1983), pp. 40–4.

'A Vicious Motive, Despicable Tricks', *Peking Review*, XVII, 5 (1 February 1974), pp. 7–10.

Althusser, Louis, and Balibar, Étienne, *Reading Capital*, trans. Ben Brewster (New Left Books, London, 1970).

Besterman, Theodore, *Voltaire* (Longman, London, 2nd revised edition, 1970).

Capon, Edmund, *Art and Archaeology in China* (Macmillan, Melbourne, Sydney, 1977).

Ch'en, Jerome, *China and the West, Society and Culture 1815–1937* (Hutchinson, London, 1979).

Cohen, Paul A., *Discovering History in China, American Historical Writing on the Recent Chinese Past* (Columbia University Press, New York, 1984).

Dawson, Raymond, *The Chinese Chameleon, An Analysis of European Conceptions of Chinese Civilization* (Oxford University Press, London, 1967).

de Rachewiltz, Igor, *Papal Envoys to the Great Khans* (Faber and Faber, London, 1971).

Delfs, Robert, 'Economic Marathon', *Far. Eastern Economic Review*, CXXIX, 34 (29 August 1985), pp. 50–3.

Epstein, Israel, 'Smedley, Strong, Snow — Bridge Builders from People to People', *Beijing Review*, XXVIII, 28 (15 July 1985), pp. 15–23.

Foucault, Michel, *Power/Knowledge, Selected Interviews and Other Writings 1972–1977, Michel Foucault*, ed. Colin Gordon, trans. Colin Gordon, Leo Marshall, John Mepham, Kate Soper (The Harvester Press, Brighton, 1980).

Franke, Wolfgang, *China and the West*, trans. R. A. Wilson (Basil Blackwell, Oxford, 1967; University of South Carolina Press, Columbia, South Carolina, 1968).

Hollander, Paul, *Political Pilgrims, Travels of Western Intellectuals to the Soviet Union, China and Cuba 1928–1978* (Oxford University Press, New York, 1981).

Holmes, Leslie, *Politics in the Communist World* (Clarendon Press, Oxford, 1986).

Hughes, E. R., *The Invasion of China by the Western World* (Adam and Charles Black, London, 1937; 1968).

Humble, Richard, *Marco Polo* (G. P. Putnam's Sons, New York, 1975).

Hunt, Michael H., 'Pearl Buck — Popular Expert on China, 1931–1949', *Modern China, An International Quarterly*, III, 1 (January 1977), pp. 33–64.

Isaacs, Harold R., *Scratches on our Minds, American Images of China and India* (John Day, New York, 1958), updated and republished as *Images of Asia, American Views of China and India* (Harper Torchbooks, New York, 1972 ed.).

Jones, Dorothy B., *The Portrayal of China and India on the American Screen 1896–1955* (MIT Center for International Affairs, Cambridge, Mass., 1955).

Kagan, Leigh, and Kagan, Richard 'Oh Say, Can You See? American Cultural Blinders on China', in Friedman, Edward, and Selden, Mark (edd.), *America's Asia: Dissenting Essays on Asian–American Relations* (Random House, New York, 1969).

Kaminski, Gerd, and Unterrieder, Else, *Von Österreichern und Chinesen* (Europaverlag, Vienna, Munich, Zürich, 1980).

Leslie, Donald D., Mackerras, Colin, and Wang Gungwu (edd.), *Essays on the Sources for Chinese History* (Australian National University Press, Canberra, 1973).

Lowe, Donald M., *The Function of 'China' in Marx, Lenin, and Mao* (University of California Press, Berkeley and Los Angeles, 1966).

Madsen, Axel, *Malraux, A Biography* (William Morrow, New York, 1976).

Mao Zedong, 'On Tactics against Japanese Imperialism', *Selected Works of Mao Tse-tung [Mao Zedong] Volume I* (Foreign Languages Press, Peking, 1965).

March, Andrew L., *The Idea of China, Myth and Theory in Geographic Thought* (Wren, Melbourne, 1974).

Morgan, Ted, *Somerset Maugham* (Jonathan Cape, London, 1980).

'Mosher Sues', *Stanford Observer*, XXI, 1 (October 1986), p. 13.

Posner, Arlene, and de Keijzer, Arne J. (edd.), *China, A Resource and Curriculum Guide* (University of Chicago Press, Chicago, 2nd revised edition 1976).

Rule, Paul A., *K'ung-tzu or Confucius? The Jesuit Interpretation of Confucianism* (Allen & Unwin, Sydney, 1986).

Said, Edward W., *Orientalism* (Random House, Vintage Books, New York, 1978; 1979).

Sawer, Marian, *Marxism and the Question of the Asiatic Mode of Production* (Martinus Nijhoff, The Hague, 1977).

Smith, Richard J., *China's Cultural Heritage, the Ch'ing Dynasty, 1644–1912* (Westview, Boulder, 1983).

Steele, A. T., *The American People and China* (McGraw-Hill, New York, 1966).

Strong, Tracy B., and Keyssar, Helene, *Right in her Soul: The Life of Anna Louise Strong* (Random House, New York, 1983).

Varg, Paul, *Missionaries, Chinese, and Diplomats, The American Protestant Missionary Movement in China, 1870–1952* (Princeton University Press, Princeton, 1958).

'Why Are We Here?', *Far Eastern Economic Review*, CXXXIII, 33 (14 August 1986), p. 103.

Wittfogel, Karl A., 'The Marxist View of China', *The China Quarterly*, 11 (July–September 1962), pp. 1–20; 12 (October–December 1962), pp. 154–69.

Young, John D., *Confucianism and Christianity The First Encounter* (Hong Kong University Press, Hong Kong, 1983).

Zhongguo tongji nianjian 1983 (Chinese Statistical Yearbook 1983) (Chinese Statistical Press, Beijing, 1983).

Zwecker, Zoe, 'Henri Cordier and the Meeting of East and West', in Pullapilly, Cyriac K. and Van Kley, Edwin J. (edd.), *Asia and the West, Encounters and Exchanges from the Age of Explorations, Essays in Honor of Donald F. Lach* (Cross Cultural Publications, Notre Dame, Indiana, 1986), pp. 309–29.

Index